CONTENTS

Llewellyn's

—1989—

MOON SIGN BOOK

& Gardening Guide

Printed in the United States of America
Typography property of Chester-Kent, Inc.

ISBN: 0-87542-404-X

Edited and Designed by Terry Buske
Cover Painting by David Egge

Contributing Writers: Louise Riotte, Sophia Mason, Stan Barker, Pat Esclavon-Hardy, Nancy Soller, Carl Llewellyn Weschcke, Terry Buske

Technical Consultant: Gary Duncan

Published by
LLEWELLYN PUBLICATIONS
P.O. Box 64383-404
St. Paul, MN 55164-0383, U.S.A.

DECEMBER 1988

S	M	T	W	T	F	S
				1	2	3
4	5	6	7	8	9	10
11	12	13	14	15	16	17
18	19	20	21	22	23	24
25	26	27	28	29	30	31

JANUARY 1989

S	M	T	W	T	F	S
1	2	3	4	5	6	7
8	9	10	11	12	13	14
15	16	17	18	19	20	21
22	23	24	25	26	27	28
29	30	31				

FEBRUARY 1989

S	M	T	W	T	F	S
			1	2	3	4
5	6	7	8	9	10	11
12	13	14	15	16	17	18
19	20	21	22	23	24	25
26	27	28				

MARCH 1989

S	M	T	W	T	F	S
			1	2	3	4
5	6	7	8	9	10	11
12	13	14	15	16	17	18
19	20	21	22	23	24	25
26	27	28	29	30	31	

APRIL 1989

S	M	T	W	T	F	S
						1
2	3	4	5	6	7	8
9	10	11	12	13	14	15
16	17	18	19	20	21	22
23	24	25	26	27	28	29
30						

MAY 1989

S	M	T	W	T	F	S
	1	2	3	4	5	6
7	8	9	10	11	12	13
14	15	16	17	18	19	20
21	22	23	24	25	26	27
28	29	30	31			

JUNE 1989

S	M	T	W	T	F	S
				1	2	3
4	5	6	7	8	9	10
11	12	13	14	15	16	17
18	19	20	21	22	23	24
25	26	27	28	29	30	

JULY 1989

S	M	T	W	T	F	S
						1
2	3	4	5	6	7	8
9	10	11	12	13	14	15
16	17	18	19	20	21	22
23	24	25	26	27	28	29
30	31					

AUGUST 1989

S	M	T	W	T	F	S
		1	2	3	4	5
6	7	8	9	10	11	12
13	14	15	16	17	18	19
20	21	22	23	24	25	26
27	28	29	30	31		

SEPTEMBER 1989

S	M	T	W	T	F	S
					1	2
3	4	5	6	7	8	9
10	11	12	13	14	15	16
17	18	19	20	21	22	23
24	25	26	27	28	29	30

OCTOBER 1989

S	M	T	W	T	F	S
1	2	3	4	5	6	7
8	9	10	11	12	13	14
15	16	17	18	19	20	21
22	23	24	25	26	27	28
29	30	31				

NOVEMBER 1989

S	M	T	W	T	F	S
			1	2	3	4
5	6	7	8	9	10	11
12	13	14	15	16	17	18
19	20	21	22	23	24	25
26	27	28	29	30		

DECEMBER 1989

S	M	T	W	T	F	S
					1	2
3	4	5	6	7	8	9
10	11	12	13	14	15	16
17	18	19	20	21	22	23
24	25	26	27	28	29	30
31						

JANUARY 1990

S	M	T	W	T	F	S
	1	2	3	4	5	6
7	8	9	10	11	12	13
14	15	16	17	18	19	20
21	22	23	24	25	26	27
28	29	30	31			

FEBRUARY 1990

S	M	T	W	T	F	S
				1	2	3
4	5	6	7	8	9	10
11	12	13	14	15	16	17
18	19	20	21	22	23	24
25	26	27	28			

FROM THE PUBLISHER

Carl Llewellyn Weschcke

GARY DUNCAN PASSES AWAY

St. Paul, MN. — Neil Llewellyn Block, known to the astrological world under pseudonym of "Gary Duncan," died suddenly of an apparent massive heart attack between 8 and 8:30 a.m. Sunday June 19, 1988.

Neil Llewellyn Block was born August 6, 1931, at 1:13 a.m. in Fullerton, California. His father, Andrew Jesse Block, was originally from Windom, Minnesota, and his mother, Eleanor Grace Norton Block, was from Rosebank, New York. Neil and his mother, later separated from his father, lived for some time at Oceanside and were active in the Rosicrucian Fellowship. Neil started teaching astrology at the Fellowship as a young teenager, and also worked part-time throughout his high school and college years for Llewellyn Publications in Culver City, California. It was in these early years that he formed a friendship and astrological association with Donald Bradley (who later wrote under the pseudonym of "Garth Allen") that lasted until Bradley's death.

I first met Neil Block at an AFA convention in 1962, which

I believe was just about the time that he chose to separate his career in computer science and plans to get a doctorate in astronomy from his interest in astrology by adopting the pseudonym of Gary Duncan. While working at the Jet Propulsion Laboratory (1960-1966) as a Senior Research Engineer, he edited and wrote most of the 1966 edition of the *Moon Sign Book*. It was in this edition that we published what I believe to be the first computer-drawn astro-geo. maps, with the planetary positions likewise generated by the computer. Another first in this issue was a computer-generated graphic ephemeris.

It was during the writing of the *1966 Moon Sign Book*, because of a very tight schedule, that we worked side by side for a week in his house in La Canada, California, and I got to know Neil better. He was an accomplished pianist, and at that time had two grand pianos in his home. He had earned part of his income during his college years by playing the piano and singing in bars. During that week, he told me a lot about his work with Llewellyn George, but it was only after his death that I discovered his given middle name was Llewellyn.

His work at the Jet Propulsion Laboratory was very high level, and in 1962 he joined with D. O. Muhleman and D. B. Holdridge in authorship of JPL Technical Report No. 32-321, "The Astronomical Unit Determined by Radar Reflections from Venus." Neil was solely responsible for the production of the basic astronomical ephemerides of the Sun, Moon and planets. It was his computer programs that provided the international standard of accuracy used by all NASA agencies.

While working as a Senior Programmer at Bendix Computer (1958-1960), he was involved with the early use of computers in electronic typesetting and production of artwork, and during one of his visits to Llewellyn in St. Paul, I introduced him to a group of investors who formed Computype, Inc., where he worked as Vice President and developed the first use of an integrated electronic typesetting system from keyboard to finished typeset pages. Computype was merged into Aspen Systems, now part of the American Can Co., and Neil went to work (1968-1970) as Executive Vice President at University Computer Corp. in Cleveland, Ohio, where he produced the first half-tone reproductions of photographs on the RCA Videocomp. He continued in the area of computer typesetting development with Addressograph-Multigraph (1970-1974) before returning to California, where he worked first with the University of California at Irvine and then with various computer and aerospace firms, including Dunegran/ Endevco, General Automation, Process Systems, and then Hughes Aircraft Co. as a Senior Project Engineer and Systems Manager (1983-1986) when Hughes was merged into General Motors, with a vast reduction in staff.

Since that time, Neil worked as a free-lance computer consultant, and relocated for a period to work as Gary Duncan with Matrix Software in Big Rapids, Michigan, and most recently as a consultant for Llewellyn Publications in St. Paul.

At 56 years of age, he recognized that re-employment in the computer field was difficult, and I personally convinced him that his best career choice now lay with his work in astrological writing, computation, and publishing. He arrived here in early May 1988, having been working on various projects for us while he lived in Washington state and then northern California, and was living with us in our home in Marine-on-St. Croix 30 miles north of St. Paul. He had an office and a computer set up here, and would commute to the main Llewellyn office as needed. Together we had planned a dozen new projects, all of which were in various stages of development—including a software program to accompany the forthcoming book *Transits in Reverse*, by Edna Rynveld, various astrological computations and a new Campanus Table of Houses, and several books, ranging from one dealing with the "Bible and Astrology" to the "Inside-Outside Theory of Delineation."

During the last year or so his health had deteriorated. All his life he had suffered from asthma and had severe allergies to tobacco smoke. While in Michigan he suffered his first heart attack, but he was on medication for this and hypertension. Last fall, while in Washington, he contracted a debilitating case of flu, from which he never seemed to fully recover, and his first days with us were totally miserable. Last Friday, June 17, he visited his doctor here and then spent a very productive day at the Llewellyn office. Friday and Saturday were days filled with plans and enthusiasm for work, and Saturday evening we had an enjoyable dinner with my mother. Except for a strange back pain, he seemed happier and healthier than he'd been in months.

Sunday morning we found him sitting, slumped, in the kitchen. Our son, Gabriel, had talked with him some minutes earlier and he'd complained that he'd had a difficult night. I found no pulse. The paramedics arrived within five minutes of our call, and worked for over an hour, gaining some pulse before moving him to the hospital. Apparently the damage was too extensive, and the failure was total by 10:30 a.m.

As Gary Duncan he will be remembered for his demands for mathematical accuracy in computation and rigorous statistical approaches to astrological research. I think he may have been in touch with more astrologers during this century than any other person, for he was actually active for nearly a half century and knew many of the big names that have long been gone: Llewellyn George, Max Heindel, Albert Benjamin (C. C. Zain), Grant Lewi, Carl Payne Tobey, Ernest Grant, Don Bradley, and on and on. He was a child prodigy—with professional accomplishments in music, mathematics, astronomy, computer science, and business, as well as astrology. And, as nearly everyone in the astrological world knows, his personal library may have been one of the finest.

Aside from his volunteer and part-time work at Llewellyn, his earliest employment, at age 13, was as Assistant Librarian (1944-1949) at the Santa Ana Public Library. In the Air Force (1951-52) Neil worked as Cryptographer and supervised accounting operations for a large-scale supply depot serving five states for all four branches of the military. During this period, he also wrote 70% of the the plug boards for the large IBM 402 and 425 machines.

From 1949 to 1953, except for the time in the Air Force, he worked as a Computational Lab Assistant at the UCLA Astronomy Dept. in Los Angeles, during which time he computed the orbits of the minor planet Icarus and the moons of Jupiter, working with the IBM-CPC. From 1953-1955 he worked as a Programmer for Douglas Aircraft Co.; 1955-1956 as Research Supervisor Servomechanism, Inc.; 1956-1957 as Advanced Programming Manager Alwac Corp.; 1957-1958 as Software Manager for Autonetics; and then to Bendix Computer in 1958.

During these years, he also served as Guest University

Lecturer in Numerical Analysis and in Celestial Mechanics at UCLA, as Instructor in Mathematics for Electronic Data Processing at Long Beach College; and on various academic committees on computer programming and software design. His computer expertise spanned the full range, from large CDC and IBM machines to a number of mini systems and microcomputers. He had "guru" expertise in Fortran and C languages, and also wrote in Pascal, PL/1, Basic, Bal, Exec, Snorol, Lisp, Pilot, Texsys, Typset, Datatext, Text 360, TE, Apt, Adapt, and Action. He was responsible for the development of both hardware and software system designs for a new 32-bit minicomputer, and for a variety of interactive systems in computer typesetting.

During his business career, he not only helped found Computype and develop its business plan but had direct supervisory responsibility for workforces of up to 250 workers.

Neil Llewellyn Block/Gary Duncan had a wide range of friends in his chosen worlds of computer science, astronomy and astrology. It is my earnest hope that I can work with enough of his computer files to salvage a major portion of his astrological work and see it through to publication. I would like to see the name Gary Duncan on one or more software products and books as a fitting memorial to a friend whose one real avocation was *scientific* and *applied astrology*. If there are readers and friends out there who have correspondence, expertise, and an interest in helping, I'd be pleased to hear from you in the hope that we can develop enough material for commercial viability.

During his last month, Gary and I had talked of a "dream" that would lead to a Llewellyn Research Center in San Diego where the Duncan Library could be established as a continuation of Llewellyn George's own dream of a foundation for scientific research and professional exchange. Gary had come to recognize that commercial applications of research results would be the only practical basis for realizing this dream. His departure from us was just too soon, but his memory will be with us for a long time.

Carl Llewellyn Weschcke
Marine-on-St. Croix, Minn.
June 20, 1988

FROM THE EDITOR

Terry Buske

Thank you for your great letters and comments. I hope that this year's book will be just as much help for you.

I hope that you have been able to get through this critical summer drought in 1988 and that you have not lost too much. Mother Nature doesn't seem to want to cooperate with us anymore, but then have we cooperated with her? We need to seriously think about our own environmental practices and do our part in keeping our planet clean and productive. We don't really have much else except Mother Earth when it comes right down to it.

I had the good fortune to be able to do some traveling in the summer of 1987, and visited many parts of the country. I traveled 5,000 miles and went to as many botanical gardens as I could. I also had a chance to meet Louise Riotte, which was one of the highlights of my trip. She is a wonderful person and her fresh figs were delicious!

I am impressed by the ways in which all of you can work with the varied climates of our country. We have included some special articles for the South in the book this year. If you have any suggestions for articles or special topics, please write to me at Llewellyn. I would love to hear from you. Until next year.

Moon Lore
by Louise Riotte

There is a "best time" to do everything. And the proper study of certain events and what happens after they occur can be an advantage to us in coping with our day-to-day activities. While it is impossible to say that all the information we have regarding Moon lore is correct and one hundred percent foolproof, still, much of it has stood the test of time. Of course it is a mixture of fact and fiction—but it does make fascinating reading—and many of the bits of old wisdom that have come down to us through the centuries are still valid today.

Everything within the patterns of nature operates in cycles. These are valid assumptions and have nothing to do with fortunetelling, soothsaying, or mysticism. They are simply a part of the harmony of nature. And it goes without question that there is a harmony between the Sun, Moon, stars and the Earth. This information has been derived from comparisons, investigations, and studies made by men for centuries concerning the relationship of things on planet Earth to the heavenly bodies above and round about the Earth. These things affect the weather as well and when something happens in nature it foretells of other things that are about to happen.

Much of Moon lore concerns planting, and those who use the Moon as their guide in farming and gardening believe that timing and rhythm are very important to these activities. It is a widely held belief that to be really successful with a farm or garden, or other enterprises using Moon phases and signs, you must learn to work in harmony with Mother Nature.

Tree Talk

When we consider the tremendous amount of Moon lore that is concerned with trees it is completely astonishing— and some of it is even contradictory. The phase of the Moon, for instance, if waxing or waning, is considered to be of very great importance when timber must be felled. This is a very ancient belief going back to the time of Caesar. The people of that era believed the very best time to fell trees was when the Moon was in conjunction with the Sun. They even had a name for this day—interlinium," which was sometimes referred to as the "Moon's silence."

Cato in *De Re Rustica* has this to say on the cutting of timber: "When you root up the elm, the pine, the nut tree, or indeed any other kind of tree, mind you do so when the moon is on the wane, after midday, and when there is no south wind blowing. The proper time for cutting a tree is when the seed is ripe, but be careful not to draw it away or plane it when the dew is falling. Never touch the timber except when the moon is on the change, or else at the end of the second quarter; at these periods you may either root up the tree or fell it as it stands. The next seven days after the full moon are the best of all for grubbing up a tree. Be particularly careful not to rough-hew timber, or indeed, to cut or touch it unless it is perfectly dry; and by no means while it is covered with frost or dew."

It is a widely held belief among many old-time woodsmen that timber should be cut only during the waning of the Moon. It is thought that as the Moon wanes, the sap in the timber moves downward and decreases, making the wood drier and much easier to cut. They believe the effect of the Moon on trees is similar to the way it affects the seas and oceans.

Early day carpenters did not like to use wood that had been cut during the waxing Moon, insisting that it was full of moisture and would shrink, warp, and be generally unsuitable for construction purposes. The general rules for cutting wood are as follows:

Cut chestnut, oak, and other hard woods before noon, after the Full Moon in the waning quarters and in the month of August.

Cut pine, maple, and white woods before noon, between the New Moon and the Full Moon phase, in the sign of Virgo and also in the month of August.

Another source has these bits of wisdom to impart: set or cut any shrub or tree that you want to have retarded growth in the dark of the Moon and in Cancer.

Cut trees you wish to grow quickly again during the first quarter of the Moon. Trees cut down during the light of the Moon will not keep.

If a tree be cut at Full Moon, it will split immediately as if torn asunder by a great force (1838).

Trees to be used for durable purposes should be cut during the first and last quarters of the Moon (1838).

Chestnut or black ash timber for fence rails is four times better if cut in the last quarter of the Moon (Feb. or Mar.) than in the first quarter. Chestnut, for firewood, snaps more when burning if cut in the first quarter. Hemlock burns better if cut in the last quarter (1833).

The ancients advised felling timber within four days after the New Moon. Pliny said to do it on the shortest day of the year. Columnella said the twentieth to twenty-eighth day; Cato, four days after the Full; Vegetius, the fifteenth to twenty-fifth day for ship timber. Never cut timber during the light of the Moon.

Bridge timbers *should* be felled during the light of the Moon.

Birch bark comes off easier during the first quarter of the Moon of June and July.

Jared Elliott believed the best time to cut brush was in June, July, or August in the dark of the Moon and in the sign of Leo.

Pruning and Grafting by the Signs

There are also a number of interesting beliefs that have grown up about these practices. One Moon-signer, Claude Johnson of Arkansas, experimented with grafting and budding trees to obtain better varieties of fruit. He believed this was best accomplished with an increasing Moon in a fruitful sign. He used grafts from good-bearing trees, taking them during the time the trees were dormant. He kept his cuttings in a cool, dark place, having cut them usually from December through February. Not wanting to let the cuttings get too dry or too damp while waiting for the right time to make the graft, he chose to store them where they would have some humidity.

It was his practice to graft just before the sap began to flow. And he always grafted while the Moon was from New to Full between the first and second quarters. If possible, he would try to do the entire job during these increasing phases when the Moon was in Cancer, the most fruitful, movable, watery, and feminine of signs. He considered the next best signs to be Scorpio, a highly rated second, Pisces, noted for fruitfulness and good rooting characteristics, and Capricorn, which has an earthy and productive nature.

He sought to produce better fruit by carefully pruning his trees. Controlling limb growth, he believed, diverted the sap to the primary branches of the tree instead of allowing it to dissipate into spreading and unwanted branches. The time he chose, if possible, was during the trees' dormant months while the sap was down. But he was always careful to choose fruitful signs in a decreasing Moon phase, and usually in the fourth quarter.

Another source says, "Don't graft trees when the moon is on the wane or not seen."

Here is another interesting bit of Moon lore: "To make a barren fruit tree bear fruit, bore a half-inch hole into the heart at sunrise, put sulfur in the hole and drive a wooden pin in it."

Another gem of wisdom says, "Apple trees should be planted during Pisces, a watery sign, and the fruit should be harvested in Libra which is also a moist sign." This is thought to produce superior apples, firm when ripe, bright of color, near perfection in shape, and "the best eatin' apple you ever tasted."

When trees are pruned during the proper signs the cuts heal quickly, cover with bark smoothly, and do not have large knobs.

Lightning is thought to strike trees that are "poor in fat" more often than "fat trees." Poor trees are considered to be cottonwood, catalpa, locust, poplar, and willow. Fat trees are bass, beech, butternut, chestnut, oak, and maple.

Many believe that fence posts will not "heave out" of the ground if set during the Fixed signs of Aquarius, Taurus, Leo, or Scorpio and in the fourth Moon quarter.

If trees need watering, irrigate when the Moon is in a watery sign, and in the increasing light of the first and second quarters.

Weather and Moon Lore

If the lower horn of the Moon is dusky, it will rain before the Full Moon. If the horns of the Moon are sharp on the third day, the whole month will be fine. If the upper horn of the Moon is dusky at setting, it will rain during the wane of the Moon. If the center is dusky it will rain at Full Moon.

If shadows are not visible when the Moon is four days old, expect bad weather.

Watch the spiders. If they are busy you will have fine weather. But if they are hiding and breaking webs, they warn of a coming storm.

Flies sting just before a storm. They also cluster on door screens.

When birds huddle together and fluff up their feathers, watch for rain.

High-flying swallows indicate good weather. Insects, their prey, venture high only in the best weather.

Watch the chickens. If they stay out in the rain it's going to rain all day.

The darker the color of caterpillars in the fall, the harder the winter will be.

Birds become hungry just before a storm and eat more.

If geese can walk on top of the snow in March, spring will arrive early.

Clear Moon, frost soon.

A silvery Moon denotes clear, cool weather.

Sweeping the house in the dark of the Moon will rid it of both moths and spiders.

Should Christmas come during a waxing Moon it is a prediction of a very good year. The closer Christmas is to the New Moon, the more prosperous the next year will be.

Should Christmas arrive during a waning Moon, it will be a difficult year and the closer the end of the waning Moon, so much harder the next year will be.

Should the New Moon fall on Monday, the "Moon day," it is generally believed to be a sign of good luck and good weather.

If two New Moons occur in one calendar month (and this occasionally happens) it is believed to bring good luck. Other beliefs concerning this say that something unusual will happen.

If the Moon change occurs on Sunday there will be a flood before the month is over.

The closer the phase change of the Moon to midnight, the fairer the weather for the next seven days. The closer the change of the Moon to noontime, the more changeable the weather for the next seven days.

A wish on the New Moon will come true, but you must not tell your wish and you must kiss the person nearest to you.

If thunder comes at the Moon's change in the spring, it is heralded as a good sign, foretelling that weather will be mild and moist and predicting good crops.

A generally held belief is that if the Full Moon and Equinox meet, there will be violent storms followed by an unusually dry spring.

Never point to the New Moon; it brings bad luck.

Rain will occur if there is a halo round the Moon. If stars are within the halo then it will rain as many days as there are stars, or rain will happen after that many days. Five or more stars within the ring means cold weather, but fewer stars predict warm weather.

Medicines and tonics will be more effective when given at Full Moon. This is particularly applicable to worm medicines for animals. Worms are always more active at the time of the Full Moon, stirring and moving about. Worm your animals at Full Moon and the treatment is more likely to be successful.

The New Moon is the most powerful phase of the waxing or increasing Moon, as it has full growth ahead. This is more fact than fiction and has repeatedly been proven. If you wish to increase something in your personal life, your garden, your business, etc., this is a good time to start making plans.

Children and Marriage

A marriage is more likely to be happy, enduring, and successful if performed on a growing Moon, and the Full Moon is the best time. The Full Moon has a direct effect on children and animals born at this time. They are almost always larger and stronger than those born when the Moon is on the wane. Spring-born children and animals are also larger and stronger than those born in other seasons.

Should a boy baby be born on the wane of the Moon, it is almost certain that a girl baby will be born next, and vice versa. If a birth takes place on the growing or waxing Moon, the next child will usually be of the same sex.

Boy babies should be weaned on the waxing or growing Moon but girl babies should be weaned on the waning or decreasing Moon. And they (either sex) should be nursed for the last time in a fruitful period. This will result in strong, sturdy boys and slender, delicate, and lovely girls.

Moon Lore and Animals

Wean a colt only when the Moon is in Capricorn, Aquarius, or Pisces. Let the colt nurse last in a fruitful period.

Set eggs so that they hatch during the light of the Moon, and in Cancer, Scorpio, or Pisces. Eggs should be set on such a date that twenty-one days later they will hatch in a fruitful period.

In his book *Powerful Planets,* Llewellyn George states: "Chicks hatched in new of Moon grow faster and are hardier than those hatched in "old" of Moon. They come out of their shells all on the same day, are strong and alert.

"Chicks hatched in new of Moon and in a fruitful sign will mature rapidly and be good layers, while those hatched in old of Moon and in a barren sign will not show such good results. They straggle out of their eggs on different days, are weak and sluggish compared to those hatched in New Moon.

"Chicks hatched when Moon is in Gemini will be restless, active, cluckers and fliers, big eaters, but not good layers. Hatched in Leo or Virgo their productiveness will be of only ordinary degree.

"Hatched in new of Moon and in sign of Cancer is best of all, for they will mature quickly, be domesticated, maternal, and very productive. Hatched in Scorpio or Pisces (fruitful signs), they will be good layers."

If these signs and laws of nature are observed, the results will be prize-winning stock and eggs that will sell at high prices to others who want well-bred stock.

Desex stock when the Moon is in Capricorn, Aquarius, or Pisces.

The best time to set hens is in February during light of the Moon.

In Europe, oysters' peak spawning time is two days after the New or Full Moon.

Proverbs regarding weather often concern poultry and unusual actions. Crowing at unusual times, violent and sudden flapping of wings, nervousness in the flock, rolling in the dirt, crowding together, frantic scratching in search of food, and other unusual behavior often are predictions of stormy weather. Barnyard fowls and especially wild birds, who are closer to nature, often become very nervous and noisy just before there is a drastic and unfavorable change in the weather. A country weather prediction says, "When the peacock loudly bawls, we'll soon have both rain and squalls."

Birds' and other animals' warnings should not be ignored. Their instinct is very often more accurately predictive and ahead of any of man's instruments for recording weather changes. It is possible that they can feel the electrical change in the atmosphere before a storm. This odd behavior has often been observed; however, it is still a mystery to us what devices they have that act as alarms. But we do know they exist.

If you raise birds, especially canaries, you should know that the sign of Taurus rules the throat, and many bird breeders believe that birds hatched under this sign will produce better than average singers. Breeders of other types of birds may profit by knowing that birds hatched under the sign of Libra will have the qualities of beauty, color, form, and grace more emphasized than will birds hatched under other signs. "Use good breeders, choose a fruitful sign with good aspects for mating, and you can considerably improve bird quality."

Egg yolks often give a clue to the diet the chickens have been on. If the yolk is bright orange (it's loaded with vitamin A), it indicates that the chickens have had free range and that they've been allowed to feed on grass and other vegetation. These chickens' eggs usually have a higher nutritional value than that of caged birds' eggs. Their eggs have light-colored yolks.

Farm and Ranch Activities

Ranchers and stockfarmers should know that they will be more successful in the following activities if they time them in harmony and rhythm with the phases of the Moon.

It is generally thought that such operations as castration, sterilization, and surgery should be performed only when the Moon is in the "feet." This is the sign of Pisces during the decrease of the Moon in the third and fourth quarters. It was customary among old-time ranchers to mark their stock from February 19th to March 21st, during which time Pisces was in effect. Another opinion believes you may operate any time the *daily* Moon sign is in Pisces, but you should avoid Virgo, Libra, Scorpio, or Sagittarius, as it is thought that if the operation is performed under these signs, there will be excessive bleeding, the wound will fail to heal properly, and the animal may even die. It is generally agreed that the optimal operation time is no earlier than twenty-four hours after the Full Moon has passed, and some stockmen schedule these activities within one week of the New Moon, either before or after.

Shearing of sheep and goats is best done when the Moon is increasing because you will have better quality and greater quantities of wool and mohair at the next clipping time.

Dehorning will be less difficult and the wounds will be quicker to heal without complications if the horns are removed at the New Moon or one week before or after. The daily Moon signs of Aries and Taurus should be avoided as the governing body zone is too near the horn area.

Butchering and slaughtering should also be dictated by careful attention to Moon signs. It is thought that meat will keep better, have a fine flavor, and be of tender quality if these operations take place the first three days after a Full Moon. Killing should never be done during the Leo sign.

Your pasture land can be greatly improved by paying attention to Moon signs. If you want the herbage to grow back quickly and with increased foliage, have the livestock graze it only during the first and second quarter phases of the Moon. Remove the stock from the time of the Full Moon through the third and fourth quarters. It is thought to be of value to time this procedure so that the grass and herbage can grow without the stock grazing it during one of the fruitful monthly signs of Pisces, Taurus, Cancer (best of all), Scorpio, or Capricorn.

Sprouts by Moon Sign

You, too, can be a gardener. Yes, even if you are an apartment dweller and do not own so much as one square foot of earth. Planting by the Moon is generally thought of as being done by those who have outdoor gardens but this is not necessarily so; those who plant indoors can profit by "Moon planting" as well. And one of the ways to bring more and better nutrition to your table is by planting sprouts. Generally speaking, you should follow the same rules as the outdoor gardener.

Here is a general guide to each sign:

Aquarius—A dry barren sign. Not good for planting.

Pisces—Third in line of the most productive signs, exceeded only by Cancer and Scorpio. Fruitful and productive. Plant sprouts in this sign.

Aries—Dry and barren, not regarded as good for planting.

Taurus—Semi-fruitful and fairly productive. Good for leafy vegetables.

Gemini—Dry and barren. Of no value for planting.

Cancer—The most fruitful sign, good for all planting and transplanting operations. Plant sprouts in this sign.

Leo—The most barren sign in the zodiac. Avoid for planting.

Virgo—Moist but next to Leo in barrenness. Don't plant or transplant.

Libra—Semi-fruitful and moist. Sprouts may be started in this sign.

Scorpio—Secondmost productive sign. Plant sprouts in this sign.

Sagittarius—Has a trend toward barrenness. Other signs better for planting.

Capricorn—Productive, earthy, and moist. Sprouts may be planted in this sign.

Note the best signs for planting sprouts and consider also the quarters. Plant leafy annuals (sprouts may be so thought of) in the first quarter (New Moon, waxing, and increasing) or in the second quarter (half Moon, first-quarter

Moon, waxing gibbous, and increasing light)—good for planting leafy annuals that yield above ground, such as beans, cereals (corn, barley, oats, rye, alfalfa, wheat, etc.).

Five thousand years ago, the Chinese began sprouting beans. The first bean they used was the mung bean and they are still sprouting it today. But don't stop at mung beans, delicious as they are; go on to soybeans, whole oats, wheat and rye, kidney, adzuki, cranberry, fava, lima, garbanzo, marrow and pinto beans, lentils and peanuts, unhulled sesame, sunflower, chia, fennel, red clover, fenugreek, alfalfa, mustard, and radish seeds, buckwheat and cress, whole corn and unpearled barley. (Only potato and tomato seeds are not recommended for sprouting, as they contain toxins. They are members of the nightshade family.)

Sprouts are considered to be "top quality" foods, being richer in most nutrients than at any other time in the plant's life cycle. Actively enzymatic and containing the same B complex as the original seeds, they also have additional vitamin C, which forms in anything that sprouts. Left to sprout in light the growing seeds become richer in chlorophyll the longer they sit. (Chlorophyll, with a molecular structure similar to hemoglobin, is useful to the human body because it helps regenerate the bloodstream. But, unfortunately, it also seems that the vitamin E content of the sprout decreases as it becomes older. To overcome this it is suggested that you combine three-day-old and six-day-old sprouts to get full vitamin and chlorophyll value.) There is also evidence of the liberation of vitamin A with sprouting.

Because of the presence of such vitamins (plus minerals), and a high water content, sprouts might serve as the green leafy vegetable in a balanced diet. Their short life cycle, and indoor cultivation, usually protect them from the ravages of insects, thus eliminating any need to treat them with pesticides. And sprouts should always be organically grown.

Enzyme activity is increased by sprouting. Legumes of all kinds, including peanuts, and all beans contain acid and gas-forming properties until sprouting occurs. Large groups of sugars (oligosaccharides) are the reason and it is only the secretion of the enzyme glactosidase, released by the germination process, that breaks down the sugars to their simple states. Proteins are also converted to amino acids by sprouting, causing the bean or seed to become more digestible by the human body.

Sprouts are relatively simple to grow. They require drainage, moisture, warmth, and ventilation. Beans or seeds should be soaked overnight in about three times their volume of water. Be sure to start them in a good sign. Keep in a dark place. In the morning, with a screen of wire mesh, nylon hose, or cheesecloth, drain the water from the jar or vessel. You may wish to save this water as it is rich in water-soluble vitamins and minerals.

Rinse the seeds and drain again. Return to a dark area. This procedure should be repeated at least twice a day (morning and night) and up to four times a day if possible. This rinsing and draining is important; the seeds will not do well in stale water. Be especially careful in warm weather.

In about two or three days, you will notice that the seeds have "popped." Now is the time to place them in indirect sunlight so that they can start accumulating chlorophyll; but continue the rinse-and-drain process until the desired length is reached. Soybeans are good at 3"-5" tall, taking 5-7 days; alfalfas 1"-2" long are edible in 3-5 days. Eat wheat sprouts when they are the length of the kernel, about 3 days, but wheat grass can go to 6". Sunflower seeds are edible from just under 2" (6-7 days), although some prefer them longer; mung 1½"-3" (5-7 days); lentils 1"; peas 2". Experiment! Your own individual taste may differ.

Sprouts will even grow well in distilled water. How pure can you get? You can also sprout different seeds in combination, choosing varieties of about the same sprouting time. For greener sprouts give them more light, but be careful they don't rot. Always be sure they have plenty of moisture, for without plenty of moisture they will send out roots to find it and this will cause a change in the taste. Seeds sprouted in darkness have a nuttier flavor but are lighter in color. Use sprouts when they're ready; otherwise, refrigerate in a covered container. Sprouts are good eaten raw, or add them to cooked food just before serving; this will retain their nutritive value but will soften them up a little and bring out their full flavor.

Psycholunology

Perhaps there is something new "under the Moon." Psycholunology is a branch of cosmobiology that maintains that the phases of the Moon affect human behavior. The Full Moon, especially, is associated with fertility, with the menstrual cycle, with murder and suicide, with births, with epilepsy, and with violence and madness. Much of this is not new; the Moon has always been associated with most of these things.

The late Dr. William F. Petersen, professor of pathology at the University of Illinois School of Medicine in Chicago, was one of the pioneers who researched the dynamic balance of life and environment. From 1920 to 1950, he performed painstaking research that revealed human biological rhythms correlated with weather patterns. He found that both human biorhythms and weather changes could be traced to natural fluctuations in the solar cycle, the lunar cycle, and the star cycle.

Much of Dr. Petersen's work involved correlating individual and population rhythms with the sunspot cycle. He was also interested in detecting lunar periodicities. His inspiration was the work of the Danish Nobel Laureate Svante Arrhenius, whose paper "Cosmic Influences on Physiological Phenomena," in 1898, marked the beginning of modern scientific studies on the cosmic effect of human organisms. Arrhenius demonstrated that clear-cut lunar cycles influenced deaths, births, menstruation, epileptic attacks, and atmospheric electric potential.

Dr. Petersen was able to identify lunar rhythms in the following data samples: birth records in New York and Chicago, the occurrence of scarlet fever and epilepsy, cardiovascular deaths due to tuberculosis, and suicides. He found that more male children were born at the Full Moon and that more female children were born at the time of New Moon.

The first practicing psycholunologist is A.L. Lieber, a Florida psychiatrist (author of *The Lunar Effect*, Anchor Press/ Doubleday) who believes that the Moon affects the human body in much the same way as the tides are affected: "Like the surface of the Earth, man is about 80 percent water and 20 percent solids. . . . the gravitational force of the Moon, acting in concert with other major forces of the Universe exerts an influence on the water in the human body . . . as it does on the oceans of the planet. Life has . . . biological high tides and low tides governed by the Moon. At new and full

Moon these tides are at their highest—and the Moon's effect on our behavior is the strongest."

Lunar folklore down through the centuries has always maintained that certain forms of behavior are intensified by a Full Moon. Maternity wards always gear up at this time because more births than usual are expected to occur. Emergency-room attendants await an upsurge in cases of bleeding and violence. Firemen, policemen, and ambulance drivers usually expect more cases of violence and accidents to occur. There are even records showing that more marriages take place during the Full Moon! Who said there was no such thing as "Moon madness"? And in past ages, the Full Moon has been associated with episodes of lycanthropy, or werewolfery—many believe that certain people can change themselves into wolves at this time.

Whether or not these lunar effects actually exist has been the subject of a great deal of study. The Moon's influence on the birth rate has probably received the most attention. Actually, results have been rather contradictory. A study at the Tallahassee Memorial Hospital between 1956 and 1958 seemed to support the hypothesis that the Full Moon does affect births: 401 babies were born within two days of the Full Moon, but only 320 were born within two days of the first quarter. A New York City study of 510,000 births during the years 1948-1958 indicated that the birth rate was one percent higher during the two weeks following the Full Moon than before.

However, a second study in 1973 showed precisely the reverse. And a third study of the years 1961-1963 showed an *excess* of births *centered* on the time of the Full Moon.

Using a complicated computer method of converting regular solar time into lunar time, Lieber analyzed cases of murder in Dade County, Florida, for the period from 1956 to 1970. His findings indicated that homicides peaked at the time of the Full Moon and rose again during the New Moon. A similar study made in Cuyahoga County, Ohio, showed a peak three days after the Full and New Moons, a result Lieber attributed to Cuyahoga's more northerly latitude.

Dr. Lieber also has this to say: "In applying lunar knowledge, we should consider using a calendar showing both lunar and solar time. We would then be able to recognize lunar and solar periodicities, especially their coincidences.

Ancient civilizations used a lunar calendar; the Israelis, the Chinese, the Hindus, and the Moslems still do. Interestingly, there is much less violent crime in these societies."

Medical Moon Lore

Most of you know which sign governs or rules a particular part of the body, but for the benefit of new Moon-signers let me give the twelve basic signs of the zodiac and their rulerships:

Aries—Head, face
Taurus—Throat, neck
Gemini—Hands, arms, chest, shoulders, lungs, nervous system
Cancer—Breast, stomach
Leo—Heart, sides, upper back
Virgo—Bowels, solar plexus

Libra—Kidneys, loins, lower back, ovaries
Scorpio—Sex organs, bladder
Sagittarius—Hips, thighs, liver, blood
Capricorn—Knees
Aquarius—Ankles, legs, body fluids
Pisces—Feet

Those who consider the Moon signs in the treatment of human and animal ailments believe that all such procedures should be in rhythm with the Moon and its various phases. It is generally agreed that proper timing should be as follows:

Dental work—Fill cavities during a waning Moon in the third or fourth quarter and in a Fixed sign (Aquarius, Taurus, Leo, Scorpio). Extract teeth during a waxing Moon in the first and second quarters, but only in the signs of Pisces, Gemini, Virgo, Sagittarius, or Capricorn. Plates should be made under a decreasing Moon in the third or fourth quarter and in a Fixed sign (Aquarius, Taurus, Leo, Scorpio).

Operations—the most favorable time for an operation, teeth extraction, tonsillectomy, or removal of a growth is at a time when the sign is one that rules the knees or feet (the best), such as Capricorn or Pisces.

Removal of unwanted growth—such as corns, calluses, superfluous hair, warts, etc. Use a barren sign such as Aquarius, Aries, Leo, Virgo, or Sagittarius with a fourth-quarter Moon.

Surgical procedures—Moon should be on the increase and in the first or second quarter. Vitality and healthy conditions prevailing, wounds will heal better and more rapidly during this time. An exception is the cutting away of unwanted growths. Do this on a decreasing Moon and in the third or fourth quarter.

All down through the centuries mankind has felt the mystery and fascination of the Moon. In story and song, myth and superstition, our nearest celestial neighbor has been credited with profound powers. And there is a wealth of evidence to show that the Moon does indeed influence behavior. Just like the sea, human biological tides respond to the Moon's pull, and for a similar reason. Our bodies, like the Earth itself, are made up of about eighty percent water.

MOON
TABLES

The Moon Tables on the following pages will tell
you the position of the Moon in phase and sign for
the coming year. The times listed are for CST. You
will also find a Lunar Aspectarian giving the aspects
that the Moon makes to the other planets for each
day. Along with this is a table of favorable and
unfavorable dates for each sign.

TABLE OF TERMS REFERRING TO LUNAR QUARTERS (PHASES)

Sun-Moon Angle	Moon Sign Book Term	Common Terms	Division by:		
		2	4	8	
0-90° after Conjunction	First Quarter	Increasing Waxing Light New	New Moon	New Moon	
				Crescent	
90-180°	Second Quarter		First Quarter	First Quarter	
				Gibbous	
180-270°	Third Quarter	Decreasing Waning Dark Old	Full Moon	Full Moon	
				Disseminating	
270-360°	Fourth Quarter		Last Quarter	Last Quarter	
				Balsamic	

THE PHASES

● **New Moon:** Finalization, rest, hidden reorganizations, incipient beginnings, or chaos, disorganization, confusion, regret, stagnation, covert revenge.

○ **Full Moon:** Fulfillment, culmination, completion, activity, social awareness, or unfulfilled longing, unrest, fretfulness, sentimentality, and overt revenge.

● **First Quarter:** Germination, emergence, beginningness, outwardly directed activity.

◗ **Second Quarter:** Growth, development and articulation of things which already exist.

○ **Third Quarter:** Maturity, fruition, assumption of full form of expression.

◗ **Fourth Quarter:** Disintegration, drawing back for reorganization, rest, reflection.

SIGNS OF THE MOON

♈ **Moon in Aries:** Good for starting things, but lacking in staying power. Things occur more rapidly, but also quickly pass away.

♉ **Moon in Taurus:** Things begun now last the longest and tend to increase in value. Things begun now become habitual and hard to alter.

♊ **Moon in Gemini:** An inconstant and fickle position for the Moon. Things begun now are easily moved by outside influences.

♋ **Moon in Cancer:** Stimulates emotional rapport between people. Pinpoints need, supports growth and nurturance.

≈ Moon in Leo: Draws emphasis to the self, to central ideas or institutions, away from connections with others and emotional needs.

≈ Moon in Virgo: Favors accomplishment of details and commands from higher up, while discouraging independent thinking and enterprise.

♎ Moon in Libra: Increases self-awareness, favoring self-examination and interaction with others but discouraging spontaneous initiative.

♏ Moon in Scorpio: Increases awareness of psychic power. Precipitates psychic crises and ends connections thoroughly.

♐ Moon in Sagittarius: Encourages expansionary flights of the imagination and confidence in the flow of life.

♑ Moon in Capricorn: Artificial, disciplined, controlled and institutional activities are favored. Develops strong structure.

♒ Moon in Aquarius: Idealized conditions lead to the potential for emotional disappointment and disruption in the natural flow of life.

♓ Moon in Pisces: Energy withdraws from the surface of life, hibernates within, secretly reorganized and realigning for a new day.

ALL TIMES GIVEN IN THE MOON SIGN BOOK ARE IN CENTRAL STANDARD TIME. YOU NEED TO ADJUST THEM TO YOUR TIME ZONE AND TO DAYLIGHT SAVING TIME.

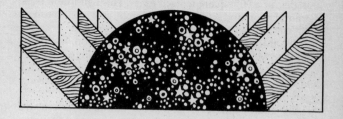

The Moon's Phases

Everyone has seen the Moon wax and wane, growing progressively larger and smaller through a period of approximately 29½ days. This circuit from New Moon, when the surface of the Moon is completely dark, to Full Moon, when it is totally lit, and back again, is called the "lunation cycle." It is the result of a relationship between the Sun, Moon and Earth. As the Moon makes one entire trip around the Earth, it reflects the light of the Sun in varying degrees, depending on the angle between the Sun and Moon as viewed from Earth. During the year, the Moon will make thirteen such trips, each called a lunation.

This cycle is divided into parts called "phases." There are several methods by which this can be done, and the system used in the *Moon Sign Book* will not necessarily correspond to those used in other almanacs and calendars. It is important, when using the Moon as a guide, to use Llewellyn's *Astrological Calendar* or *Moon Sign Book*, as these books have been designed for astrological use.

The method of division used by Llewellyn divides the lunation cycle into four phases or quarters. These are measured as follows.

The **first quarter** begins when the Sun and Moon are in the same place, or *conjunct*. The Moon is not visible at first, since it rises at the same time as the Sun. But toward the end of this phase, a silver thread can be seen just after sunset as the Moon follows the Sun over the western horizon.

The **second quarter** begins halfway between the New

Moon and Full Moon, when the Sun and Moon are at right
angles, or a 90° square to each other. This half-moon rises
around noon, and sets around midnight, so it can be seen in
the western sky during the first half of the night.

The **third quarter** begins with the Full Moon, when the
Sun and Moon are opposite one another and the full light of
the Sun can shine on the full sphere of the Moon. The round
Moon can be seen rising in the east at sunset, and then rising
progressively a little later each evening.

The **fourth quarter** begins about halfway between the
Full Moon and New Moon, when the Sun and Moon are
again at 90°, or right angles. This decreasing Moon rises at
midnight, and can be seen in the east during the last half of
the night, reaching the overhead position just about as the
Sun rises.

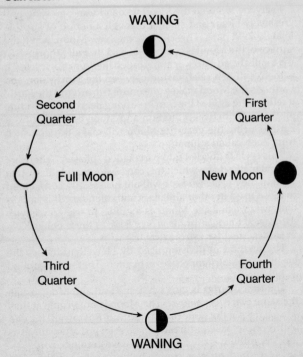

How To Use Your Moon Sign Book

Timing your activities is one of the most important things you can do to ensure success. In many Eastern countries, timing by the planets is so important that practically no event takes place without first setting up a chart for it. Many times weddings take place in the middle of the night because that is when the influences are the best. You may not want to take it that far, and you don't really need to set up a chart for each activity, but you may as well make use of the influences of the Moon whenever possible. It's easy and it works!

In the *Moon Sign Book* you will find all of the information you need to plan just about any important activity: weddings, fishing, buying a car or house, cutting your hair, traveling and more. Not all of the things you need to do will fall on particularly favorable days, but we can give you the guidelines you need to pick the best day out of the several you have to choose from.

Let's run through some examples. Say you need to set up an appointment to have your hair cut. You have thin hair and would like to have it look thicker. Look in the **Health & Beauty** section under **Hair Care.** You will see that you should cut it during a Full Moon (marked FM in the Moon Tables or under the Sun in the Lunar Aspectarian). You should, however, avoid the Moon in Virgo. We'll say that it's the month of June. Look up June in the **Moon Tables** section.

The Full Moon falls on June 19th. It is in Capricorn, which is fine. Because the Full Moon occurs at just after midnight

(Central Time), any time would be good during the day. If
the Full Moon were to fall later in the day, you could have it
cut early on the 20th. Because it does happen so early in the
morning, you could also cut your hair late on the 18th. It is
fairly flexible. You do not have to use the exact time listed.

That was an easy one. Let's move on to an example that
takes in a phase and sign of the Moon. You want to buy a
house for your permanent home. Look in the **Home &
Family** section under **House.** It says that you should buy
when the Moon is in Taurus, Leo, Scorpio or Aquarius. You
will need to get a loan so you look in the **Business and
Finance** section under **Loans.** Here it says that in the 3rd and
4th quarters it favors the borrower (you). Let's say that you
will be buying in March. Look at the March tables. The
Moon is in the 3rd and 4th quarters from March 1st through
the 6th and from the 23rd through the 31st. It is in Aquarius
(a fixed sign) on the 4th and 5th, and in Scorpio (fixed) on
the 24th, 25th and 26th. Those would be the best dates to
wheel and deal.

With all activities, be sure to check the *Favorable and Unfavorable Dates* for your Sun Sign listed next to the *Lunar
Aspectarian.* If there is a choice of several dates that are
equally good, go with the one marked **F** under your sign.

OK. Now you have that down. Let's go to an example
where you need to figure aspects along with the other
things. You will find the aspects listed in the **Lunar Aspectarian.** You need to fix your car. Let's use August as the
month. Look in the **Home and Family** section under **Automobile Repair.** It says that it is best when the Moon is in a
fixed sign, 1st or 2nd quarter and well aspected to the Sun.
Avoid bad aspects to Mars, Saturn, Uranus, Neptune or
Pluto if possible. Bad aspects are indicated as Sq or O in the
Lunar Aspectarian. First find out when the Moon is in the proper quarter. The dates for August would be the 2nd through
the 15th and the 31st. It is in a fixed sign (Leo) on the 2nd,
Scorpio on the 8th and 9th, and Aquarius on the 15th. Now
look at the *Lunar Aspectarian* under the *Sun.* There are no
aspects between the Sun and Moon on the 2nd, 8th or 15th.
There is a square on the 9th, so avoid that date. Now look
under *Mars.* There are no aspects on the 2nd or 15th and a
sextile (positive) on the 8th. All of these dates are still in the
running. Now look under the planet *Saturn.* Again,

there are no aspects on the 2nd and 15th and a positive sextile on the 8th. All dates are fine. Look under the planet *Uranus* next. Again, the same thing occurs. The same holds true for *Neptune* and *Pluto*. After you have looked under all of the planets listed for the activity and eliminated those dates that have negative aspects under those planets, you are ready to make your appointment. Use the *Favorable and Unfavorable* table for your Sun Sign in choosing between dates.

You have just gone through the entire process of choosing the best date for a special event. With practice, you will be able to scan the information in the tables and do it very quickly. You will also begin to get a feel for what works best for you. Everyone has his or her own high and low cycle.

Gardening activities are dependent on many outside factors, weather being one of the major ones. Obviously you can't go out and plant when there is still a foot of snow on the ground or when it is raining cats and dogs. You have to adjust to the conditions at hand. If the weather was bad or you were on vacation during the 1st quarter when it was best to plant, do it during the 2nd quarter while the Moon is in a fruiful sign instead. If the Moon is not in a fruitful sign during the 1st or 2nd quarter, choose a day when it is in a semi-fruitful sign. The best advice is to choose either the sign or the phase that is *most* favorable when the two don't coincide.

So, to summarize, in order to make the most of your plans and activities, check with the *Moon Sign Book*. First, look up the authority in the corresponding section under the proper heading. Then, look for the information given there in the proper table (the *Moon Table, Lunar Aspectarian* or *Favorable and Unfavorable Dates*, or all three). Choose the best date according to the number of positive factors in effect. If most of the dates are favorable, then there is no problem choosing the one that will best fit your schedule. However, if there just don't seem to be any really good dates, pick the one with the least number of negative influences. We guarantee that you will be very pleased with the results if you use nature's influences to your advantage.

For a quick reference, look at the *Astro-Almanac*. This is a *general guide* and does not take into account all of the factors.

HOW TO USE THE MOON TABLES
AND ASPECTARIAN

First, read the preceding section on how to use your *Moon Sign Book*. You will be using the tables on the following pages in conjunction with the information given in the individual sections: **Home & Family, Business & Finance, Health & Beauty, Leisure & Recreation** and **Farm & Garden.**

The **Moon Tables** pages include the date, day, sign the Moon is in, the element of that sign, the nature of the sign, the Moon's phase and the times that it changes sign or phase. **FM** signifies Full Moon and **NM** signifies New Moon. The times listed directly after the day are the times when the Moon changes sign. The times listed after the phase indicate the times when the Moon changes phase. All times are listed in **Central Standard Time.** You need to change them to your own time zone. See the conversion tables.

On the page next to the *Moon Table* you will find the **Lunar Aspectarian** and the **Favorable and Unfavorable Dates.** To use the *Lunar Aspectarian,* find the planet that the activity lists and run down the column to the date desired. If you want to find a favorable aspect to Mercury, run your finger down the column under Mercury until you find an **Sx** or **T.** Positive or good aspects are signified by an Sx or T. Negative or adverse aspects are signified by an **Sq** or **O.** The conjunction, or **C,** is sometimes good, sometimes bad, depending on the activity or planets involved. The *Lunar Aspectarian* gives the *aspects of the Moon to the other planets.*

The *Favorable and Unfavorable Days* table lists all of the Sun Signs. To find out if a day is positive for you, find your sign and then look down the column. If it is marked **F** it is very favorable. If it is marked **f,** it is slightly favorable. A **U** means very unfavorable and a small **u** means slightly unfavorable.

SYMBOL KEY

SX: sextile/positive   **T:** trine/positive
SQ: square/negative   **O:** opposition/negative
C: conjunction/positive/negative/neutral

To find out the exact times of the daily aspects, see *Llewellyn's 1989 Daily Planetary Guide & Astrologer's Datebook.*

Sign	Glyph	Dates	Ruler	Element	Quality	Nature
Aries	♈	Mar 21–Apr 20	Mars	Fire	Cardinal	Barren
Taurus	♉	Apr 20–May 21	Venus	Earth	Fixed	Semi-Fruitful
Gemini	♊	May 21–June 21	Mercury	Air	Mutable	Barren
Cancer	♋	June 21–July 23	Moon	Water	Cardinal	Fruitful
Leo	♌	July 23–Aug 23	Sun	Fire	Fixed	Barren
Virgo	♍	Aug 23–Sept 22	Mercury	Earth	Mutable	Barren
Libra	♎	Sept 22–Oct 23	Venus	Air	Cardinal	Semi-Fruitful
Scorpio	♏	Oct 23–Nov 22	Pluto	Water	Fixed	Fruitful
Sagittarius	♐	Nov 22–Dec 22	Jupiter	Fire	Mutable	Barren
Capricorn	♑	Dec 22–Jan 20	Saturn	Earth	Cardinal	Semi-Fruitful
Aquarius	♒	Jan 20–Feb 18	Uranus	Air	Fixed	Barren
Pisces	♓	Feb 18–Mar 21	Neptune	Water	Mutable	Fruitful

TIME ZONE

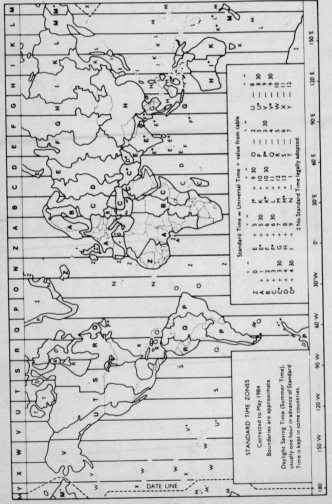

CONVERSIONS

WORLD TIME ZONES
Compared to Central Standard Time

( ) From Map
(S) CST - Used
(R) EST - Add 1 hour
(Q) Add 2 hours
(P) Add 3 hours
(O) Add 4 hours
(N) Add 5 hours
(Z) Add 6 hours
(T) MST - Subtract 1 hour
(U) PST - Subtract 2 hours
(V) Subtract 3 hours
(W) Subtract 4 hours
(X) Subtact 5 hours

(Y) Subtract 6 hours
(A) Add 7 hours
(B) Add 8 hours
(C) Add 9 hours
(D) Add 10 hours
(E) Add 11 hours
(F) Add 12 hours
(G) Add 13 hours
(H) Add 14 hours
(I) Add 15 hours
(K) Add 16 hours
(L) Add 17 hours
(M) Add 18 hours

Standard Time = Universal Time + value from table

	h m		h m		h m
Z	0 00	H	+ 8 00	Q	− 4 00
A	+ 1 00	I	+ 9 00	R	− 5 00
B	+ 2 00	I*	+ 9 30	S	− 6 00
C	+ 3 00	K	+10 00	T	− 7 00
C*	+ 3 30	K*	+10 30	U	− 8 00
D	+ 4 00	L	+11 00	U*	− 8 30
D*	+ 4 30	M	+12 00	V	− 9 00
E	+ 5 00	M*	+13 00	V*	− 9 30
E*	+ 5 30	N	− 1 00	W	−10 00
F	+ 6 00	O	− 2 00	W*	−10 30
F*	+ 6 30	P	− 3 00	X	−11 00
G	+ 7 00	P*	− 3 30	Y	−12 00

JANUARY

Date	Moon's Sign	Element	Nature	Moon's Phase
1 Sun. 3:35 pm	Scorpio	Water	Fruitful	4th
2 Mon.	Scorpio	Water	Fruitful	4th
3 Tues.	Scorpio	Water	Fruitful	4th
4 Wed. 1:12 am	Sagit.	Fire	Barren	4th
5 Thurs.	Sagit.	Fire	Barren	4th
6 Fri. 7:15 am	Capri.	Earth	Semi-fruit	4th
7 Sat.	Capri.	Earth	Semi-fruit	NM 1:23 pm
8 Sun. 10:31 am	Aquar.	Air	Barren	1st
9 Mon.	Aquar.	Air	Barren	1st
10 Tues. 12:32 pm	Pisces	Water	Fruitful	1st
11 Wed.	Pisces	Water	Fruitful	1st
12 Thurs. 2:37 pm	Aries	Fire	Barren	1st
13 Fri.	Aries	Fire	Barren	1st
14 Sat. 5:37 pm	Taurus	Earth	Semi-fruit	2nd 7:59 am
15 Sun.	Taurus	Earth	Semi-fruit	2nd
16 Mon. 9:58 pm	Gemini	Air	Barren	2nd
17 Tues.	Gemini	Air	Barren	2nd
18 Wed.	Gemini	Air	Barren	2nd
19 Thurs. 3:58 am	Cancer	Water	Fruitful	2nd

The SUN enters Aquarius at 8:08 pm

Date	Moon's Sign	Element	Nature	Moon's Phase
20 Fri.	Cancer	Water	Fruitful	2nd
21 Sat. 12:03 pm	Leo	Fire	Barren	FM 3:35 pm
22 Sun.	Leo	Fire	Barren	3rd
23 Mon. 10:33 am	Virgo	Earth	Barren	3rd
24 Tues.	Virgo	Earth	Barren	3rd
25 Wed.	Virgo	Earth	Barren	3rd
26 Thurs. 11:02 am	Libra	Air	Semi-fruit	3rd
27 Fri.	Libra	Air	Semi-fruit	3rd
28 Sat. 11:50 pm	Scorpio	Water	Fruitful	3rd
29 Sun.	Scorpio	Water	Fruitful	4th 8:03 pm
30 Mon.	Scorpio	Water	Fruitful	4th
31 Tues. 10:31 am	Sagit.	Fire	Barren	4th

JANUARY 1989
Lunar Aspectarian

Favorable & Unfavorable Days

	SUN	MERCURY	VENUS	MARS	JUPITER	SATURN	URANUS	NEPTUNE	PLUTO	ARIES	TAURUS	GEMINI	CANCER	LEO	VIRGO	LIBRA	SCORPIO	SAGITTARIUS	CAPRICORN	AQUARIUS	PISCES
1		Sq						Sx		U		f	u	f		F			f	u	f
2	Sx					Sx		Sx	C		U		f	u	f		F		f	u	f
3				O							U		f	u	f		F		f	u	f
4		Sx								f		U		f	u	f		F		f	u
5			C	T						f		U		f	u	f		F		f	u
6						C	C			u	f		U		f	u	f		F		f
7	C							C	Sx	u	f		U		f	u	f		F		f
8				Sq	T					f	u	f		U		f	u	f		F	
9		C							Sq	f	u	f		U		f	u	f		F	
10			Sx	Sx	Sq	Sx	Sx			f	u	f		U		f	u	f		F	
11								Sx	T		f	u	f		U		f	u	f		F
12	Sx		Sq		Sx		Sq				f	u	f		U		f	u	f		F
13		Sx				Sq		Sq		F		f	u	f		U		f	u	f	
14	Sq			C			T			F		f	u	f		U		f	u	f	
15		Sq	T			T		T	O		F		f	u	f		U		f	u	f
16	T				C						F		f	u	f		U		f	u	f
17		T								f		F		f	u	f		U		f	u
18										f		F		f	u	f		U		f	u
19			Sx			O	O	O		u	f		F		f	u	f		U		f
20			O						T	u	f		F		f	u	f		U		f
21	O			Sq	Sx					u	f		F		f	u	f		U		f
22		O							Sq	f	u	f		F		f	u	f		U	
23					Sq					f	u	f		F		f	u	f		U	
24				T		T	T	T			f	u	f		F		f	u	f		U
25			T						Sx		f	u	f		F		f	u	f		U
26		T			T		Sq			U		f	u	f		F		f	u	f	
27	T					Sq		Sq		U		f	u	f		F		f	u	f	
28		Sq	Sq							U		f	u	f		F		f	u	f	
29	Sq			O		Sx	Sx	Sx			U		f	u	f		F		f	u	f
30									C		U		f	u	f		F		f	u	f
31		Sx	Sx		O					f		U		f	u	f		F		f	u

FEBRUARY

Date	Moon's Sign	Element	Nature	Moon's Phase
1 Wed.	Sagit.	Fire	Barren	4th
2 Thurs. 5:30 pm	Capri.	Earth	Semi-fruit	4th
3 Fri.	Capri.	Earth	Semi-fruit	4th
4 Sat. 8:52 pm	Aquar.	Air	Barren	4th
5 Sun.	Aquar.	Air	Barren	4th
6 Mon. 9:53 pm	Pisces	Water	Fruitful	NM 1:38 am
7 Tues.	Pisces	Water	Fruitful	1st
8 Wed. 10:19 pm	Aries	Fire	Barren	1st
9 Thurs.	Aries	Fire	Barren	1st
10 Fri. 11:46 pm	Taurus	Earth	Semi-fruit	1st
11 Sat.	Taurus	Earth	Semi-fruit	1st
12 Sun.	Taurus	Earth	Semi-fruit	2nd 5:16 pm
13 Mon. 3:23 am	Gemini	Air	Barren	2nd
14 Tues.	Gemini	Air	Barren	2nd
15 Wed. 9:41 am	Cancer	Water	Fruitful	2nd
16 Thurs.	Cancer	Water	Fruitful	2nd
17 Fri. 6:34 pm	Leo	Fire	Barren	2nd
18 Sat.	Leo	Fire	Barren	2nd

The SUN enters Pisces at 10:22 am

Date	Moon's Sign	Element	Nature	Moon's Phase
19 Sun.	Leo	Fire	Barren	2nd
20 Mon. 5:35 am	Virgo	Earth	Barren	FM 9:33 am
21 Tues.	Virgo	Earth	Barren	3rd
22 Wed. 6:06 pm	Libra	Air	Semi-fruit	3rd
23 Thurs.	Libra	Air	Semi-fruit	3rd
24 Fri.	Libra	Air	Semi-fruit	3rd
25 Sat. 6:58 am	Scorpio	Water	Fruitful	3rd
26 Sun.	Scorpio	Water	Fruitful	3rd
27 Mon. 6:30 pm	Sagit.	Fire	Barren	3rd
28 Tues.	Sagit.	Fire	Barren	4th 2:09 pm

FEBRUARY 1989
Lunar Aspectarian

Favorable & Unfavorable Days

Day	SUN	MERCURY	VENUS	MARS	JUPITER	SATURN	URANUS	NEPTUNE	PLUTO	ARIES	TAURUS	GEMINI	CANCER	LEO	VIRGO	LIBRA	SCORPIO	SAGITTARIUS	CAPRICORN	AQUARIUS	PISCES
1	Sx									f		U		f	u	f		F		f	u
2								C		f		U		f	u	f		F		f	u
3				T		C		C	Sx	u	f		U		f	u	f		F		f
4		C			T					u	f		U		f	u	f		F		f
5			C	Sq					Sq	f	u	f		U		f	u	f		F	
6	C				Sq					f	u	f		U		f	u	f		F	
7				Sx		Sx	Sx	Sx	T		f	u	f		U		f	u	f		F
8		Sx		Sx							f	u	f		U		f	u	f		F
9			Sx			Sq	Sq	Sq		F		f	u	f		U		f	u	f	
10	Sx	Sq								F		f	u	f		U		f	u	f	
11			Sq	C		T	T	T			F		f	u	f		U		f	u	f
12	Sq				C				O		F		f	u	f		U		f	u	f
13		T								f		F		f	u	f		U		f	u
14			T							f		F		f	u	f		U		f	u
15	T							O		u	f		F		f	u	f		U		f
16			Sx			O		O	T	u	f		F		f	u	f		U		f
17				Sx						u	f		F		f	u	f		U		f
18		O								f	u	f		F		f	u	f		U	
19			O	Sq					Sq	f	u	f		F		f	u	f		U	
20	O			Sq			T				f	u	f		F		f	u	f		U
21				T		T		T	Sx		f	u	f		F		f	u	f		U
22				T							f	u	f		F		f	u	f		U
23		T				Sq	Sq	Sq		U		f	u	f		F		f	u	f	
24										U		f	u	f		F		f	u	f	
25	T		T				Sx				U		f	u	f		F		f	u	f
26		Sq				Sx		Sx	C		U		f	u	f		F		f	u	f
27			Sq	O	O						U		f	u	f		F		f	u	f
28	Sq									f		U		f	u	f		F		f	u

MARCH

Date	Moon's Sign	Element	Nature	Moon's Phase
1 Wed.	Sagit.	Fire	Barren	4th
2 Thurs. 2:59 am	Capri.	Earth	Semi-fruit	4th
3 Fri.	Capri.	Earth	Semi-fruit	4th
4 Sat. 7:37 am	Aquar.	Air	Barren	4th
5 Sun.	Aquar.	Air	Barren	4th
6 Mon. 9:00 am	Pisces	Water	Fruitful	4th
7 Tues.	Pisces	Water	Fruitful	NM 12:20 pm
8 Wed. 8:37 am	Aries	Fire	Barren	1st
9 Thurs.	Aries	Fire	Barren	1st
10 Fri. 8:26 am	Taurus	Earth	Semi-fruit	1st
11 Sat.	Taurus	Earth	Semi-fruit	1st
12 Sun. 10:17 am	Gemini	Air	Barren	1st
13 Mon.	Gemini	Air	Barren	1st
14 Tues. 3:28 pm	Cancer	Water	Fruitful	2nd 4:12 am
15 Wed.	Cancer	Water	Fruitful	2nd
16 Thurs.	Cancer	Water	Fruitful	2nd
17 Fri. 0:14 am	Leo	Fire	Barren	2nd
18 Sat.	Leo	Fire	Barren	2nd
19 Sun. 11:40 am	Virgo	Earth	Barren	2nd
20 Mon.	Virgo	Earth	Barren	2nd

The SUN enters Aries at 9:29 am

Date	Moon's Sign	Element	Nature	Moon's Phase
21 Tues.	Virgo	Earth	Barren	2nd
22 Wed. 0:25 am	Libra	Air	Semi-fruit	FM 3:59 am
23 Thurs.	Libra	Air	Semi-fruit	3rd
24 Fri. 1:11 pm	Scorpio	Water	Fruitful	3rd
25 Sat.	Scorpio	Water	Fruitful	3rd
26 Sun.	Scorpio	Water	Fruitful	3rd
27 Mon. 0:55 am	Sagit.	Fire	Barren	3rd
28 Tues.	Sagit.	Fire	Barren	3rd
29 Wed. 10:26 am	Capri.	Earth	Semi-fruit	3rd
30 Thurs.	Capri.	Earth	Semi-fruit	4th 4:22 am
31 Fri. 4:46 pm	Aquar.	Air	Barren	4th

MARCH 1989
Lunar Aspectarian

Favorable & Unfavorable Days

Day	SUN	MERCURY	VENUS	MARS	JUPITER	SATURN	URANUS	NEPTUNE	PLUTO	ARIES	TAURUS	GEMINI	CANCER	LEO	VIRGO	LIBRA	SCORPIO	SAGITTARIUS	CAPRICORN	AQUARIUS	PISCES
1		Sx								f		U		f	u	f		F		f	u
2			Sx				C			u	f		U		f	u	f		F		f
3	Sx					C		C	Sx	u	f		U		f	u	f		F		f
4				T	T					f	u	f		U		f	u	f		F	
5		C							Sq	f	u	f		U		f	u	f		F	
6				Sq	Sq		Sx				f	u	f		U		f	u	f		F
7	C		C			Sx		Sx	T		f	u	f		U		f	u	f		F
8				Sx	Sx		Sq			F		f	u	f		U		f	u	f	
9						Sq		Sq		F		f	u	f		U		f	u	f	
10		Sx	Sx				T				F		f	u	f		U		f	u	f
11	Sx		Sx			T		T	O		F		f	u	f		U		f	u	f
12		Sq		C	C					f		F		f	u	f		U		f	u
13			Sq							f		F		f	u	f		U		f	u
14	Sq									f		F		f	u	f		U		f	u
15		T				O	O	O	T	u	f		F		f	u	f		U		f
16	T		T							u	f		F		f	u	f		U		f
17				Sx	Sx					f	u	f		F		f	u	f		U	
18									Sq	f	u	f		F		f	u	f		U	
19				Sq	Sq		T				f	u	f		F		f	u	f		U
20		O				T		T	Sx		f	u	f		F		f	u	f		U
21			O								f	u	f		F		f	u	f		U
22	O			T	T		Sq			U		f	u	f		F		f	u	f	
23						Sq		Sq		U		f	u	f		F		f	u	f	
24						Sx				U		f	u	f		F		f	u	f	
25						Sx		Sx	C		U		f	u	f		F		f	u	f
26		T									U		f	u	f		F		f	u	f
27	T		T	O	O					f		U		f	u	f		F	-	f	u
28										f		U		f	u	f		F		f	u
29		Sq					C			u	f		U		f	u	f		F		f
30	Sq		Sq			C		C	Sx	u	f		U		f	u	f		F		f
31					T					u	f		U		f	u	f		F		f

APRIL

Date	Moon's Sign	Element	Nature	Moon's Phase
1 Sat.	Aquar.	Air	Barren	4th
2 Sun. 7:38 pm	Pisces	Water	Fruitful	4th
3 Mon.	Pisces	Water	Fruitful	4th
4 Tues. 7:52 pm	Aries	Fire	Barren	4th
5 Wed.	Aries	Fire	Barren	NM 9:34 pm
6 Thurs. 7:08 pm	Taurus	Earth	Semi-fruit	1st
7 Fri.	Taurus	Earth	Semi-fruit	1st
8 Sat. 7:32 pm	Gemini	Air	Barren	1st
9 Sun.	Gemini	Air	Barren	1st
10 Mon. 10:59 pm	Cancer	Water	Fruitful	1st
11 Tues.	Cancer	Water	Fruitful	1st
12 Wed.	Cancer	Water	Fruitful	2nd 5:14 pm
13 Thurs. 6:32 am	Leo	Fire	Barren	2nd
14 Fri.	Leo	Fire	Barren	2nd
15 Sat. 5:40 pm	Virgo	Earth	Barren	2nd
16 Sun.	Virgo	Earth	Barren	2nd
17 Mon.	Virgo	Earth	Barren	2nd
18 Tues. 6:32 am	Libra	Air	Semi-fruit	2nd
19 Wed.	Libra	Air	Semi-fruit	2nd

The SUN enters Taurus at 8:40 pm

Date	Moon's Sign	Element	Nature	Moon's Phase
20 Thurs. 7:14 pm	Scorpio	Water	Fruitful	FM 9:14 pm
21 Fri.	Scorpio	Water	Fruitful	3rd
22 Sat.	Scorpio	Water	Fruitful	3rd
23 Sun. 6:39 am	Sagit.	Fire	Barren	3rd
24 Mon.	Sagit.	Fire	Barren	3rd
25 Tues. 4:16 pm	Capri.	Earth	Semi-fruit	3rd
26 Wed.	Capri.	Earth	Semi-fruit	3rd
27 Thurs. 11:34 pm	Aquar.	Air	Barren	3rd
28 Fri.	Aquar.	Air	Barren	4th 2:47 pm
29 Sat.	Aquar.	Air	Barren	4th
30 Sun. 4:04 am	Pisces	Water	Fruitful	4th

APRIL 1989
Lunar Aspectarian

Favorable & Unfavorable Days

	SUN	MERCURY	VENUS	MARS	JUPITER	SATURN	URANUS	NEPTUNE	PLUTO	ARIES	TAURUS	GEMINI	CANCER	LEO	VIRGO	LIBRA	SCORPIO	SAGITTARIUS	CAPRICORN	AQUARIUS	PISCES
1	Sx	Sx	Sx	T					Sq	f	u	f		U		f	u	f		F	
2										f	u	f		U		f	u	f		F	
3				Sq	Sq	Sx	Sx	Sx	T		f	u	f		U		f	u	f		F
4											f	u	f		U		f	u	f		F
5	C		C	Sx	Sx	Sq	Sq	Sq		F		f	u	f		U		f	u	f	
6		C								F		f	u	f		U		f	u	f	
7						T	T	T	O		F		f	u	f		U		f	u	f
8											F		f	u	f		U		f	u	f
9					C					f		F		f	u	f		U		f	u
10	Sx	Sx	Sx	C						f		F		f	u	f		U		f	u
11							O	O		u	f		F		f	u	f		U		f
12	Sq		Sq			O			T	u	f		F		f	u	f		U		f
13		Sq		Sx						f	u	f		F		f	u	f		U	
14									Sq	f	u	f		F		f	u	f		U	
15	T		T	Sx						f	u	f		F		f	u	f		U	
16		T			Sq	T	T	T	Sx		f	u	f		F		f	u	f		U
17			Sq								f	u	f		F		f	u	f		U
18				T		Sq				U		f	u	f		F		f	u	f	
19					Sq		Sq			U		f	u	f		F		f	u	f	
20	O			T						U		f	u	f		F		f	u	f	
21			O			Sx	Sx	Sx	C		U		f	u	f		F		f	u	f
22		O									U		f	u	f		F		f	u	f
23					O					f		U		f	u	f		F		f	u
24										f		U		f	u	f		F		f	u
25			O							f		U		f	u	f		F		f	u
26	T		T			C	C	C	Sx	u	f		U		f	u	f		F		f
27		T								u	f		U		f	u	f		F		f
28	Sq			T						f	u	f		U		f	u	f		F	
29			Sq						Sq	f	u	f		U		f	u	f		F	
30	Sx	Sq		T	Sq		Sx				f	u	f		U		f	u	f		F

MAY

Date	Moon's Sign	Element	Nature	Moon's Phase
1 Mon.	Pisces	Water	Fruitful	4th
2 Tues. 5:51 am	Aries	Fire	Barren	4th
3 Wed.	Aries	Fire	Barren	4th
4 Thurs. 5:56 am	Taurus	Earth	Semi-fruit	4th
5 Fri.	Taurus	Earth	Semi-fruit	NM 5:47 am
6 Sat. 6:04 am	Gemini	Air	Barren	1st
7 Sun.	Gemini	Air	Barren	1st
8 Mon. 8:20 am	Cancer	Water	Fruitful	1st
9 Tues.	Cancer	Water	Fruitful	1st
10 Wed. 2:24 pm	Leo	Fire	Barren	1st
11 Thurs.	Leo	Fire	Barren	1st
12 Fri.	Leo	Fire	Barren	2nd 8:21 am
13 Sat. 0:31 am	Virgo	Earth	Barren	2nd
14 Sun.	Virgo	Earth	Barren	2nd
15 Mon. 1:08 pm	Libra	Air	Semi-fruit	2nd
16 Tues.	Libra	Air	Semi-fruit	2nd
17 Wed.	Libra	Air	Semi-fruit	2nd
18 Thurs. 1:48 am	Scorpio	Water	Fruitful	2nd
19 Fri.	Scorpio	Water	Fruitful	2nd
20 Sat. 12:53 pm	Sagit.	Fire	Barren	FM 12:17 pm

The SUN enters Gemini at 7:55 pm

Date	Moon's Sign	Element	Nature	Moon's Phase
21 Sun.	Sagit.	Fire	Barren	3rd
22 Mon. 9:55 pm	Capri.	Earth	Semi-fruit	3rd
23 Tues.	Capri.	Earth	Semi-fruit	3rd
24 Wed.	Capri.	Earth	Semi-fruit	3rd
25 Thurs. 5:02 am	Aquar.	Air	Barren	3rd
26 Fri.	Aquar.	Air	Barren	3rd
27 Sat. 10:14 am	Pisces	Water	Fruitful	4th 10:02 pm
28 Sun.	Pisces	Water	Fruitful	4th
29 Mon. 1:26 pm	Aries	Fire	Barren	4th
30 Tues.	Aries	Fire	Barren	4th
31 Wed. 3:00 pm	Taurus	Earth	Semi-fruit	4th

MAY 1989
Lunar Aspectarian

Favorable & Unfavorable Days

	SUN	MERCURY	VENUS	MARS	JUPITER	SATURN	URANUS	NEPTUNE	PLUTO	ARIES	TAURUS	GEMINI	CANCER	LEO	VIRGO	LIBRA	SCORPIO	SAGITTARIUS	CAPRICORN	AQUARIUS	PISCES
1			Sx			Sx		Sx	T		f	u	f		U		f	u	f		F
2		Sx		Sq	Sx		Sq			F		f	u	f		U		f	u	f	
3						Sq		Sq		F		f	u	f		U		f	u	f	
4			Sx				T				F		f	u	f		U		f	u	f
5	C		C			T		T	O		F		f	u	f		U		f	u	f
6		C								f		F		f	u	f		U		f	u
7				C						f		F		f	u	f		U		f	u
8			C				O			u	f		F		f	u	f		U		f
9	Sx							O	T	u	f		F		f	u	f		U		f
10			Sx							u	f		F		f	u	f		U		f
11		Sx			Sx				Sq	f	u	f		F		f	u	f		U	
12	Sq									f	u	f		F		f	u	f		U	
13		Sq	Sq	Sx			T				f	u	f		F		f	u	f		U
14				Sq	T			T	Sx		f	u	f		F		f	u	f		U
15	T						Sq				f	u	f		F		f	u	f		U
16		T	T	Sq	T	Sq		Sq		U		f	u	f		F		f	u	f	
17										U		f	u	f		F		f	u	f	
18						Sx					U		f	u	f		F		f	u	f
19			T		Sx		Sx		C		U		f	u	f		F		f	u	f
20	O	O									U		f	u	f		F		f	u
21			O		O					f		U		f	u	f		F		f	u
22										f		U		f	u	f		F		f	u
23					C	C	C		Sx	u	f		U		f	u	f		F		f
24				O						u	f		U		f	u	f		F		f
25	T	T								f	u	f		U		f	u	f		F	
26			T		T				Sq	f	u	f		U		f	u	f		F	
27	Sq	Sq				Sx					f	u	f		U		f	u	f		F
28			T	Sq	Sx			Sx	T		f	u	f		U		f	u	f		F
29		Sx	Sq				Sq				f	u	f		U		f	u	f		F
30	Sx			Sq	Sx	Sq		Sq		F		f	u	f		U		f	u	f	
31			Sx				T			F		f	u	f		U		f	u	f	

JUNE

Date	Moon's Sign	Element	Nature	Moon's Phase
1 Thurs.	Taurus	Earth	Semi-fruit	4th
2 Fri. 4:03 pm	Gemini	Air	Barren	4th
3 Sat.	Gemini	Air	Barren	NM 1:54 pm
4 Sun. 6:18 pm	Cancer	Water	Fruitful	1st
5 Mon.	Cancer	Water	Fruitful	1st
6 Tues. 11:29 pm	Leo	Fire	Barren	1st
7 Wed.	Leo	Fire	Barren	1st
8 Thurs.	Leo	Fire	Barren	1st
9 Fri. 8:30 am	Virgo	Earth	Barren	1st
10 Sat.	Virgo	Earth	Barren	1st
11 Sun. 8:32 pm	Libra	Air	Semi-fruit	2nd 1:00 am
12 Mon.	Libra	Air	Semi-fruit	2nd
13 Tues.	Libra	Air	Semi-fruit	2nd
14 Wed. 9:12 am	Scorpio	Water	Fruitful	2nd
15 Thurs.	Scorpio	Water	Fruitful	2nd
16 Fri. 8:13 pm	Sagit.	Fire	Barren	2nd
17 Sat.	Sagit.	Fire	Barren	2nd
18 Sun.	Sagit.	Fire	Barren	2nd
19 Mon. 4:42 am	Capri.	Earth	Semi-fruit	FM 0:58 am
20 Tues.	Capri.	Earth	Semi-fruit	3rd
21 Wed. 10:58 am	Aquar.	Air	Barren	3rd

The SUN enters Cancer at 3:54 am

Date	Moon's Sign	Element	Nature	Moon's Phase
22 Thurs.	Aquar.	Air	Barren	3rd
23 Fri. 3:37 pm	Pisces	Water	Fruitful	3rd
24 Sat.	Pisces	Water	Fruitful	3rd
25 Sun. 7:07 pm	Aries	Fire	Barren	3rd
26 Mon.	Aries	Fire	Barren	4th 3:10 am
27 Tues. 9:46 pm	Taurus	Earth	Semi-fruit	4th
28 Wed.	Taurus	Earth	Semi-fruit	4th
29 Thurs.	Taurus	Earth	Semi-fruit	4th
30 Fri. 0:09 am	Gemini	Air	Barren	4th

JUNE 1989
Lunar Aspectarian — Favorable & Unfavorable Days

Day	SUN	MERCURY	VENUS	MARS	JUPITER	SATURN	URANUS	NEPTUNE	PLUTO	ARIES	TAURUS	GEMINI	CANCER	LEO	VIRGO	LIBRA	SCORPIO	SAGITTARIUS	CAPRICORN	AQUARIUS	PISCES
1						T		T	O		F		f	u	f		U		f	u	f
2		C		Sx							F		f	u	f		U		f	u	f
3	C				C					f		F		f	u	f		U		f	u
4			C							f		F		f	u	f		U		f	u
5						O	O	O	T	u	f		F		f	u	f		U		f
6		Sx		C						u	f		F		f	u	f		U		f
7									Sq	f	u	f		F		f	u	f		U	
8	Sx			Sx						f	u	f		F		f	u	f		U	
9		Sq	Sx				T				f	u	f		F		f	u	f		U
10				Sq	T			T	Sx		f	u	f		F		f	u	f		U
11	Sq	T		Sx							f	u	f		F		f	u	f		U
12			Sq			Sq	Sq	Sq		U		f	u	f		F		f	u	f	
13	T				T					U		f	u	f		F		f	u	f	
14				Sq			Sx				U		f	u	f		F		f	u	f
15			T			Sx		Sx	C		U		f	u	f		F		f	u	f
16			T	T							U		f	u	f		F		f	u	f
17		O								f		U		f	u	f		F		f	u
18				O						f		U		f	u	f		F		f	u
19	O						C			u	f		U		f	u	f		F		f
20			O			C		C	Sx	u	f		U		f	u	f		F		f
21				O						f	u	f		U		f	u	f		F	
22	T								Sq	f	u	f		U		f	u	f		F	
23	T				T		Sx				f	u	f		U		f	u	f		F
24		Sq				Sx		Sx	T		f	u	f		U		f	u	f		F
25			T		Sq						f	u	f		U		f	u	f		F
26	Sq	Sx		T		Sq	Sq	Sq		F		f	u	f		U		f	u	f
27			Sq		Sx					F		f	u	f		U		f	u	f
28	Sx			Sq		T	T	T	O	F		f	u	f		U		f	u	f
29										F		f	u	f		U		f	u	f
30			Sx	Sx						f		F		f	u	f		U		f	u

JULY

Date	Moon's Sign	Element	Nature	Moon's Phase
1 Sat.	Gemini	Air	Barren	4th
2 Sun. 3:20 am	Cancer	Water	Fruitful	NM 11:00 pm
3 Mon.	Cancer	Water	Fruitful	1st
4 Tues. 8:38 am	Leo	Fire	Barren	1st
5 Wed.	Leo	Fire	Barren	1st
6 Thurs. 5:05 pm	Virgo	Earth	Barren	1st
7 Fri.	Virgo	Earth	Barren	1st
8 Sat.	Virgo	Earth	Barren	1st
9 Sun. 4:31 am	Libra	Air	Semi-fruit	1st
10 Mon.	Libra	Air	Semi-fruit	2nd 6:20 pm
11 Tues. 5:10 pm	Scorpio	Water	Fruitful	2nd
12 Wed.	Scorpio	Water	Fruitful	2nd
13 Thurs.	Scorpio	Water	Fruitful	2nd
14 Fri. 4:32 am	Sagit.	Fire	Barren	2nd
15 Sat.	Sagit.	Fire	Barren	2nd
16 Sun. 1:02 pm	Capri.	Earth	Semi-fruit	2nd
17 Mon.	Capri.	Earth	Semi-fruit	2nd
18 Tues. 6:36 pm	Aquar.	Air	Barren	FM 11:42 am
19 Wed.	Aquar.	Air	Barren	3rd
20 Thurs. 10:08 pm	Pisces	Water	Fruitful	3rd
21 Fri.	Pisces	Water	Fruitful	3rd
22 Sat.	Pisces	Water	Fruitful	3rd
The SUN enters Leo at 2:46 pm				
23 Sun. 0:41 am	Aries	Fire	Barren	3rd
24 Mon.	Aries	Fire	Barren	3rd
25 Tues. 3:11 am	Taurus	Earth	Semi-fruit	4th 7:32 am
26 Wed.	Taurus	Earth	Semi-fruit	4th
27 Thurs. 6:16 am	Gemini	Air	Barren	4th
28 Fri.	Gemini	Air	Barren	4th
29 Sat. 10:33 am	Cancer	Water	Fruitful	4th
30 Sun.	Cancer	Water	Fruitful	4th
31 Mon. 4:42 pm	Leo	Fire	Barren	4th

JULY 1989
Lunar Aspectarian

Favorable & Unfavorable Days

	SUN	MERCURY	VENUS	MARS	JUPITER	SATURN	URANUS	NEPTUNE	PLUTO	ARIES	TAURUS	GEMINI	CANCER	LEO	VIRGO	LIBRA	SCORPIO	SAGITTARIUS	CAPRICORN	AQUARIUS	PISCES
1		C				C				f		F		f	u	f		U		f	u
2	C					O	O	O		u	f		F		f	u	f		U		f
3									T	u	f		F		f	u	f		U		f
4			C							f	u	f		F		f	u	f		U	
5				C					Sq	f	u	f		F		f	u	f		U	
6		Sx				Sx		T		f	u	f		F		f	u	f		U	
7						T		T	Sx		f	u	f		F		f	u	f		U
8	Sx				Sq						f	u	f		F		f	u	f		U
9		Sq					Sq			U		f	u	f		F		f	u	f	
10	Sq		Sx	Sx		Sq		Sq		U		f	u	f		F		f	u	f	
11					T		Sx			U		f	u	f		F		f	u	f	
12		T				Sx		Sx	C		U		f	u	f		F		f	u	f
13	T		Sq	Sq							U		f	u	f		F		f	u	f
14										f		U		f	u	f		F		f	u
15			T	T						f		U		f	u	f		F		f	u
16					O		C			f		U		f	u	f		F		f	u
17						C		C	Sx	u	f		U		f	u	f		F		f
18	O	O								u	f		U		f	u	f		F		f
19									Sq	f	u	f		U		f	u	f		F	
20			O	O	T					f	u	f		U		f	u	f		F	
21						Sx	Sx	Sx	T		f	u	f		U		f	u	f		F
22				Sq							f	u	f		U		f	u	f		F
23	T	T				Sq	Sq	Sq		F		f	u	f		U		f	u	f	
24				T						F		f	u	f		U		f	u	f	
25	Sq	Sq	T			Sx	T	T	T		F		f	u	f		U		f	u	f
26			Sq						O		F		f	u	f		U		f	u	f
27	Sx		Sq							f		F		f	u	f		U		f	u
28		Sx								f		F		f	u	f		U		f	u
29			Sx	Sx	C			O		u	f		F		f	u	f		U		f
30						O		O	T	u	f		F		f	u	f		U		f
31										u	f		F		f	u	f		U		f

AUGUST

Date	Moon's Sign	Element	Nature	Moon's Phase
1 Tues.	Leo	Fire	Barren	NM 10:07 am
2 Wed.	Leo	Fire	Barren	1st
3 Thurs. 1:20 am	Virgo	Earth	Barren	1st
4 Fri.	Virgo	Earth	Barren	1st
5 Sat. 12:29 pm	Libra	Air	Semi-fruit	1st
6 Sun.	Libra	Air	Semi-fruit	1st
7 Mon.	Libra	Air	Semi-fruit	1st
8 Tues. 1:06 am	Scorpio	Water	Fruitful	1st
9 Wed.	Scorpio	Water	Fruitful	2nd 11:29 am
10 Thurs. 1:03 pm	Sagit.	Fire	Barren	2nd
11 Fri.	Sagit.	Fire	Barren	2nd
12 Sat. 10:17 pm	Capri.	Earth	Semi-fruit	2nd
13 Sun.	Capri.	Earth	Semi-fruit	2nd
14 Mon.	Capri.	Earth	Semi-fruit	2nd
15 Tues. 4:00 am	Aquar.	Air	Barren	2nd
16 Wed.	Aquar.	Air	Barren	FM 9:07 pm
17 Thurs. 6:46 am	Pisces	Water	Fruitful	3rd
18 Fri.	Pisces	Water	Fruitful	3rd
19 Sat. 8:00 am	Aries	Fire	Barren	3rd
20 Sun.	Aries	Fire	Barren	3rd
21 Mon. 9:11 am	Taurus	Earth	Semi-fruit	3rd
22 Tues.	Taurus	Earth	Semi-fruit	3rd

The SUN enters Virgo at 9:47 pm

Date	Moon's Sign	Element	Nature	Moon's Phase
23 Wed. 11:40 am	Gemini	Air	Barren	4th 12:41 pm
24 Thurs.	Gemini	Air	Barren	4th
25 Fri. 4:14 pm	Cancer	Water	Fruitful	4th
26 Sat.	Cancer	Water	Fruitful	4th
27 Sun. 11:13 pm	Leo	Fire	Barren	4th
28 Mon.	Leo	Fire	Barren	4th
29 Tues.	Leo	Fire	Barren	4th
30 Wed. 8:30 am	Virgo	Earth	Barren	NM 11:45 pm
31 Thurs.	Virgo	Earth	Barren	1st

AUGUST 1989
Lunar Aspectarian

Favorable & Unfavorable Days

	SUN	MERCURY	VENUS	MARS	JUPITER	SATURN	URANUS	NEPTUNE	PLUTO	ARIES	TAURUS	GEMINI	CANCER	LEO	VIRGO	LIBRA	SCORPIO	SAGITTARIUS	CAPRICORN	AQUARIUS	PISCES
1	C								Sq	f	u	f		F		f	u	f		U	
2		C								f	u	f		F		f	u	f		U	
3				C	Sx	T	T	T			f	u	f		F		f	u	f		U
4			C						Sx		f	u	f		F		f	u	f		U
5					Sq		Sq				f	u	f		F		f	u	f		U
6	Sx					Sq		Sq		U		f	u	f		F		f	u	f	
7										U		f	u	f		F		f	u	f	
8		Sx		Sx	T	Sx	Sx	Sx			U		f	u	f		F		f	u	f
9	Sq		Sx						C		U		f	u	f		F		f	u	f
10				Sq							U		f	u	f		F		f	u	f
11		Sq								f		U		f	u	f		F		f	u
12	T		Sq							f		U		f	u	f		F		f	u
13				T	O	C	C	C	Sx	u	f		U		f	u	f		F		f
14		T	T							u	f		U		f	u	f		F		f
15										f	u	f		U		f	u	f		F	
16	O								Sq	f	u	f		U		f	u	f		F	
17				O	T	Sx	Sx	Sx			f	u	f		U		f	u	f		F
18		O						T			f	u	f		U		f	u	f		F
19			O		Sq	Sq	Sq			F		f	u	f		U		f	u	f	
20							Sq			F		f	u	f		U		f	u	f	
21	T			Sx	T	T					F		f	u	f		U		f	u	f
22			T				T	O			F		f	u	f		U		f	u	f
23	Sq	T								f		F		f	u	f		U		f	u
24			T	Sq						f		F		f	u	f		U		f	u
25	Sx	Sq				O				f		F		f	u	f		U		f	u
26			Sq	Sx	C	O		O	T	u	f		F		f	u	f		U		f
27										u	f		F		f	u	f		U		f
28		Sx							Sq	f	u	f		F		f	u	f		U	
29			Sx							f	u	f		F		f	u	f		U	
30	C				Sx	T	T			f	u	f		F		f	u	f			U
31				C				T	Sx	f	u	f		F		f	u	f			U

SEPTEMBER

Date	Moon's Sign	Element	Nature	Moon's Phase
1 Fri. 7:48 pm	Libra	Air	Semi-fruit	1st
2 Sat.	Libra	Air	Semi-fruit	1st
3 Sun.	Libra	Air	Semi-fruit	1st
4 Mon. 8:24 am	Scorpio	Water	Fruitful	1st
5 Tues.	Scorpio	Water	Fruitful	1st
6 Wed. 8:52 pm	Sagit.	Fire	Barren	1st
7 Thurs.	Sagit.	Fire	Barren	1st
8 Fri.	Sagit.	Fire	Barren	2nd 3:50 am
9 Sat. 7:14 am	Capri.	Earth	Semi-fruit	2nd
10 Sun.	Capri.	Earth	Semi-fruit	2nd
11 Mon. 2:03 pm	Aquar.	Air	Barren	2nd
12 Tues.	Aquar.	Air	Barren	2nd
13 Wed. 5:08 pm	Pisces	Water	Fruitful	2nd
14 Thurs.	Pisces	Water	Fruitful	2nd
15 Fri. 5:39 pm	Aries	Fire	Barren	FM 5:52 am
16 Sat.	Aries	Fire	Barren	3rd
17 Sun. 5:23 pm	Taurus	Earth	Semi-fruit	3rd
18 Mon.	Taurus	Earth	Semi-fruit	3rd
19 Tues. 6:17 pm	Gemini	Air	Barren	3rd
20 Wed.	Gemini	Air	Barren	3rd
21 Thurs. 9:51 pm	Cancer	Water	Fruitful	4th 8:11 pm
22 Fri.	Cancer	Water	Fruitful	4th

The SUN enters Libra at 7:21 pm

Date	Moon's Sign	Element	Nature	Moon's Phase
23 Sat.	Cancer	Water	Fruitful	4th
24 Sun. 4:45 am	Leo	Fire	Barren	4th
25 Mon.	Leo	Fire	Barren	4th
26 Tues. 2:33 pm	Virgo	Earth	Barren	4th
27 Wed.	Virgo	Earth	Barren	4th
28 Thurs.	Virgo	Earth	Barren	4th
29 Fri. 2:16 am	Libra	Air	Semi-fruit	NM 3:48 pm
30 Sat.	Libra	Air	Semi-fruit	1st

Favorable & Unfavorable Days

Day	SUN	MERCURY	VENUS	MARS	JUPITER	SATURN	URANUS	NEPTUNE	PLUTO	ARIES	TAURUS	GEMINI	CANCER	LEO	VIRGO	LIBRA	SCORPIO	SAGITTARIUS	CAPRICORN	AQUARIUS	PISCES
1								Sq			f		u	f	F		f	u	f		U
2		C			Sq	Sq		Sq		U		f		u	f	F		f	u	f	
3			C							U		f		u	f	F		f	u	f	
4					T	Sx	Sx				U		f		u	f	F		f	u	f
5	Sx							Sx	C		U		f		u	f	F		f	u	f
6				Sx						f		U		f		u	f	F		f	u
7		Sx								f		U		f		u	f	F		f	u
8	Sq		Sx	Sq						f		U		f		u	f	F		f	u
9					O	C	C			u	f		U		f		u	f	F		f
10	T	Sq						C	Sx	u	f		U		f		u	f	F		f
11			Sq	T						f	u	f		U		f		u	f	F	
12		T							Sq	f	u	f		U		f		u	f	F	
13			T				Sx				f	u	f		U		f		u	f	F
14					T	Sx		Sx	T		f	u	f		U		f		u	f	F
15	O			O			Sq				f	u	f		U		f		u	f	F
16		O			Sq	Sq		Sq		F		f	u	f		U		f		u	f
17							T	T	O	f	F		f	u	f		U		f		u
18			O		Sx	T		T	O	f	F		f	u	f		U		f		u
19	T			T						f	F		f	u	f		U		f		u
20		T								u	f	F		f	u	f		U		f	
21	Sq									u	f	F		f	u	f		U		f	
22		Sq	T	Sq	C	O	O	O	T		u	f	F		f	u	f		U		f
23											u	f	F		f	u	f		U		f
24	Sx	Sx		Sx						f		u	f	F		f	u	f		U	
25			Sq							f		u	f	F		f	u	f		U	
26							T				f		u	f	F		f	u	f		U
27				Sx	T			T	Sx		f		u	f	F		f	u	f		U
28		C	Sx							U		f		u	f	F		f	u	f	
29	C			C	Sq	Sq	Sq	Sq		U		f		u	f	F		f	u	f	
30										U		f		u	f	F		f	u	f	

OCTOBER

Date	Moon's Sign	Element	Nature	Moon's Phase
1 Sun. 2:54 pm	Scorpio	Water	Fruitful	1st
2 Mon.	Scorpio	Water	Fruitful	1st
3 Tues.	Scorpio	Water	Fruitful	1st
4 Wed. 3:30 am	Sagit.	Fire	Barren	1st
5 Thurs.	Sagit.	Fire	Barren	1st
6 Fri. 2:46 pm	Capri.	Earth	Semi-fruit	1st
7 Sat.	Capri.	Earth	Semi-fruit	2nd 6:53 pm
8 Sun. 11:07 pm	Aquar.	Air	Barren	2nd
9 Mon.	Aquar.	Air	Barren	2nd
10 Tues.	Aquar.	Air	Barren	2nd
11 Wed. 3:38 am	Pisces	Water	Fruitful	2nd
12 Thurs.	Pisces	Water	Fruitful	2nd
13 Fri. 4:42 am	Aries	Fire	Barren	2nd
14 Sat.	Aries	Fire	Barren	FM 2:33 pm
15 Sun. 3:53 am	Taurus	Earth	Semi-fruit	3rd
16 Mon.	Taurus	Earth	Semi-fruit	3rd
17 Tues. 3:20 am	Gemini	Air	Barren	3rd
18 Wed.	Gemini	Air	Barren	3rd
19 Thurs. 5:10 am	Cancer	Water	Fruitful	3rd
20 Fri.	Cancer	Water	Fruitful	3rd
21 Sat. 10:48 am	Leo	Fire	Barren	4th 7:20 am
22 Sun.	Leo	Fire	Barren	4th
23 Mon. 8:16 pm	Virgo	Earth	Barren	4th

The SUN enters Scorpio at 4:36 am

Date	Moon's Sign	Element	Nature	Moon's Phase
24 Tues.	Virgo	Earth	Barren	4th
25 Wed.	Virgo	Earth	Barren	4th
26 Thurs. 8:12 am	Libra	Air	Semi-fruit	4th
27 Fri.	Libra	Air	Semi-fruit	4th
28 Sat. 8:57 pm	Scorpio	Water	Fruitful	4th
29 Sun.	Scorpio	Water	Fruitful	NM 9:28 am
30 Mon.	Scorpio	Water	Fruitful	1st
31 Tues. 9:24 am	Sagit.	Fire	Barren	1st

OCTOBER 1989
Lunar Aspectarian

Favorable & Unfavorable Days

	SUN	MERCURY	VENUS	MARS	JUPITER	SATURN	URANUS	NEPTUNE	PLUTO	ARIES	TAURUS	GEMINI	CANCER	LEO	VIRGO	LIBRA	SCORPIO	SAGITTARIUS	CAPRICORN	AQUARIUS	PISCES
1								Sx		U		f	u	f		F		f	u	f	
2					T	Sx		Sx	C		U		f	u	f		F		f	u	f
3		Sx	C								U		f	u	f		F		f	u	f
4				Sx						f		U		f	u	f		F		f	u
5	Sx									f		U		f	u	f		F		f	u
6		Sq					C			f		U		f	u	f		F		f	u
7	Sq			Sq	O	C		C	Sx	u	f		U		f	u	f		F		
8		T								u	f		U		f	u	f		F		
9			Sx	T						f	u	f		U		f	u	f		F	
10	T								Sq	f	u	f		U		f	u	f		F	
11			Sq		T	Sx	Sx	Sx			f	u	f		U		f	u	f		F
12									T		f	u	f		U		f	u	f		F
13		O	T		Sq	Sq	Sq	Sq		F		f	u	f		U		f	u	f	
14	O			O						F		f	u	f		U		f	u	f	
15					Sx	T	T	T			F		f	u	f		U		f	u	f
16									O		F		f	u	f		U		f	u	f
17		T	O							f		F		f	u	f		U		f	u
18	T			T						f		F		f	u	f		U		f	u
19					C	O	O	O		u	f		F		f	u	f		U		f
20		Sq		Sq					T	u	f		F		f	u	f		U		f
21	Sq									f	u	f		F		f	u	f		U	
22		Sx	T						Sq	f	u	f		F		f	u	f		U	
23	Sx			Sx						f	u	f		F		f	u	f		U	
24					Sx	T	T	T			f	u	f		F		f	u	f		U
25			Sq						Sx		f	u	f		F		f	u	f		U
26						Sq				U		f	u	f		F		f	u	f	
27				Sq	Sq			Sq		U		f	u	f		F		f	u	f	
28		C	Sx	C						U		f	u	f		F		f	u	f	
29	C				T	Sx	Sx	Sx			U		f	u	f		F		f	u	f
30									C		U		f	u	f		F		f	u	f
31										f		U		f	u	f		F		f	u

NOVEMBER

Date	Moon's Sign	Element	Nature	Moon's Phase
1 Wed.	Sagit.	Fire	Barren	1st
2 Thurs. 8:47 pm	Capri.	Earth	Semi-fruit	1st
3 Fri.	Capri.	Earth	Semi-fruit	1st
4 Sat.	Capri.	Earth	Semi-fruit	1st
5 Sun. 6:10 am	Aquar.	Air	Barren	1st
6 Mon.	Aquar.	Air	Barren	2nd 8:12 am
7 Tues. 12:26 pm	Pisces	Water	Fruitful	2nd
8 Wed.	Pisces	Water	Fruitful	2nd
9 Thurs. 3:09 pm	Aries	Fire	Barren	2nd
10 Fri.	Aries	Fire	Barren	2nd
11 Sat. 3:10 pm	Taurus	Earth	Semi-fruit	2nd
12 Sun.	Taurus	Earth	Semi-fruit	FM 11:52 pm
13 Mon. 2:20 pm	Gemini	Air	Barren	3rd
14 Tues.	Gemini	Air	Barren	3rd
15 Wed. 2:52 pm	Cancer	Water	Fruitful	3rd
16 Thurs.	Cancer	Water	Fruitful	3rd
17 Fri. 6:47 pm	Leo	Fire	Barren	3rd
18 Sat.	Leo	Fire	Barren	3rd
19 Sun.	Leo	Fire	Barren	4th 10:45 pm
20 Mon. 2:55 am	Virgo	Earth	Barren	4th
21 Tues.	Virgo	Earth	Barren	4th
22 Wed. 2:26 pm	Libra	Air	Semi-fruit	4th

The SUN enters Sagittarius at 2:06 am

Date	Moon's Sign	Element	Nature	Moon's Phase
23 Thurs.	Libra	Air	Semi-fruit	4th
24 Fri.	Libra	Air	Semi-fruit	4th
25 Sat. 3:14 am	Scorpio	Water	Fruitful	4th
26 Sun.	Scorpio	Water	Fruitful	4th
27 Mon. 3:31 pm	Sagit.	Fire	Barren	4th
28 Tues.	Sagit.	Fire	Barren	NM 3:42 am
29 Wed.	Sagit.	Fire	Barren	1st
30 Thurs. 2:27 am	Capri.	Earth	Semi-fruit	1st

NOVEMBER 1989
Lunar Aspectarian

Favorable & Unfavorable Days

	SUN	MERCURY	VENUS	MARS	JUPITER	SATURN	URANUS	NEPTUNE	PLUTO	ARIES	TAURUS	GEMINI	CANCER	LEO	VIRGO	LIBRA	SCORPIO	SAGITTARIUS	CAPRICORN	AQUARIUS	PISCES
1										f		U		f	u	f		F		f	u
2			C	Sx						f		U		f	u	f		F		f	u
3	Sx	Sx			O	C	C	C		u	f		U		f	u	f		F		f
4									Sx	u	f		U		f	u	f		F		f
5				Sq						f	u	f		U		f	u	f		F	
6	Sq	Sq							Sq	f	u	f		U		f	u	f		F	
7			Sx	T			Sx			f	u	f		U		f	u	f		F	
8	T	T			T	Sx		Sx	T		f	u	f		U		f	u	f		F
9			Sq				Sq				f	u	f		U		f	u	f		F
10					Sq	Sq		Sq		F		f	u	f		U		f	u	f	
11				O			T			F		f	u	f		U		f	u	f	
12	O		T		Sx	T		T	O		F		f	u	f		U		f	u	f
13		O									F		f	u	f		U		f	u	f
14										f		F		f	u	f		U		f	u
15							O			f		F		f	u	f		U		f	u
16			O	T	C	O		O	T	u	f		F		f	u	f		U		f
17	T	T								u	f		F		f	u	f		U		f
18				Sq					Sq	f	u	f		F		f	u	f		U	
19	Sq									f	u	f		F		f	u	f		U	
20		Sq			Sx		T	T			f	u	f		F		f	u	f		U
21			T	Sx		T			Sx		f	u	f		F		f	u	f		U
22	Sx						Sq				f	u	f		F		f	u	f		U
23		Sx			Sq	Sq		Sq		U		f	u	f		F		f	u	f	
24			Sq							U		f	u	f		F		f	u	f	
25					T		Sx				U		f	u	f		F		f	u	f
26			Sx	C		Sx		Sx	C		U		f	u	f		F		f	u	f
27											U		f	u	f		F		f	u	f
28	C									f		U		f	u	f		F		f	u
29		C								f		U		f	u	f		F		f	u
30					O		C	C		u	f		U		f	u	f		F		f

DECEMBER

Date	Moon's Sign	Element	Nature	Moon's Phase
1 Fri.	Capri.	Earth	Semi-fruit	1st
2 Sat. 11:43 am	Aquar.	Air	Barren	1st
3 Sun.	Aquar.	Air	Barren	1st
4 Mon. 6:49 pm	Pisces	Water	Fruitful	1st
5 Tues.	Pisces	Water	Fruitful	2nd 7:27 pm
6 Wed. 11:12 pm	Aries	Fire	Barren	2nd
7 Thurs.	Aries	Fire	Barren	2nd
8 Fri.	Aries	Fire	Barren	2nd
9 Sat. 1:00 am	Taurus	Earth	Semi-fruit	2nd
10 Sun.	Taurus	Earth	Semi-fruit	2nd
11 Mon. 1:16 am	Gemini	Air	Barren	2nd
12 Tues.	Gemini	Air	Barren	FM 10:31 am
13 Wed. 1:50 am	Cancer	Water	Fruitful	3rd
14 Thurs.	Cancer	Water	Fruitful	3rd
15 Fri. 4:42 am	Leo	Fire	Barren	3rd
16 Sat.	Leo	Fire	Barren	3rd
17 Sun. 11:20 am	Virgo	Earth	Barren	3rd
18 Mon.	Virgo	Earth	Barren	3rd
19 Tues. 9:46 pm	Libra	Air	Semi-fruit	4th 5:55 pm
20 Wed.	Libra	Air	Semi-fruit	4th
21 Thurs.	Libra	Air	Semi-fruit	4th

The SUN enters Capricorn at 3:23 pm

Date	Moon's Sign	Element	Nature	Moon's Phase
22 Fri. 10:19 am	Scorpio	Water	Fruitful	4th
23 Sat.	Scorpio	Water	Fruitful	4th
24 Sun. 10:38 pm	Sagit.	Fire	Barren	4th
25 Mon.	Sagit.	Fire	Barren	4th
26 Tues.	Sagit.	Fire	Barren	4th
27 Wed. 9:11 am	Capri.	Earth	Semi-fruit	NM 9:20 pm
28 Thurs.	Capri.	Earth	Semi-fruit	1st
29 Fri. 5:39 pm	Aquar.	Air	Barren	1st
30 Sat.	Aquar.	Air	Barren	1st
31 Sun.	Aquar.	Air	Barren	1st

DECEMBER 1989
Lunar Aspectarian

Favorable & Unfavorable Days

	SUN	MERCURY	VENUS	MARS	JUPITER	SATURN	URANUS	NEPTUNE	PLUTO	ARIES	TAURUS	GEMINI	CANCER	LEO	VIRGO	LIBRA	SCORPIO	SAGITTARIUS	CAPRICORN	AQUARIUS	PISCES
1				Sx		C			Sx	u	f		U		f	u	f		F		f
2			C							f	u	f		U		f	u	f		F	
3	Sx								Sq	f	u	f		U		f	u	f		F	
4		Sx		Sq						f	u	f		U		f	u	f		F	
5	Sq				T	Sx	Sx	Sx	T		f	u	f		U		f	u	f		F
6		Sq	Sx	T							f	u	f		U		f	u	f		F
7					Sq	Sq	Sq	Sq		F		f	u	f		U		f	u	f	
8	T									F		f	u	f		U		f	u	f	
9		T	Sq		Sx	T	T	T			F		f	u	f		U		f	u	f
10				O					O		F		f	u	f		U		f	u	f
11			T							f		F		f	u	f		U		f	u
12	O									f		F		f	u	f		U		f	u
13		O			C		O	O		u	f		F		f	u	f		U		f
14						O			T	u	f		F		f	u	f		U		f
15			O	T						f	u	f		F		f	u	f		U	
16									Sq	f	u	f		F		f	u	f		U	
17	T			Sq			T			f	u	f		F		f	u	f			U
18		T			Sx	T		T	Sx	f	u	f		F		f	u	f			U
19	Sq									f	u	f		F		f	u	f			U
20			T	Sx	Sq		Sq	Sq		U		f	u	f		F		f	u	f	
21		Sq				Sq				U		f	u	f		F		f	u	f	
22	Sx		Sq		T		Sx				U		f	u	f		F		f	u	f
23						Sx		Sx	C		U		f	u	f		F		f	u	f
24		Sx									U		f	u	f		F		f	u	f
25			Sx	C						f		U		f	u	f		F		f	u
26										f		U		f	u	f		F		f	u
27	C				O		C			u	f		U		f	u	f		F		f
28						C		C	Sx	u	f		U		f	u	f		F		f
29		C								u	f		U		f	u	f		F		f
30			C	Sx						f	u	f		U		f	u	f		F	
31									Sq	f	u	f		U		f	u	f		F	

LUNAR ACTIVITY GUIDE

ACTIVITY	MOON'S SIGN	MOON'S PHASE
Buy animals		New Moon, 1st
Baking	Aries, Cancer, Libra, Capricorn	1st or 2nd
Hair care:		
Permanent waves hair straightening coloring	Aquarius	1st quarter
Cut hair to stimulate growth	Cancer, Scorpio, Pisces	1st or 2nd
Cut hair for thickness	Any sign except Virgo	Full Moon
Cut hair to decrease growth	Gemini, Leo, Virgo	3rd or 4th
Start a diet to lose weight	Aries, Leo, Virgo, Sagit., Aquarius	3rd or 4th
Start a diet to gain weight	Cancer, Scorpio, Pisces	1st or 2nd
Buy clothes	Taurus, Libra	1st or 2nd
Buy antiques	Cancer, Scorpio, Capricorn	
Borrow money	Leo, Sagittarius, Aquarius, Pisces	3rd or 4th
Start a savings account	Taurus, Scorpio, Capricorn	1st or 2nd
Join a club	Gemini, Libra, Aquarius	
Give a party	Gemini, Leo, Libra, Aquarius	
Travel for pleasure	Gemini, Leo, Sagittarius, Aquarius	1st or 2nd
Begin a course of study	Gemini, Virgo, Sagittarius	1st or 2nd
Enter a new job	Taurus, Virgo, Capricorn	1st or 2nd
Can fruits and vegetables	Cancer, Scorpio, Pisces	3rd or 4th
Preserves, jellies	Taurus, Scorpio, Aquarius	3rd or 4th
Dry fruits and vegetables	Aries, Leo, Sagit.	3rd
Remove teeth	Gemini, Virgo, Sagittarius, Capricorn, Pisces	1st or 2nd
Fill teeth	Taurus, Leo, Scorpio, Aquarius	3rd or 4th

ACTIVITY	MOON'S SIGN	MOON'S PHASE
Dressmaking, mending		1st or 2nd
Buy health foods	Virgo	
Buy medicines	Scorpio	
Buy permanent home	Taurus, Leo, Scorpio, Aquarius	
Buy property for speculation	Aries, Cancer, Libra, Capricorn	
Send mail	Gemini, Virgo, Sagittarius, Pisces	
Wood cutting	Any sign but Cancer, Scorpio,	3rd or 4th
Beauty treatments	Taurus, Cancer, Leo, Libra, Scorpio, Aquarius	1st or 2nd
Brewing	Cancer, Scorpio, Pisces	3rd or 4th
Start building	Taurus, Leo, Aquarius	3rd or 4th
Bulbs for seed	Cancer, Scorpio, Pisces	2nd or 3rd
Canning	Cancer, Scorpio, Pisces	3rd or 4th
Pour cement	Taurus, Leo, Aquarius	Full Moon
Plant cereals	Cancer, Scorpio, Pisces	1st or 2nd
Cultivation	Aries, Gemini, Leo, Virgo, Sagit., Aquarius	4th
Breaking habits	Gemini, Leo, Virgo	3rd or 4th
Fix your car	Taurus, Virgo	1st or 2nd
Weddings	Taurus, Cancer, Leo, Libra, Pisces	2nd
Move	Taurus, Leo, Scorpio, Aquarius	
Painting	Taurus, Leo, Scorpio, Aquarius	3rd or 4th
Train a pet	Taurus	3rd or 4th
Buy a car	Taurus, Leo, Scorpio, Aquarius	3rd or 4th
Collect debts	Aries, Cancer Libra, Capricon	3rd or 4th

ASTRO-ALMANAC

How to Use the ASTRO-ALMANAC

Llewellyn's unique Astro-Almanac is provided for quick reference. Because the dates indicated may not be the best for you personally, be sure to read the instructions on page 33 and then go to the proper section of the book and read the detailed description provided for each activity.

Most of the time, the dates given in the Astro-Almanac will correspond to the ones you can determine for yourself from the detailed instructions. But just as often, the dates given may not be favorable for your Sun Sign or for your particular interests. That's why it's important for you to learn how to use the entire process to come up with the most beneficial dates *for you*.

The following pages are provided for easy reference for those of you who do not need detailed descriptions. The dates provided are determined from the sign and phase of the Moon and the aspects to the Moon.

In this year's edition, we have increased the number of activities covered in the Astro-Almanac. We hope this helps you get quick information for most of your needs. Please read the instructions on how to come up with the dates yourself, though. This is very important in some instances (such as for planning surgery or making big purchases). You will find other lists of dates in the proper sections of *The Moon Sign Book*. We list Fishing and Hunting Dates, Gardening Dates, Dates for Destroying Plant and Animal Pests, and other types of activities. See the Table of Contents for a complete listing.

What to Do When in JANUARY

Entertain: 1, 8-10, 17-18, 22-23, 26-28
Sports activities: 22
Marriage for happiness: None
End a romance of file for divorce: 22-23
Cut hair to increase growth: 11, 19
Cut hair to retard growth: 22-23
Cut hair for added thickness: 21
Permanents and hair coloring: 8-9
Start a weight loss program: 4-5, 22-25, 31
Stop a bad habit: 22-25
See dentist for fillings: 2, 22, 30
See dentist for extractions: 7, 11, 17-18
Consult physician: 1, 6-7, 13-14, 19-21, 26-28
Purchase major appliances: None
Buy a car or have repairs done: 3, 9
Purchase electronic equipment: 1, 10
Buy antiques or jewelry: 7, 16, 20
Buy real estate for speculation: 1, 6-7, 13-14, 19-21, 26-28
Buy permanent home: 2-3, 8-10
Selling home, property, or possessions: 4-5, 9-10, 12, 14, 16-17, 24, 26, 31
Sign important papers: 9
Building: None
Ask for credit or loan: None
Start new ventures or advertise: 9-10
Apply for job: None
Ask for raise or promotion: 4, 9, 17, 26, 31
Collect money: 26
Move into new home: 10, 15
Do roofing: 2-3, 22-23, 29-30
Pour concrete: 8-10, 15-16, 22-23
Painting: 2-3, 22-23, 29-30
Cut timber: 1, 4-6, 31
Travel for business: 1-5, 7, 9-12
Travel for pleasure: 2, 10, 12
Air travel: 1
Buy animals: 8, 11
Neutering or spaying an animal: 6, 8-10
Dock or dehorn animals: 1-10, 29-31
Make sauerkraut: 21
Brewing: 2-3, 21, 29-30
Canning: 2-3, 21, 29-30
Mow lawn to retard growth: 1-6, 21-31

What to Do When in FEBRUARY

Entertain: 5-6, 13-14, 18-19, 23-24
Sports activities: 18
Marriage for happiness: 8, 17
End a romance of file for divorce: None
Cut hair to increase growth: 7-8, 15-17
Cut hair to retard growth: None
Cut hair for added thickness: None
Permanents and hair coloring: 6
Start a weight loss program: 1-2, 5, 20-22, 28
Stop a bad habit: 20-22
See dentist for fillings: 25-26
See dentist for extractions: 7-8, 13-14
Consult physician: 3-4, 9-10, 15-17, 23-24
Purchase major appliances: None
Buy a car or have repairs done: 6, 12, 18, 25
Purchase electronic equipment: 13
Buy antiques or jewelry: 12, 15, 17
Buy real estate for speculation: 3-4, 9-10, 15-17, 23-24
Buy permanent home: 5-6, 11-12, 18-19, 25-27
Selling home, property, or possessions: 3-4, 7-8, 11-13, 17, 21-22
Sign important papers: None
Building: None
Ask for credit or loan: None
Start new ventures or advertise: 6, 12, 15, 17
Apply for job: None
Ask for raise or promotion: 4, 8, 13
Collect money: 4, 17
Move into new home: 25
Do roofing: 5, 25-27
Pour concrete: 5-6, 11-12, 18-19
Painting: 5, 25-27
Cut timber: 1-5, 28
Travel for business: 6-8, 10, 12-15, 17-18, 20-22, 24-26, 28
Travel for pleasure: 8, 10, 14-15, 17, 22, 25
Air travel: 13-14, 24
Buy animals: None
Neutering or spaying an animal: 3-5, 7-9
Dock or dehorn animals: 1-6, 28
Make sauerkraut: 25-27
Brewing: None
Canning: 25-27
Mow lawn to retard growth: 1-5, 20-28

What to Do When in MARCH

Entertain: 4-5, 12-14, 17-18, 22-24
Sports activities: 17-18
Marriage for happiness: 16
End a romance of file for divorce: None
Cut hair to increase growth: 7, 15-16
Cut hair to retard growth: None
Cut hair for added thickness: 22
Permanents and hair coloring: None
Start a weight loss program: 1, 4-5, 27-28
Stop a bad habit: None
See dentist for fillings: 4-5, 25-26
See dentist for extractions: 7, 12-14, 20-21
Consult physician: 2-3, 8-9, 15-16, 22-24, 29-31
Purchase major appliances: 4-5
Buy a car or have repairs done: 5, 10, 18, 26
Purchase electronic equipment: 24
Buy antiques or jewelry: 10, 16
Buy real estate for speculation: 2-3, 8-9, 15-16, 22-24, 29-31
Buy permanent home: 4-5, 10-11, 17-18, 25-26
Selling home, property, or possessions: 1, 4-5, 8, 10, 12, 17, 22, 26, 31
Sign important papers: 5, 10, 26
Building: None
Ask for credit or loan: 4
Start new ventures or advertise: 10-11, 16
Apply for job: 10
Ask for raise or promotion: 1, 5, 10, 26
Collect money: 2, 8, 16, 22, 31
Move into new home: 11
Do roofing: 4-5, 25-26
Pour concrete: 4-5, 10-11, 17-18
Painting: 4-5, 25-26
Cut timber: 1-5, 30-31
Travel for business: 1-2, 4-5, 7-8, 10-11, 13-14, 16-18, 20-22, 24-26, 28-29, 31
Travel for pleasure: 2, 4, 8, 11, 16-17, 22, 31
Air travel: 12-14, 24
Buy animals: 8
Neutering or spaying an animal: 4-6, 8-10
Dock or dehorn animals: 1-5, 12-13, 30-31
Make sauerkraut: 25-26
Brewing: 6
Canning: 6, 25-26
Mow lawn to retard growth: 1-6, 22-31

What to Do When in APRIL

Entertain: 1-2, 9-10, 13-15, 18-20, 28-29
Sports activities: 13-15
Marriage for happiness: 13
End a romance of file for divorce: None
Cut hair to increase growth: 11
Cut hair to retard growth: None
Cut hair for added thickness: 20
Permanents and hair coloring: None
Start a weight loss program: 1-2, 23-25, 28-29
Stop a bad habit: None
See dentist for fillings: 1-2, 21-22, 28-29
See dentist for extractions: 9-10
Consult physician: 5-6, 11-12, 18-20, 26-27
Purchase major appliances: 1-2, 28-29
Buy a car or have repairs done: 2, 8, 13-14, 22, 28-29
Purchase electronic equipment: 1, 10
Buy antiques or jewelry: 8, 11, 18
Buy real estate for speculation: 5-6, 11-12, 18-20, 26-27
Buy permanent home: 1-2, 7-8, 13-15, 21-22, 28-29
Selling home, property, or possessions: 1, 6, 9-10, 13, 15-16, 18, 20, 27-28, 30
Sign important papers: 1
Building: None
Ask for credit or loan: 1, 28
Start new ventures or advertise: 7-8, 11
Apply for job: None
Ask for raise or promotion: 6, 27
Collect money: 18, 26
Move into new home: 1, 15
Do roofing: 1-2, 21-22, 28-29
Pour concrete: 1-2, 7-8, 13-15, 28-29
Painting: 1-2, 21-22, 28-29
Cut timber: 1-2, 28-29
Travel for business: 1-2, 4, 6-9, 11, 13-16, 18, 20-24, 27-30
Travel for pleasure: 1, 13, 15, 18, 28, 30
Air travel: 9-10, 20
Buy animals: 8-9, 11
Neutering or spaying an animal: 2-4, 6-8
Dock or dehorn animals: 1-2, 9-11, 28-29
Make sauerkraut: 21-22
Brewing: 3-4, 30
Canning: 3-4, 21-22, 30
Mow lawn to retard growth: 1-4, 20-30

What to Do When in MAY

Entertain: 6-7, 11-12, 16-17, 25-26
Sports activities: 11-12
Marriage for happiness: 10
End a romance of file for divorce: None
Cut hair to increase growth: 8-10, 18-19
Cut hair to retard growth: None
Cut hair for added thickness: 20
Permanents and hair coloring: None
Start a weight loss program: 2-3, 21-22, 25-26, 30-31
Stop a bad habit: None
See dentist for fillings: 4, 20, 25-26
See dentist for extractions: 6-7, 13
Consult physician: 2-3, 8-10, 16-17, 23-24, 30-31
Purchase major appliances: None
Buy a car or have repairs done: 11
Purchase electronic equipment: None
Buy antiques or jewelry: 10, 17
Buy real estate for speculation: 2-3, 8-10, 16-17, 23-24, 30-31
Buy permanent home: 4-5, 11
Selling home, property, or possessions: 4, 6-8, 11, 13, 19, 25-26, 28-29
Sign important papers: 11
Building: 20
Ask for credit or loan: 1
Start new ventures or advertise: 5, 10
Apply for job: None
Ask for raise or promotion: 6, 11, 25, 29
Collect money: 10, 31
Move into new home: 26
Do roofing: 4, 20, 25-26
Pour concrete: 4-5, 11-12, 25-26
Painting: 4, 20, 25-26
Cut timber: 2-4, 30-31
Travel for business: 1, 4-7, 10-11
Travel for pleasure: 1, 10-11
Air travel: 6-7
Buy animals: 7-8
Neutering or spaying an animal: 2-4, 6-8, 31
Dock or dehorn animals: 6-11
Make sauerkraut: 20
Brewing: 1, 20, 27-29
Canning: 1, 20, 27-29
Mow lawn to retard growth: 1-4, 20-31

What to Do When in JUNE

Entertain: 3-4, 7-8, 12-13, 21-23, 30
Sports activities: 7-8
Marriage for happiness: 8, 13
End a romance of file for divorce: None
Cut hair to increase growth: 5-6, 14-16
Cut hair to retard growth: 30
Cut hair for added thickness: 19
Permanents and hair coloring: None
Start a weight loss program: 21-23, 26-27
Stop a bad habit: 30
See dentist for fillings: 1-2, 22-23, 29
See dentist for extractions: 3-4, 9, 11
Consult physician: 5-6, 12-13, 19-20, 26-27
Purchase major appliances: 22-23
Buy a car or have repairs done: 7-8, 22-23, 29
Purchase electronic equipment: 22-23
Buy antiques or jewelry: 13
Buy real estate for speculation: 5-6, 12-13, 19-20, 26-27
Buy permanent home: 7-8, 14-16, 21-23, 28-29
Selling home, property, or possessions: 2-3, 6, 8, 11, 13, 16, 22-23, 27, 30
Sign important papers: 22
Building: None
Ask for credit or loan: None
Start new ventures or advertise: 17-18
Apply for job: 11
Ask for raise or promotion: 22
Collect money: 13
Move into new home: 15
Do roofing: 1-2, 21-23, 28-29
Pour concrete: 1-2, 7-8, 21-23, 28-29
Painting: 1-2, 21-23, 28-29
Cut timber: 1-2, 26-30
Travel for business: 7-11, 13, 15-19, 22-25, 27, 29-30
Travel for pleasure: 8-9, 13, 15, 23, 25, 27, 30
Air travel: 13, 30
Buy animals: 7
Neutering or spaying an animal: 1-2, 4-6, 29-30
Dock or dehorn animals: 3-10, 30
Make sauerkraut: 24-25
Brewing: None
Canning: 24-25
Mow lawn to retard growth: 1-2, 19-30

What to Do When in JULY

Entertain: 1, 4-6, 9-11, 19-20, 27-28
Sports activities: 4-6
Marriage for happiness: None
End a romance of file for divorce: None
Cut hair to increase growth: 2-3, 12
Cut hair to retard growth: 1, 28
Cut hair for added thickness: 18
Permanents and hair coloring: None
Start a weight loss program: 19-20, 23-24
Stop a bad habit: 1, 27-28
See dentist for fillings: 19, 25
See dentist for extractions: 7, 17
Consult physician: 2-3, 9-11, 17-18, 23-24, 29-31
Purchase major appliances: 19
Buy a car or have repairs done: 4, 6, 19
Purchase electronic equipment: 11, 28
Buy antiques or jewelry: 3, 9, 11
Buy real estate for speculation: 2-3, 9-11, 17-18, 23-24, 29-31
Buy permanent home: 4-6, 12-13, 19-20, 25-26
Selling home, property, or possessions: 1, 5-6, 11-12, 15, 24-
    25, 28-29
Sign important papers: 6, 12
Building: None
Ask for credit or loan: None
Start new ventures or advertise: 3, 14-16
Apply for job: None
Ask for raise or promotion: 1, 6, 28
Collect money: 11, 29
Move into new home: 25
Do roofing: 19-20, 25-26
Pour concrete: 4-6, 19-20, 25-26
Painting: 19-20, 25-26
Cut timber: 1, 25-28
Travel for business: 1, 3-4, 6-9, 11-12, 14-16, 18-19, 21-22,
    24-25, 27-29, 31
Travel for pleasure: 6, 8, 11, 15, 25, 27, 29
Air travel: 1, 11, 27-28
Buy animals: 3, 5
Neutering or spaying an animal: 1, 3-5, 29-31
Dock or dehorn animals: 1-9, 27-31
Make sauerkraut: 21-22
Brewing: 29-31
Canning: 21-22, 29-31
Mow lawn to retard growth: 1, 18-31

What to Do When in AUGUST

Entertain: 1-2, 6, 15-16, 23-25, 28-29
Sports activities: 1-2, 28-29
Marriage for happiness: None
End a romance of file for divorce: 28-29
Cut hair to increase growth: 8-10
Cut hair to retard growth: 23-25, 28-29
Cut hair for added thickness: 16
Permanents and hair coloring: None
Start a weight loss program: 16, 19-20, 28-29
Stop a bad habit: 23-25, 28-29
See dentist for fillings: 16, 21-22, 28-29
See dentist for extractions: 3-4, 14, 30-31
Consult physician: 6, 13-14, 19-20, 26-27
Purchase major appliances: 16
Buy a car or have repairs done: 1-2, 9, 15-16, 28-29
Purchase electronic equipment: 23
Buy antiques or jewelry: 14
Buy real estate for speculation: 6, 13-14, 19-20, 26-27
Buy permanent home: 1-2, 8-10, 15-16, 21-22, 28-29
Selling home, property, or possessions: 2-3, 8, 13-14, 21-23, 28, 30-31
Sign important papers: 2, 8, 28
Building: 16
Ask for credit or loan: 29
Start new ventures or advertise: 11-12, 15
Apply for job: 3, 14, 30
Ask for raise or promotion: 2, 14, 23, 28
Collect money: 14
Move into new home: 9, 29
Do roofing: 16, 21-22, 28-29
Pour concrete: 1-2, 15-16, 21-22, 28-29
Painting: 16, 21-22, 28-29
Cut timber: 23-25, 28-29
Travel for business: 1-2, 4-5, 8-9, 11-12, 14-16, 18, 20-23, 25, 27-30
Travel for pleasure: 8-9, 12, 14, 21, 25, 29-30
Air travel: 23
Buy animals: 5, 31
Neutering or spaying an animal: 2, 27-29
Dock or dehorn animals: 1-6, 8, 23-31
Make sauerkraut: 17-18
Brewing: 26-27
Canning: 17-18, 26-27
Mow lawn to retard growth: 16-29

What to Do When in SEPTEMBER

Entertain: 2-3, 12-13, 20-21, 24-26, 29-30
Sports activities: 24-26
Marriage for happiness: None
End a romance of file for divorce: 24-26
Cut hair to increase growth: 4-6, 14
Cut hair to retard growth: 20-21, 24, 26
Cut hair for added thickness: 15
Permanents and hair coloring: None
Start a weight loss program: 16-17, 24-28
Stop a bad habit: 20-21, 24-28
See dentist for fillings: 18-19, 24-26
See dentist for extractions: 10-11, 14
Consult physician: 2-3, 9-11, 16-17, 22-23, 29-30
Purchase major appliances: None
Buy a car or have repairs done: 5
Purchase electronic equipment: None
Buy antiques or jewelry: 3, 10, 30
Buy real estate for speculation: 2-3, 9-11, 16-17, 22-23, 29-30
Buy permanent home: 4-6
Selling home, property, or possessions: 4, 6-7, 11-12, 14, 18-20, 24, 27-28
Sign important papers: None
Building: None
Ask for credit or loan: None
Start new ventures or advertise: 7
Apply for job: None
Ask for raise or promotion: 7, 12, 20, 28
Collect money: None
Move into new home: 13
Do roofing: 18-19, 24-26
Pour concrete: 12-13, 18-19, 24-26
Painting: 18-19, 24-26
Cut timber: 21, 24-28
Travel for business: 1, 3-7, 10
Travel for pleasure: 4-5, 10
Air travel: 3
Buy animals: 1, 6, 30
Neutering or spaying an animal: 26
Dock or dehorn animals: 1-7, 21-30
Make sauerkraut: 15
Brewing: 15, 22-23
Canning: 15, 22-23
Mow lawn to retard growth: 15-28

What to Do When in OCTOBER

Entertain: 1, 9-10, 17-18, 21-23, 26-28
Sports activities: 21-23
Marriage for happiness: None
End a romance of file for divorce: 21-23
Cut hair to increase growth: 2-3, 12, 29-30
Cut hair to retard growth: 18, 21-23
Cut hair for added thickness: 14
Permanents and hair coloring: None
Start a weight loss program: 14, 21-25
Stop a bad habit: 17-18, 21-25
See dentist for fillings: 15-16, 21-23
See dentist for extractions: 8, 11-12
Consult physician: 1, 7-8, 13-14, 19-20, 26-28
Purchase major appliances: None
Buy a car or have repairs done: 3, 10, 16, 21-22, 30
Purchase electronic equipment: 17
Buy antiques or jewelry: 1, 8
Buy real estate for speculation: 1, 7-8, 13-14, 19-20, 26-28
Buy permanent home: 3, 9-10, 15-16, 21-23, 29-30
Selling home, property, or possessions: 2-4, 8-9, 11, 15, 17-18, 22-24, 28-29
Sign important papers: 3, 22
Building: None
Ask for credit or loan: 22
Start new ventures or advertise: 4-6, 9-10, 31
Apply for job: 8
Ask for raise or promotion: 3, 8, 17, 22
Collect money: 28
Move into new home: 9, 22
Do roofing: 15-16, 21-23
Pour concrete: 9-10, 15-16, 21-23
Painting: 15-16, 21-23
Cut timber: 21-28
Travel for business: 3-6, 8-12, 15-18, 21-26, 29-31
Travel for pleasure: 5, 9-11, 15, 18, 22-24, 29
Air travel: 17-18, 28
Buy animals: 1, 4, 30-31
Neutering or spaying an animal: None
Dock or dehorn animals: 1-6, 21-31
Make sauerkraut: 19-20
Brewing: None
Canning: 19-20
Mow lawn to retard growth: 14-28

What to Do When in NOVEMBER

Entertain: 5-7, 14-15, 18-19, 23-24
Sports activities: 19
Marriage for happiness: None
End a romance of file for divorce: 18-19
Cut hair to increase growth: 8
Cut hair to retard growth: 14-15, 18-19
Cut hair for added thickness: 12
Permanents and hair coloring: 5
Start a weight loss program: 18-22
Stop a bad habit: 14-15, 18-22
See dentist for fillings: 12-13, 19, 25-27
See dentist for extractions: 4, 8
Consult physician: 3-4, 10-11, 16-17, 23-24, 30
Purchase major appliances: None
Buy a car or have repairs done: 6, 13, 19, 25, 27
Purchase electronic equipment: 7, 23
Buy antiques or jewelry: 4, 30
Buy real estate for speculation: 3-4, 10-11, 16-17, 23-24, 30
Buy permanent home: 5-7, 12-13, 18-19, 25-27
Selling home, property, or possessions: 2-3, 7-8, 12, 17, 20-21, 25-26, 29
Sign important papers: None
Building: 12
Ask for credit or loan: 25-26
Start new ventures or advertise: 1-2, 6-7, 28-29
Apply for job: None
Ask for raise or promotion: 17, 29
Collect money: None
Move into new home: 7, 12, 26
Do roofing: 12-13, 18-19, 25-27
Pour concrete: 5-7, 12-13, 18-19
Painting: 12-13, 18-19, 25-27
Cut timber: 19-24
Travel for business: 1-2, 4, 6-9, 12-15, 17, 19-22, 24-25, 27-30
Travel for pleasure: 7-8, 12, 17, 20-22, 25
Air travel: 14, 24
Buy animals: 1, 4-5, 30
Neutering or spaying an animal: 30
Dock or dehorn animals: 1-5, 19-30
Make sauerkraut: 16-17
Brewing: 25-27
Canning: 16-17, 25-27
Mow lawn to retard growth: 12-27

What to Do When in DECEMBER

Entertain: 2-4, 11-12, 15-16, 20-21, 30-31
Sports activities: 15-16
Marriage for happiness: None
End a romance of file for divorce: 15-16
Cut hair to increase growth: 5-6
Cut hair to retard growth: 12, 16
Cut hair for added thickness: 12
Permanents and hair coloring: 2-4, 31
Start a weight loss program: 15-19, 25-26
Stop a bad habit: 12, 15-19
See dentist for fillings: 15-16, 22-24
See dentist for extractions: 1, 5-6, 11, 28-29
Consult physician: 1, 7-8, 13-14, 20-21, 27-29
Purchase major appliances: None
Buy a car or have repairs done: 2-3, 16, 22, 24
Purchase electronic equipment: 4
Buy antiques or jewelry: 27, 29
Buy real estate for speculation: 1, 7-8, 13-14, 20-21, 27-29
Buy permanent home: 2-4, 9-10, 15-16, 22-24
Selling home, property, or possessions: 1, 5-6, 9, 13, 15, 18, 20, 22, 24-25, 29-30
Sign important papers: 4, 9, 24
Building: None
Ask for credit or loan: 25
Start new ventures or advertise: 2-3, 9
Apply for job: 1, 9
Ask for raise or promotion: 24, 29
Collect money: None
Move into new home: None
Do roofing: 15-16, 22-24
Pour concrete: 2-4, 9-10, 15-16, 30-31
Painting: 15-16, 22-24
Cut timber: 19-21, 25-26
Travel for business: 2-3, 5-6, 8-9, 11-13, 15-16, 18-20, 22-24, 26-27, 29
Travel for pleasure: 3, 5-6, 8-9, 11, 18, 20, 22
Air travel: 11-12
Buy animals: 31
Neutering or spaying an animal: 1, 28-30
Dock or dehorn animals: 1-4, 19-31
Make sauerkraut: 13-14
Brewing: 22-24
Canning: 13-14, 22-24
Mow lawn to retard growth: 12-26

HOME, FAMILY & PETS

HOME, FAMILY & PETS

Automobiles

Choose a favorable date for your Sun Sign, when the Moon is in a fixed sign (Taurus, Leo, Scorpio, Aquarius), well-aspected by the Sun and not aspected by Mars and Saturn (the planets of accidents).

Several years ago a reader wrote to say that she bought her car according to the directions in the Special Activities section, that it now had over 100,000 miles on it, and had never had any major repairs.

Automobile Repair

Repair work is more successful when begun with the Moon in a fixed sign (Taurus, Leo, Scorpio or Aquarius), and well-aspected to the Sun. First and Second Quarters are the best Moon phases. Avoid unfavorable aspects with Mars, Saturn, Uranus, Neptune or Pluto.

Baking

Baking should be done when the Moon is in the movable signs, Aries, Cancer, Libra or Capricorn. Bakers who have experimented with these rules say that dough rises higher and bread is lighter during the increase of the Moon.

Brewing

It is best to brew during the Full Moon and the Fourth Quarter. Plan to have the Moon in a water sign (Cancer, Scorpio, Pisces).

Building

Turning the first sod for the foundation of a home or laying the cornerstone for a public building marks the beginning of the building. Excavate, lay foundations, and pour cement when the Moon is full and in a fixed sign, Taurus, Leo, or Aquarius. Saturn should be aspected but not Mars, for Mars aspects may indicate accidents.

Canning

Can fruits and vegetables when the Moon is in either the Third or Fourth Quarters, and when it is in one of the water signs, Cancer, Scorpio or Pisces. For preserves and jellies, use the same quarters, but see that the Moon is in one of the fixed signs: Taurus, Scorpio or Aquarius.

Cement and Concrete

Pour cement for foundations and concrete for walks and pavements during the Full Moon. It is best too for the Moon to be in one of the fixed signs, Taurus, Leo or Aquarius.

Dressmaking

Design, cut, repair or make clothes during the First and Second Quarters on a day marked favorable for your Sun Sign. Venus, Jupiter and Mercury should be aspected, but avoid Mars or Saturn aspects.

Williams Lily wrote in 1676, "make no new clothes, or first put them on when the Moon is in Scorpio or afflicted by Mars, for they will be apt to be torn and quickly worn out." (Also see *Buying Clothing* in the Business Section.)

Fence Posts and Poles

Set the posts or poles when the Moon is in the Third or Fourth Quarters. The fixed signs Taurus, Leo and Aquarius are best for this.

House

If you desire a permanent home, buy when the Moon is in one of the fixed signs, Taurus, Leo, Scorpio or Aquarius. If you're buying for speculation and a quick turnover, be certain that the Moon is not in a fixed sign, but in one of the cardinal signs, Aries, Cancer, Libra, or Capricorn.

House Furnishings

Follow the same rules for buying clothing, avoiding days when Mars is aspected. Days when Saturn is aspected make things wear longer and tend to a more conservative purchase. Saturn days are good for buying, and Jupiter days are good for selling.

Lost Articles

Search for lost articles during the First Quarter and when your Sun Sign is marked favorable. Also check to see that the planet ruling the lost item is trine, sextile, or conjunct the Moon. The Moon governs household utensils, Mercury letters and books, and Venus clothing jewelry and money.

Marriage

As general rule, the best time for marriage to take place is during the increase of the Moon, just past the first quarter. Such marriages will tend more towards optimism. Good signs for the Moon to be in are Taurus, Cancer, Leo, Libra and Pisces. Moon in Taurus produces the most steadfast marriages, but if the partners later want to separate they may have a very difficult time. Avoid Aries, Gemini, Virgo, Scorpio and Aquarius. Make sure that the Moon is well-aspected, especially to Venus or Jupiter. Avoid aspects to Mars, Uranus or Pluto.

Moving into a House or Office

Make sure that Mars is not aspected to the Moon. Try to move on a day which is favorable to your Sun sign, or when the Moon is conjunct, sextile or trine the Sun.

Mowing the Lawn

Mow the lawn in the First or Second quarters to increase growth. If you wish to retard growth, mow in the Third or Fourth quarters.

Painting

The best time to paint buildings is during the decrease of the Moon (Third and Fourth quarters).

If the weather is hot do the painting while the Moon is in Taurus; if the weather is cold, paint while the Moon is in Leo. By painting in the Fourth Quarter, the wood is dryer and the paint will penetrate, while painting around the New Moon the wood is damp and the paint is subject to scalding when hot weather hits it. It is not advisable to paint while the Moon is in a water sign if the temperature is below 70 degrees, as it is apt to creep, check, or run.

Pets

Take home new pets when the date is favorable to your Sun sign, or the Moon is well-aspected by the Sun, Venus, Jupiter, Uranus or Neptune. Avoid days when the Moon is afflicted by the Sun, Mars, Saturn, Uranus, Neptune or Pluto. Train pets starting when the Moon is in Taurus. Neuter them in any sign but Virgo through Sagittarius. Avoid the week before and after the Full Moon.

When selecting a new pet it is good to have the Moon well aspected by the planet which rules the animal. Cats are ruled by the Sun, Dogs by Mercury, birds by Venus, horses by Jupiter, and fish by Neptune.

Romance

The same principles hold true for starting a relationship as for marriage. However, since there is less control over when a romance starts it is sometimes necessary to study it after the fact. Romances begun under an increasing Moon are more likely to be permanent, or at least satisfying. Those started on the waning Moon will more readily transform the participants. The general tone of the relationship can be guessed from the sign the Moon is in. For instance, those begun when the Moon is in Capricorn will take greater effort to bring to a desirable conclusion, but may be very rewarding. Those begun when the Moon is in Aries may be impulsive and quick to burn out. Good aspects between the Moon and Venus are excellent influences. Avoid those of Mars, Uranus and Pluto. Ending relationships is facilitated by a decreasing Moon, particularly in the Fourth Quarter. This causes the least pain and attachment.

Sauerkraut

The best tasting sauerkraut is made just after the Full Moon in a fruitful sign.

Shingling

Shingling should be done in the decrease of the Moon when it is in a fixed sign. If shingles are laid during the New Moon, they have a tendency to curl at the edges.

Weaning Children

This should be done when the Moon is in Sagittarius, Capricorn, Aquarius or Pisces. The mother should nurse the child in a fruitful period the last time. Venus should then be trine, sextile or conjunct the Moon.

Wine and Other Drinks Besides Beer (See Brewing)

For wine and spirits it is best to start when the Moon is in Pisces or Taurus. Good aspects with Venus are favorable. Avoid aspects with Mars or Saturn.

Best Days For Your Special Purposes

When you wish to choose a favorable day for something other than matters governed by your own ruling planet, read the following list and note the planet which rules the matter in question. Turn to the list of *Favorable and Unfavorable Days* in the **Moon Tables** section of the *Moon Sign Book*. Choose a date for the activity listed below that is both marked "favorable" (F or f) for your Sun Sign and one that is marked with an "Sx" or "T" in the *Lunar Aspectarian* under the planet described. Never choose a date for any of these activities which is marked with an "O" or "Sq" under Saturn, Mars or Uranus, as these are negative aspects. They tend to counteract the good results promised.

The more good aspects in operation on the date you choose, the better the outlook for your affairs. "The better the day the better the deed." To recapitulate: Choose a date from the proper lists of dates marked "Sx" or "T" under the planet ruling the activity and also marked "F" or "f" to your own Sign, but *never* a date marked "O" or "Sq" in the *Lunar Aspectarian* to Mars, Saturn or Uranus.

Moon

For doing housecleaning or a big baking, putting up preserves, washing, using liquids or chemicals, for matters connected with babies or small children, and to deal with the public in general, choose the good aspects of the Moon.

Sun

To gain favors of persons of high rank, title or prominent social standing, or those in responsible government office, to make a change or try for promotion, choose the good dates of Sun.

Mercury

For writing or signing an important document seeking news or information, shopping, study, dealing with literary matters, choose the good dates of Mercury.

Venus

To give a successful party, ball or entertainment, to marry, for matters of courtship, art, beauty, adornment; to cultivate the friendship of a woman, choose the good dates of Venus.

Mars

For dealing with surgeons, dentists, hair stylists, assayers, contractors, mechanics, lumbermen, police, personnel of army or navy, choose the good dates of Mars.

Jupiter

To deal with physicians, educators, sportspeople, bankers, brokers, philanthropists; to collect money or make important changes, choose the good dates of Jupiter.

Saturn

For dealing with plumbers, excavators or miners, for starting a new building, letting or leasing a house or dealing in land, choose the good dates of Saturn.

Uranus

For successful work on an invention, for dealing with inventors, metaphysicians, astrologers or new thought people, for new methods, or starting a journey, choose the good dates of Uranus.

Neptune

For all affairs connected with the deep sea or liquids in general, for practicing psychometry or developing mediumship, photography, tobacco and drugs, choose the good dates of Neptune.

Pluto

For uncovering errors, overcoming habits, healing, fumigation, pasteurizing, pest control, choose the good dates of Pluto. Also for matters related to the affairs of the dead, taxes, inheritance, etc.

Plan Your Yard Sale
By The Moon
by Terry Buske

Whether you are having a yard or garage sale, advertising items for sale in the paper or planning an estate sale or auction, timing your sale by the Moon works to your advantage.

The general rules for selling are: sell on days when Jupiter, Mercury, or Mars are trine, sextile or conjunct the Moon and avoid days when Saturn is square or opposite the Moon. Look in the *Moon Tables* section under the *Lunar Aspectarian* for this information. Find a date when as many of these aspects as possible are in effect and when your Sun sign is favorable. If there are no good dates with all of these, the most important ones to look for are the sextile or trine to Jupiter, with no square or opposition to Saturn. Jupiter is the planet of good fortune, so positive aspects to it will bring more money and people to your sale.

When advertising specific items in the paper, you have a little more flexibility because you can choose the date the ad will appear.

If you are selling kitchen or dining room furniture or appliances, having the Moon in Libra or Taurus will probably bring more calls as these signs have to do with fine dining, the senses and other such things that go along with cooking and entertaining. Libra is also a good sign for the Moon to be in when selling art, expensive and designer goods, and any fine jewelry.

If you are selling antiques, the best signs for the Moon are Scorpio, Cancer and Capricorn. Taurus is also an alternative. When the Moon is in one of these signs and the above instructions are followed, you will have a good turnout at your auction or estate sale. You will be flooded with calls from your ad. People like to buy older things when the Moon is in one of these signs.

If you are selling a car, choose a date when the Moon is in Taurus, Leo, Scorpio or Aquarius.

Sporting goods seem to sell quickly in Virgo, Sagittarius, Gemini and Capricorn. Leo is a good alternative. Virgo is a health-conscious sign, and people are more inclined to buy exercise equipment during that time.

Whatever you are selling, try to time it according to the sign that rules that particular article or activity. You will have better luck and will not have to reduce your price.

What Sex Will The Baby Be?

by Louise Riotte

This question has always been of great interest to parents—perhaps even more so when the child is a first-born. Nowadays we have all sorts of medical methods by which physicians can at least hazard a good educated guess, but it may still be of interest to many to know how the baby's sex may be determined by using astrology.

Judgment of the 5th House of a parent indicates whether the first child will be male or female. Also, the time of conception, if known, and the planets in the signs at that time are to be considered, along with the nature of the signs and planets. The Sun, Moon, Ascendant, and the planets that have prerogative over them are to be observed principally. If the Sun, Moon, and Ascendant are femininely constituted, then judge a female child. The masculine planets are the Sun, Uranus, Saturn, and Mars. The Moon and Venus are feminine.

The odd signs—Aries, Gemini, Leo, etc.—are considered masculine, and the even signs—Taurus, Cancer, Virgo, etc.—are feminine. In judging the sex, remember to keep the degrees of the signs in mind too.

In the father's horoscope the 5th House denotes the first child and the possible sex. The 7th House denotes the second child, the 9th House the third child, and the 11th House the fourth child, etc.

Thus if there are malefics in the 5th House of the father

the first child is apt to be sickly, or die early; if the malefics are in the 7th House, the second child may die; if in the 9th House, the third child, etc.

Benefics in these houses would show which of the children would be more fortunate, honorable, useful, a blessing, etc. In a female nativity the first child is denoted by the 4th House, the second child by the 6th House, and the 3rd child by the 8th House, etc. The nature and possible destiny of each child, from the mother's standpoint, is to be judged from the nature of the planets in these houses in her map. Uranus, Saturn, or Mars in the 5th House of the father or in the 4th House of the mother indicates accidents, injuries, sickness, or death, etc., of the first child. Malefics in other houses, as stated, indicate hurt, loss of, or detriment to the second or third child.

Cancer (a feminine sign) on the cusp of the 5th House, and with the Moon or Venus, and feminine planets also in Cancer in the 5th House indicate a daughter in a male nativity. Sagittarius on the cusp of the 5th House and masculine planets in the 5th would indicate a son as the first child in a male nativity, etc. When the 7th House is dominated and influenced by masculine planets and a masculine sign, it indicates that the second child, in a male nativity, would be a boy.

These rules, of course, apply to the natural order of conceptions, and where conception has not been interfered with or prevented in any way.

Grandchildren are indicated when the maps of the parents are fruitful, and when good influences in the houses of children indicate good health and long life for children.

Multiple births, such as twins, triplets, etc., are especially produced and influenced by the sign of Gemini, which is also known as the sign of "The Twins" and of Castor and Pollux.

Saturn is a barren sign and tends to promote barrenness and to deny children when in the houses of children at birth.

Many believe that spring-born children are stronger and healthier and have a greater chance of longevity.

It is also believed that children born in the Full Moon are larger and stronger than those born in the wane of the Moon.

LEISURE &
RECREATION

Fishing	Sports	Writing
Hunting	Travel	Entertainment
Friends	Flying	Games
Parties		

LEISURE & RECREATION

Fishing

During the summer months the best time of the day for fishing is from sunrise to two or three hours after, and from about two hours before sunset until one hour after. In the cooler months, the fish are not actively biting until the air is warmed by the Sun. At this time the best hours are from noon to three o'clock. Warm and cloudy days are good for fishing. The most favorable winds are from the south and southwest while easterly winds are the most unfavorable. The best days of the month for fishing are those on which the Moon changes quarters, and especially if the change occurs on a day when the Moon is in a watery sign, Cancer, Scorpio, or Pisces. The best period in any month is the day after the Full Moon. See the article on Fishing and Hunting.

Friends

The need for friendship is greater when Uranus aspects the Moon, or the Moon is in Aquarius. Friendship prospers when Venus or Uranus is trine, sextile, or conjunct the Moon. The chance meeting of informed acquaintances and friends is facilitated by the Moon in Gemini.

Parties, Giving or Going To

The best time for parties is when the Moon is in Gemini, Leo, Libra, or Sagittarius with good aspects to Venus and Jupiter. There should be no aspects to Mars or Saturn.

Sports

The Sun rules physical vitality, Mars rules coordination and competition, and Saturn rules strategy but hinders co-ordination. Plan activities to coincide with good aspects from the appropriate planets. Specific sports are ruled by specific planets, from which they benefit. Archery is ruled by Jupiter, as is horse racing. Mars rules baseball, football, boxing, shooting and wrestling. Automobile racing is ruled by the Sun, Mars and Uranus. Exercising is ruled by the Sun. Swimming is ruled by Neptune and the Moon. Accidents are associated with squares or oppositions to Mars,

Saturn, or Uranus.

Travel

Short journeys are ruled by Mercury, long ones by Jupiter. The Sun rules the actual journey itself. Long trips which threaten to exhaust the traveller are best begun when the Sun is well-aspected to the Moon and the date is favorable for the traveller. If travelling with other people, good aspects from Venus are desirable. For enjoyment, aspects to Jupiter are profitable. For visiting, aspects to Mercury. To avoid accidents, avoid squares or oppositions to Mars, Saturn, Uranus or Pluto, and again, look for good aspects from the Sun.

When to Fly

Choose a day when the Moon is in Gemini or Libra, and well-aspected by Mercury and/or Jupiter. Avoid adverse aspects of Mars, Saturn or Uranus.

Writing

Writing for pleasure or publication is best done when the Moon is in Gemini. Mercury should be direct. Favorable aspects to Mercury, Uranus and Neptune promote ingenuity.

RECREATION ACTIVITIES

Everyone is affected by their lunar cycle. Your lunar high occurs when the Moon is in your Sun Sign, and your lunar low occurs when the Moon is in the sign opposite your Sun Sign. The handy *Favorable and Unfavorable Dates* tables in the Moon Tables section give the lunar highs and lows for each Sun Sign every day of the year.

This lunar cycle influences all your activities: your physical strength, mental alertness, and manual dexterity are all affected.

Astrological Rulership

By combining the *Favorable and Unfavorable Dates* tables and the *Lunar Aspectarian* tables with the information given below in the list of astrological rulerships of leisure-time activities, you can choose the best time for a variety of activities.

The best time to perform an activity is when its ruling

planet is in favorable aspect to the Moon or when the Moon
is in its ruling sign—that is, when its ruling planet is trine,
sextile, or conjunct the Moon, marked with a T, Sx, or C, in
the *Lunar Aspectarian,* or when its ruling sign is marked *F* in
the *Favorable and Unfavorable Dates* tables.

For example, go bicycling when Uranus or Mercury are
marked with a T, Sx, or C, or when Gemini is marked with an
F. Ice skating is enjoyed more when Neptune is trine, sextile,
or conjunct the Moon, and films are more rewarding when
Neptune or Uranus is marked T, Sx, or C or when Leo or
Aquarius is marked *F.*

ARTS
Acting, actors   Neptune, Pisces, Sun, Leo
Art in General   Venus, Libra
Ballet   Neptune, Venus
Ceramics   Saturn
Crafts   Mercury, Venus
Dancing   Venus, Taurus, Neptune, Pisces
Drama   Venus, Neptune
Embroidery   Venus
Etchings   Mars
Films, filmmaking   Neptune, Leo, Uranus, Aquarius
Literature   Mercury, Gemini
Music   Venus, Libra, Taurus, Neptune
Painting   Venus, Libra
Photography   Neptune, Pisces, Uranus, Aquarius
Printing   Mercury, Gemini
Theaters   Sun, Leo, Venus

HUNTING AND PETS
Animals in general   Mercury, Jupiter, Virgo, Pisces
   Game animals   Sagittarius
   Animal training   Mercury, Virgo
Cats   Leo, Sun, Virgo, Venus
Dogs   Mercury, Virgo
Firearms   Uranus, Mars
Fish   Neptune, Pisces, Moon, Cancer
Pet birds   Mercury, Venus
Horses, trainers, riders   Jupiter, Sagittarius
Hunters   Jupiter, Sagittarius

SPORTS
Acrobatics,   Mars, Aries
Archery   Jupiter, Sagittarius

Ball games in general   Venus
    Baseball   Mars
    Football   Mars
Bicycling   Uranus, Mercury, Gemini
Calisthenics   Mars, Neptune
Deep-sea diving   Neptune, Pisces
Horseracing   Jupiter, Sagittarius
Jogging   Mercury, Gemini
Polo   Uranus, Jupiter, Venus, Saturn
Racing   (other than horse)   Sun, Uranus
Ice Skating   Neptune
Roller skating   Mercury
Sports in general   Sun, Leo
    Competitive sports in general   Mars
    Sporting equipment   Jupiter, Sagittarius
Swimming   Neptune, Pisces, Moon, Cancer
Tennis   Mercury, Venus, Uranus, Mars
TRAVEL
Air travel   Mercury, Sagittarius, Uranus
Automobile travel   Mercury, Gemini
Boating   Moon, Cancer, Neptune
Camping   Leo
Helicopters   Uranus
Highways   Uranus, Gemini
Hotels   Cancer, Venus
Motorcycle travel   Uranus, Aquarius
Parks   Sun, Leo
Picnics   Venus, Leo
Restaurants   Moon, Cancer, Virgo, Jupiter
Rail Travel   Uranus, Mercury, Gemini
Long journeys   Jupiter, Sagittarius
Short journeys   Mercury, Gemini
Vacations, holidays   Venus, Neptune
OTHER ENTERTAINMENTS
Barbeques   Moon, Mars
Casinos   Venus, Sun, Jupiter
Chess   Mercury, Mars
Collections   Moon, Cancer
Festivals   Venus
Gambling   Sun, Leo, Jupiter
Parades   Jupiter, Venus
Parties   Venus, Leo

Lucy Rhea Hagen, a devoted "Moon signer" of Ardmore, Oklahoma, is a fisher lady extraordinary and the winner of many prizes and trophies for her catches. It is also a tribute to her genuine friendliness and helpfulness to others, that she has also been selected to receive several "Best Sport" awards.

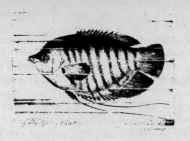

Does The Moon Really Influence Fish And Game?

by Louise Riotte

Moon signers are enthusiastic in their belief that the phases of the Moon influence their take when fishing or hunting. Others claim that it's pure lunacy. Somewhere caught in the middle are a whole bunch of people who don't know exactly what to think. A lot of fishermen and hunters "believe" but don't want to admit it!

Even so, many in-betweeners wonder how a ball of dust and rock 250,000 miles out into space can possibly have an influence on the earth, and on the creatures of the earth.

But, without question, it has been proven over and over again that the Moon does have influences on the Earth. Each time it is "overhead", a high tide occurs on our larger bodies of water that is readily discernible. It occurs on smaller bodies as well, but is less noticeable. And many farmers and gardeners also believe it influences the water in the Earth.

It also causes tides in the atmosphere and even on the land itself, perhaps not as dramatically noticeable, but there nonetheless.

Evidence keeps building that these lunar forces affect earth's creatures as well, though perhaps on a much smaller scale than the oceans or continents. Research has shown that when animals—including people—are isolated from the sun, clocks and calendars, they gradually adjust their daily cycles to exactly that of the Moon's (24.9 hours). Under the same conditions, most women will assimilate their menstrual cycles to exactly the lunar month (29.3) days. One report, using the records of 250,000 births, found that the average length of human gestation (the time from a baby's conception to birth) is exactly nine lunar months (265.8 days). It also revealed that more births occurred during a Full Moon than any other phase.

Oysters are known to open their shells at every high tide in coastal waters. The California grunion breeds only on those nights immediately following the Full or New Moon. The sea urchin reproductive cycle follows the lunar cycle exactly. Largemouth bass in Silver Springs, Florida, were noted laying their eggs on the day of the Full Moon. The palolo worm of Samoa and Fiji, a creature that lives almost all its life inside coral reefs, emerges to mate only on the night before the last quarter of the Moon in October and November. Bursting with egg and sperm cases, the long tails of these worms break off and swarm to the surface, where the islanders scoop them up by the basketful. For the islanders these are feast days, and the coincidence of the worm harvest with feast days is possible because lunar calendar timing is *precise*. Timing does not depend on maximum tidal pull, which would be stronger at Full Moon, but on a particular sequence in the lunar cycle.

Fishermen's traditional knowledge of the lunar timing of sea creatures has been modernized. A man named, appropriately enough, John S. Haddock produced a Fish Biting Hours Computer Calendar. According to this calendar, there are four daily periods of lunar feeding stimuli. These stimuli periods are never at the same daily clock time because the lunar day is somewhat longer than the solar day. The Haddock calendar converts lunar time to solar time and provides for geographical correction. It enables the fisherman to tell by the clock when his chances are best. Mr. Haddock claims most record fish catches are made during a lunar feeding-stimulus period. It is well to note that solar time alone would offer no clue at all to the useful feeding rhythm of fish.

Like the earth, animals are made up mostly of water and this leads some scientists to believe that they, too, "feel" the gravitational pull of the Moon. Appropriately enough, this phenomenon is called a "biological tide." However, Dr. George Abell of UCLA, author of a popular astrophysics college textbook, points out that the total pull on our body water, compared to that on the oceans, is about 30 trillion times less.

Other scientists theorize that the effect could be the Moon's electromagnetic field interacting with the electromagnetic field surrounding every living organism. Dr. Brown, famous for his oyster experiments, found, for instance, that ordinary bean seeds had a rhythm of drawing in water that peaked with each New and Full Moon. But the degree of the water uptake could be changed by simply turning the beans in a new direction. He believes that the beans' electromagnetic fields may tune into the earth's field, and both are affected by the Moon's. When the beans are turned they're temporarily thrown out of synchronization.

Dr. Harry Rounds of Wichita State University found that the heart rate of animals under stress (again including humans) would increase shortly after a New or Full Moon. (Hunters should take note of this.) He speculates that a change in the earth's electromagnetic field, caused by the Moon, is responsible.

Here, I think it might be safe to say that, while we don't know exactly what the force is, *something* from the Moon *can* influence earthly life forms. Llewellyn George, author of *Powerful Planets,* believed that it was the *unseen* rays of the Moon that were effective. He further stated that it was the *quality* of the rays which the Moon transmits which are so significant.

This brings up the question of why earthly life forms, including fish and game, sometimes seem to be following a Moon pattern, yet at other times do not.

First, all species are different. It's very possible that while one may be influenced by the Moon, the other may not. Experiment with this idea yourself by taking a drive out in the country sometime during any Moon phase. In one pasture the cows may be feeding. In another a flock of sheep are lying down and resting.

And again, not all members of the same species march to the same drummer. Some birds may be pecking at the corn, while others are resting in the trees. Some bass are in the throes of spawning, while others are merrily busting shad on yonder flat.

Some scientists theorize that the reason may be related to

how receptive the individual is to lunar influences. Also other factors, such as the weather and the Sun, along with the subject's own biological instincts, condition and needs may be having a greater effect at any given time.

The seeming imbalances that affect people must also be considered when determining the best times to fish and hunt. The effect that weather has on our quarries is obvious. The Moon could be exerting its strongest force of the year, yet not be enough to override a cold front that drove the base out of the shallows and into deep water.

Temperature has to be a particularly strong, overriding factor to a fish. Being cold-blooded its metabolism is regulated mostly by water temperature and, consequently its feeding habits. A two-pound bass, for instance, may need to eat only once a week in 40° water. So it's logical to assume that it won't be as likely to follow the four-feedings-a-day schedule (that most fishing tables forecast) in the winter as in the summer.

And then, there's the stress factor, or the lack of one. It would seem that when a fish is content, the Moon—or any external force, for that matter—basically has no effect.

Finally, to further complicate matters, there is a factor that we can't control. The day that is ultra good for fishing may not be good for you personally. If you happen to be at the low of your own lunar cycle on a day that is tops for fishing, the fish may ignore your line, or possibly get away before you land them. It's something to think about. On the other hand, if the best fishing days coincide with your own best days—just think what might happen if you went fishing. Especially if you happen to be a Piscean.

Something else to consider is season. A certain type of fish will have a season at a certain place, and you should not expect to catch that type of fish out of season. Or, if you are a hunter, one of your best hunting days may come along when you are not allowed to hunt because it is legally out of season.

Opinions differ on which lunar phase and sign are best for fishing. However, most old-timers generally agree that the day of and the day after the phase change are usually best. Some say that the three days before and three days after the Full Moon are also favorable, with the day after the Full Moon being the best.

The Moon in Pisces and the Moon in Cancer are considered

good for both fishing and planting, along with the association of these two signs in particular with eating and drinking. Possibly the appetites of fish are greater when the Moon is in Pisces and Cancer, and when fish or animals are hungry their tendency is to become careless—even the older and larger ones becoming less cautious. This may be the reason we catch more fish when the Moon is in these two signs, and it is particularly noticeable that larger fish are caught at these times. Usually these bigger ones have more fish "wisdom," but they get hooked just the same when the Moon goes into Pisces and Cancer.

As to the time of day, many feel that fishing is best when the Moon is directly overhead, and the two hours on either side of this time. At the New Moon, the beginning of the First Quarter (Sun and Moon conjunct), both the Sun and Moon are directly overhead at noon (halfway between dawn and dusk). At the beginning of the Second Quarter (the Sun and Moon square), the Moon is overhead at midnight (halfway between dusk and dawn). At the beginning of the Fourth Quarter (Sun and Moon again square), the Moon is overhead at dawn, when the Sun is rising.

This theory holds that the next best time for fishing is when the Moon is straight "down" on the other side of the Earth. This is midnight at the New Moon, dawn at the beginning of the Second Quarter; noon at the Full Moon; and dusk at the beginning of the Fourth Quarter. It should also be considered that the rising and setting of the Moon varies as you go north and south.

In general, during the summer the best fishing times are one or two hours before and after sunrise and sunset. Fish are also likely to bite before either a warm front or a cold front moves in. In fall and winter, fish aren't likely to bite until warmed by the Sun, making the hours from noon to 3 p.m. the most likely to give you a catch.

Fishermen generally agree that warm, close, cloudy days are best for fishing—the reason for this being that fish have no eyelids! On a cloudy day there is no bright light to distress them, so they feed nearer the surface.

And, speaking of stress, this is not necessarily a human commodity, brought on by being intelligent enough to know that things are going badly. Scientists say that animals experience their own kind of stress. Hunger and reproduction are the two most probable causes.

Fish are believed by many old-timers to be able to sense weather change and to be particularly active three days before a storm. But on the day of the actual weather change the fish will not bite. This may be because winds often stir up the water, inducing the little fish to come out. And little fish are followed by big fish which prey on them. These, in turn, are followed by fishermen. Folklore further maintains that fish aren't likely to bite after heavy rains.

The symbols of the zodiacal signs are thousands of years old—nobody really knows how many thousands. Thus, it is interesting to observe that only two of the twelve signs were symbolized by two fish, and Cancer, symbolized by a crab.

There's another factor, sometimes overlooked, in determining the day's best feeding times—the Sun. We give a lot of power to the Moon's travel across the heavens, then ignore the Sun and maybe pretend it isn't there! This could be a big mistake, considering that the Sun has 150 times more gravitational pull than the Moon. It's also our largest source of electromagnetic energy, which includes radio waves, X-rays, ultraviolet and infrared radiation, and, of course, light—which is 400,000 times brighter than any Full Moon. In short, whatever the Moon can do, some believe the Sun can do better.

Can it? Again we come to the postulation of Llewellyn George, "It is not the light of the Moon that is the source of its power. It is the vibratory influence of the Moon. Its invisible rays are far more potent than its light rays." This wonderful man tapped great sources of knowledge; perhaps he is right.

To be successful in fishing it helps to understand fish. Let me give you a "for instance." A friend of mine who has a catfish pond feeds them regularly. He claims that they come in answer to his call when he approaches the pond at feeding time. This is not likely because a fish's sense of hearing is not keen, but they are very sensitive to vibrations, and have probably learned to associate the vibration caused by his individual footstep with food. This may be the reason why, in certain fishing situations, quietness is important.

Fish depend heavily on the sense of smell, and it is also believed that a sense of taste exists on the outer parts of their bodies.

What is sometimes regarded as a *sixth sense* is a special

sense located in the *lateral line*. This is a row of tubes and pores over a nerve that runs along the side of the body from the head to the tail fin. This is the sense organ that feels vibrations that are too low to be heard by the human ear— and it is the lateral line sense of a fish that registers the vibrations from the footstep of a person on the bank of a stream. Good fishermen know that a footstep is more likely to frighten fish than the human voice.

While I'm talking about fishing and hunting, I'd like to mention that these two sports are likely to become even more popular as we become more and more diet and health conscious. Fish is a very healthy, low fat food; some even believe it is "brain food." It is a good source of niacin, protein, vitamin D. Ocean fish are a reliable source of iodine. Rabbit, which is also low in fat, is an excellent health food, but be sure they are disease free. Deer meat, called venison, is delicious if properly cared for after the kill, and cooked correctly. My husband hunted deer in Colorado for many years and I learned how to cook a roast to perfection. Sear the roast and place it in a large dutch oven, add one can of mushroom soup and one can of onion soup, and roast in a slow oven setting.

The Moon and Deer Hunting

Skeptics often claim that the phases of the Moon do not affect deer habits. I think they're wrong, and careful and knowledgeable hunters pay attention to the night sky and plan their hunting accordingly.

A dark night—either because of the Moon's phase or an overcast sky—usually signals increased foraging at dawn and dusk. My husband always hunted at these times and seldom indeed did he fail to bag his kill.

Scoffers might dismiss this information as an old wives' tale, but wildlife biologists give some convincing reasons why hunters should keep an eye on nighttime conditions.

First, biologists note, deer prefer foraging at night, a habit for which they're well-equipped. In each deer eye, hundreds of thousands of "rod" cells interpret colorless light, enabling them to move about and feed in extremely dark surroundings.

The abundance of rod cells causes deer eyes to glow when hit by light. (You will notice this if a deer crosses in front of you at night and the eyes are hit by the car's lights.)

Rod cells allow deer to forage during Full or Half-Moon nights, but they don't permit deer to see in the total darkness encountered on a moonless, cloudy or rainy night.

Since a deer can't feed during such nights, it chooses other low-light periods such as dawn, during and just after dusk, figuring these are relatively safe times.

Of course, under certain conditions deer will start feeding in late afternoon, anyway, and keep browsing until dawn or later. During a dry year when forage is scarce, for instance, deer must search longer and wander more to keep themselves satisfied, even during periods of bright moonlight. During extremely dry prolonged periods many deer starve.

If food is abundant, however, the lunar phase will exert more influence on their feeding habits, so plan tactics with Moon positions in mind. Following bright nights, take a stand so that you can watch deer heading for cover. If there's no activity, try still-hunting. Following dark nights, though, stay on the stand until at least 9 a.m.

Following a bright night, some sportsmen choose to diligently hunt during *midday*. Deer that feed and roam much of the night grow restless by then. They get up to relieve themselves, they move into better shade as the Sun's angle changes. This movement triggers hunger, so they also begin to feed. To find them, watch and still-hunt edges and cover from 11 am to 2 pm during the days.

While the night sky does influence deer habits during daylight hours, don't expect emphatic signs of deer movement. They're still wary creatures, cautious even when overcome by the urge to eat.

But only one deer in an entire stretch of woods needs to be slightly more active—if you're in the right place—to translate the sky's influence into venison on the table.

═══ Hunting and Fishing Dates ═══

Dates	Sign	Phase
Jan 1, 3:35 pm-Jan 4, 1:12 am	Scorpio	4th qtr.
Jan 10, 12:32 pm-Jan 12, 2:37 pm	Pisces	1st qtr.
Jan 19, 3:58 am-Jan 21, 12:03 pm	Cancer	2nd qtr.
Jan 21, 3:35 pm	Leo	Full Moon
Jan 28, 11:50 pm-Jan 31, 10:31 am	Scorpio	3rd/4th
Feb 6, 9:53 pm-Feb 8, 10:19 pm	Pisces	1st qtr.

Feb 15, 9:41 am-Feb 17, 6:34 pm	Cancer	2nd qtr.
Feb 20, 9:33 am	Virgo	Full Moon
Feb 25, 6:58 am-Feb 27, 6:30 pm	Scorpio	3rd qtr.
Mar 6, 9:00 am-Mar 8, 8:37 am	Pisces	4th/1st
Mar 14, 3:28 pm-Mar 17, 0:14 am	Cancer	2nd qtr.
Mar 22, 3:59 am	Libra	Full Moon
Mar 24, 1:11 pm-Mar 27, 0:55 am	Scorpio	3rd qtr.
Apr 2, 7:38 pm-Apr 4, 7:52 pm	Pisces	4th qtr.
Apr 10, 10:59 pm-Apr 13, 6:32 am	Cancer	1st/2nd
Apr 20, 7:14 pm-Apr 20, 9:14 pm	Scorpio	2nd qtr.
Apr 20, 9:14 pm	Scorpio	Full Moon
Apr 20, 9:14 pm-Apr 23, 6:39 am	Scorpio	3rd qtr.
Apr 30, 4:04 am-May 2, 5:51 am	Pisces	4th qtr.
May 8, 8:20 am-May 10, 2:24 pm	Cancer	1st qtr.
May 18, 1:48 am-May 20, 12:17 pm	Scorpio	2nd qtr.
May 20, 12:17 pm	Scorpio	Full Moon
May 20, 12:17 pm-May 20, 12:53 pm	Scorpio	3rd qtr.
May 27, 10:14 am-May 29, 1:26 pm	Pisces	3rd/4th
Jun 4, 6:18 pm-Jun 6, 11:29 pm	Cancer	1st qtr.
Jun 14, 9:12 am-Jun 16, 8:13 pm	Scorpio	2nd qtr.
Jun 19, 0:58 am	Sagit.	Full Moon
Jun 23, 3:37 pm-Jun 25, 7:07 pm	Pisces	3rd qtr.
Jul 2, 3:20 am-Jul 4, 8:38 am	Cancer	4th/1st
Jul 11, 5:10 pm-Jul 14, 4:32 am	Scorpio	2nd qtr.
Jul 18, 11:42 am	Capricorn	Full Moon
Jul 20, 10:08 pm-Jul 23, 0:41 am	Pisces	3rd qtr.
Jul 29, 10:33 am-Jul 31, 4:42 pm	Cancer	4th qtr.
Aug 8, 1:06 am-Aug 10, 1:03 pm	Scorpio	1st/2nd
Aug 16, 9:07 pm	Aquarius	Full Moon
Aug 17, 6:46 am-Aug 19, 8:00 am	Pisces	3rd qtr.
Aug 25, 4:14 pm-Aug 27, 11:13 pm	Cancer	4th qtr.
Sep 4, 8:24 am-Sep 6, 8:52 pm	Scorpio	1st qtr.
Sep 13, 5:08 pm-Sep 15, 5:52 am	Pisces	2nd qtr.
Sep 15, 5:52 am	Pisces	Full Moon
Sep 15, 5:52 am-Sep 15, 5:39 pm	Pisces	3rd qtr.

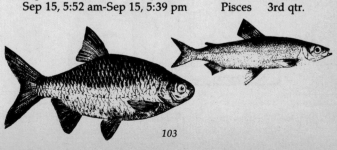

Sep 21, 9:51 pm-Sep 24, 4:45 am	Cancer	4th qtr.
Oct 1, 2:54 pm-Oct 4, 3:30 am	Scorpio	1st qtr.
Oct 11, 3:38 am-Oct 13, 4:42 am	Pisces	2nd qtr.
Oct 14, 2:33 pm	Aries	Full Moon
Oct 19, 5:10 am-Oct 21, 10:48 am	Cancer	3rd/4th
Oct 28, 8:57 pm-Oct 31, 9:24 am	Scorpio	4th/1st
Nov 7, 12:26 pm-Nov 9, 3:09 pm	Pisces	2nd qtr.
Nov 12, 11:52 pm	Taurus	Full Moon
Nov 15, 2:52 pm-Nov 17, 6:47 pm	Cancer	3rd qtr.
Nov 25, 3:14 am-Nov 27, 3:31 pm	Scorpio	4th qtr.
Dec 4, 6:49 pm-Dec 6, 11:12 pm	Pisces	1st/2nd
Dec 12, 10:31 am	Gemini	Full Moon
Dec 13, 1:50 am-Dec 15, 4:42 am	Cancer	3rd qtr.
Dec 22, 10:19 am-Dec 24, 10:38 pm	Scorpio	4th qtr.

Horse Racing

by Louise Riotte

Horse racing has been called the "sport of kings" and while it certainly may be that, it is also the favorite sport of lots of lesser mortals as well. In the early days when the Spaniards first brought horses to the Americas, the Indians were not long in seeing the advantages of this mode of travel. They proceeded to steal horses from the white man, and this was counted a great honor for the tribe. Indians love to gamble and racing became very popular with both men and women. It was not unusual for the brave to return home and find that during his absence, his squaw had gambled away the family teepee, blankets, cooking pots and other possessions! When she got started, she just couldn't stop! Lots of other people have the same problem.

Many ideas have been used for picking winners; one of which is the "astrological hunch" method, which consists of equal parts astrological symbolism, sympathetic magic, and intuition. Best-suited to horse racing (as opposed to other sports), this method was perfected by Sydney Omar and is more fully explained in Jess Stearn's *A Time for Astrology*.

First it is necessary to know the Moon's sign (see the *Moon Tables*) and the Ascendant. At dawn, the rising sign is the same as the Sun's sign, and it advances one sign every two hours. (See the *Horoscope* section.)

The hours of the day are ruled by the planets. There are 24 planetary hours in each day. The time from sunrise to sunset is divided by 12, which gives the time of the daytime planetary hours. The planetary hours at night are from sunset to sunrise, and this time, also divided by 12, gives the length of the night planetary hours. The planets rule these hours, from sunrise to sunset, in the following order.

On Sunday, the first hour after sunrise is ruled by the Sun; the 2nd planetary hour by Venus; the third hour by Mercury; the fourth hour by the Moon; the fifth hour by Saturn; the sixth hour by Jupiter; the seventh hour by Mars; the eighth hour by the Sun again, etc., and in this order on through the 24 hours.

The first planetary hour of each day is ruled by the planet that rules the day. Thus on Sunday (ruled by the Sun), the first hour of the day is ruled by the Sun. The Moon, ruling Monday, rules the first planetary hour after sunrise. Tuesday is ruled by Mars, and Mars rules the first hour after sunrise; Mercury on Wednesday; Jupiter on Thursday; Venus on Friday; and Saturn on Saturday.

The planetary hours are longer in the daytime in the summer, as the days are longer, and shorter at night. In the wintertime, the night planetary hours are longer, with shorter daytime hours.

The happenings of each hour are said to be of the nature of the planet ruling the hour. Keeping this information in mind, here is an example of the way a horse-race winner might be picked. If, let us say, a race is to take place at noon on March 14, the Moon will be in Aries, the Sun in Pisces, and the Ascendant in Gemini. (The Ascendant is in Pisces at dawn, around 6:00 a.m., changes to Aries at 8:00 a.m., to Taurus at 10:00 a.m., and enters Gemini at noon.) We would then study the racing form for names of horses and jockeys that tie in with the Aries Moon and Gemini Ascendant. Examples might be horses named Man O' War (Aries rules war) or Secretariat (Gemini rules clerical work) or jockeys named Grant (a famous soldier) or Castor (one of the Gemini twins). To carry this idea on, you might wish to consult *The Rulership Book*, by Rex Bills (published by Macoy Publishing & Masonic Supply Co., Inc., Richmond, Virginia).

Here is a general list of the types of names ruled by the planets. You can find lots more if you consult *The Rulership Book* as suggested.

The Sun (ruler of Leo)—short names, names derived

from nature or royalty.

The Moon (ruler of Cancer)—family names of the rural variety, suggesting simplicity, domesticity, or collective life.

Mercury (ruler of Gemini and Virgo)—common, conventional names.

Venus (ruler of Taurus and Libra)—long names, names pleasant to the ear or suggestive of glamour.

Mars (ruler of Aries)—short names; names that are concise, blunt, militant; names that are popular among fiction writers as typical names of heroes.

Jupiter (ruler of Sagittarius)—short names, royal or Biblical names.

Saturn (ruler of Capricorn)—long names, names suggestive of dignity, tradition or history.

Uranus (ruler of Aquarius)—unusual, startling names, either ultramodern or archaic.

Neptune (ruler of Pisces)—names that lend a note of mystery to the imagination.

Pluto (ruler of Scorpio)—names associated with the underworld or politics.

Care of Race Horses

Most of the finest horses today are descendants of horses having Arabian bloodlines. And the Arabs, who were also addicted to horse racing, are said to have fed their finest race horses honey as an aid to strength and stamina.

D. C. Jarvis, M.D., tells this story in his book *Folk Medicine.*

"From Dr. William Weston of South Carolina and his experience with race horses wintered there, I gained interesting and valuable insight into the value of iodine in the body, and its relation to endurance.

"About 100 race horses are wintered where he lives. Two years previous to a visit I paid him, the man in charge of the horses came to him saying that a horse was under his care which had everything it takes to win the Kentucky Derby. If they could just learn precisely how to feed this horse to maintain its speed capability, he believed the horse would have an outstanding racing season. Would Dr. Weston help him by planning the feeding of the horse?

"Dr. Weston was greatly interested and consented to do so. As a first step he asked for samples of any and all foods given the horse. The samples were analyzed at the South Carolina Food Research Laboratory. As a result of the analysis, Dr. Weston advised increasing the iodine content of the ration, by incorporating into it foods, such as kelp, specifically rich in iodine. This was done. In the ensuing season the horse won every race in which it was entered.

"As a result of the experience, two wealthy race-horse owners invited Dr. Weston to come to their horse farms to discuss the feeding of their stock. Again iodine-rich foods were added to the usual rations, with the same result; every horse fed an iodine-rich diet won every race in which it was entered. This seems to be a complete demonstration of the relation of iodine to energy and endurance."

The interesting suggestions put forth here are simply that. There are no guarantees—but if you would like to try them . . . go for it!

HEALTH & BEAUTY

Beauty care
Dental Work
Dieting

Eye exams
Habits
Hair care

Health
Surgery
Herbs

HEALTH & BEAUTY

Beauty Care

For beauty treatments, skin care and massage, the Moon should be in Taurus, Cancer, Leo, Libra, Scorpio or Aquarius and sextile, trine, or conjunct Venus and/or Jupiter. Plastic Surgery should be done in the increase of the Moon, when the Moon is not in square or opposition to Mars. Nor should the Moon be in the sign ruling the area to be operated on. Avoid days when the Moon is square or opposite Saturn or the Sun.

Finger nails should be cut when the Moon is not in any aspect with Mercury or Jupiter. Saturn and Mars must not be marked Sq or O because this makes the nails grow showly or thin and weak. The Moon should be in Aries, Taurus, Cancer, or Leo. For toenails, the Moon should not be in Gemini or Pisces. Corns are best cut when the Moon is in the Third or Fourth Quarter.

Dieting. Weight gain occurs more readily when the Moon is in a Water Sign, Cancer, Scorpio or Pisces. Experience has shown that weight may be lost though, if a diet is started when the Moon is decreasing in light (Third and Fourth Quarters), and when it is in Aries, Leo, Virgo, Sagittarius or Aquarius. The lunar cycle should be favorable on the day you wish to begin your diet.

Dental Work

For this pick a day that is marked favorable for your Sun Sign. Mars should be marked Sx, T, or C and Saturn, Uranus and Jupiter should not be marked Sq, or O.

Teeth are best removed during the increase of the Moon in the First or Second Quarters in Gemini, Virgo, Sagittarius, Capticorn or Pisces. The day should be favorable for your lunar cycle and Mars and Saturn should be marked C, T, or Sx.

Filling should be done when the Moon is in a fixed sign and decreasing in light. The same applies for having impressions made for plates.

Dieting

Weight gain occurs more readily when the Moon is in a Water Sign; Cancer, Scorpio or Pisces. Experience has shown that weight may be lost though if a diet is started when the Moon is decreasing in light (Third and Fourth

Quarters), and when it is in Aries, Leo, Virgo, Sagittarius or Aquarius. The lunar cycle should be favorable on the day you wish to begin your diet.

Eyeglasses

Eyes should be tested and glasses fitted on a day marked favorable for your Sun Sign and on a day which falls during your favorable lunar cycle. Mars should not be in aspect with the Moon. The same applies for any treatment of the eyes, which should also be started during the increase of the Moon.

Habits

To end any habit you wish to eliminate, start on a day when the Moon is in the Third or Fourth Quarters and in a barren sign. Gemini, Leo or Virgo are the best times, while Aries and Capricorn are suitable too. Make sure your lunar cycle is favorable. Avoid lunar aspects to Mars or Jupiter. Aspects to Neptune or Saturn are helpful. These rules apply to smoking and will produce a good start. Every time you wish to overcome a habit, watch for these positions of the Moon to help you.

Hair Care

Haircuts are best when the Moon is in a mutable or earthy sign, well-placed and aspected, but not in Virgo, which is barren. For **faster** growth, the Moon should be in a water sign. To make hair grow **thicker,** cut it when the Moon is in opposition to the Sun, or when it is a Full Moon, which is marked O in the Lunar Aspectarian. However, if you want your hair to grow more **slowly,** the Moon should be in Gemini or Leo in the Third or Fourth Quarters with Saturn square or opposite the Moon.

Permanent waves, straightening and *hair coloring* will take well if the Moon is in Aquarius and Venus is marked T or Sx. You should avoid doing your hair if Mars is marked Sq or O, especially if heat is to be used. For permanents, a trine to Jupiter is helpful. The Moon also should be in the First Quarter and at the same time check the lunar cycle for a favorable day in relation to your Sun Sign.

Health

Diagnosis is more likely to be successful when the

Moon is in a cardinal sign (Aries, Cancer, Libra, Capricorn) and less so when in a mutable sign. Begin a program for recuperation or recovery when the Moon is in a cardinal or fixed sign and the day is favorable to your sign. Enter hospitals at these times. For surgery, see "Surgical Operations." Buy medicines when the Moon is in Scorpio if they are made from natural substances.

Surgical Operations

The flow of blood, like the ocean tides, appears to be regulated by the Moon's phases. *Time* magazine (page 74, June 6, 1960) reports on 1,000 tonsilectomy case histories analyzed by Dr. Edson J. Andrews, only 18% of associated hemorrhaging occurred in the Fourth and First Quarters. This, a new astrological rule: To reduce the hazard of hemorrhage after a surgical operation, plan to have the surgery within one week before or after the New Moon. Avoid where possible surgery within one week before or after the Full Moon. Select, too, a date when the Moon is not in the sign governing the part of the body involved in the operation. The farther removed the Moon sign is from the sign ruling the afflicted part of the body, the better for healing. There should be no lunar aspects to Mars, and favorable aspects to Venus and Jupiter should be present.

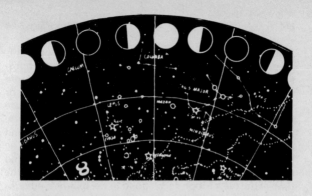

Medical Astrology
by Louise Riotte

In his book *Powerful Planets*, Llewellyn George, one of the greatest and most respected astrologers of all time, stated, "Medical astrology in its relation to diagnosis and the prevention and cure of disease, is a valuable adjunct to metaphysicians, doctors, surgeons and dentists." What he said in 1931 is just as true today.

And physicians in the days of old, such as Hippocrates, "the Father of Medicine," used a knowledge of planetary influences to perform their wonders. They well knew the subject of sympathy and antipathy; they knew that the angle of crystallization at sixty degrees, called sextile, was *creative*; they knew that bodies in opposite points of the zodiac were disintegrative in their effects. They knew that sulphur corresponds to the planet Mercury, and, being students of astrology, they knew many other facts that will not be clear to modern scientists until they, too, take up a serious study of planetary influences.

And so it may be readily seen that the subject of medical astrology takes in much more than the title implies. This fact is readily evidenced by many physicians, surgeons, non-drug-oriented practitioners, and dentists who are now using knowledge of astrology to enhance their skills and to assure more definite and satisfactory results by acting in harmony with the duly timed workings of nature.

By examining a person's natal chart, the physician skilled

in medical astrology can see what disorders the patient is predisposed to at birth; by examining the progressed horoscope he can see which tendencies are now coming into expression, whether complications are about to set in, or whether the sickness is about to break up. He can calculate the time of crisis in advance, for he knows that in acute situations the crises come about on the 7th, 14th, 21st, and 28th days from the time his patient was taken sick. The Moon makes a revolution in her orbit in about 28 days, and the 7th, 14th, 21st days, and her return to her place at the time of the New Moon correspond to the quarters, adverse aspects, and crisis times in the illness. Therefore, the first, second, and third quarters of the Moon from the time the illness began are crisis days in acute diseases and fevers.

If the patient lives through these crises, and until the Moon returns to her place, the disease will dissolve itself. The crisis days are the dangerous ones. The most serious crisis day is the 14th, as a rule, when the Moon arrives at the opposite aspect to her place at the beginning of the illness. This crisis day is called the "Criticus Primus," the one of prime importance. More patients usually die on the 14th day of a serious illness than on the other crisis days, and if they survive, their chances for recovery are usually good.

The knowledgeable physician can also tell whether an operation is necessary or simply a change of diet, whether to treat by sympathy or by antipathy, as well as tell which remedies will be most acceptable to the patient's system and therefore the most efficacious.

One of the simple but potent rules that is interesting to surgeons is as follows: "Pierce not with steel that part of the body represented by the sign which the Moon occupies on that day." Another astrological rule may also be invoked: "To reduce the hazard of hemorrhage after a surgical operation, plan to have the surgery occur within one week before or after the New Moon; avoid, whenever possible, submitting to surgery within one week before or after the Full Moon."

These rules are best applied to cases where one can "elect" whether or not to have surgery at a given time; in emergency cases, of course, they cannot be applied as the delay of one or two weeks might prove fatal.

In his book Llewellyn George tells a most interesting

story of what occurred at the time when he was located in Portland, Oregon. "I was called upon frequently for some years by two prominent surgeons to make the charts of patients and determine the best date and time for surgical operations. During that period each of the operations was a success—and the patients recovered.

"I recall one extreme case of a lady who had already been operated on five times by other surgeons. Because she was in great distress on account of serious adhesions it was necessary to operate again. As she was very ill and weak, another operation would obviously be precarious.

"As usual, it became my duty to find the proper time for this operation. A task it proved to be. The lady had so many planetary afflictions that it was difficult to find a good place in her chart. I worked all night on it and at last found a spot wherein if the Moon was located it gave promise of success— but that time would be at midnight! Fortunately the patient was willing to have the operation when the Moon was favorable if it promised relief.

"But midnight is a difficult time for securing the use of the operating room. However, the doctors went to the Good Samaritan hospital and frankly told the Sister Superior in charge the reason for wanting the operation at that unusual hour. Somewhat to their surprise she said, 'Certainly you may have the room, for we understand the importance of the Moon.'

"The operation proved satisfactory to all concerned. In fact, the patient was so delighted with the results that she became a student of astrology—and so did the surgeons; now they draw all such horoscopes themselves."

Dr. H.L. Cornell, author of the *Encyclopedia of Medical Astrology*, has stated that statistics show that surgical operations, including operations on the eyes, are apt to be most successful when the Moon is increasing in light, that is, between the New and Full moons, and that the patients heal more rapidly and have fewer complications than when the Moon is decreasing.

During the decrease of the Moon the vitality is usually less, and the bodily fluids at low ebb; these fluids rise and fill the vessels of the body to a greater fullness when the Moon is increasing.

The Rules for Operations Are As Follows

1. Operate in the increase of the Moon if possible.
2. Do not operate at the exact time of the Full Moon, as the fluids are running high at this time.
3. Never operate when the Moon is in the same sign as at the patient's birth (the Sun Sign).
4. Never operate upon that part of the body ruled by the sign through which the Moon is passing at the time, but wait a day or two until the Moon passes into the next sign below—this rule is of great importance in major operations.
5. Let the Moon be in a fixed sign, but not in the sign ruling the part to be operated on, and such sign of the Moon also not on the Ascendant.
6. Do not operate when the Moon is applying to (moving toward) any aspect of Mars, as such tends to promote the danger of inflammation and complications after the operation.
7. There should be good aspects to Venus and Jupiter (sextile or trine).
8. Avoid, when possible, operations when the Sun is in the sign ruling the part upon which the operation is to be performed.
9. The Moon should be free from all manner of impediment.
10. Fortify the sign ruling the part of the body to be operated on.
11. A Mars hour is not desirable for surgical operations.
12. Do not cut a nerve when Mercury is afflicted (square or opposition).
13. When the Moon is under the Sun's beams and opposed by Mars, it is a dangerous time for amputations.
14. Avoid abdominal operations when the Moon is passing through Virgo, Libra, or Scorpio. Good times are when the Moon is passing through Sagittarius, Capricorn, or Aquarius.

Consideration of the Moon's phases is also of great importance in the practice of dentistry. Teeth are best extracted in either the first or second quarter—waxing Moon—which promotes healing. Best signs for extractions are Gemini (which rules the arms), Virgo (the bowels), Sagittarius (the thighs), Capricorn (the knees), and Pisces (the feet). Note that all those signs are some distance from the head. Mars and Saturn should be marked C, T, or Sx. Avoid extractions when the Moon is passing through Aries, Cancer, Libra, Taurus, Leo, Scorpio, or Aquarius.

My son had a most interesting experience involving his teeth. As so often happens, a wisdom tooth was impacted. Treating it was somewhat beyond the skill of our family dentist, who sent him to a surgeon skilled in such difficulties. Upon removal of the tooth the surgeon found a cyst, which was also removed. The surgeon sent the cyst to the lab for analysis and it was found to be precancerous. In light of this discovery my son was told to return once each year for X-rays and a checkup to see if there was any development.

Now it also happened that the date when the tooth and cyst were removed was an excellent time for removing noxious growths. To be sure that all was well my son returned for three years for checkups, and on each occasion it was found that the space was gradually filling in with healthy bone tissue, and he has experienced no further difficulty.

Fillings should be done when the Moon is waning in the third and fourth quarters, and in a fixed sign, such as Taurus (which rules the neck), Leo (the heart), Scorpio (the genitals), or Aquarius (the legs).

Metabolism Directed by Planetary Vibrations

"Metabolism is defined as the act or process by which living tissues or cells take up and convert into their own proper substances the nutritive material brought to them by the blood, or by which they transform their cell protoplasm into simpler substances, which are fitted either for excretion or for some special purpose, as in the manufacture of the digestive ferments. Therefore, metabolism may be either constructive (anabolism) or destructive (katabolism)."
—Webster.

In astrology metabolic bodily processes are understood to receive their direction from planetary vibrations; the influence of some planets and aspects is constructive and others destructive, *both* operations being necessary to well-being. The *benign* influences direct anabolism, or constructive processes; the *malign* influences affect katabolism, or destructive processes.

For instance, Saturn is commonly symbolized as "The Reaper," an old man bearing a scythe, who is usually believed to indicate death but in reality signifies the decay, dissolution, and demise of old worn-out tissue that must be excreted. In this we see that the office of Saturn is just as beneficial as that of any other planet; without the influence of Saturn the human system would soon become congested with non-functioning matter.

Blood Transfusions

Of course we have long known that for a blood transfusion to be successful the blood of the patient and the blood-giver must match; generally speaking, human beings are divided into *four* blood groups, these coinciding with the four astrological groupings—Fire, Earth, Air, and Water. These are called triplicities, each group being comprised of three signs of the same nature. For instance, the fiery group is Aries, Leo, and Sagittarius. They have many qualities and characteristics in common and may be called sympathetic to one another. Aries people are born between March 21 and April 19; Leo, July 23 to August 22; Sagittarius, November 22 to December 21.

In this ancient astrological arrangement there may be found an idea to aid in determining definitely whether or not a patient and a blood-giver belong to a similar blood group, with more facility than by the trial-and-error method.

A blood transfusion is something most of us don't think about until it actually becomes necessary. Now, in addition to the care that must be taken to get a correct match, we have something else to worry about—AIDS. Great care is now being taken but many people may have received this virus in years past, before it was realized that a person could become infected through a transfusion.

The Sun gives oxygen to the blood, and Mars gives the iron and hemoglobin. In the astral body Jupiter has direct relation to the blood. The activity of Mars in the blood tends to promote hemorrhages, rupture of blood vessels, hemorrhoids, and excessive menses.

The Arterial System

Those who are concerned with the arterial system may also wish to know the astrological significance of the various signs. The Sun, the sign of Leo, and the opposite sign, Aquarius, have much to do with the disturbance and morbid condition of the arteries. Jupiter in Aries especially affects the arteries of the head; Jupiter and Taurus rule the arteries of the neck and throat. Jupiter in Taurus, Gemini, or Cancer rules and affects the arteries and veins of the respiratory system; Jupiter in Cancer rules the arteries of the stomach; Jupiter in Leo rules and affects the arteries and right ventricle of the heart; Jupiter in Virgo rules the arteries of the bowels and abdomen, etc.

The excess of mineral deposits laid down by the pathological action of Saturn tends to promote diseases of the arteries, hardening, crystallization, etc., and to impair their elasticity and ability to accommodate the different volumes of the blood stream.

This narrowing of the arteries, which constricts the natural flow of the blood, is sometimes called "hardening of the arteries." We know now that there is a great deal that we can do through eating a correct diet to prevent this condition from occurring. The American Heart Association recommends that we consume less meat (though small quantities of lean meat are permitted), eggs, cheese, whole milk and cream, and saturated fat, and more fruits and vegetables. Low-fat dairy products, such as low-fat cottage cheese and low-fat milk, are permitted.

Foods low in cholesterol are also recommended. Here I would like to mention *Weight Watchers Quick Start Program Cookbook* by Jean Nidetch (A Plume Book, published by New American Library), which has a number of excellent recipes. What makes this book special is the breakdown per serving into calories, protein, fat, carbohydrate, calcium, sodium, and cholesterol.

In astrological lore herbs have always played an important part in preventing and curing various illnesses. In 1926 in Germany, it was found that garlic helped in 19 of 20 cases of advanced arterial disease, and was also helpful in cases of high blood pressure. In England in 1931, garlic relieved hypertension in 25 uniformly successful experiments. In Paris, France, it was noted that there was a blood pressure fall of 10 to 40 mm. after two days' dosage with garlic.

Dr. W. H. Graves, in his book *Medicinal Value of Natural Foods*, also recommends garlic for hardening of the arteries and high blood pressure. Many people hesitate to use garlic because of the social aspects. Yes, it does have an odor, but you can overcome this to a great extent by chewing parsley, mint, or orange peeling after the meal. But why chew garlic at all? My own favorite way is to peel a garlic clove, slice it several times, and swallow the pieces just as I would a vitamin pill, without chewing it at all!

Those who are troubled with high cholesterol, thought to contribute to arterial disease, are usually told to eliminate starchy foods. Occasionally you might like to try a *breadless sandwich*—slice firm cabbage crosswise and use your favorite spread. And shredded cabbage is, in itself, good for a lot of things such as constipation, asthma, skin eruptions and poor complexion, obesity, gout, diabetes, etc., as well as being a good muscle builder and blood cleanser.

In our stress-filled lives we are becoming more and more conscious of the detrimental effects of high blood pressure. Often there is just no way we can reduce the stress that comes from outside factors we are subjected to as we go about our daily lives. But there are certain foods we can eat that are helpful, such as carrots, celery, cranberries, cucumbers, dandelion, desert tea (Ephedra), endive, garlic, huckleberries, kumquats, melons, nectarines, oranges, parsley, peaches, pears, pineapple, pomegranates, raspberries, sauerkraut juice, spinach, summer squash, strawberries, tangerines, and tomatoes.

For a more comprehensive list of foods to use and foods to avoid, you may wish to write to the American Heart Association, National Center, 7320 Greenville Ave., Dallas, TX 75231. They also have two helpful cookbooks, *American Heart Association Cookbook* and *Cooking Without Your Salt Shaker*.

Homeopathic Remedies

In her most excellent book, *The American Book of Nutrition and Medical Astrology* (published by Astro Computing Services, Inc., P.O. Box 16430, San Diego, CA 92116-0430), Eileen Nauman has this to say about homeopathic remedies: "A medical astrologer in cooperation with a homeopathic doctor may also recommend certain homeopathic remedies after tests have corroborated the findings in a natal chart.

'Homeopathic remedies are made in a liquid, dry, soluble or insoluble state. Three different processes are used in the making of a remedy; trituration, solution, and attenuation. The vehicles used for that purpose are sugar of milk or milk lactose, water and alcohol. Homeopathic pharmacies are especially careful to get only the finest and purest alcohol and distilled water is used as a solvent.

"The man who modernized the use of cell-salt therapy was Dr. William H. Schuessler of Oldenburg, Germany, a homeopath looking for a simple, unified method of treatment." Cell salts are the inorganic minerals that live in the cells of the body, and are instrumental in maintaining health. They have been known in Europe since the early 1800's— but in India they have been known since Vedic times.

Cell salts constitute only five percent of the body but this inorganic matter is nevertheless very important to the body's functioning. Every cell in our bodies contains many of these mineral salts, which are necessary for all metabolism. Although there are hundreds of minerals in our bodies, Schuessler considered twelve mineral salts essential to health, and astrologers have traditionally assigned each of these cell salts to one of the signs of the zodiac, as follows:

Aries—kali phosphoricum (potassium). This salt is a constituent of all fluids and tissues, notably of the brain, nerves, muscles, and blood cells.

A deficiency is characterized by mental fatigue and nervous exhaustion; addition of this cell salt to the diet helps to rejuvenate and soothe. Headaches are another symptom of deficiency and there may also be a humming or buzzing in the ears. In women, menstruation may be late and scanty. Mental depression and bodily weakness are other signals of a deficiency. Those who are easily frightened or prone to hysteria will often respond favorably to this tissue salt as it brings about a restabilization process, lifting people up from depression and bringing them down from the heights of exaggerated emotional stress.

Taurus—natrum sulphuricum (nat. sulph., sulphate of sodium, and Glauber's salt). This salt does not appear in the cells, only in the intercellular fluid. It aids and regulates the elimination of superfluous water.

With a lack of this salt, there may be an accumulation of water in the connective tissue. There may be yellow water secretions on the skin, and a coating at the base of the tongue. You may have a bitter taste in your mouth. Your eyelids might contain granular sand, and you may have a sensation of burning at the corners of the eyes. Headaches may be caused by poor digestion, a bloated feeling, and excessive bile. Damp weather tends to emphasize problems as well as bring on others, such as humid asthma, difficulty in breathing, and a proclivity for contracting influenza.

Gemini—kali muriaticum (potassium chloride). This salt is found in the blood, muscles, nerve and brain cells, as well as in the intercellular fluid.

Deficiency may be characterized by a coated tongue and discharges from mucous surfaces. Cold or chest congestion may also indicate a deficiency of this cell salt. Lymph glands may swell and be sore. There may be hoarseness or loss of voice as well as earaches and other middle ear problems; snapping sounds may take place within the ear. Constipation and indigestion may occur after eating foods containing fat. There may be dark clotting during a woman's menstruation; and there may also be rheumatic fever, including swelling around the joints.

Cancer—calcarea fluorica (calcium fluoride, fluoride of lime). This salt is found in the surface layer of the bones and teeth, and in the elastic fibers of the skin, connective tissue, and vascular walls.

A deficiency of calcarea fluorica is indicated when any part of the body cracks or splits when ordinary folding or bending takes place. This may include cracked lips, cold sores, a fissured tongue, and loss of tooth enamel. Or chapped hands and skin that feels hard and thickened. Other symptoms indicating the need for this cell salt are hardening of the arteries or veins, especially in cases involving varicose veins, and enlargement of the knuckles and other joints. There may be receding gums and loosened teeth or eye problems such as blurred vision, pain in the eyes, and even cataracts.

Leo—magnesia phosphorica (magnesium phosphate). This salt is an earthy constituent of muscles, nerves, bones, brain, spine, sperm, teeth, and blood.

If the body lacks enough magnesia phosphorica to form a liquid with albumin, cramping of the muscles and inflammation of the nerves may occur. When cramps exist there may also be spasms and shooting pains. The cramps most often occur in the calves, where the sciatic nerve becomes inflamed. Gastric disorders are another indication of a deficiency. Flatulent colic may occur, causing a person to bend over double with pain.

Heart spasms, as well as palpitations and constricting pains across the chest, may be noted. Furthermore, angina pectoris may occur. Women may experience menstrual problems such as a great deal of neuralgic pain in the ovaries, or menses that come too early.

Virgo—kali sulphuricum (potassium sulphate). This salt is an oxygen carrier of particular importance to the skin and the covering of mucous and serous membranes.

Skin conditions that may indicate a deficiency include scaling, burning and itching skin, a light, crusty dryness on the surface, wet eczema, psoriasis, nettle-rash eruptions and seborrhea.

The person may also experience chills and inflammatory pain because the cells are not receiving sufficient oxygen. Respiratory infections may occur, characterized by hoarseness and clogged nasal passages.

People who have a deficiency of kali sulphuricum usually are uncomfortable in warm or overheated rooms, escaping if possible to the out-of-doors. Pain is often experienced, which tends to shift and wander, sometimes being felt at the nape of the neck, in the back, or in the limbs—confusing to both patient and doctor.

Libra—natrum phosphoricum (sodium phosphate). This salt is found in blood, muscles, nerve and brain cells as well as in intercellular fluid. Its leading role is in the catalysis of lactic acid and emulsification of fatty acids.

Acidosis is a symptom that may occur if the acid-alkaline metabolism is out of balance. A person wearing jewelry may find that his/her skin turns green or black from the chemical interaction of the metal against the skin—a primary signal that the acid level in the body is abnormally high. If the gastric system is affected there may be heartburn, burping, a tight sensation in the chest, or an ulcerated stomach. Such problems are best eliminated by taking natrum phosphoricum rather than an antacid tablet.

Other indications of a lack of this cell salt are feet that

are cold during the day and burning at night. Hives, another way for excess acid to be released through skin pores, are fairly common.

Scorpio—calcarea sulphurica (calcium sulphate, gypsum). The function of this salt is to control suppuration. It is responsible for the destruction of worn-out red blood cells, which, if not effectively dealt with, may cause a lag in healing. The sulphates are derivatives of sulphur, the prime cleanser in the human body.

Deficiency may result in prolonged suppuration. Silicea hastens the process of suppuration in a normal manner. Calcarea sulphurica closes up the process at the proper time if present in the blood in sufficient quantity. The orifices of the body can be greatly affected by a lack of this cell salt—because it is through them that the body sloughs off its dead cells. Clogging caused by dead cells can induce other symptoms, such as boils, abscesses, and external and internal ulcers.

Sagittarius—silicea (silica, oxide of silicon). This salt is found abundantly in the vegetable kingdom, but in much smaller amount in animals, especially the higher vertebrates. However, it is essential to the body and particularly to the bones, joints, glands, skin, and mucous surfaces.

Deficiency may delay the normal healing process by retarding suppuration. Silicea is a cleanser and eliminator. An insufficient amount of this cell salt may be indicated by abscesses, boils, or other festering skin conditions; eyes may develop sties, ulcers of the cornea, or eventually even cataracts.

Loss of hair and hair that loses its sheen are also symptoms. You may have roaring sounds in the ears, swelling of the parotid glands, icy cold or sweating feet, hands, or underarms, and cracking skin at the ends of the fingers. Another symptom is sleepwalking.

Capricorn—calcarea phosphorica (calcium phosphate, phosphate of lime). This cell salt is the most abundant in the body and is essential to proper growth and nutrition. It gives solidity to the bones and has an affinity for albumin, with which it builds new blood cells. Calcarea phosphorica has quick restorative powers for broken bones and for teeth that are not forming correctly or are decaying before their time. Since it helps to build new blood corpuscles, it is a great aid to rapid recovery.

Any type of bone trouble in any part of the body may be caused by a deficiency of this cell salt. Even bones around the ears may be painful. In infants there may be teething problems or poor tooth formation, even decay. Infants who perspire heavily in the head region may also need calcarea phosphorica.

Simple anemia caused by the onset of menstruation, as well as other types of anemia, has responded well to treatment with calcarea phosphorica. Lower back pain caused by the menstrual cycle has also responded favorably.

A lack of this cell salt may also cause digestive problems. There may also be flatulence and abdominal swelling as well as a craving for bacon, ham, and salted or smoked meats.

You may buy the cell salts mentioned herein from the Standard Homeopathic Company, P.O. Box 61067, Los Angeles, CA 90061. It is suggested also that the cell salts be used in combination. With a complete set of the individual salts, you can put any combination together to treat a problem, and then recombine salts as conditions change, with no wasted tablets.

The cell salts are also available in different potencies— 3X, 6X, 12X, and 30X. Some authorities recommend only 6X for nutritional purposes. Bioplasma (twelve salts in one tablet) is a balanced combination of Dr. Schuessler's 12 Tissue Remedies. In this tablet nine of the remedies are in the 3X potency, the exceptions being cakcarea fluor 6X, natrum mur 6X, and silicea 6X.

Symptomatology

Homeopathic medicine is based on symptomatology and the law of similars, "let likes be treated by likes." A very minute amount of a substance is used to treat the symptoms since similar symptoms will be produced by the same substance in massive doses. The cell salts are twelve among over 1000 homeopathic substances used in the treatment of disease. Their therapeutic use as remedies in homeopathy is quite different from their use according to the biochemic theory of Dr. Schuessler. Dr. Schuessler believed that symptoms resulted from a deficiency of one or more of these twelve biochemic remedies of cell salts. The patient could be restored to health by taking one or more of these salts in minute quantities as indicated by the symptoms.

I personally have great faith in homeopathic remedies. My son is severely allergic to poison ivy, and when he was a young boy he loved hunting, fishing, and just roaming about the woods. These activities often resulted in a severe case of poisoning. A homeopathic physician practicing in our area provided the only remedy that was effective in curing his condition and in doing so very rapidly. It was rumored that Dr. Boyd made his own remedies (no one ever really knew for sure), but he was extremely popular as a doctor, for his remedies not only worked but also cost a dollar or less!

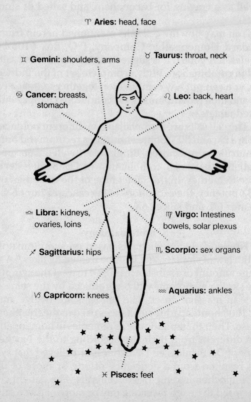

♈ **Aries:** head, face

♊ **Gemini:** shoulders, arms

♉ **Taurus:** throat, neck

♋ **Cancer:** breasts, stomach

♌ **Leo:** back, heart

♎ **Libra:** kidneys, ovaries, loins

♍ **Virgo:** Intestines bowels, solar plexus

♐ **Sagittarius:** hips

♏ **Scorpio:** sex organs

♑ **Capricorn:** knees

♒ **Aquarius:** ankles

♓ **Pisces:** feet

The Magic Of Herbal Remedies

by Louise Riotte

Today, it is almost impossible to turn on the radio without hearing, somewhere between music or broadcasts, a voice telling us to "take an aspirin a day to keep the doctor away"! Yes, I know, it used to be an "apple," but times have changed. Now they are telling us that if we will take an aspirin a day we are less likely to have a heart attack. And, as a nation, we are all becoming conscious of high blood pressure, high cholesterol, and diets of all types, as well as being adjured by the Surgeon General to cut down on cigarette smoking. While, at the same time, our oh-so-peculiar-government keeps right on subsidizing the tobacco growers. It is indeed a strange world.

But what about aspirin? Aspirin, and products containing aspirin, is a household word. Television sings its praise as a painkiller, and it is now in practically every medicine closet—there is even a special one for kids.

Aspirin is a white crystalline solid formed by the action of acetic anhydride on salicylic acid. Today, salicylic acid is obtained from phenol, a coal-tar derivative. But this was not always so—the original source of salicylic acid was the bark of the willow tree. *Salix* is the botanical name for willows, from which we have arrived at *salicylic*.

Salicylic acid obtained from phenol is no better than that derived from willow bark. We use it because the synthetic product is cheaper to produce than that occurring in nature—but, nevertheless, the willow bark is still there to be used should the necessity ever arise.

The use of salicylic acid in the treatment of pain and fever is far from new. Old records show that the Romans were obtaining it as early as 400 B.C. Our pioneers moving westward found that the North American Indians have long used willow bark as a remedy. As often happens early users knew what the natural product did, but not *why* it did it. Without going into the "hows" and "whys" of discovery, let us explore some common and popular herbal remedies which have stood the test of time as well as aspirin.

Acacia (*Acacia Senegal, acacia Arabica, a. vera, a. decurrens*). Also known as Gum Arabic, it is found in Northern Africa, Egypt and Middle East countries. There is also a type of this species found in Texas.

Acacia, because of its high tannic acid content, has been widely used in the treatment of burns. Applied to the burned area it has a soothing effect, preventing air from contacting the burn, nourishing the tissue and preventing blistering.

Used to treat ulcers it has an astringent effect, causing contraction of tissues and tending to arrest discharges. It is of particular value for ulcers of the mouth and gums. It may also be used to fasten loose teeth. Placed in boiling water it becomes an adhesive mucilage and the combination of the contracting tissue effect and the mucilage effect helps to fasten the teeth.

It is also helpful in the condition known as dysentery, characterized by loose bowels resulting from inflammation of the mucous membranes of the intestines. In addition to a liquid diet and rest in bed, the patient should drink a small amount of acacia in liquids. Acacia is also used to soothe coughs and is good for hoarseness of the throat.

Alder, Black, American (*Prinos verticillatus*). The bark of this tree, steeped in hot water, produces a solution that has a strong, laxative effect. It has been highly recommended for constipation. Dosage should be about one teaspoon of the powdered bark to a cup of hot water.

Allspice (*Pimenta officinalis*). This is one of the deliciously aromatic herbs that is both good and "good for you." It is atomachic in that it excites stomach activity, carminative in that it tends to remove gases from the upper intestinal tract and, inasmuch as it imparts flavor to almost any food, it is also a condiment. It is useful also in cases of diarrhea.

The part of the herb used is the round, brown fruits, which are powdered after drying. Dosage, sufficient for average use, would be some powder equivalent to that of a seven-grain tablet or pill.

Aloes (Liliacae Family; *aloe socotrina*). A pot of aloes on the kitchen windowsill is a familiar sight. Just about everybody knows about this famous burn remedy which I sometimes call a "drugstore in a flower pot"! But did you know the juice is also an excellent remedy for sunburn? Also, it acts as a purgative in constipation of the colon, having a tendency to drastically cleanse mucous membranes reached by it—and it is also cleansing to the stomach. As a tonic laxative, a dose of one-quarter grain is the usual amount prescribed.

Barley (*Hordeum distichon*). I can't say enough nice things about barley. It is valuable as a food for the sick and convalescent, and valuable as a diet for conditions where it is desirable for food to be easily digested.

Take two ounces of the barley grains, wash, pour a pint of cold water on them and boil for twenty minutes. Allow to cool. The barley water remaining is a non-irritating food, ideal for children suffering from diarrhea. Barley, used in soup, is not only nourishing but also delicious. And, here is another use not generally known—barley water is exceedingly good for the skin, promoting softness and soothing to either sunburn or chapped skin. I have an old book of early day beauty preparations, and barley water is mentioned in many of them.

Blackberry (*Rubus Villosus*, of the rose family Rosaceae). Is there anyone among us who hasn't come upon a patch of wild blackberries and greeted it with a whoop of joy? Shrubby and prickly though they are, the juicy fruit makes it well worthwhile to wade in and start picking. Medicinally the fruit, bark or rhizome, roots and leaves may all be used.

The berry is a popular food and has been used as a remedy for loose bowels, especially for children during the heat of summer. The bark, roots and leaves are also valuable for this purpose, having an astringent and tonic effect. To relieve diarrhea, pour cold water on ground or bruised root, bark or leaves and boil for twenty minutes to one-half hour. Cool and strain. Use one ounce of the herb to one pint of water. You may also wish to add extra water to allow for the boiling away. Average dose is from two teaspoonfuls to one cup.

Juliette de Bairacli Levy, in her *Herbal Handbook for Farm and Stable*, mentions blackberries as a famed Spanish Gypsy tonic for horses and mules, being given two handfuls of the leaves or fruits daily. It can be used as a decoction of the young leaves in red wine, the horse being given a pint draught daily until health is restored. Blackberry fruits are also a tonic herb in pregnancy for human or animal use. Externally, leaves are used for curing all types of eczema. The Gypsies say that fresh-plucked leaves, warmed over a fire, will heal most diseased places.

Bloodroot (Sanguinaria canadensis). This North American plant grows mainly in rich forest soil. It needs rich soil, ample water, warmth and sunshine. A low-growing perennial herb, the leaves have from seven to nine lobes with red-colored veins. It has a large white flower with eight to twelve white petals. My mother often spoke of having gathered this plant when she was a young farm girl in Indiana.

The part used is the dried rhizome which should be collected in early spring and carefully dried. It is then ground into powder—which may be placed in capsules or compressed into pill form.

A small dose (1/12th grain) is useful as an expectorant, tending to loosen and detach from mucous membranes loose fragments and loose phlegm. A smaller dose (1/20th) will stimulate gastric and intestinal secretions.

Castor Oil Plant (Ricinus communis). You probably remember this one as a child—and not too happily! Yet it has always been considered valuable because it works—so don't fault it too much! Actually, it has a mild action and is highly recommended for young children and child-bearing women. Taken with warm milk or in orange juice, the flavor may be somewhat disguised. It is not only valuable for constipation but also in cases of colic in young infants. It may be applied externally for itches, ringworm and cutaneous complaints—some even say it will cause warts to disappear. In some areas, native women are said to use the fresh leaves of the castor oil plant as a poultice for application to increase milk secretion.

Planted around the vegetable garden area, castor oil plants are said to repel moles. Be warned, however, that the seeds of this plant may be fatal. If you plant it, remove the seeds before they mature—they are very attractive to look at and some child might come upon them.

Catnip (Nepeta cataria). This is a herb I grow every year—both for myself and for my cats. The fresh leaves are delicious in mixed salads and helpful in removing gases from the intestinal tract.

Catnip is also a tonic, strengthening tissues and acting as a refrigerant, relieving thirst and reducing fever. (Parks' catalog lists catnip seeds.)

Chamomile (Anthemis nobilis). Once upon a time, a lady with a headache drank a cup of chamomile tea, much as we take an aspirin today, and it was a quite pleasant remedy which was reputed to also lift the spirits as well. To make the tea, the flowers and leaves of this herb are dried and powdered. An ounce of the powder is then stirred into one pint of boiling water to obtain a solution that excites action of the stomach. The dose should not exceed one-half cup. Chamomile is well known as a remedy for nervous conditions of women, and is also used to stimulate the menstrual function. The flower may be used to make a poultice for the relief of pain, by external application. The lotion may also be used for toothache, earache and other nerve pains by direct application to the affected part. The solution is also tonic and strengthening.

Comfrey (Symphytum officinale). Comfrey is the famous "Knitbone" herb which is easily grown in practically any garden soil, needing only to be well watered and with a fair amount of sunshine. The parts used are the root and leaves. Comfrey is probably used for more different purposes than any other herb. Space does not permit going into details, but it is often used for the following purposes: Pulmonary diseases; Scrofular diseases; Diarrhea, Leucorrhea; Calcium deficiency; Colds and coughs; Sores, Stomach conditions; Arthritis; Gall and liver conditions; Asthma; Tonsils, General cleanser, Gastric and duodenal ulcers; *Pruritus ani*; Cuts and wounds; Traumatic eye injuries; Headaches; Breasts; Hemorrhoids; Gout; Gangrene; Burns; Nutritive; Kidney stones; Anemia; Bloody Urine; Tuberculosis; Female debility; and Skin protection.

Dandelion (Taraxacum officinale). This humble little herb is often looked down upon, even fiercely hated by those who despise them when they come up in their lawns. Yet it is not only nutritious and chock full of vitamins, but is also tonic and laxative. In the spring I gather the buds and cook them with my leeks, thinly sliced, and seasoned with oregano and basil—a delicious and healthful "pottage." Dandelions are high in vitamin C.

Dandelion is chiefly used in kidney and liver disorders. Once dandelion coffee was quite popular. Gather roots, allow them to dry and roast them in the oven, then grind and use just as you would coffee, allowing it to percolate or steep in boiling hot water for about fifteen minutes.

Eyebright (Euphrasia officinalis). Eyebright has just been re-discovered in the last few years. One-half teaspoonful of the fluid extract of eyebright combined with an equal amount of the fluid extract of Golden Seal has been found to be an excellent lotion for irritating disorders of the eyes. The effect is slightly tonic and astringent, the tissues being drawn together and discharges halted.

Fig (Ficus carica). There is a legend that says that "when Adam became aware of good and evil he covered himself with a fig leaf." Perhaps it is because of this legend that we sometimes see a fig leaf tastefully arranged on a statue. Whatever the reason for this, fig leaves are indeed quite large, and they are also somewhat rough in texture though attractive in shape and color. I was gifted with a rooted cutting of an everbearing fig some fifty years ago and it is still growing in my garden and bearing abundantly every year, starting in early July and continuing on until frost, usually in early November.

Figs like good soil, hot, very hot Sun, and an ample water supply. They can be grown indoors in colder climates than mine (Southern Oklahoma) and will do well if placed out of doors in summer.

Figs are nutritious (absolutely delicious), laxative and demulcent (soothing to irritated surfaces). They contain dextrose (grape sugar) for energy (62 percent), fat, proteins, starch and other vitamin and mineral elements.

Figs are useful for boils, constipation and the milk from a broken branch is said to remove warts. This milk is also helpful in healing sores, and a tea made from the fig leaves may be used to wash the sores. For nose and throat conditions, the tea may be sniffed into the nose. Several drops of the warm tea are also useful for dropping into the ear for earache. The tea is made by taking one heaping teaspoonful of finely cut leaves to a cup of boiling water.

Garlic (Allium sativum). This humble but pungent herb has many uses. It increases perspiration and also serves as a diuretic, aiding and increasing functions of the kidneys. It is also an expectorant, useful for removing mucus from the throat and lungs. Garlic is very helpful in treating animals as well as humans and may be used in the treatment of all fevers, pulmonary, gastric and skin complaints, rheumatism, all worms, also liver-fluke, mange, ringworm, ticks and lice. It is the supreme immunizer of stock against infectious diseases. For animals, the dose is two bulbs, or whole plants, or two handfuls of leaves when in season, given twice daily in a bran mash with molasses. In fevers and pulmonary ailments, make a brew from two bulbs or finely chopped whole plants to 1½ pints water, plus two tablespoons of honey added. Give one cupful morning and night. For external use, omit honey.

When dosing milking animals, feed the herb at milking time and its pungent aroma will then have left the bloodstream by the time of the next milking and will not alter the flavor of the milk.

Dried, powdered garlic, plain or in water solution, is presently becoming a popular agricultural insecticide spray.

Hazel (Corylus avellana). This small nut tree of hedges and woods is distinguished by its shiny, crisp, round leaves and attractive flower catkins of yellow-green touched with red, and its autumn nuts contained in green "Bonnets" with cut edges.

Known as a tree of special magic, it is the one which gives the famed (and much used) water-divining rod, *virgula devinata*. Hazel is of special benefit to farm animals as a general tonic. The foliage fed to milk animals increases their milk yield, and the nuts fatten them.

Jewel Weed (Impatiens aurea) is a "jewel" indeed, for the juice of this plant will alleviate the suffering and discomfort of poison ivy—and oddly, it is often found growing near poison ivy. Euell Gibbons in his book *Stalking the Healthful Herbs* suggests that after extraction the juice be frozen into ice cubes, the cubes stored in the freezer, and kept handy in case a roam in the woods results in a case of poison oak or ivy.

The juice of the plant is also reported effective for removal of warts, corns and similar growths on the skin. Also, it is said to relieve ringworm. It is also recommended for cases of jaundice (liver ailment) and dropsy. For jaundice and dropsy, a drink (½ cup of which is taken three times a day) is prepared by mixing an ounce of the powdered herb with a pint of boiling water.

Marigold (Calendula officinalis). This is a stimulant which is helpful when used as a local remedy for direct application to varicose veins, chronic ulcers and similar ailments. By increasing perspiration, it flushes poisons from the body. A solution for both internal and external use may be prepared by pouring a pint of boiling water over an ounce of the powdered flowers and stems of the herb. Taking a dose of one tablespoonful two or three times a day internally will aid the external effect.

Oats (Avena sativa). Oats has many healing properties, but is especially recommended for the heart. An authoritative work on herbs states that oats "seem to exert a very beneficial action upon heart muscles." The plentiful taking of oatmeal and/or oatmeal water has been considered as a preventative for heart disease as well as for helping to remedy heart disease.

Oats in the form of oatmeal has also been recommended for insomnia because of its beneficial effect on the nervous system, and is reported to facilitate sleep. For the same reasons it is recommended as a nerve tonic, as a restorative in nervous prostration and following exhaustion as the result of diseases accompanied by fever. The presence of phosphorus in oats makes it valuable for the formation of brain and nerve tissue—it was once believed (and may well be true) that ample use of oatmeal helped children become more adept in their studies.

Do you have freckles? It has been reported that boiling oats in vinegar and then applying the resulting mash to the face or other parts of the body will remove the spots.

Onion (Allium Cepa). The not-so-humble onion has a lot of therapeutic uses—one of the effects being as a diuretic; that is, it serves to stimulate the action of the kidneys and promotes the flow of urine.

Roasted onion may be used as a poultice for tumors or ulcers, especially where there is pus formation. When placed against the ear, such a poultice is said to relieve earaches. Mixed with honey, onion juice may be used to cure a cough. And the boiled onion, when eaten, is helpful in relieving a cold. Put it in chicken soup!

Rosemary (Rosmarinus officinalis). One of our most pleasant herbs, it is a tonic, strengthening and toning muscles—and it is also an astringent, drawing tissues together and causing a cessation of fluid discharges. It is diaphoretic, increasing perspiration. It has excellent effects on the stomach, increasing action and aiding digestion. Rosemary acts as a nervine, lessening irritability of the nerves, and is useful as a nerve sedative. It has also been used to relieve headaches.

Further, rosemary has been recommended for use in preventing premature baldness by combining a solution of this herb with Borax. For treating the hair, pour a pint of boiling water over an ounce of the dried herb or powder and mix the solution. Rosemary oil was popular with our grandmothers as a hair treatment to keep their "crowning glory" in a state of shining good health.

The herbs mentioned here are but a few of the hundreds, possibly thousands (many plants have properties still undiscovered), of plants that can bless and heal, most of them gently, over a period of time which does not shock the system as stronger drugs sometimes do. Many helpful herbs grow wild, or may easily be grown in your flower or vegetable garden. Others may be obtained from Indiana Botanic Gardens, Inc., Box 5, Hammond, Indiana 46325.

It is also important to know that specific herbs are ruled by specific planets. Jupiter, for instance, rules aloes, aniseed, apricots, balm, Blue Flag, dandelion, etc. The therapeutic properties of the Jupiter group are alexipharmic, analeptic, anthelmintic, antispasmodic, balsamic, emollient.

Typical herbs of Mars include *Allium sativum*, basil, catmint, cresses, mustard and red pepper. The therapeutic properties of the Mars group are aphrodisiac, caustic, escharotic, resolvent, rubefacient, stimulant, tonic and vesicant.

The Mercury group has bittersweet, elfwort, male fern, horehound, and southernwood as typical herbs. The therapeutic properties of the Mercury group are alterative, antiperiodic, cephalic and nervine.

The Moon group includes cabbage, cucumbers, lettuce,

lily, moonwort, water arrowhead, watercress, waterflag, water lily, and willows—all strongly associated with water. The Moon group's therapeutic properties are alterative, attenuant, and emetic.

The planet Neptune is said to have rule over herbs which are of a narcotic, soporific and sleep-producing, anesthetic nature, such as opiates, tobacco, cocaine, morphine, heroin, etc. The therapeutic properties are analgesic, anodyne, hypnotic, soporific and suggestive. The poppy plant, from which opium is derived, is undoubtedly strongly ruled or influenced by Neptune. Coffee also comes under the rule of Neptune, as well as mosses, mushrooms, sponges and vegetable fungus growths.

Typical herbs ruled by Saturn include belladonna, barley, boneset, *cannabis sativa*, goutwort, *Helleborus niger*, hemlock, henbane, Indian hemp, and Solomon's seal—many helpful and also many poisonous plants. Saturn's therapeutic properties are antiphlogistic, antipyretic, astringent, febrifuge, refrigerant, sedative and styptic.

Typical herbs ruled by the Sun are almond, *Calendula officinalis*, helianthus, heliotrope, marigold, mustard, olive, orange, and, of course, the sundew and sunflower. The therapeutic properties are cardiac, anticachetic and sudorific.

The rulerships of the more distant planets such as Uranus over plants and herbs have not, as yet, been clearly defined. Their influences as so far observed seem to be mostly mental or spiritual, and affect the mind or nervous system. The therapeutic action of the drugs and herbs of Uranus is observed to be electric and vibrational. Of the herbs, croton oil, the oil expressed from the seed of the *Croton tigilum* tree, is listed as a typical herb of Uranus. Actually, more minerals and metals are listed under Uranus than herbs.

The Venus group of herbs includes apples, archangel, artichoke, asparagus, bearberry, cherry, cloves, columbines, cowslip, daisy, foxglove, goldenrod, herb Robert, indigo plant, ladies' mantle, mallow, marsh mallow, mints, parsley, plums, verbena, violets, wheat and yarrow. The therapeutic properties of the Venus group are antinephritic, diuretic, demulcent and emetic.

Let Astrology
Help You Diet
by Louise Riotte

First of all, get rid of your guilt feelings. The desire to have an alluring figure is a laudable one; you will add beauty to the world by improving your appearance. And, whether you need to add pounds or lose them, astrology can help you toward your goal.

Usually, overweight is caused simply by overeating. A great many of us overeat for reasons other than actual hunger. The stay-at-home person is apt to eat out of boredom, and food is readily at hand. Many who work are tempted to have a doughnut or a piece of pie during coffee breaks, even when they're not hungry. Perhaps you see a co-worker having a little treat and you feel entitled to have one too. But remember, *calories do count*, in spite of some theories of reducing.

All of us are a bit weak when it comes to food. We need some help in reinforcing our will power. To begin to overcome any habit you wish to break, such as overeating, *start on a day when the Moon is in the third or fourth quarter and in a barren sign*. Gemini, Leo, and Virgo are considered the best signs, yet Aries and Capricorn are suitable as well. Make sure your lunar cycle is favorable. Avoid days when lunar aspects to Mars or Jupiter are unfavorable, but aspects to Neptune or Saturn can be helpful.

If you feel you should not embark on a dietary program without first consulting your doctor or having a general checkup, remember that diagnosis is more likely to be accurate when the Moon is in a Cardinal sign (Aries, Cancer, Libra, Capricorn), and less so when in a Mutable sign (Gemini, Virgo, Sagittarius, Pisces); the Moon should also be favorable to your Sun sign. Since your pre-diet checkup is not an emergency, you can schedule your appointment for a suitable day and choose the right time at your leisure.

Ten Steps To A Trimmer You

1. When grocery shopping, prepare a list and stick to it. And shop when your stomach is full.
2. Never skip meals—controlling your appetite at the next meal may be too difficult. Eat breakfast like a queen, lunch like a princess, and dinner like a pauper.
3. Make a list of why you want to lose those extra pounds— this seems to help us maintain our motivation and willpower. Weigh yourself only once a week and you'll be less apt to get discouraged.
4. When you start to lose, give yourself a reward. But not a treat related to food. Perhaps a new article of clothing or a movie.
5. Being only human, you may slip occasionally and eat something fattening. Don't punish yourself by going on a binge. Forgive yourself and start again. A friend of mine put a sign on her refrigerator, "Think fat." It helps!
6. Learn to enjoy your meals for themselves, without reading, watching TV, or listening to the radio while you are eating. Eat slowly. Relax and enjoy each mouthful. Try eating from a smaller plate. Plan to have an attractive table setting—you are just as important as "company."
7. Chew each mouthful well before swallowing and you will be satisfied with smaller quantities. This will also aid your digestive process.
8. Recognize that there may be certain times of day when the temptation to overeat is stronger. Try to create a set of activities you can turn to at such times.
9. Serve food directly on individual plates, instead of having family style meals and passing big bowls of food around the table. Keep seconds on the stove and out of sight.
10. Keeping a food diary will also be helpful in keeping track of your daily calorie and carbohydrate intake. This will aid you in becoming aware of why you overeat.

Timing Your Sprouts By Moon Sign

by Louise Riotte

Sprouts, especially those grown in water, are completely Moon ruled—even more so than other plants usually grown in earth. And sprouts have a lot going for them. For a fast kitchen crop they are unbeatable, and everyone can "play"; children, apartment dwellers, young or old—and you can grow sprouts just about anywhere. You can be a gardener even if you do not own one inch of soil.

Sprouts are a healthy and economical source of extra protein and vitamins, and they are far, far better nutrition-wise than many foods found on the American table. The equipment takes up little space, so you may have an easy-care garden on your kitchen counter which will give you a maximum return for a minimum outlay. Moreover, the equipment is very inexpensive. All you need are a few jars and some seeds.

Sprouts are tasty. There is a wide variety of seeds which may be sprouted to add a great variety of flavors to our usual foods, lifting them out of the ordinary at a time of year when we are hungry for something green and fresh. Sprouts have no "season". . .you can grow them winter and summer, spring and fall and all the times in-between if you will just follow a few simple rules.

Sprouting is fun and practically foolproof. With just a little care and attention to detail it is almost impossible to make a mistake. You don't even need to have a "green

139

thumb" to be an effective sprouter.

Let's begin by getting down to the nitty gritty. . .just what are sprouts? Sprouts are seeds of grains or legumes which, germinated through the process known as sprouting, convert their fats and starches into vitamins, sugars and proteins. Under proper conditions you can sprout any viable seed, but some are more palatable than others and have more varied uses.

Perhaps the key word here should be "viable". Your seeds must be fresh and untreated with chemicals. Such seeds are comparatively easy to buy and probably may be purchased at your nearest health store, or by mail order from any one of the large natural food suppliers. Some of the nursery catalogs even carry them. (Vermont Bean Seed Co., Garden Lane, Bomoseen, Vermont 05732, is an excellent source. They carry Alfalfa seeds, Mung beans, Chinese Red Peas, Radish seeds, Mustard, Yellow soybeans and California Red Clover)

Sprouted seeds are considered the very best source of vitamins after sea vegetation (such as kelp); also Moonruled. Besides vitamin B complex, they contain D, C, and vitamin E. Sprouted seed protein is ready to work for your body without going through the long breaking-down process animal protein requires—they are nature's way to good health.

In purchasing your seeds you may figure that one pound of seeds will equal approximately four pounds of sprouts. When your seeds arrive be sure to store properly those you will not use immediately. Kept in dry and airtight jars, they will maintain their viability for years. Don't store them, though, use them!

The equipment you will need for sprouting is simple and may be homemade. You may start, if you like, with two widemouthed fruit jars. Next, cut two pieces of screening (which may be aluminum, plastic or nylon) to fit the jar openings, using the regular fruit jar ring to hold these in place.

Mung beans or lentils are among the easiest sprouters so I would suggest you start with one of these. Wash the beans and remove any broken seeds. Put one-half cup beans in one jar, filling it with four times the amount of water. Let the beans soak overnight. In the morning you will find they have doubled in bulk. Now, place screen and jar ring over the jar opening and drain the water off the beans.

Your next step is to put half the beans into the other jar with a screen top, rinsing both sets of beans with fresh, cool water. Take care not to leave any water in the container for seeds should be just damp, not soaked. Lay jars on their sides in a dark place, never in direct sunlight. But remember good ventilation is important. A handy corner of your kitchen counter will be a good place. Two or three times each day rinse with cool water, pouring it completely out each time.

You will be delighted to see sprouts appearing on the second day and they will be ready to use by the third or fourth day. You will also be happily surprised at just how many sprouts you have—perhaps more than you can use at once. If this happens, refrigerate them in a covered container. Such sprouts as mung beans will be usable for about three days before they begin to deteriorate.

There are a few things you should know for best results. Sprouts will not grow well at room temperatures much above 80 degrees, but high humidity is even more of a deterrent. The water you use for sprouting your seeds is important too and should be the purest possible. Avoid flouridated water which will not grow good sprouts. If your city water is treated, catch rain water and store it in glass or plastic jugs. Water, too, is Moon ruled.

Timing your sprouts astrologically for growth is also important. As with outdoor plants, sprouts will grow with a waning Moon but will grow faster as the Moon waxes, 1st and 2nd quarters. And you may expect them to grow fastest of all just after the New Moon. Besides these lunar phases also take note of the days when the Moon is passing through the three water signs of Cancer, Scorpio and Pisces, which are considered the most fertile signs for plant growth. For most seeds Moon-ruled Cancer is the best, but for cereal grains used as sprouting material (such as barley, wheat or triticale) you may also use the sign of Libra. Sprouts may be considered as "annuals" and you may use any other growing advice which applies to these.

What seeds will you wish to sprout? And, having duly arrived with a successful harvest, how will you use them? Let's start again with Mung beans. These are delicious when combined with meat and other vegetables in chowders, seafood dishes or delicate omelets. Try them in rice dishes to add a different flavor and texture, combine them with other foods in stuffings. They will even perk up baked goods and biscuits.

Crisp, delectable sprouted lentils are good eaten raw in salads or in place of lettuce in sandwiches. Cook them with tomatoes or in an eggplant dish and you will find they lend a sweet, nutty flavor. They become something special when combined with onions, herbs and a bit of meat for a really great soup. Rolled into a meat loaf they will lift it into the realm of a gourmet treat. If you have access to mushrooms, combine them with lentils for a very special dish.

Soybeans are just chockful of vitamin B, stretching the nutritional value of any dish in which they are included. And here's a new twist—try roasting and grinding some of your sprouts, using them as a substitute for peanut butter in cookies, muffins or cupcakes. Alfalfa is good for you, too, containing thirty-five percent protein and, when sprouted, vitamins D, E, K and C, as well as such minerals as phosphorus, iron and silicon. And, right here, let me emphasize again just how much sprouting improves a seed's nutritional value, over and above that of the dry, unsprouted, seed. You can use the dried sprouts of Alfalfa in recipes calling for nuts.

Wheat sprouts are sweet and crunchy. Use them as toppings for fruit pies or, dried and ground, in cake or cookie batters. Wheat, containing little fat, is a good source of protein, a valuable source of vitamins; nicotinic acid, B_6, pantothenic acid and E. Triticale, a new plant development, may be used like wheat. When sprouted, it doubles in protein. It is an exciting new seed and a natural for adding to breads, muffins and waffles.

Radishes sprout as quickly and easily indoors as they do in your garden, and they give a tangy, peppery flavor to salads and sandwiches. Containing vitamins B_1 and C, they are beneficial for teeth, nerves, gums, hair and nails. Don't leave out mustard seeds, as they are a great source of vitamin A. But use them sparingly with other greens for they have a lot of character. Barley is one of our best bodybuilders. It contains vitamins B_1 and B_2, is blood cooling and tonic, and has long been considered a remedy for ailments of kidneys and bladder. It is also a very special taste treat.

That sun-worshipping plant, the Sunflower, produces one of our best sprouts, containing vitamins B_1, A, D, and F—another good body-building food helpful in countering weak eyes, arthritis and problems of tooth decay or dryness of skin.

This one may be entirely new to you—Fenugreek. Fenugreek is derived from a Latin word that means "Greek hay", but don't let that turn you away. The excellent flavor of this sprouted seed is just the opposite of that sweet grain; it is spicy and slightly bitter. Perhaps, for many, it might even be called an "acquired taste". However if you buy a packaged mixture of seeds for sprouting, fenugreek quite likely will be included and you might find it interesting to experiment a little.

As with many seeds or grains of ancient origin, fenugreek is supposed to have curative powers of value in the treatment of ulcers (far from the bland diet cure) and as a gargle when made into tea. It is rich in iron, high in protein and vitamin A. And, if you know that fenugreek is a component of curry powder, and have experienced the throat-searing results of a strong curry dish, its medicinal claims may not seem too far-fetched. But watch it. This one is strong!

The list of seeds that can be sprouted would not be complete without corn, containing vitamins B_1, C, A and B_2—another great body-builder which adds both flavor and nutritional value to everyday dishes. Still other seeds you may wish to try are beans, such as garbanzo, lima and red kidney. Pinto, Great Northern, White or Fava beans will also sprout well. Haricot or Broad beans are believed to be especially helpful in stimulating energy, strength and sexual vigor.

Sprouting can become a household habit, whether we try it for nutrition, occuational therapy or economy. And it can all be done without adding chemicals or fertilizers, without weeding and without bug sprays!

Crises: The Turning Points In Disease

by Louise Riotte

Hippocrates, "the Father of Medicine," was an authority on diagnoses and treatments of disease that were deduced from astronomical correlations. In fact, the famous Hippocratic crises are based on the hexagonal angles of the Moon's monthly motion in the case of fevers, diseases, and even surgical operations. The timing of the crises is still observed by modern medical people; many of whom seem to have forgotten their celestial origin.

Crises are brought about by the changes of the Moon, by transits, by progressed Moon aspects, or a New Moon, and by directions. Judgment should not be based upon any one affliction; all should be taken into consideration. And the fundamental vitality should be considered too. The time of death usually comes at a crisis time, but should never be intimated to the sick person, even though certain death may be indicated by the planetary influences. The map of birth shows the days when crises are due.

In acute diseases the 7th, 14th, 21st, and 28th days from the time the patient became ill are crisis days of the disease, being based upon the four quarters of the Moon. The Moon makes a revolution in her orbit in about 28 days, and the 7th, 14th, and 21st days and her return to her place at the time of the New Moon correspond to her quarters, adverse aspects, and the crisis times in acute diseases. Therefore the first, second, third, and fourth quarters of the Moon, from the time the illness began, are crisis days. A person taken sick with a fever exactly at the New Moon would have the crises on the exact quarters of the Moon as given in the Moon Tables.

In acute diseases and fevers the crisis days are the dangerous ones. The most serious crisis day is the 14th day, as a rule, when the Moon arrives at the opposition aspect to her place at the beginning of the illness. This crisis day is called the "Criticus Primus," the one of prime importance. More patients die on the 14th day of a serious fever than on the other crisis days, and if they do not die on the 14th day their chances for recovery or for moderation of the disease are usually good. The patient is usually worse on the 7th and 21st days of the disease, but these crises are considered of minor importance as compared to the 14th-day crisis. Improvements in the patient's condition are due on the 9th, 10th, 18th, and 19th days of the disease, as these days correspond to the trine aspects of the Moon, her good aspects, from the day the illness began.

The patient takes a turn for the better when the Moon is in good aspect to the Benefics (the planets Jupiter and Venus). Even if it's a crisis day, the patient's condition will improve if the Moon is in sextile (60°) or trine (120°) aspect to Jupiter and/or Venus. Both of these aspects signal harmony and good health. The Lords (rulers) of the Ascendant 9th, 10th, or 11th houses also herald an interval of ease and relief, particularly if the Lord of the Ascendant is in good aspect to the Sun on a crisis day, and if the Sun does not have the power of dominion over the disease. So if the patient lives through all the crisis days, the disease will dissolve itself or become chronic.

Regarding disease, there has always been much superstition in times past, but Hippocrates showed that disease had only natural causes, and took treatment of disease out of the hands of religion. He objected to the use of strong drugs without careful tests of their curative values. He insisted that "our natures are the physicians of our diseases." He treated his patients with proper diet, fresh air, change in climate, and attention to habits and living conditions. His favorite diet for sick people was a barley gruel. His favorite medicine was honey: "the drink to be employed should there be any pain is vinegar and honey. If there be great thirst, give water and honey."

Herbs And Health

At the dawn of history, most physicians were also herbalists. Over time, herbs have been replaced by pharmaceuticals for healing, even though many of our modern medicines are actually made from herbal extracts. Here are a few of the herbal remedies that you can use at home for common ailments. For serious ailments be sure to see a health professional.

Insect Bites: apply eucalyptus oil, thyme oil or distilled witch hazel extract.

Burns: use a poultice of comfrey, mustard or yarrow. Salves can be made from elderberry blossoms, golden seal or red clover. Wheat germ oil also helps, and of course there is aloe vera, which when applied immediately after a burn occurs, helps stop blistering and pain.

Diarrhea: raw apples and bananas; teas of crowfoot, peppermint, red raspberry or slippery elm.

Fever: teas of chamomile, yarrow, catnip, elderberry or peppermint. Spearmint tea is good for children.

Headache: hot teas of perppermint, catnip, spearmint or chamomile. A very hot foot bath of one tablespoon dry mustard, lemon juice, onion, honey and water for 5-10 minutes.

Stomach Ache: chew on fennel seeds or drink teas of caraway and sweet cicely, sage, chamomile, mints, slippery elm or yarrow.

Sunburn: make an ointment of glycerine, witch hazel and sunflower seed oil. Aloe vera works well.

Encouraging Hair Growth: eat wheat germ, cod-liver oil or lecithin daily. Cut it during the Full Moon.

Sprains: poultices of chamomile and hops or caraway and hyssop.

Insomnia: These teas are the best for making you sleepy: chamomile, catnip, hops, lady's slipper.

Colds: Teas or capsules of golden seal are considered to work the fastest (no more than a tablespoon per day). Other remedies include teas of balsam, catnip, elderberry and peppermint, mullien, rosemary or sarsaparilla.

Any of the teas, herbs, and ingredients listed here can be found in most reputable health food stores or co-ops. Some mail-order companies also specialize in herbal remedies. Some of the ingredients are as close as your local grocery.

BUSINESS, FINANCE & LEGAL

Advertising
Business
Buying
Electronics
Clothes
Collecting
Employment

Furniture
Legal matters
Loans
Machinery
Mailing
Mining
News

Photog./radio/TV
Selling
Signing papers
Travel
Flying
Writing
Wills

BUSINESS, FINANCE & LEGAL

Advertising

Write advertisements when it is a favorable day for your Sun Sign and Mercury or Jupiter is conjunct, sextile or trine the Moon. Mars and Saturn should not be aspecting the Moon by square, opposition or conjunction. Advertising campaigns are best begun when the Moon is in Taurus, Cancer, Sagittarius, or Aquarius, and well aspected. Advertise to give away pets when the Moon is in Sagittarius or Pisces.

Business

As you begin training for any occupation, see that your lunar cycle is favorable that day and that the planet ruling your occupation is marked C, T, or Sx.

In starting a business of your own, see that the Moon is free of afflictions and that the planet ruling the business is marked C, T, or Sx.

When you take up a new job, Jupiter and Venus should be sextile, trine, or conjunct the Moon.

To make contracts, see that the Moon is in a fixed sign and sextile, trine, or conjunct Mercury.

Buying

Buy during the Third Quarter, when the Moon is in Taurus for quality, in a mutable sign for savings. Good aspects from Venus or the Sun (C, Sx, T) are desirable. If you are buying for yourself it is good if the day is favorable to your Sign. See also machinery, appliances, tools.

Buying Electronic Equipment

Choose a day when the Moon is in an Air Sign (Gemini, Libra or Aquarius) and well-aspected by Mercury and/or Uranus. A favorable Saturn aspect aids with sound equipment.

Clothes Buying

For buying clothes, there are several astrological guidelines. First see that the Moon is sextile or trine to the Sun, and that the Moon is in the First or Second Quarters.

When the Moon is in Taurus, buying clothes will bring pleasure and satisfaction. Do not buy clothing or jewelry or wear them for the first time when the Moon is in Scorpio or Aries. Buying clothes on a favorable day for your Sun sign and when Venus or Mercury are well aspected is best; but avoid aspects to Mars and Saturn.

Collections

Try to make collections on days when your sun is well aspected. Avoid days in which Mars or Saturn are aspected. If possible, the Moon should be in a cardinal sign: Aries, Cancer, Libra or Capricorn. It is more difficult to collect when the Moon is in Taurus and Scorpio.

Employment, Promotion or Favors

Choose a day when your sign is favorable. Mercury should be marked C, T, or Sx. Avoid days when Mars or Saturn are aspected.

Furniture

Follow the rules for Machinery and Appliances but buy when the Moon is in Libra. Sell furniture when the Moon is in Libra as well.

Legal Matters

In general, a good aspect between the Moon and Jupiter is the best influence for a favorable decision. If you are starting a lawsuit to gain damages, begin during the increase of the Moon (1st and 2nd quarters). If you are seeking to avoid payment, get a court date when the Moon is decreasing (3rd and 4th quarters). A good Moon-Sun aspect strengthens your chance of success. In divorce cases, a favorable Moon-Venus aspect may produce a more amicable settlement. Moon in Cancer or Leo and well-aspected by the Sun brings the best results in custody cases.

Loans

Moon in the First and Second Quarters favors the lender, in the Third and Fourth it favors the borrower. Good aspects of Jupiter and Venus to the Moon are favorable to both, as is the Moon in Leo, Sagittarius, Aquarius or Pisces.

Machinery, Appliances, Tools

Tools, machinery and other implements should be bought on days when your lunar cycle is favorable and when Mrs and Uranus are trine, sextile, or conjunct the Moon. Any quarter of the Moon is suitable. When buying gas or electrical appliances, the Moon should be in Aquarius. The same applies for electronic equipment.

Mailing

For best results, send mail on favorable days for your Sun Sign. The Moon in Gemini is good, while Virgo, Sagittarius and Pisces are helpful, too.

Mining

Saturn rules drilling and mining. Begin this work on a day when Saturn is marked C, T, or Sx. If mining for gold, pick a day in which the Sun is also marked C, T, or Sx. Mercury rules quicksilver, Venus copper, Jupiter tin, Saturn lead and coal, Uranus radioactive elements, Neptune oil, and the Moon water. Choose a day when the planet ruling whatever is being drilled for is marked C, T or Sx.

New Ventures

Things usually get off to a better start during the increase of the Moon, the First and Second quarter. If there is impatience, anxiety or deadlock, it can often be broken at the Full Moon. Agreements can be reached then.

News

The handling of news is related to Uranus, Mercury, and all of the air signs. When Uranus is aspected, there is always an increase in the spectacular side of the news. Collection of news is related to Saturn.

Photography, Radio, T.V., Film and Video

For all these actiities, it is best to have Neptune, Venus, and Mercury well aspected, that is, trine, sextile, or conjunct the Moon. The act of photographing is not dependent on any particular phase of the Moon, but Neptune rules photography while Venus is related to beauty in line, form, and color.

Selling or Canvassing

Contacts for these activities will be better during a day

favorable to your Sun Sign. Otherwise, make strong efforts to sell on days when Jupiter, Mercury, or Mars are trine, sextile, or conjunct the Moon. Avoid days when Saturn is square or opposite the Moon.

Signing Important Papers

Sign contracts or agreements when the Moon is increasing (First and Second Quarter) in a fruitful sign, and on a day when Moon-Mercury aspects are operating. Avoid days when Mars, Saturn, or Neptune are square or opposite the Moon. Don't sign anything if it is an unfavorable day for you.

Travel

Short journeys are ruled by Mercury, long ones by Jupiter. The Sun rules the actual journey itself. Long trips which threaten to exhaust the traveller are best begun when the Sun is well-aspected to the Moon and the date is favorable for the traveller. If travelling with other people, good aspects from Venus are desirable. For employment, aspects to Jupiter are profitable. For visiting, aspects to Mercury. To avoid accidents, avoid afflictions from Mars, Saturn, Uranus or Pluto, and again, look for good aspects from the Sun.

When to Fly

Choose a day when the Moon is in Gemini or Libra, and well-aspected by Mercury and/or Jupiter. Avoid adverse aspects of Mars, Saturn or Uranus.

Writing

Writing for pleasure or publication is best done when the Moon is in Gemini. Mercury should be direct. Favorable aspects to Mercury, Uranus and Neptune promote ingenuity.

Writing A Will

The Moon should be in a fixed sign in the First or Second Quarters. There should be favorable aspects to Saturn, Venus and Mercury and no afflictions from Pluto.

FLYING BY THE LIGHT
OF THE MOON

Most of you will have to schedule at least one flight this year for business or pleasure. Knowing the best dates for flying can alleviate some of the fears you may have about the airplane disasters that are occurring with alarming frequency.

Travel by air is best done when the Moon is in Gemini or Libra and well aspected by Mercury (for short trips) and Jupiter (for long trips). Well aspected means that the Moon is Trine or Sextile Mercury or Jupiter (listed as Sx or T in the *Lunar Aspectarian*). Avoid dates when the Moon is Square or Opposite (Sq or O) Mars, Saturn or Uranus. Also look for a favorable day for your Sun Sign.

If you will be doing business, a sextile or trine to Jupiter is favorable, even if it is just a short trip. Positive aspects to Mercury make for good communication and pleasant visits with friends. The Quarter or phase of the Moon doesn't really come into play in air travel.

For 1989, the *best dates* for scheduling flights are:

    January: 17th, 18th
    February: 13th, 14th, 22nd (after 6:06 pm CST), 24th
    March: 13th
    April: 8th (after 7:32 pm CST), 9th
    May: 6th, 7th, 17th
    June: 3rd, 4th (before 6:18 pm CST), 13th, 30th
    July: 1st 11th (before 5:10 pm CST), 28th
    August: 7th
    September: 3rd, 19th (after 6:17 pm CST), 20th, 30th
    October: 18th
    November: 14th, 25th (before 3:14 am CST)
    December: 11th

These dates are the *most favorable.* If you must schedule a flight on a different date, look for a majority of positive influences and avoid squares and oppositions to Mars, Saturn and Uranus where possible. Conjunctions still have not been proven to be positive or negative, so for these dates they have been avoided. It is better to go with a different sign of the Moon and avoid the negative aspects if a choice must be made. Happy flying!

Starting A New Business Or Business Venture

When starting a new business or any type of new venture, check to make sure that the Moon is in the first or second quarter. This will help it get off to a better start. If there is a deadlock or anxiety, it will often be broken during the Full Moon. Agreements can then be reached.

You should also check the aspects of the Moon to the type of venture you are becoming involved in or with. Look for positive aspects to the planet that rules the activity (listed as Sx or T in the *Lunar Aspectarian*).

Activities ruled by the **Sun** are advertising, executive positions, acting, banking, finance, government, jewelry, law and public relations.

Activities ruled by **Mercury** are accounting, brokerage, clerical, disc jockey, doctor, editor, inspector, librarian, linguist, medical technician, scientist, teaching, writing, publishing, communication and mass media.

Activities and occupations ruled by **Venus** are architect, art and artists, beautician, dance, design, fashion and marketing, music, poetry and chiropractors.

Activities ruled by **Mars** are barber, butcher, carpenter, chemist, construction, dentist, metal worker, surgeon and the military.

Activities and occupations that are ruled by **Jupiter** are counseling, horse training, jockey, judge, lawyer, legislator, minister, pharmacist, psychologist, public analyst, social clubs, research and self-improvement.

Activities and occupations ruled by **Saturn** are agronomy, math, mining, plumbing, real estate, repairperson, printers, paper making and dealing with older people.

Activities and occupations ruled by **Uranus** are aeronautics, broadcasting, electricians, inventing, lecturing, radiology, and computers.

Activities and occupations ruled by **Neptune** are photography, investigators, religious institutions, shipping, pets, movies, wine merchants, health foods, resorts, travel by water and welfare.

Activities and occupations ruled by **Pluto** are acrobatics, athletic managers, atomic energy, research, speculation, sports, stockbrokers, and any purely personal endeavors.

If you follow the guidelines given above and apply them to the occupations or activities listed for each planet, you should have excellent results in your new business ventures. Even if it is not a new venture, check the aspects to the ruler of the activity before making moves in your business. Avoid any dates marked Sq or O to that planet ruler in the *Lunar Aspectarian*. You are sure to have trouble with the client or deal.

FARM &
GARDEN

LOUISE RIOTTE

Louise Riotte has been gardening by the Moon for several decades. She is knowledgeable in all phases of both timing by the Moon and growing plants. She writes a monthly gardening column for her local newspaper as well as articles for such magazines as *Organic Gardening*. She has written seven books to date, some of them familiar to Llewellyn readers. *Planetary Planting* (ACS, San Diego) is about using the planets in your gardening tasks, while *Roses Love Garlic* and *Carrots Love Tomatoes* (Storey Communications, Pownal, N.Y.) are all about companion planting. Her new book, *Sleeping with a Sunflower*, about old-time planting legends, is already a very popular book (Storey Communications).

Louise is an avid gardener, using only organic methods. She is a prolific writer and has contributed greatly to the *Moon Sign Book*. You will find her articles on a variety of subjects scattered throughout this edition. You will find that her writings are fun to read as well as being very informative.

Gardening
By The Moon

by Louise Riotte

Since writing my book, *Planetary Planting* (published by Astro Computing Services), I am frequently asked to explain just what astrological-organic gardening, or "Moon gardening" is.

Many of you have known and loved the *Moon Sign Book* for many years but for those who are new to gardening by the Signs of the Zodiac, a brief explanation of what it is, and what it is not, may be in order.

Moon planting is not a form of magic, or a cure-all for careless gardening practices, nor is it a guarantee of complete success. Rather, it is the study and use of the forces of nature as an *aid* in obtaining the highest possible degree of success.

"Organic gardening" teaches us HOW to plant in harmony with nature, " Moon gardening", along with the proper Sign, teaches us WHEN. Furthermore, this knowledge of how to plant, combined with when to plant, will give much better results than when one is used without the other.

So, all you organic and other gardeners, go right on doing what you have been doing—plant your gardens, build your compost heaps, water, weed, prune, cultivate and harvest. But, instead of doing these things in a hit or miss manner, do them when the Signs are right. Try it, it's fun!

Lunar gardening should never be considered as something which will produce a miracle cure for inescapable problems, for even Moon-planted crops can't completely withstand drought or get along without a program of weeding, watering, mulching, composting and fertilizing as is normally necessary. And remember also that there is a proper time for each of these gardening activities and if they are done in the proper Moon sign and quarter they will be even more effective. Given the same odds and care, you will find that growth will advance at a more rapid, satisfactory rate.

Moon Quarters Are Important Too

One of the reasons for failure in using Moon gardening techniques is the fact that many people do not take into consideration the Moon quarters when using the zodiacal Signs.

Let me explain first of all just what I mean by "Moon Quarters." The Moon is considered to be on the increase from New Moon to Half Moon to Full Moon, on the decrease from Full Moon to Dark of Moon to New Moon. Simplifying further, the first quarter and the second quarter are considered increasing, the third and fourth quarters decreasing.

Combine these divisions with the correct sign and you will increase your accuracy when you time planting and other gardening practices to coincide with natural rhythms.

Many gardeners simply follow the old practice of planting crops that produce above ground during Moon increase and crops producing below the ground at Moon decrease. However, following this practice without consulting the signs may lead to possible selection of planting days governed (ruled in the sense of affecting), by barren signs.

Here are some suggestions for using the right quarters for gardening operations, being sure to also check the appropriate sign for what you are planning to do.

First Quarter: Plant asparagus, broccoli, Brussel Sprouts, barley, cabbage, cauliflower, celery, cucumbers, corn, cress, endive, kohlrabi, lettuce, leek, oats, parsley, onions, spinach and seeds of herbs and flowering plants.

Avoid the first day of the New Moon for planting, also the days on which it changes quarters.

Second Quarter: Plant beans, eggplant, muskmelons, peas, peppers, pumpkins, squash, tomatoes, watermelon. In both the First and Second Quarters it is best to plant seed while the Moon is in the fruitful signs of **Cancer, Scorpio or Pisces.** The next best signs are Taurus and Capricorn. For flowers use Libra. Onions and Garlic seeds may be planted in Sagittarius.

Third Quarter: Plant artichoke, beets, carrots, chicory, parsnips, potatoes, radish, rutabaga, turnip and all bulbous flowering plants. Good also for planting apple trees, beech trees, biennials, deciduous trees, maple, oak tree, onion sets, peach trees, peanuts, pear trees, perennials, plum trees, rhubarb (under Aries), sage, strawberries, tubers for seed, and sunflowers.

These instances are given as rather broad suggestions, planting by the rulership of the Signs is a little more complicated. According to a simple plan worked out by Rudolph Steiner, the founder of the Anthroposophical movement, there is a system of correspondences between the four elements of what he saw as the four primordial organs of the plant: seed/fruit, flower, leaf/stem and root. The root, which grows in the earth, corresponds to the earth element. The water element is always associated with growth. The flower is ruled by the air because it reaches out into the atmosphere to receive pollen from either air-borne insects or the wind. The seed contains the basic blueprint for life, the genetic material, and is therefore associated with the fire element, which accounts for the determining quality in biological life.

Aries: Ram, Head—A movable fire sign governed by the sun: seeds if planted in this sign produce vines or stalks. Since Aries rules the seeds, plants germinated when the Moon is in Aries are quick to bolt (go to seed). Bitterness, a quality of the fire signs may also become apparent. Aries, since it gives the fastest maturity, can be used advantageously by market gardeners to get an early crop. It is unfortunate, however, that the Aries Moon only occurs in the waxing phases from January to March.

Taurus: Bull, Neck — A fixed, earthly sign governed by Mercury and Earth, good for all root crops where quick growth is an advantage. Taurus rules food storage as evidenced in the root of potatoes, or the stem of the Kohlrabi. Good for most plants, especially root crops, such as those needing to survive winter in the root system. The feeding process in the root which continues all winter long, despite the dormancy of the top growth, is ruled by Taurus. According to Charles Hooks, Taurus and Capricorn plants have short vine growth, "similar to Moon in Pisces, but less productive." Taurus is advantageous to root growth and for transplanting. A Canadian gardener writes that the Second Quarter Taurus Moon promotes excellent root growth, "short nodes and strength of plant intensified." A professional flower grower finds that Taurus gives superb substance to petals.

Gemini: Heavenly Twins, Arms—Even though this is a barren sign it is good for planting melon seeds. And it is a good sign for cultivating the soil to destroy weeds. Gemini rules the vascular system (xylem and phloem) in which water and sap flow through the plant. Planting in Gemini produces long, stringy, weak plants which it rules. Jewelweed, Elm and Celery, for example, have the ability to grow in overly moist places, and may do well if planted in this sign.

Cancer: Crab, Breast—Cancer is a Cardinal Water Sign ruled by the Moon. Under this fruitful, movable Sign seeds germinate quickly. Favorable to growth it ensures an abundant yield. For Moon planters it is the most productive sign, ruling the principles of growth in the green foliage, stalk, leaf or vine. If it comes at the Full of the Moon it is a good sign to plant beans; if at time of New Moon, lentils. Sow peas if the day follows the New Moon, they will grow quickly, have abundant flowers and yield. Peas, sown immediately after the second quarter will bear but little; if sown a day or two after the Full Moon they will bloom and fruit in abundance but yield little; if sown a day or two after the Full Moon is out they will do little more than break through the ground.

Cancer is a good earth sign to prune grape vines.

Leo: Lion, Heart—This is a barren fiery sign, favorable only to the destruction of noxious growth. If weeds, briars and bushes are cut off in the 4th quarter of the Moon in August when its place is in Leo they will be more certainly destroyed than at any other time.

Leo rules a curtailing function in the cycle of a plant's growth which is most necessary. Under Cancer, which rules the vegetative growth, we find great productiveness, with replication of leaf after leaf. But, for the plant to blossom and set fruit this process cannot continue. As the time for the flower to appear arrives the leaves become smaller and compacted together on the stalk. They end eventually in a whorl called the "calyx", consisting of atrophied leaves called "sepals" which form a green base around the nascent flower.

This curtailing influence is under the rulership of Leo, along with the calyx and sepals. As this process slows growth we can easily understand why Leo is considered to be the most barren sign for planting. A test of seedlings transplanted while the Moon was in Leo had a zero survival rate, while those transplanted under Cancer were very successful.

Virgo: Virgin, Bowels—This, too, is generally considered a barren sign, making many and beautiful flowers, but not favorable to growth of seed or transplanting. Yet, Virgo is favorable to vine growth if that is desired and for many, vertical gardening has become increasingly important. Vines on a west fence can be used in the garden to great advantage to shield plants from a too hot afternoon sun, especially in a dry summer. They also provide a windbreak, taking the place of trees whose roots may reach out into the garden.

Virgo rules the process of "digestion" in the plant (glycolysis and the Kreb's cycle). Thinking this process out we can see why Virgo is the only earth sign which is considered barren. Almost all the vegetable food we eat consists of "stored food" in the plant, such as the edible parts of apples, cabbages, potatoes, carrots, etc. These consist of stored food (sugar and carbohydrates). Even grains consist predominantly of stored food. Digestion of this will produce energy for plant growth during the season but at the end of the year there will be no food stored up. Resulting plants will be tough and vinelike, without having the redeeming values of a Capricorn plant in added structure and tap root development.

Libra: Balance-Scales, Reins—Libra is a strong, movable sign. Seeds planted in Libra produce vigorous pulp growth and roots and a reasonable amount of grain. It is also the sign under which to plant flowers. And, since Libra is the sign of beauty and attractiveness it is not surprising that it should be the ruler of the blossom or flower petals. It is also semi-fruitful for other crops. It is of interest to note that the petals are the only part of the plant which need and absorb oxygen from the air, evidencing the rulership of the air element. Libra is a masculine sign and may produce over blooming, and the seeds or bulbs are poor germinators. Over-blooming is hard on bulb growth.

If you want to grow prize-winning roses, take first prize at the garden club, or just have the prettiest yard on the block, plant your flowers in Libra.

Scorpio: Scorpion, Eagle, Secrets, Genitals—This is the second most fruitful sign, producing watery effects. Oddly it is the sign with the greatest potential for good or evil. For the gardener it is an especially good sign to plant corn.

Scorpio rules sexual reproduction, especially the sexual organs of the flower. It is, therfore, a fertile producer setting much fruit. It also rules the buds, and in company with Taurus, is the best sign for winter-hardiness. It fosters regeneration and regrowth after winterkill and protection against early and late frosts. As the best sign for regeneration it is a good sign for transplanting tomatoes, which are ruled by Scorpio. They are actually stimulated to produce more fruit by being pruned back just after the flowers set. Scorpio's special gift to the gardener is sturdiness, so this sign is also fine for vine growth.

Scorpio is one of the best signs for planting and transplanting all crops, including flowers.

As a water sign, Scorpio is one of the most "fruitful" placements for planting. It retains water well, and with Capricorn, is the best sign for drought resistance (Pisces is good for dry garden sites, but not so much for drought-survival). Hooks wrote that Scorpio is used where length of vine is desirable. Squash as well as tomatoes are ruled by Scorpio. Tomatoes benefit from the Moon in Scorpio because it gives them more resistance to drought and cold, problems to which they are very sensitive. Squash and pumpkins form best when planted under Scorpio.

Sagittarius: Archer, Bowman, the thighs—A fiery masculine sign, generally believed a poor time to plant or transplant. However, some believe that if the moon is dark or on the wane, root crops such as potatoes or radishes may be planted, as they are thought to do well if planted in signs of the lower part of the body.

Sagittarius rules fruit, and is therefore sometimes used for planting apple trees or other fruit crops. Hay and onions may also be planted when the Moon is in Sagittarius.

Capricorn: Goat, Knees—This sign is somewhat productive, favoring root crops such as beets, potatoes, turnips, etc. Ruled by Saturn its element is earth. Moist and movable it produces rapid growth of pulp stalks or roots, but not much grain.

Capricorn rules the bark and structural material in the plant, either wood or fiber, above ground or below. Good for grafting and pruning as the wood heals well. Capricorn also rules the hormones which control "apical dominance" (the dominance of top branches, so that the former grow faster and produce a symmetrical shape). It is ideal for planting ornamental trees or shrubs.

Aquarius: Water Bearer, Legs—This is an airy, masculine sign. Seed not only does not grow well, but is likely to rot. Aquarius does, however, favor the tilling of the soil. This sign rules the base of the stem, the point from which the stem grows up and the root grows down. It also rules clones and asexual reproduction. It rules the Onion clan and pine trees, and both would probably benefit from being planted under the Moon in Aquarius.

The sign is beneficial in situations involving shock and this would certainly be a good sign to try for transplanting onion sets. Aquarian people are generally "tall and lofty" (both in appearance and idealism) or "bulb-like" in build. Thus, the sign will probably promote good growth in pine stands and onions.

Pisces: Fish, Feet—A watery, fruitful productive sign similar to Cancer, favorable to all kinds of planting. It is one of the best signs for producing the fruit of the earth. Being a watery sign, it assists vegetation to withstand drought.

Pisces rules hydrotropism (water-seeking) in the root system. This is the sign for planting in dry soils where deep root penetration is desired. It is believed to produce the shortest top growth of Moon in any sign. The strong underground nutrition supports a healthy, plentiful fruit crop, somewhat better than Scorpio, less so than Cancer. Because Pisces encourages growth in the root system it is a very poor sign for potatoes, as some Moon-planters have noticed. The plant's energy is always seeking to go beyond the storage tuber into the growing roots. Potatoes planted under a Pisces Moon tend to sprout buds at the eye. I once experimented and planted potatoes in Pisces and then forgot about it. When I dug the potatoes I was astonished at the large number of little protruberances the potatoes in that row showed. A neighbor said, "We call those 'little toes'."

Hydroponic Gardening

Favorable results are attained when the Moon is in a fruitful sign (Cancer, Scorpio, Pisces) and increasing in light (1st and 2nd quarters). Avoid the exact dates of the Full, New and Quarter Moons, and adverse Moon-Neptune aspects. Choose crops with an affinity for the Moon, Jupiter and Neptune; Venus-ruled plants may also do well.

Planting Guide

Plant	Phase	Sign
Annuals	1st or 2nd	
Apple Trees	2nd or 3rd	Sagittarius
Artichokes	1st	Cancer, Pisces, Virgo
Asparagus	1st	Cancer, Scorpio, Pisces
Asters	1st or 2nd	Virgo
Barley	1st or 2nd	Cancer, Scorpio, Pisces, Libra, Capricorn
Beans	2nd	Cancer, Scorpio, Pisces, Libra, Taurus
Beech trees	3rd	Capricorn
Beets	3rd	Cancer, Scorpio, Pisces, Libra, Capricorn
Berries	2nd	Cancer, Scorpio, Pisces
Biennials	3rd or 4th	
Broccoli	1st	Cancer, Scorpio, Pisces, Libra
Brussel Sprouts	1st	Cancer, Scorpio, Pisces, Libra
Buckwheat	1st or 2nd	Capricorn
Bulbs	3rd	Cancer, Scorpio, Pisces
Bulbs for seed	2nd or 3rd	
Cabbage	1st	Cancer, Scorpio, Pisces, Libra, Taurus
Cactus		Taurus, Capricorn
Cantaloupes	1st or 2nd	Cancer, Scorpio, Pisces, Libra
Carrots	3rd	Cancer, Scorpio, Pisces, Libra
Cauliflower	1st	Cancer, Scorpio, Pisces, Libra
Celery	1st	Cancer, Scorpio, Pisces
Cereals	1st or 2nd	Cancer, Scorpio, Pisces, Libra
Chard	1st or 2nd	Cancer, Scorpio, Pisces, Libra
Chicory	2nd or 3rd	Cancer, Scorpio, Pisces, Sagittarius
Chrysanthe-mums	1st or 2nd	Virgo
Clover	1st or 2nd	Cancer, Scorpio, Pisces
Corn	1st	Cancer, Scorpio, Pisces
Corn for fodder	1st or 2nd	Libra
Coryopsis	2nd or 3rd	Libra
Cosmos	2nd or 3rd	Libra
Cress	1st	Cancer, Scorpio, Pisces
Crocus	1st or 2nd	Virgo
Cucumbers	1st	Cancer, Scorpio, Pisces

Daffodils	1st or 2nd	Libra, Virgo
Dahlias	1st or 2nd	Libra, Virgo
Deciduous trees	2nd or 3rd	Cancer, Scorpio, Pisces
Egg Plant	2nd	Cancer, Scorpio, Pisces, Libra
Endive	1st	Cancer, Scorpio, Pisces, Libra
Flowers for		Virgo, Gemini, Sagittarius
beauty	1st	Libra
abundance	1st	Cancer, Pisces, Virgo
sturdiness	1st	Scorpio
hardiness	1st	Taurus
Garlic	1st or 2nd	Scorpio, Sagittarius
Gladiolas	1st or 2nd	Libra, Virgo
Golden glow	2nd or 3rd	Libra
Gourds	1st or 2nd	Cancer, Scorpio, Pisces, Libra
Grapes	2nd or 3rd	Cancer, Scorpio, Pisces
Hay	1st or 2nd	Cancer, Scorpio, Pisces, Libra, Taurus, Sagittarius
Herbs	1st or 2nd	Cancer, Scorpio, Pisces
Honeysuckle	1st or 2nd	Scorpio, Virgo
Hops	1st or 2nd	Scorpio, Libra
Horseradish	1st or 2nd	Cancer, Scorpio, Pisces
House plants	1st	Libra (flowering), Cancer, Scorpio Pisces, (vines: Scorpio)
Iris	1st or 2nd	Cancer, Virgo
Kohlrabi	1st	Cancer, Scorpio, Pisces, Libra
Leeks	2nd or 3rd	Sagittarius
Lettuce	1st	Cancer, Scorpio, Pisces, Libra, Taurus (late sowings)
Lilies	1st or 2nd	Cancer, Scorpio, Pisces
Maple trees	2nd or 3rd	Sagittarius
Melons	2nd	Cancer, Scorpio, Pisces
Moon Vine	1st or 2nd	Virgo
Morning glory	1st or 2nd	Cancer, Scorpio, Pisces, Virgo
Oak trees	2nd or 3rd	Sagittarius
Oats	1st or 2nd	Cancer, Scorpio, Pisces, Libra
Okra	1st	Cancer, Scorpio, Pisces, Libra
Onion seeds	2nd	Scorpio, Sagittarius
Onion sets	3rd or 4th	Libra, taurus, Pisces
Pansies	1st or 2nd	Cancer, Scorpio, Pisces
Parsley	1st	Cancer, Scorpio, Pisces, Libra
Parsnips	3rd	Cancer, Scorpio, Pisces, Libra
Peach trees	2nd or 3rd	Taurus, Libra
Peanuts	3rd	Cancer, Scorpio, Pisces
Pear trees	2nd or 3rd	Taurus, Libra

Peas	2nd	Cancer, Scorpio, Pisces, Libra
Peonies	1st or 2nd	Virgo
Peppers	2nd	Scorpio, Sagittarius
Perennials	3rd	
Petunias	1st or 2nd	Libra, Virgo
Plum trees	2nd or 3rd	Taurus, Libra
Pole beans	1st or 2nd	Scorpio
Poppies	1st or 2nd	Virgo
Portulaca	1st or 2nd	Virgo
Potatoes	3rd	Cancer, Scorpio, Taurus, Libra, Capricorn, Sagittarius
Privet	1st or 2nd	Taurus, Libra
Pumpkins	2nd	Cancer, Scorpio, Pisces, Libra
Quinces	1st or 2nd	Capricorn
Radishes	3rd	Libra, Taurus, Pisces, Sagittarius Capricorn
Rhubarb	3rd	Aries
Rice	1st or 2nd	Scorpio
Roses	1st or 2nd	Cancer
Rutabagas	3rd	Cancer, Scorpio, Pisces, Taurus
Saffron	1st or 2nd	Cancer, Scorpio, Pisces
Sage	3rd	Cancer, Scorpio, Pisces
Salsify	1st or 2nd	Cancer, Scorpio, Pisces
Spinach	1st	Cancer, Scorpio, Pisces
Squash	2nd	Cancer, Scorpio, Pisces, Libra
Strawberries	3rd	Cancer, Scorpio, Pisces
String beans	1st or 2nd	Taurus
Sweet peas	1st or 2nd	Cancer, Scorpio, Pisces
Tomatoes	2nd	Cancer, Scorpio, Pisces
Trees		
Shade	1st	Taurus, Capricorn
Ornamental	2nd	Libra, Taurus
Erosion Control	3rd	Cancer, Scorpio, Pisces, Taurus, Capricorn
Trumpet vines	1st or 2nd	Cancer, Scorpio, Pisces
Tubers for seed	3rd	Cancer, Scorpio, Pisces, Libra
Tulips	1st or 2nd	Libra, Virgo
Turnips	3rd	Cancer, Scorpio, Pisces Taurus, Capricorn, Libra
Valerian	1st or 2nd	Virgo, Gemini
Watermelons	1st or 2nd	Cancer, Scorpio, Pisces, Libra
Wheat	1st or 2nd	Cancer, Scorpio, Pisces, Libra

An Organic Gardening Guide

by Louise Riotte

January with its wintery blast, snow and ice, is the best gardening month of the year. Janus, the two-faced Roman god whose name was given to this month, could look forward and backward at the same time. Planning, while seated before the fireplace warm and cozy, a flower garden with its brilliant colors; a garden of succulent vegetables; a grove of fruit trees laden with red and golden globes; and last but not least, a lush green carpet lawn is pure joy!

Now is the time to check your seed catalogs for new and better varieties. For January is the very best time for planning, and the best plans are made by looking forward and also backward. While the garden rests, a good gardener should cultivate his plans for the coming year by evaluating last season's crops and making New Year's resolutions for the garden to come. Remove the bare spots by planning your garden now.

Looking Backward

Was last year a good gardening year for you? If you kept records on last year's calendar, or in a log or diary, they can help you make 1989 even better. Did something go wrong last year, and what went unusually well? Note if certain seed varieties produced abundantly so that you can reorder them. And, while we are on the subject of ordering seed, you might also think about what you would like to order for your fall garden also. By the time autumn rolls around, many local seed racks are empty and you can't find your favorites.

Think also if there are poor-bearing areas in your garden that may need more rock powder or compost this year. What insects or diseases caused your vegetables problems and how could biological controls or better crop timing help? If you used a trick of many think-ahead gardeners, you probably have, in addition to written records, photographs of your garden at different stages in the season. (And these photographs and records can be mighty important, too, if you plan to enter any competitions.) They can also help you spot crop gaps you can eliminate.

I'll also tell you how to plan and plant for fresh vegetables all season long for the longest possible season. By planning you can also avoid having all the canning and freezing to do at the same time, if that is one of the nightmares you remember from last year.

Check your food inventory book or survey your storage areas. Is the freezer still full of broccoli while the canned tomatoes are almost gone? Home management, like economics, should have supply and demand related, but often we need experience to teach us how.

Looking Forward

After you've looked over last season's garden map, draw up a new one. Take advantage of what experience has taught you about what grows best where—but also start rotating crops. Check to see what grows well in combination—in other words, "companion planting." You'll find this given in great detail in my books *Carrots Love Tomatoes: Secrets of Companion Planting*, for vegetables, and *Roses Love Garlic*, for flowers. Both books are published by Storey Communications.

Cabbage, tomatoes, and peppers, for example, can be grown in about the same space as a single crop because they all grow well together. Also, as mentioned in my newest book, *Sleeping With A Sunflower: A Treasury of Old Time Gardening Wisdom* (Storey Communications), you who have very limited space may find it advantageous to practice "two-level gardening," such as onions with lettuce, kohlrabi with beets, or carrots with tomatoes.

Choose the right time to buy seeds or plants for your garden by doing so when the Moon is passing from the Full Moon to the last quarter. The Moon should be in conjunction or good aspect (sextile or trine) with Mercury. Mars should not be afflicted or in aspect with the Moon, but Venus should be marked good and your lunar cycle favorable. See the *Moon Table* section.

"Man does not live by bread (or vegetables) alone," and many of you will also want to plan for a pretty flower garden. If you want lots of flowers for cutting, annuals—planted under Libra—are by far the best. Here are some likely candidates to choose from when you are placing your order. To save time and effort, purchase flower plants rather than seeds.

Ageratum	Hollyhock	Phacelia
Baby's breath	Larkspur	Phlox
Burning bush	Lavatera	Poppy
Calendula	Love-in-a-mist	Salpiglosis
Candytuft	Love-lies-	Satin flower
Chinese forget-	bleeding	Statice
me-not	Lupine	Strawflower
Chrysanthemum	Marigold	Sunflower
Clarkia	Mignonette	Snapdragon
Cockscomb	Monkey flower	Stock
Dianthus	Morning glory	Verbena
Dimorphotheca	Nasturtium	Zinnia
Gaillardia	Nicotiana	
Geranium	Petunia	

Perennials, generally speaking, should be planted in the 3rd quarter. Consult your *Moon Sign Book* for specific varieties. Perennials have a lot going for them, too, because you can expect to see their pretty faces "same time next year."

Here are some that may be depended upon to do well in shady locations: coral bells, day lily, globe flower, ferns (all kinds), lily of the valley, monkshood, and plantain lily.

Perennials for sandy soil include black-eyed Susan, blue indigo, camomile, cattail gayfeather, coreopsis, gaillardia, goldentuft, Iceland poppy, moss rose, red yarrow, rockcress, rose campion, snow-in-summer, soapwort, stonecrop, tunic-flower, Washington lupine.

In my book *Planetary Planting* (Astro-Computing Services), I have devoted a whole chapter to vine and perennial ground covers and how to grow them. Vines do best when planted under Virgo. Here are some suggestions: woodruff, liverleaf (hepatica), vinca (periwinkle), box huckleberry, sedum acre, partridge berry, bugle (ajuga), pachysandra, bearberry, and thyme.

Planting the Cemetery Plot

Before we leave ornamental plants I would like to touch briefly upon a subject about which I am often asked—cemetery-plot planting. Many of us have lost loved ones and would like to beautify their final resting place, but we also would like to plant something that will not necessitate a great deal of care. An excellent evergeen ground cover would be sedum acre or sedum sexangulare, both low growers and both thriving in full Sun without watering. Perhaps you have tried English ivy but have some bare spots where it has died out. To replace it you need only young plants. They must be removed from their pots before planting, and the soil should be prepared by digging in some humus, leaf mold, peat moss, or bone meal. Spring is the best time to plant the ivy and sedum.

The only plants that are of any value for decorating a grave during the winter months are evergreens. Among the best of these are pachysandra, English ivy, creeping euonymus, creeping myrtle, low-growing yews (taxus), and low junipers. These evergreens are attractive all year round.

In the Southwest, where cedars do well, the Indians have a very beautiful custom of planting a young cedar by a new grave so "that it may point upward and guide the soul to heaven."

If you have the time and desire to tend them, there are some colorful flowers and low plants that would bloom for a short season—evergreen candytuft, moss pink, and plumbago. Making the last resting place of a loved one beautiful often gives comfort to the hearts of those left behind.

Keeping Your Hens Laying in Winter

January is often a difficult month for animals and poultry. Your laying hens may just decide to take a winter vacation, but you may be able to change their minds. "An egg in January may be worth two in June." Layers normally go into a seasonal slump in mid-winter. Here's how to keep them on the job. In addition to their regular ration, provide hens with oats (or oatmeal) soaked in warm water. A good supply of clean, lukewarm water helps, too. Make sure litter on the chicken house floor is thick, clean and dry; hens may become discouraged if they have wet, cold feet. Insulating the poultry house helps also, even if you only have discarded, opened-up, cardboard boxes to do it with. Furniture and appliances come in big boxes; find a dealer and ask him to save you some.

Here's another hint that will help both the chickens and you later on in the year. Here, where I live in Southern Oklahoma, there are many ranches. It is often possible to get spoiled hay for mulch from beef farmers in the area. If this is done you won't have to worry about it sprouting and turning your garden into a pasture, thanks to your chickens. When the farmers clean out the old hay, spread as much in the coop and outdoor run as you can. Then stack the rest near the garden. After a late-fall garden clean-up, you can spread the hay from the chicken's area and some of the stacked hay in the poultry house and also over the garden plot. Feed your chickens right in the garden. As soon as they've shredded down the hay, add more from the stack. Gradually use up the last few bales to re-carpet the henhouse; then shut up the chickens and start gardening. The end result of this operation is finely shredded mulch, on-site nitrogen fertilizer, and, very important, *no weeds!* Your chickens can be your "winter garden helpers."

Save Those Wood Ashes

Ashes from the stove or fireplace are a valuable element to add to your garden soil. Ashes contain high levels of potash and calcium, and improve the pH (acidity) of soil. Store ashes under a roof so that moisture will not leach out valuable properties.

Now Is the Time to Prune

Some trees and shrubs can be pruned at almost any season, while others will suffer extensive damage unless you do the job at precisely the right time. Experienced gardeners and orchardists say that dormant pruning is best done during January, February, or March, but that the later it can be done during the dormant season the better, as the wounds heal more quickly.

Pruning is the operation that checks limb growth, prevents too much spreading of the branches, and produces better fruit. Trees should be pruned during the decrease of the Moon while it is in a fruitful sign. The 3rd quarter and the sign of Scorpio are an ideal combination.

Except for formal treatment, the natural shape of the tree should be given every consideration. Each type has a typical form and pruning should emphasize this. And, remember also, any tree will attempt to regain its normal form, regardless of trimming done to change it. Trees have a will of their own.

Most shade trees require relatively little pruning. Removal of dead, interfering branches is usually all that is needed. All cuts should be made with a short saw as close to the crotch as possible and parallel with the adjoining trunk or branch. Leaving even a short stub will make proper healing of the cut difficult or impossible and may result in decay.

On smaller branches, the first cut should be made part way up from the bottom and then the second cut made from the top down. If the cuts are not made in this manner, a tear that is very difficult to heal may result. Larger branches should be given even more care and small branches can be trimmed with a snap-cut pruner. Any jagged edges should be shaved off and the wound painted thoroughly with tree paint. Painting seals the cut and prevents moisture and decay from setting in before live wood covers the wound. Larger cuts should be painted each year because the cut portion may have a tendency to dry and crack.

Starting Seeds Indoors

There are many ways to get an early start with your garden—hot beds, seed beds, cold frames, paper pots, drinking cups, wooden boxes (flats), and many others. However, I'm partial to flats for many seeds. Whatever you use, make sure it's sterile.

Flats should be about three inches deep, with several holes in the bottom or along the sides for drainage. Cover the holes with small pieces of flower pots, putting the curved surface downward. Fill the flats with sand, fine peat moss and loam (you may also use vermiculite or perlite). Firm the mixture in the flats, and then fill within one inch of the top. Make sure your planting medium is also sterile.

Sow the seeds thinly in rows about two inches apart. Cover the seeds to a depth three times the diameter of the seeds (unless they need light for germination). Use a small board to firm. Mark the rows on the end of the box with a crayon to identify the different flowers or vegetables.

Water from the bottom by placing the flats in a tub or sink. Put the flats in a warm, dark place until the seeds germinate, and then place them in direct sunlight or under fluorescent lights. Most vegetable and annual flower seeds are best planted in Cancer, Scorpio, or Pisces, flowers in Libra. Most do best if planted in the 1st or 2nd quarter. If in doubt consult the *Best Gardening Dates* section.

Succession Planting

This is something I highly recommend, especially for those who have small gardens. Well-planned succession planting can give you twice as much production from your plot and use your compost advantageously as well. However, the technique of succession planting demands restraint. It is tempting to celebrate the first perfect warm day of spring by planting every seed you can lay your hands on—tempting but not "garden wise." If you want to keep a supply of fresh vegetables coming over the longest possible season, start planting very early and continue planting at frequent intervals, taking care to consider the frost dates in your area (your county agent can probably tell you this or give you some U.S.D.A. bulletins giving this information) and the maturing time each crop needs. Don't let a crop linger too long. When it is past its bearing prime, replace it with new crops.

Nature's Own "Refrigerator" Can Be Useful

Many vegetables are frost resistant and can be planted early, or planted in midsummer and kept in the ground late into the fall. Lettuce, celery, collards, kale, broccoli, Brussels sprouts, mustard greens, cress, escarole, Chinese cabbage, parsnips, endive, and chervil all fit this category. In my mild climate I can often keep spinach, parsley, lettuce, and Chinese cabbage going all winter if I give some attention to *mulching* and if I plant them in a protected area. Remember what I told you about "letting the chickens do your weeding" when you are using spoiled hay.

Some gardeners have success in planting two crops of peas—one early, one late—though the late crop, planted in summer's decline, is seldom as successful as the spring one. Even so, those little green peas taste delicious. Pea pods do well as a second crop.

Midsummer-planted fall crops may require special protection from the Sun in the form of deeper planting and paper collars or a cheesecloth screen. Sprinkling the cheesecloth with water in the morning protects against wilt. Seeds may be soaked before planting, and they will need frequent watering for successful germination.

I always plant my potatoes in February in the 3rd quarter under Cancer, Scorpio, Taurus, Libra, Capricorn, or Sagittarius. Once, I even did this in a sleet storm because it was the right day and the right sign. I had to, because like so many of you I was a "week-end gardener" and had to make the most of the time at my disposal. It was the biggest potato crop I ever had! Moon signers take notice.

How to Succeed with Succession

Succession planting saves space and makes full use of the land. It also conserves storage space and promotes healthy nutrition, for it allows you to consume a larger proportion of your food in its freshest form.

Also, taking an idea from *Sleeping With A Sunflower*, it enables you to get a long-playing run for your compost by planting the heavy feeders such as broccoli, Brussels sprouts, cabbage, cauliflower, celeriac, celery, etc., with less-demanding beets, carrots, radishes, rutabagas, or turnips. Legumes, the third in the food chain of succession planting, include broad and lima beans, bush and pole beans, peas, and soybeans. These soil improvers collect nitrogen from the air and restore it to the earth.

February and March are also good times to buy and plant shrubs; give heed to the correct times previously mentioned. You may want to dig the hole in the fall before the ground freezes.

When buying shrubs it is better to buy the balled and burlapped type, if your pocketbook permits. If you can't do this, it's better to buy those that have had their roots disturbed as little as possible. Shrubs with bare roots will generally survive if they are small, and the small ones are usually a bit more reasonable in price.

When you're ready to plant your shrub, cut off any broken or bruised parts and place in a prepared hole. Never leave the shrub exposed to air longer than necessary. The hairs which cover the roots are so tiny that they quickly shrivel if too much air strikes them. Place the shrub in the hole a little lower than ground level. Spread the roots so that soil can sift down between them. Fill the hole about half full of topsoil, working the shrub up and down enough to get the soil around the roots.

If the roots are dried out, submerge them in a tub of water and leave them there for a day or two. Should the branches be shriveled, bury the entire plant and soak with water until the bark is smooth.

If there is a delay in planting—a few days or a week—dig a trench in the shade, with one side sloping, and put the roots in the bottom with the rest of the shrub above ground but resting against the sloping side. Cover the roots with soil and water.

Pruning Shrubs

Remember, if you are dealing with spring-blooming shrubs, that their buds were formed in the preceding fall. Removing these in the spring means loss of bloom for the year. Such shrubs should be pruned in July, or directly after the bloom is over. If they bloom in summer they should be pruned while dormant, or very early, before growth starts in the spring. Moreover, when pruning is done recklessly and everything is cut to a few inches in height, the form of the plant, which is often an integral part of the charm, is destroyed.

Growing Roses for Their Hips

Many of you know that rose hips are an excellent source of vitamin C, but sometimes it is helpful to be reminded of this. Rugosa roses, a species of the flower and not just a variety, produce the largest hips, measuring up to two inches in diameter. Harvest the fruits when rosy red, before they turn dark and wrinkled. Harvest in a dry sign—Aries, Leo, Sagittarius, Gemini, or Aquarius—and in the 3rd or 4th quarter. Here are some recommended varieties: Hansa, Frau Dagmar Hastrup, Delicata and Rugosa magnifica.

All roses, but especially those grown for their beautiful blossoms, appreciate good drainage, abundance of food, and a sunny location. Given these three requisites, the plants are almost certain to grow and bloom until frost. Give them compost or well-rotted manure for best results. Fertilize in the 3rd or 4th quarter under Cancer, Scorpio, or Pisces. About the first of July, mulch rose bed with peat moss or lawn clippings as this will keep down weeds, conserve moisture, and keep roots cool.

Some Hints for March and April

If space is a limiting factor for you, try choosing compact and especially productive varieties of vegetables. Plant leaf lettuce instead of the heading varieties, and you will have a long harvesting season if you pull just the outer leaves for your salads and sandwiches. They will be replaced right up until midsummer.

Broccoli, too, will give you many cuttings. Harvest the central blossom head when ripe and smaller buds will appear along the stem—smaller but just as tasty. Brussels sprouts produce a second, though smaller, crop in much the same way.

Some Transplanting Can Be Done in April

Indoor head starts are particularly wise for cool-weather-sensitive plants that transplant well. And if you grow your own you can have exactly the varieties you want. Sturdy small tomato, eggplant, pepper, bean, and okra plants can be ready to go into the garden when frost danger is over (again check the date of the last frost in your area) if their seeds are started inside six to nine weeks before. Figure the seed-planting date for cool-weather crops like broccoli and the other coles and for head lettuce at six to eight weeks before the right time for setting the garden. Peppers, an unusually slow crop to germinate, can be started up to 3½ months before their set-out date.

Seeds can be given their initial start in almost anything that will hold two inches of dirt when filled to the top and that has some, but not too much, drainage.

Here is how an 1880 gardener did it: "Take eggshells cut in half, make two or three small holes in bottom of each, fill with sifted soil, sink in a box of sand, sow seeds and cover with glass, of course keeping them in the right light. Water only the sand, for they will absorb enough through the holes. In transplanting all you have to do is break off the shells, leaving the lump of earth intact without the roots being jarred or disturbed" (*Sleeping With A Sunflower*). This idea is still cheap and practical. And, may I suggest, you can use a milk carton, cut in half, for your "box of sand."

Planting mediums are also a matter of choice and experience. One favorite consists of layers or a mix of crumbled sphagnum or peat moss (for its drainage and root-encouraging looseness), potting or fine compost-enriched soil (for nourishment), and sterile vermiculite (to prevent fungus-caused damping-off disease). Pack the soil down and cover the seed tightly to prevent its washing away. Never plant seeds too close together, for the competition for space is exhausting for small plants.

Most seeds germinate quickly in darkness with even moisture and in warmth of 70°–80°F. Cover the flats, pots, or whatever with plastic (try grocery-store vegetable bags) or glass to retain warmth and moisture, and check often for tiny plants and to catch possible mold under the plastic. Move to a sunny place when growth appears, but keep the soil moist and remove the glass or plastic cover.

Back in the beginning of this article I also mentioned planting seed in flats, and I still think this is one of the best ways to accomplish early starting of plants. The area in which you live has, of course, a bearing on when you will start seeding indoors by whatever method you choose. Those of us who live in the Southern and Southwestern states should start sooner and set plants out earlier so that they mature before the heat of summer. Northern gardeners should start later so that their tender plants, such as tomatoes and peppers and eggplant, will escape the cold.

A Small Garden Can Be a Little Heaven

A tidy, well-managed little garden delights and satisfies us like a miniature portrait, and don't forget that the varieties of miniature vegetables are steadily being enlarged by our seedsmen. It is no wonder that the fad for patio and apartment roof plots keeps returning. Use the same signs for planting and harvesting that you would if you had forty acres instead of your tiny plot. But, even so, the larger landholder, too, finds reasons to make the most of his space. Energy, water, and compost are saved, and secondary benefits come in the way some plants in close proximity help one another.

If you can't go out, go up. Vertical growing, often very ornamental in itself, is another way to save space. It also exposes vegetables to the Sun for quick ripening and prevents damage from decay, insects, and diseases associated with damp ground. Wire stakes, trellises, fences, cages, and other supporting structures allow you to provide upward mobility for your vine crops.

Cucumbers, if trained to a trellis, will grow straighter. Make a teepee out of long poles for your climbing beans and peas and get twice as much production. Cage your tomatoes and they are less likely to rot than if they touch the ground. Peppers, often very brittle, will benefit if cage grown or tied to a trellis. Firm staking also helps to prevent wind damage.

Interplanting Gives Dividends

Interplanting is a bit different from succession planting, but if carefully managed, it can double or even triple the use of garden space. However, since extra strain is put on the soil, it is important that the interplanted area be enriched with compost, watered with fish emulsion, manure, or seaweed solution, and mulched when the ground is warm.

Any vegetables can be interplanted, but some combinations do better in "togetherness" than others. One crop may be used to support, shade, nurse or eventually replace another. Here are some suggestions. Beets and kohlrabi—the kohlrabi shades the beets, producing a much more tender and succulent vegetable. Cabbage, tomato, and pepper—a terrific combination either cooked or grown together. Black-eyed peas and corn—but give the corn a head start, for these peas are rampant climbers. Lettuce, onion, and carrot are great salad-bowl favorites but spare the lettuce seed. Onions will shoot above the lettuce, and carrot tops permit the Sun but give a bit of shade. Onions and snap beans fit well in the same space and there is some evidence that one protects the other from pests. Radishes and carrots—the fast-growing radishes are used and out of the way when the carrots need more space. Climbing cucumbers and sunflowers—a clear case of natural support but give the sunflowers a head start. Squash, corn, and beans—an old custom that goes back to the Indians who taught this to the pioneers. All members of the squash family will shade the weeds out under corn, and pole beans will climb corn stalks. Let the beans dry and you can harvest them all at once.

Poor Man's Nursery

To beautify their barren lawns, many people go to the nursery to choose trees known to be bona fide ornamentals. But if you can find a friendly farmer or rancher, most small trees can be transported from the wild if they do not have long taproots running deep into the earth. Trees should be pruned on top to compensate for roots and root hairs lost in the transplanting process. It is best to move them with a ball of dirt around the roots.

Good choices include the red maple, lovely in its vivid autumn dress and very adaptable; the sweet gum, equally lovely in fall dress of vivid yellow, orange and violet; the shagbark hickory; the redbud, and the small, lovely dogwood.

May Could Be the Month for Moving

When seedlings have developed their first *true* leaves (leaves like the mature plant), they should be given more growing room in deeper, richer soil. There, while given about 14 hours of Sun or light a day, they can be weaned from constant dampness to drier soil.

Feed the rapidly growing seedlings diluted fish emulsion every two weeks. Cole crops need a cooler spot on the ledge than do tomatoes or peppers.

Give your still-potted seedlings a week or two of hardening off outdoors before you put them in the garden, but do this in a spot sheltered from wind and strong Sun. When the actual transplanting day comes, wait until the Sun is low and provide temporary screening from the Sun if the weather is hot.

Temporary tin can or paper collars will discourage some of the pests that attack new seedlings, and watering with emulsion by the puddling method is generally recommended at the beginning.

Also try to transplant under Cancer, Scorpio, or Pisces for the best results. The moist signs and the 1st or 2nd quarter do help in transplanting success.

Something many gardeners do not realize is that lettuce, when it comes up too thick, can be transplanted. The outer leaves of the plant may wilt and die but the plant will put out new leaves and go right on growing.

Foiling the Insects

Most insect pests start appearing in greater numbers in May—and do so at just about the same time each year. Timing may be the answer to outwitting them. It may help to keep a log to remind you the following year when the infestation first became apparent and how long it lasted.

The planning you put into gardening should benefit you and not them, so try not to lay out a welcoming feast of favorite young vegetables for the insects' arrival. The experience of gardeners who have foiled the bugs is still more complete than the scientific evidence to back it up, but several observations may be of value.

The spring hatch of the carrot fly will not bother your root crops if you delay planting them until mid-June, but to do this you should provide extra water. (And it is always best to water plants on a day favorable to Cancer, Scorpio, Pisces, or Libra. In a pinch, you can also use Taurus.)

Mid- to late-July plantings of squash, cucumbers, and pumpkins escape the vine borer (keep a log; this may differ in your area). Corn earworm cycles need to be observed and recorded before planting dates are arranged, but usually if you make successive plantings, at least one of them escapes damage between cycles.

Cantaloupes are safer if started in pots inside and set out in late spring in some areas. Sometimes early plantings of cabbage and its relatives will avoid cabbage worm, looper and aphids. The cucumber beetle seems to vanish during the last week in June in some areas, while bean beetles prefer early to late beans in the Southwest. Radishes planted early escape maggots. Again, it is sensible to keep an insect log not only to time your next year's planting but to make sure that whatever biological means you use against pests (and do not forget companion planting) strikes its target or nabs its prey.

If, in the process, you become interested enough in insect habits, maybe you won't mind them so much!

Try June for Budding Peach Trees

T-budding, a favorite way to propagate peach and apricot trees, should be done in early summer when the buds for next year's growth are formed. Select wood for budding them from firm, undamaged branches. With a sharp knife, make a scooped-out cut that takes about a half inch of bark both above and below the bud. Make the T slits in the rootstock with two motions of the knife blade, lift the corners of the slits, and insert the new bud. Wrap rubber strips around the graft, leaving the bud exposed. Leave the branch and leaves above the bud until fall, to shade the bud, and then break the branch over just above the new bud, to force growth.

Carpentry Garden Helpers to Make

Rings and cages are helpful for keeping plants such as tomatoes off the ground and for supporting brittle plants such as peppers to keep them from breaking in a high wind. Cages also serve as frames for plastic covers to prevent frost damage. And well-made rings and cages, once made or purchased, can be re-used year after year. The initial cost is usually the last one.

Frames and arbors are useful as in-garden fences for providing support for beans, peas, cucumbers, and other vining crops. String two or three strands of stout wire between heavy eight-foot posts set two feet into the ground. Keep the ends taut by guy wiring the posts. As plants grow, drop strands of soft material from the horizontal wires. Plants with this type of support can grow 24 inches apart.

Another popular method of support is hog netting strung in double-fencing rows between heavy posts with the plants set between the rows. Rows can be about 16 inches apart when using this method. Some gardeners also use single hog-wire-netting fences and train tomatoes from both sides onto the fence.

When setting posts, do so when the Moon is in the 3rd or 4th quarter. The Fixed signs—Taurus, Leo, or Aquarius—should be used.

Divide Iris in July

There are many different types of iris, the most popular and the easiest grown being the "bearded." There is also the small spring, fall-blooming Japanese or rainbow iris, and the Siberian, all of which should be separated every two or three years. The iris grows from a rootstock called a rhizome, often called (wrongly) a bulb or root. The real root grows from this rootstock.

Using the signs of Cancer, Scorpio, or Pisces, and the 1st or 2nd quarter, dig up the clumps of bearded iris in July (after blooming season is over) and pull rhizomes apart. Iris is very easy to separate. Select only firm, healthy sections with four "arms" for replanting. If the divisions are too small, there will be no blossoms the next year. (If the iris is especially rare or lovely, I often save even the small rhizomes, planting them in some out-of-the-way place. If they do well they can be transplanted again in a few years to a better location for viewing.)

With scissors, cut off half the foliage to reduce evaporation of moisture from the plant. In the hole in which the iris is to be planted, add a handful of dry bone meal or rotted manure. Bone meal is always a good fertilizer to use as it does not burn the roots. Wood ashes and lime are also good to mix with soil. The bearded iris grows "as a duck swims," part of its back out of the ground. Cover the iris with one to two inches of soil, firming it around the roots. Five or six inches between rhizomes is sufficient but set the rhizomes so that the growing ends face the same way.

Time to Take Root Cuttings

Many new shrubs and flowers may be obtained at little expense and labor by rooting cuttings, "vegetative propagation." Plants such as roses, begonias, hydrangeas, coleus, geraniums, delphinium, evergreens and deciduous shrubs may be propagated this way.

If cuttings are dipped in a hormone preparation, the rooting time will be cut considerably. Take the cuttings under Cancer, Scorpio, or Pisces and in the 1st or 2nd quarter, plant in good but not overly rich soil, and keep them shaded and damp for two or three weeks. If roses are being rooted, cover with a jar for the winter. My mother always used a fruit jar. Shrubs such as snowball, wiegels, and highbush cranberry may be rooted by layering. I have also tried this successfully with my ever-bearing fig.

Seed Saving

Way back in January we were planning for July. Now, at the very height of the growing season, we should begin to think of January, and then, once more, of next year's garden.

By now you may have picked a perfect tomato or a uniformly tender lot of beans. Just as success breeds success, perfect vegetables sometimes reproduce more of their kind. July is a good time to decide whether the chanciness and bother of seed collecting is justified by the satisfaction and economic savings it brings.

There are three reasons for raising vegetables from seed you collect. It saves money; it preserves unusual and hard-to-find varieties (like the "lemon" cucumber); and it is a way of making sure your seed has not been treated chemically. To this I would add a fourth reason—if the vegetable has done particularly well in your area, the seed may be worth saving. But remember, hybrid seed does not always "come true."

No one doubts that seed prices have been rising rapidly lately, but commercially packaged seed is still a bargain when compared to supermarket vegetables. R.H. Shumway, Seedsman, P.O. Box 1, Graniteville, SC 29829, specializes in open-pollinated flower and vegetable seeds.

For hard-to-find seeds you may contact Central Prairie Seed Exchange, 6984 Thorstenborg Rd., Falun, KS 67442. For seeds of native American plants and wildflowers, try Plants of the Southwest, 1812 Second St., Santa Fe, NM 87501, or Applewood Seed Co., 5380 Vivian St., Arvada, CO 80002. For hard-to-find herb seeds, try Nichols Garden Nursery, 1190 N. Pacific Hwy., Albany, OR 97321.

More seed companies are growing organically to produce seed and then refraining from using chemicals to treat seed. Consumer pressure from organic gardeners has already made itself felt in seed catalogs, where some companies have special listings of untreated seeds. Unfortunately, it is true that often these seeds are more costly than others.

One overlooked argument for seed collecting is a human,

not a scientific, one. A main motive for gardening in this age of forced and artificial interdependence is that it gives people a sense of self-sufficiency; and to some gardeners, and, I think, especially Moon signers, self-sufficiency is diminished when what is almost the first act of gardening—acquiring seed—is a mercantile transaction.

Simple Rules for Seed Collecting

1. Take seed from the best of your crop, using five or ten plants selected for yield as well as size and, if important to you, for early or late bearing qualities.
2. Use overmature vegetables. Discard irregular seed.
3. Wash moist seeds thoroughly and spread on paper towels to dry. If you place seeds outdoors, bring them in at night.
4. Dry thoroughly on racks during dry weather for two to three weeks, stirring occasionally to prevent mold.
5. Store in labeled envelopes or dry jars in a cold dry place. Your refrigerator is fine.
6. Test samples for germination before using them. This may be done in January by wrapping seeds in moist paper and setting them in a warm place for a few days.

August Is Turnip-Planting Time

In the Southwest, August, no matter how hot and dry, is turnip-planting time—though some people like to do this in July, which may be better farther north. Often we have a light rain sometime during August which brings the seed up. Then, if we have no further moisture, watering becomes necessary to keep the plants going until cooler days later in the fall. Give water under the moist signs of Cancer, Scorpio, Pisces, or Libra.

In August I also like to start other crops for my fall garden, such as Chinese cabbage, broccoli, Brussels sprouts, etc., by planting the seeds in flats much as I did in the spring and nursing them along until cooler weather gives me an opportunity for setting them out into the garden. The started plants will mature much faster than garden-sown seed and likely will give me a crop before cold weather kills them later on.

Making a New Lawn

Early September is the best time for making a new lawn and renovating an old one, as this is nature's time for seeding grass. Besides, weeds do not grow as fast as in the spring. The first step is to get rid of all weeds. Mow the lawn closely, remove clippings and debris, and dispose of them. Rake the lawn thoroughly or cultivate in such a way as to loosen the soil on the surface. If the soil has not been limed for several years, it is safe to assume that it is acid and needs lime. Spread it carefully in order to avoid caking and burning the grass. Lime and fertilizer (compost) should not be applied at the same time when making a new lawn. Apply them three or four days apart, applying the compost first.

After this time has elapsed, smooth the soil with a short toothed rake and make it as even as possible. Sow the seeds on a calm day. Allow four pounds of seed to one thousand square feet. Divide seeds and sow each half in opposite directions. This is also a good rule to follow in applying fertilizer. Rake lightly and use a light roller. Keep soil watered (using a moist sign) until long after germination. Use a fine spray so that seeds will not be washed into clumps or completely away.

Start cutting when the grass is two inches high and have mower set 1½ inches high. Never let it grow more than two or three inches. More lawns die from lack of water than from any other cause; a light sprinkling is better than none at all. But it is best to soak to a depth of four inches when watering. However, don't let water run faster than the soil can absorb it.

You can increase lawn growth if you mow in the 1st or 2nd quarter and use the signs of Cancer, Scorpio, or Pisces. If retarding gowth is desirable mow in the 3rd or 4th quarter and under the signs of Leo, Virgo, or Gemini.

Drying Vegetables

September still sees an abundant harvest of late-planted vegetables in the fall garden and drying is an excellent method of preserving them. Nothing is added and 80 to 90 percent of the water content is removed, so storage space is saved. One pound of dried fruit is equivalent to five pounds of fresh. With the exception of small quantities of vitamins A and C, fruits and vegetables retain their nutritional values after drying, as well as their flavors. Dried fruit is sweeter than fresh, because its natural sugar is concentrated, but with the water content almost gone, bacteria won't attack dried food if it is stored in tightly closed containers.

Drying Fruits

Apples, berries, apricots, peaches, prunes, cherries, coconut, dates, figs, pears, plums, and rhubarb all dry well. Choose fruits of the best quality and at the peak of maturity. Dry small fruits like strawberries whole, and if eaten that way, they resemble candy and will be great treats for your children—and much more wholesome. Cut larger fruit into uniform wedges, leaving skin and seeds intact. Fruit is sufficently dehydrated when it becomes leathery and shriveled on the outside. Store in plastic bags in the refrigerator, or in sealed jars in a cool place. Check occasionally for mold. It's nice to use dried fruits for snacks or salads. (But you can rehydrate them either by simmering in water to cover for ten to twenty minutes or by soaking them immersed in hot water for two to three hours.)

Drying Vegetables for Winter

Beans, cabbage, carrots, corn, mushrooms, okra, onions, peas, peppers, spinach, and squash dry well. Beans and peas may be left in the shell to dry either before or after harvesting. And remember, with either fruits or vegetables you will have the best results and less spoilage if you harvest them under the dry signs of Aries, Leo, Sagittarius, Gemini or Aquarius and in the 3rd or 4th quarter.

Some gardeners cut and hang the whole plant in a dry place; others prefer to shell mature legumes and set them in an attic or shed, or on a covered porch. Before storing beans, place them on shallow trays in a 180° F. oven for ten to fifteen minutes. Snap beans are dried whole and then chopped into one-inch pieces. They may be strung on twine and hung in an attic or other warm, dry place.

Shred or cut cabbage fine; carrots, white onions, peppers, squash, and pumpkin should be cut in ¼-inch strips or slices. Leave the skin on and the seeds in okra when you slice it. Red or hot peppers may be strung whole. Mushrooms dry well if tender. Spinach and other greens should be chopped into uniform pieces and stirred as they dry. Corn should be blanched ten minutes to set the milk, and then the kernels should be removed, chilled and dried in a 140° F. oven. Kernels will be transparent and hard and make wonderful, chewy snacks for you and the kids.

To revitalize dried vegetables, add three cups of liquid for every cup of veggies and soak until the liquid is absorbed (overnight for dried shelled beans).

How to Condition Dried Food

Conditioning is important to guarantee safe storage of dried produce. Fruits do especially well when stored in nettle hay. Pour cool, dry vegetables in large one-gallon open-mouthed containers of glass, crockery, or enamel. Store the open containers in a warm, dry room for ten to fourteen days, stirring the contents daily and inspecting for mold. If the produce passes inspection, it is ready to pasteurize to assure that no insect eggs or latent spoilage is present. To pasteurize, spread dry fruits or vegetables one inch thick on a cookie sheet and bake ten to fifteen minutes at 175° F. Cool thoroughly and store sealed.

October Is Bulb-Planting Time

Though Northerners may wish to do this earlier, here in Southern Oklahoma, I find October to be the ideal time for getting my flowering bulbs into the ground. The flowering bulbs are the most beautiful of all flowers and require little work, other than planting. Scatter them under trees, in front of shrubs, in flower beds with your annuals and perennials. They will have bloomed long before the trees and shrubs are in full leaf, and before your annuals are ready to be planted.

Try planting them in groups of a dozen or more bulbs of the same color—this is much more affecting and eye-arresting than a mixed planting. Select your own bulbs; weigh each one in your hand and (as you would with a head of lettuce) choose those that are firm and heavy.

If a bed of one kind of bulb is to be planted, dig in bone meal, place the bulb at the proper depth, and cover with soil. All bulbs require well-drained soil. If necessary, dig in sand, sifted coal ashes, or use a soil conditioner such as gypsum. If individual holes must be dug be sure they are large enough and are rounded at the bottom, with soil loosened and compost underneath. If a V-shaped hole is dug, the bulb will hang there with no soil touching the base, and rot. Cover bulbs with compost after the ground freezes.

All Is Not Lost

Some vegetables have a natural resistance to cold, and a few actually grow better and have improved flavor if grown as cold-weather crops. If you've been caught off-guard by frost this year, you may want to plan next year's garden so that it is, by frost time, devoted entirely to those plants that thrive in cold—just jot all this down in your garden log so that you will remember. This will mean, perhaps, that your frost-tender species, like tomatoes, will need to be ready to bear earlier. You can make this possible by giving yourself a head start inside with seedlings, or by using a cold frame. When the seed catalogs arrive in your mailbox, you may wish to look for early bearing varieties for next year.

I would also like to suggest that those of you who live in the northern tier of states order a catalog from McFayden Seeds, Box 1800, Brandon, Manitoba, Canada R7A 6N4. Cold-hardy varieties that grow well in Canada might just be the very vegetable seeds you are looking for.

Cold-Tolerant Vegetables

Cold-hardy vegetables include cabbage, Brussels sprouts, kale, turnips, rutabagas, kohlrabi, collards, sprouting broccoli, horseradish, spinach, beets, and parsnips.

Cold-season crops but injured by freezing: heading broccoli, cauliflower, lettuce, carrots, Chinese cabbage, celery, peas, and potatoes.

Tolerant of frost but preferring hotter temperatures: onions, garlic, leeks, and shallots. These will survive at 20° F.

Not tolerant of frost: muskmelons, cucumbers, squash, pumpkin, beans, tomatoes, corn, and most peppers.

Hot-weather-only crops: watermelons, sweet potatoes, eggplant, okra, and some peppers.

Putting the Garden to Bed

November and December are the months for final work. Take care of your evergreens! Mulch with leaves, manure, or grass clippings as this helps keep moisture in the ground. The evaporation of moisture from leaves continues all winter, and if your evergreens lose too much moisture, they will be winter-killed.

The greatest damage is done during the month of March, when the winds are high and the Sun warmer. It is important to tie up branches of trees that have several stems, such as arborvitaes. Single branches that have a tendency to get laden with snow may be propped by a forked stick. Be careful when dislodging snow from trees and shrubs; they are brittle and may break.

If you have hydrangea plants, tip a bushel basket over them after you have given them a heavy mulch. My fig tree survives most of our mild Southern Oklahoma winters but I always mulch it heavily anyway. If the top branches die, the roots are saved and will send out new growth in the spring.

Put Your Tools Away Clean

Wash and clean all earth from your tools and oil them to prevent rust. Some may need sharpening—do all this before hanging or storing them. Be ready for spring, when there is so much to be done all at one time.

Don't Forget the Birds!

Birds are a gardener's best friends, because they consume tons of insects. Without their help insects would, in a few years, consume every green thing, and the world would be without food as well as beauty.

Set up bird feeders, if possible, and keep them well stocked. If that isn't possible put the birdseed on an outdoor table or on the ground. During the winter more birds are killed from thirst than from starvation. Place warm water out for them occasionally. And place your feeders where you can watch the birds enjoying themselves. It will make you happy, too, some cold winter day!

OTHER GARDENING ACTIVITIES

Animals: Easiest to handle when the Moon is in Taurus, Cancer, Libra or Pisces. Avoid the Full Moon. Buy animals during the first quarter. Castrate in any sign except Leo, Scorpio or Sagittarius. Avoid the Full Moon.

Compost: Start compost when Moon is in fourth quarter in a water sign, especially Scorpio.

Cultivating: Best when Moon is in a barren sign and waning. Fourth quarter in Aries, Gemini, Leo, Virgo or Aquarius are best.

Dry Crops: Best in the third quarter when the Moon is in a fire sign.

Fertilize: Do this when the Moon is in a fruitful sign (Cancer, Scorpio or Pisces). Organic Fertilizers are best used when the Moon is in the third and fourth quarter; chemical fertilizers: first and second quarters.

Grafting: Do this during Capricorn, Cancer or Scorpio while the Moon is in the first or second quarters.

Harvesting: Harvest root crops when the Moon is in a dry sign (Aries, Leo, Sagittarius, Gemini or Aquarius) and in the third or fourth quarters. Harvest root crops intended for seed when the Moon is Full. Harvest grain which will be stored just after the Full Moon, avoiding the water signs (Cancer, Scorpio and Pisces). Fire signs are best for cutting down on water content. Harvest fruits in the third and fourth quarters in the dry signs.

Irrigation: Irrigate when the Moon is in a water sign.

Lawn Mowing: Mow in the first and second quarters to increase growth and for lushness, in the third and fourth quarters to decrease growth.

Pick Mushrooms: Gather at the Full Moon.

Prune: Prune during the third and fourth quarters in Scorpio for retarding growth and to promote better fruit, and in Capricorn to promote better healing.

Slaughter for Food: Do this in the first three days after the Full Moon in any sign except Leo.

Spraying: Destroy pests and weeds during the fourth quarter when the Moon is in a barren sign.

Transplanting: This should be done when the Moon is increasing and preferably in Cancer, Scorpio or Pisces.

Cut Timber: Cut during the third and fourth quarters while the Moon is not in a water sign. This will diminish the rotting.

GARDENING DATES

Dates	What to Do
Jan 1, 3:35 pm– Jan 4, 1:12 am Scorpio, 4th qtr.	Plant biennials, perennials, bulbs and roots. Irrigate. Fertilize (organic). Prune.
Jan 4, 1:12 am– Jan 6, 7:15 am Sagittarius, 4th qtr.	Cultivate. Destroy weeds and pests. Harvest fruits and root crops. Trim to retard growth.
Jan 6, 7:15 am– Jan 7, 1:23 pm Capricorn, 4th qtr.	Plant potatoes and tubers. Prune.
Jan 7, 1:23 pm– Jan 8, 10:31 am Capricorn, 1st qtr.	Graft or bud plants. Trim to increase growth.
Jan 10, 12:32 pm– Jan 12, 2:37 pm Pisces, 1st qtr.	Plant annuals, grains. Irrigate. Fertilize (chemical). Trim to increase growth. Graft or bud plants.
Jan 14, 5:37 pm– Jan 16, 9:58 pm Taurus, 2nd qtr.	Plant annuals for hardiness. Trim to increase growth.
Jan 19, 3:58 am– Jan 21, 12:03 pm Cancer, 2nd qtr.	Plant annuals, grains. Irrigate. Fertilize (chemical). Trim to increase growth. Graft or bud plants.

Jan 21, 3:35 pm Full Moon, Leo	Gather mushrooms. Harvest root crops for seed.
Jan 21, 3:35 pm- Jan 23, 10:33 pm Leo, 3rd qtr.	Cultivate. Destroy weeds and pests. Harvest fruits and root crops. Trim to retard growth.
Jan 23, 10:33 pm- Jan 26, 11:02 am Virgo, 3rd qtr.	Cultivate, especially medicinal plants. Destroy weeds and pests. Trim to retard growth.
Jan 28, 11:50 pm- Jan 31, 10:31 am Scorpio, 3-4th qtr.	Plant biennials, perennials, bulbs and roots. Irrigate. Fertilize (organic). Prune.
Jan 31, 10:31 am- Feb 2, 5:30 pm Sagittarius, 4th qtr.	Cultivate. Destroy weeds and pests. Harvest fruits and root crops. Trim to retard growth.
Feb 2, 5:30 pm- Feb 4, 8:52 pm Capricorn, 4th qtr.	Plant potatoes and tubers. Prune.
Feb 4, 8:52 pm- Feb 6, 1:38 am Aquarius, 4th qtr.	Cultivate. Destroy weeds and pests. Harvest fruits and root crops. Trim to retard growth.
Feb 6, 9:53 pm- Feb 8, 10:19 pm Pisces, 1st qtr.	Plant annuals, grains. Irrigate. Fertilize (chemical). Trim to increase growth. Graft or bud plants.
Feb 10, 11:46 pm- Feb 13, 3:23 am Taurus, 1-2nd qtr.	Plant annuals for hardiness. Trim to increase growth.
Feb 15, 9:41 am- Feb 17, 6:34 pm Cancer, 2nd qtr.	Plant annuals, grains. Irrigate. Fertilize (chemical). Trim to increase growth. Graft or bud plants.

Feb 20, 9:33 am Full Moon, Virgo	Gather mushrooms. Harvest root crops for seed.
Feb 20, 9:33 am– Feb 22, 6:06 pm Virgo, 3rd qtr.	Cultivate, especially medicinal plants. Destroy weeds and pests. Trim to retard growth.
Feb 25, 6:58 am– Feb 27, 6:30 pm Scorpio, 3rd qtr.	Plant biennials, perennials, bulbs and roots. Irrigate. Fertilize (organic). Prune.
Feb 27, 6:30 pm– Mar 2, 2:59 am Sag., 3–4th qtr.	Cultivate. Destroy weeds and pests. Harvest fruits and root crops. Trim to retard growth.
Mar 2, 2:59 am– Mar 4, 7:37 am Capricorn, 4th qtr.	Plant potatoes and tubers. Prune.
Mar 4, 7:37 am– Mar 6, 9:00 am Aquarius, 4th qtr.	Cultivate. Destroy weeds and pests. Harvest fruits and root crops. Trim to retard growth.
Mar 6, 9:00 am– Mar 7, 12:20 pm Pisces, 4th qtr.	Plant biennials, perennials, bulbs and roots. Irrigate. Fertilize (organic). Prune.
Mar 7, 12:20 pm– Mar 8, 8:37 am Pisces, 1st qtr.	Plant annuals, grains. Irrigate. Fertilize (chemical). Trim to increase growth. Graft or bud plants.
Mar 10, 8:26 am– Mar 12, 10:17 am Taurus, 1st qtr.	Plant annuals for hardiness. Trim to increase growth.
Mar 14, 3:28 pm– Mar 17, 0:14 am Cancer, 2nd qtr.	Plant annuals, grains. Irrigate. Fertilize (chemical). Trim to increase growth. Graft or bud plants.
Mar 22, 0:25 am– Mar 22, 3:59 am Libra, 2nd qtr.	Plant annuals for fragrance and beauty. Trim to increase growth.

Mar 22, 3:59 am Full Moon, Libra	Gather mushrooms. Harvest root crops for seed.
Mar 24, 1:11 pm– Mar 27, 0:55 am Scorpio, 3rd qtr.	Plant biennials, perennials, bulbs and roots. Irrigate. Fertilize (organic). Prune.
Mar 27, 0:55 am– Mar 29, 10:26 am Sagittarius, 3rd qtr.	Cultivate. Destroy weeds and pests. Harvest fruits and root crops. Trim to retard growth.
Mar 29, 10:26 am– Mar 31, 4:46 pm Capricorn, 3-4th qtr.	Plant potatoes and tubers. Prune.
Mar 31, 4:46 pm– Apr 2, 7:38 pm Aquarius, 4th qtr.	Cultivate. Destroy weeds and pests. Harvest fruits and root crops. Trim to retard growth.
Apr 2, 7:38 pm– Apr 4, 7:52 pm Pisces, 4th qtr.	Plant biennials, perennials, bulbs and roots. Irrigate. Fertilize (organic). Prune.
Apr 4, 7:52 pm– Apr 5, 9:34 pm Aries, 4th qtr.	Cultivate. Destroy weeds and pests. Harvest fruits and root crops. Trim to retard growth.
Apr 6, 7:08 pm– Apr 8, 7:32 pm Taurus, 1st qtr.	Plant annuals for hardiness. Trim to increase growth.
Apr 10, 10:59 pm– Apr 13, 6:32 am Cancer, 1-2nd qtr.	Plant annuals, grains. Irrigate. Fertilize (chemical). Trim to increase growth. Graft or bud plants.
Apr 18, 6:32 am– Apr 20, 7:14 pm Libra, 2nd qtr.	Plant annuals for fragrance and beauty. Trim to increase growth.
Apr 20, 7:14 pm– Apr 20, 9:14 pm Scorpio, 2nd qtr.	Plant annuals, grains. Irrigate. Fertilize (chemical). Trim to increase growth. Graft or bud plants.

Apr 20, 9:14 pm Full Moon, Scorpio	Gather mushrooms. Harvest root crops for seed.
Apr 20, 9:14 pm- Apr 23, 6:39 am Scorpio, 3rd qtr.	Plant biennials, perennials, bulbs and roots. Irrigate. Fertilize (organic). Prune.
Apr 23, 6:39 am- Apr 25, 4:16 pm Sagittarius, 3rd qtr.	Cultivate. Destroy weeds and pests. Harvest fruits and root crops. Trim to retard growth.
Apr 25, 4:16 pm- Apr 27, 11:34 pm Capricorn, 3rd qtr.	Plant potatoes and tubers. Prune.
Apr 27, 11:34 pm- Apr 30, 4:04 am Aquarius, 3-4th qtr.	Cultivate. Destroy weeds and pests. Harvest fruits and root crops. Trim to retard growth.
Apr 30, 4:04 am- May 2, 5:51 am Pisces, 4th qtr.	Plant biennials, perennials, bulbs and roots. Irrigate. Fertilize (organic). Prune.
May 2, 5:51 am- May 4, 5:56 am Aries, 4th qtr.	Cultivate. Destroy weeds and pests. Harvest fruits and root crops. Trim to retard growth.
May 4, 5:56 am- May 5, 5:47 am Taurus, 4th qtr.	Plant potatoes and tubers. Prune.
May 5, 5:47 am- May 6, 6:04 am Taurus, 1st qtr.	Plant annuals for hardiness. Trim to increase growth.
May 8, 8:20 am- May 10, 2:24 pm Cancer, 1st qtr.	Plant annuals, grains. Irrigate. Fertilize (chemical). Trim to increase growth. Graft or bud plants.

May 15, 1:08 pm– May 18, 1:48 am Libra, 2nd qtr.	Plant annuals for fragrance and beauty. Trim to increase growth.
May 18, 1:48 am– May 20, 12:17 pm Scorpio, 2nd qtr.	Plant annuals, grains. Irrigate. Fertilize (chemical). Trim to increase growth. Graft or bud plants.
May 20, 12:17 pm Full Moon, Scorpio	Gather mushrooms. Harvest root crops for seed.
May 20, 12:17 pm– May 20, 12:53 pm Scorpio, 3rd qtr.	Plant biennials, perennials, bulbs and roots. Irrigate. Fertilize (organic). Prune.
May 20, 12:53 pm– May 22, 9:55 pm Sagittarius, 3rd qtr.	Cultivate. Destroy weeds and pests. Harvest fruits and root crops. Trim to retard growth.
May 22, 9:55 pm– May 25, 5:02 am Capricorn, 3rd qtr.	Plant potatoes and tubers. Prune.
May 25, 5:02 am– May 27, 10:14 am Aquarius, 3rd qtr.	Cultivate. Destroy weeds and pests. Harvest fruits and root crops. Trim to retard growth.
May 27, 10:14 am– May 29, 1:26 pm Pisces, 3-4th qtr.	Plant biennials, perennials, bulbs and roots. Irrigate. Fertilize (organic). Prune.
May 29, 1:26 pm– May 31, 3:00 pm Aries, 4th qtr.	Cultivate. Destroy weeds and pests. Harvest fruits and root crops. Trim to retard growth.
May 31, 3:00 pm– Jun 2, 4:03 pm Taurus, 4th qtr.	Plant potatoes and tubers. Prune.
Jun 2, 4:03 pm– Jun 3, 1:54 pm Gemini, 4th qtr.	Cultivate. Destroy weeds and pests. Harvest fruits and root crops. Trim to retard growth.

Jun 4, 6:18 pm– Jun 6, 11:29 pm Cancer, 1st qtr.	Plant annuals, grains. Irrigate. Fertilize (chemical). Trim to increase growth. Graft or bud plants.
Jun 11, 8:32 pm– Jun 14, 9:12 am Libra, 2nd qtr.	Plant annuals for fragrance and beauty. Trim to increase growth.
Jun 14, 9:12 am– Jun 16, 8:13 pm Scorpio, 2nd qtr.	Plant annuals, grains. Irrigate. Fertilize (chemical). Trim to increase growth. Graft or bud plants.
Jun 19, 0:58 am Full Moon, Sag.	Gather mushrooms. Harvest root crops for seed.
Jun 19, 0:58 am– Jun 19, 4:42 am Sagittarius, 3rd qtr.	Cultivate. Destroy weeds and pests. Harvest fruits and root crops. Trim to retard growth.
Jun 19, 4:42 am– Jun 21, 10:58 am Capricorn, 3rd qtr.	Plant potatoes and tubers. Prune.
Jun 21, 10:58 am– Jun 23, 3:37 pm Aquarius, 3rd qtr.	Cultivate. Destroy weeds and pests. Harvest fruits and root crops. Trim to retard growth.
Jun 23, 3:37 pm– Jun 25, 7:07 pm Pisces, 3rd qtr.	Plant biennials, perennials, bulbs and roots. Irrigate. Fertilize (organic). Prune.
Jun 25, 7:07 pm– Jun 27, 9:46 pm Aries, 3-4th qtr.	Cultivate. Destroy weeds and pests. Harvest fruits and root crops. Trim to retard growth.
Jun 27, 9:46 pm– Jun 30, 0:09 am Taurus, 4th qtr.	Plant potatoes and tubers. Prune.
Jun 30, 0:09 am– Jul 2, 3:20 am Gemini, 4th qtr.	Cultivate. Destroy weeds and pests. Harvest fruits and root crops. Trim to retard growth.

Jul 2, 3:20 am– Jul 2, 11:00 pm Cancer, 4th qtr.	Plant biennials, perennials, bulbs and roots. Irrigate. Fertilize (organic). Prune.
Jul 2, 11:00 pm– Jul 4, 8:38 am Cancer, 1st qtr.	Plant annuals, grains. Irrigate. Fertilize (chemical). Trim to increase growth. Graft or bud plants.
Jul 9, 4:31 am– Jul 11, 5:10 pm Libra, 1-2nd qtr.	Plant annuals for fragrance and beauty. Trim to increase growth.
Jul 11, 5:10 pm– Jul 14, 4:32 am Scorpio, 2nd qtr.	Plant annuals, grains. Irrigate. Fertilize (chemical). Trim to increase growth. Graft or bud plants.
Jul 16, 1:02 pm– Jul 18, 11:42 am Capricorn, 2nd qtr.	Graft or bud plants. Trim to increase growth.
Jul 18, 11:42 am Full Moon, Cap.	Gather mushrooms. Harvest root crops for seed.
Jul 18, 11:42 am– Jul 18, 6:36 pm Capricorn, 3rd qtr.	Plant potatoes and tubers. Prune.
Jul 18, 6:36 pm– Jul 20, 10:08 pm Aquarius, 3rd qtr.	Cultivate. Destroy weeds and pests. Harvest fruits and root crops. Trim to retard growth.
Jul 20, 10:08 pm– Jul 23, 0:41 am Pisces, 3rd qtr.	Plant biennials, perennials, bulbs and roots. Irrigate. Fertilize (organic). Prune.
Jul 23, 0:41 am– Jul 25, 3:11 am Aries, 3rd qtr.	Cultivate. Destroy weeds and pests. Harvest fruits and root crops. Trim to retard growth.
Jul 25, 3:11 am– Jul 27, 6:16 am Taurus, 3-4th qtr.	Plant potatoes and tubers. Prune.

Jul 27, 6:16 am- Jul 29, 10:33 am Gemini, 4th qtr.	Cultivate. Destroy weeds and pests. Harvest fruits and root crops. Trim to retard growth.
Jul 29, 10:33 am- Jul 31, 4:42 pm Cancer, 4th qtr.	Plant biennials, perennials, bulbs and roots. Irrigate. Fertilize (organic). Prune.
Jul 31, 4:42 pm- Aug 1, 10:07 am Leo, 4th qtr.	Cultivate. Destroy weeds and pests. Harvest fruits and root crops. Trim to retard growth.
Aug 5, 12:29 pm- Aug 8, 1:06 am Libra, 1st qtr.	Plant annuals for fragrance and beauty. Trim to increase growth.
Aug 8, 1:06 am- Aug 10, 1:03 pm Scorpio, 1-2nd qtr.	Plant annuals, grains. Irrigate. Fertilize (chemical). Trim to increase growth. Graft or bud plants.
Aug 12, 10:17 pm- Aug 15, 4:00 am Capricorn, 2nd qtr.	Graft or bud plants. Trim to increase growth.
Aug 16, 9:07 pm Full Moon, Aquar.	Gather mushrooms. Harvest root crops for seed.
Aug 16, 9:07 pm- Aug 17, 6:46 am Aquarius, 3rd qtr.	Cultivate. Destroy weeds and pests. Harvest fruits and root crops. Trim to retard growth.
Aug 17, 6:46 am- Aug 19, 8:00 am Pisces, 3rd qtr.	Plant biennials, perennials, bulbs and roots. Irrigate. Fertilize (organic). Prune.
Aug 19, 8:00 am- Aug 21, 9:11 am Aries, 3rd qtr.	Cultivate. Destroy weeds and pests. Harvest fruits and root crops. Trim to retard growth.
Aug 21, 9:11 am- Aug 23, 11:40 am Taurus, 3rd qtr.	Plant potatoes and tubers. Prune.

Aug 23, 11:40 am- Aug 25, 4:14 pm Gemini, 3-4th qtr.	Cultivate. Destroy weeds and pests. Harvest fruits and root crops. Trim to retard growth.
Aug 25, 4:14 pm- Aug 27, 11:13 pm Cancer, 4th qtr.	Plant biennials, perennials, bulbs and roots. Irrigate. Fertilize (organic). Prune.
Aug 27, 11:13 pm- Aug 30, 8:30 am Leo, 4th qtr.	Cultivate. Destroy weeds and pests. Harvest fruits and root crops. Trim to retard growth.
Aug 30, 8:30 am- Aug 30, 11:45 pm Virgo, 4th qtr.	Cultivate, especially medicinal plants. Destroy weeds and pests. Trim to retard growth.
Sep 1, 7:48 pm- Sep 4, 8:24 am Libra, 1st qtr.	Plant annuals for fragrance and beauty. Trim to increase growth.
Sep 4, 8:24 am- Sep 6, 8:52 pm Scorpio, 1st qtr.	Plant annuals, grains. Irrigate. Fertilize (chemical). Trim to increase growth. Graft or bud plants.
Sep 9, 7:14 am- Sep 11, 2:03 pm Capricorn, 2nd qtr.	Graft or bud plants. Trim to increase growth.
Sep 13, 5:08 pm- Sep 15, 5:52 am Pisces, 2nd qtr.	Plant annuals, grains. Irrigate. Fertilize (chemical). Trim to increase growth. Graft or bud plants.
Sep 15, 5:52 am Full Moon, Pisces	Gather mushrooms. Harvest root crops for seed.
Sep 15, 5:52 am- Sep 15, 5:39 pm Pisces, 3rd qtr.	Plant biennials, perennials, bulbs and roots. Irrigate. Fertilize (organic). Prune.
Sep 15, 5:39 pm- Sep 17, 5:23 pm Aries, 3rd qtr.	Cultivate. Destroy weeds and pests. Harvest fruits and root crops. Trim to retard growth.

Sep 17, 5:23 pm– Sep 19, 6:17 pm Taurus, 3rd qtr.	Plant potatoes and tubers. Prune.
Sep 19, 6:17 pm– Sep 21, 9:51 pm Gemini, 3-4th qtr.	Cultivate. Destroy weeds and pests. Harvest fruits and root crops. Trim to retard growth.
Sep 21, 9:51 pm– Sep 24, 4:45 am Cancer, 4th qtr.	Plant biennials, perennials, bulbs and roots. Irrigate. Fertilize (organic). Prune.
Sep 24, 4:45 am– Sep 26, 2:33 pm Leo, 4th qtr.	Cultivate. Destroy weeds and pests. Harvest fruits and root crops. Trim to retard growth.
Sep 26, 2:33 pm– Sep 29, 2:16 am Virgo, 4th qtr.	Cultivate, especially medicinàl plants. Destroy weeds and pests. Trim to retard growth.
Sep 29, 3:48 pm– Oct 1, 2:54 pm Libra, 1st qtr.	Plant annuals for fragrance and beauty. Trim to increase growth.
Oct 1, 2:54 pm– Oct 4, 3:30 am Scorpio, 1st qtr.	Plant annuals, grains. Irrigate. Fertilize (chemical). Trim to increase growth. Graft or bud plants.
Oct 6, 2:46 pm– Oct 8, 11:07 pm Cap., 1-2nd qtr.	Graft or bud plants. Trim to increase growth.
Oct 11, 3:38 am– Oct 13, 4:42 am Pisces, 2nd qtr.	Plant annuals, grains. Irrigate. Fertilize (chemical). Trim to increase growth. Graft or bud plants.
Oct 14, 2:33 pm Full Moon, Aries	Gather mushrooms. Harvest root crops for seed.
Oct 14, 2:33 pm– Oct 15, 3:53 am Aries, 3rd qtr.	Cultivate. Destroy weeds and pests. Harvest fruits and root crops. Trim to retard growth.

Oct 15, 3:53 am- Oct 17, 3:20 am Taurus, 3rd qtr.	Plant potatoes and tubers. Prune.
Oct 17, 3:20 am- Oct 19, 5:10 am Gemini, 3rd qtr.	Cultivate. Destroy weeds and pests. Harvest fruits and root crops. Trim to retard growth.
Oct 19, 5:10 am- Oct 21, 10:48 am Cancer, 3-4th qtr.	Plant biennials, perennials, bulbs and roots. Irrigate. Fertilize (organic). Prune.
Oct 21, 10:48 am- Oct 23, 8:16 pm Leo, 4th qtr.	Cultivate. Destroy weeds and pests. Harvest fruits and root crops. Trim to retard growth.
Oct 23, 8:16 pm- Oct 26, 8:12 am Virgo, 4th qtr.	Cultivate, especially medicinal plants. Destroy weeds and pests. Trim to retard growth.
Oct 28, 8:57 pm- Oct 29, 9:28 am Scorpio, 4th qtr.	Plant biennials, perennials, bulbs and roots. Irrigate. Fertilize (organic). Prune.
Oct 29, 9:28 am- Oct 31, 9:24 am Scorpio, 1st qtr.	Plant annuals, grains. Irrigate. Fertilize (chemical). Trim to increase growth. Graft or bud plants.
Nov 2, 8:47 pm- Nov 5, 6:10 am Capricorn, 1st qtr.	Graft or bud plants. Trim to increase growth.
Nov 7, 12:26 pm- Nov 9, 3:09 pm Pisces, 2nd qtr.	Plant annuals, grains. Irrigate. Fertilize (chemical). Trim to increase growth. Graft or bud plants.
Nov 11, 3:10 pm- Nov 12, 11:52 pm Taurus, 2nd qtr.	Plant annuals for hardiness. Trim to increase growth.
Nov 12, 11:52 pm Full Moon, Taurus	Gather mushrooms. Harvest root crops for seed.

Nov 12, 11:52 pm– Nov 13, 2:20 pm Taurus, 3rd qtr.	Plant potatoes and tubers. Prune.
Nov 13, 2:20 pm– Nov 15, 2:52 pm Gemini, 3rd qtr.	Cultivate. Destroy weeds and pests. Harvest fruits and root crops. Trim to retard growth.
Nov 15, 2:52 pm– Nov 17, 6:47 pm Cancer, 3rd qtr.	Plant biennials, perennials, bulbs and roots. Irrigate. Fertilize (organic). Prune.
Nov 17, 6:47 pm– Nov 20, 2:55 am Leo, 3-4th qtr.	Cultivate. Destroy weeds and pests. Harvest fruits and root crops. Trim to retard growth.
Nov 20, 2:55 am– Nov 22, 2:26 pm Virgo, 4th qtr.	Cultivate, especially medicinal plants. Destroy weeds and pests. Trim to retard growth.
Nov 25, 3:14 am– Nov 27, 3:31 pm Scorpio, 4th qtr.	Plant biennials, perennials, bulbs and roots. Irrigate. Fertilize (organic). Prune.
Nov 27, 3:31 pm– Nov 28, 3:42 am Sagittarius, 4th qtr.	Cultivate. Destroy weeds and pests. Harvest fruits and root crops. Trim to retard growth.
Nov 30, 2:27 am– Dec 2, 11:43 am Capricorn, 1st qtr.	Graft or bud plants. Trim to increase growth.
Dec 4, 6:49 pm– Dec 6, 11:12 pm Pisces, 1-2nd qtr.	Plant annuals, grains. Irrigate. Fertilize (chemical). Trim to increase growth. Graft or bud plants.
Dec 9, 1:00 am– Dec 11, 1:16 am Taurus, 2nd qtr.	Plant annuals for hardiness. Trim to increase growth.
Dec 12, 10:31 am Full Moon, Gemini	Gather mushrooms. Harvest root crops for seed.

Dec 12, 10:31 am– Dec 13, 1:50 am Gemini, 3rd qtr.	Cultivate. Destroy weeds and pests. Harvest fruits and root crops. Trim to retard growth.
Dec 13, 1:50 am– Dec 15, 4:42 am Cancer, 3rd qtr.	Plant biennials, perennials, bulbs and roots. Irrigate. Fertilize (organic). Prune.
Dec 15, 4:42 am– Dec 17, 11:20 am Leo, 3rd qtr.	Cultivate. Destroy weeds and pests. Harvest fruits and root crops. Trim to retard growth.
Dec 17, 11:20 am– Dec 19, 9:46 pm Virgo, 3-4th qtr.	Cultivate, especially medicinal plants. Destroy weeds and pests. Trim to retard growth.
Dec 22, 10:19 am– Dec 24, 10:38 pm Scorpio, 4th qtr.	Plant biennials, perennials, bulbs and roots. Irrigate. Fertilize (organic). Prune.
Dec 24, 10:38 pm– Dec 27, 9:11 am Sagittarius, 4th qtr.	Cultivate. Destroy weeds and pests. Harvest fruits and root crops. Trim to retard growth.
Dec 27, 9:11 am– Dec 27, 9:20 pm Capricorn, 4th qtr.	Plant potatoes and tubers. Prune.
Dec 27, 9:20 pm– Dec 29, 5:39 pm Capricorn, 1st qtr.	Graft or bud plants. Trim to increase growth.

DATES TO DESTROY WEEDS AND PESTS

There are certain dates, according to the Moon's Sign and Phase, when it is better to remove or kill weeds, pests, insects, plow, use weed killer on your lawn, spray for pests and diseases, etc. Following is a list of dates for 1989 when these activities will be most effective.

Dates	Sign	Phase
Jan 4, 1:12 am-Jan 6, 7:15 am	Sagit.	4th qtr.
Jan 21, 3:35 pm-Jan 23, 10:33 pm	Leo	3rd qtr.
Jan 23, 10:33 pm-Jan 26, 11:02 am	Virgo	3rd qtr.
Jan 31, 10:31 am-Feb 2, 5:30 pm	Sagit.	4th qtr.
Feb 4, 8:52 pm-Feb 6, 1:38 am	Aquarius	4th qtr.
Feb 20, 9:33 am-Feb 22, 6:06 pm	Virgo	3rd qtr.
Feb 27, 6:30 pm-Mar 2, 2:59 am	Sagit.	3rd/4th
Mar 4, 7:37 am-Mar 6, 9:00 am	Aquarius	4th qtr.
Mar 27, 0:55 am-Mar 29, 10:26 am	Sagit.	3rd qtr.
Mar 31, 4:46 pm-Apr 2, 7:38 pm	Aquarius	4th qtr.
Apr 4, 7:52 pm-Apr 5, 9:34 pm	Aries	4th qtr.
Apr 23, 6:39 am-Apr 25, 4:16 pm	Sagit.	3rd qtr.
Apr 27, 11:34 pm-Apr 30, 4:04 am	Aquarius	3rd/4th
May 2, 5:51 am-May 4, 5:56 am	Aries	4th qtr.
May 20, 12:53 pm-May 22, 9:55 pm	Sagit.	3rd qtr.
May 25, 5:02 am-May 27, 10:14 am	Aquarius	3rd qtr.
May 29, 1:26 pm-May 31, 3:00 pm	Aries	4th qtr.
Jun 2, 4:03 pm-Jun 3, 1:54 pm	Gemini	4th qtr.
Jun 19, 0:58 am-Jun 19, 4:42 am	Sagit.	3rd qtr.

Jun 21, 10:58 am-Jun 23, 3:37 pm	Aquarius	3rd qtr.
Jun 25, 7:07 pm-Jun 27, 9:46 pm	Aries	3rd/4th
Jun 30, 0:09 am-Jul 2, 3:20 am	Gemini	4th qtr.
Jul 18, 6:36 pm-Jul 20, 10:08 pm	Aquarius	3rd qtr.
Jul 23, 0:41 am-Jul 25, 3:11 am	Aries	3rd qtr.
Jul 27, 6:16 am-Jul 29, 10:33 am	Gemini	4th qtr.
Jul 31, 4:42 pm-Aug 1, 10:07 am	Leo	4th qtr.
Aug 16, 9:07 pm-Aug 17, 6:46 am	Aquarius	3rd qtr.
Aug 19, 8:00 am-Aug 21, 9:11 am	Aries	3rd qtr.
Aug 23, 11:40 am-Aug 25, 4:14 pm	Gemini	3rd/4th
Aug 27, 11:13 pm-Aug 30, 8:30 am	Leo	4th qtr.
Aug 30, 8:30 am-Aug 30, 11:45 pm	Virgo	4th qtr.
Sep 15, 5:39 pm-Sep 17, 5:23 pm	Aries	3rd qtr.
Sep 19, 6:17 pm-Sep 21, 9:51 pm	Gemini	3rd/4th
Sep 24, 4:45 am-Sep 26, 2:33 pm	Leo	4th qtr.
Sep 26, 2:33 pm-Sep 29, 2:16 am	Virgo	4th qtr.
Oct 14, 2:33 pm-Oct 15, 3:53 am	Aries	3rd qtr.

Oct 17, 3:20 am-Oct 19, 5:10 am	Gemini	3rd qtr.
Oct 21, 10:48 am-Oct 23, 8:16 pm	Leo	4th qtr.
Oct 23, 8:16 pm-Oct 26, 8:12 am	Virgo	4th qtr.
Nov 13, 2:20 pm-Nov 15, 2:52 pm	Gemini	3rd qtr.
Nov 17, 6:47 pm-Nov 20, 2:55 am	Leo	3rd/4th
Nov 20, 2:55 am-Nov 22, 2:26 pm	Virgo	4th qtr.
Nov 27, 3:31 pm-Nov 28, 3:42 am	Sagit.	4th qtr.
Dec 12, 10:31 am-Dec 13, 1:50 am	Gemini	3rd qtr.
Dec 15, 4:42 am-Dec 17, 11:20 am	Leo	3rd qtr.
Dec 17, 11:20 am-Dec 19, 9:46 pm	Virgo	3rd/4th
Dec 24, 10:38 pm-Dec 27, 9:11 am	Sagit.	4th qtr.

BREEDING ANIMALS AND SETTING EGGS

EGGS should be set and animals mated so that the young will be born when the Moon is increasing and in a fruitful sign. The fruitful signs are Cancer, Scorpio and Pisces. Young born during the fruitful signs are generally healthier, mature faster and make better breeding stock. Those born during the semi-fruitful signs, Taurus and Capricorn, will generally still mature fast, but will produce leaner meat. The sign of Libra yields beautiful, graceful animals, for showing and racing.

To determine the best date to mate animals or set eggs, subtract the number of days given for incubation or gestation from the fruitful dates given in the following tables. For example, cats and dogs are mated sixty-three days previous to the desired birth date, as shown; chicken eggs are set twenty-one days previous.

Gestation and Incubation figures

Animal	No. of Young	Gestation
Horse	1	346 days
Cow	1	283 days
Monkey	1	164 days
Goat	1 to 2	151 days
Sheep	1 to 2	150 days
Pig	10	112 days
Chinchilla	2	110 days
Fox	5 to 8	63 days
Dog	6 to 8	63 days
Cat	4 to 6	63 days

Guinea Pig	2 to 6	62 days
Ferret	6 to 9	40 days
Rabbit	4 to 8	30 days
Rat	10	22 days
Mouse	10	22 days

Domestic Fowl	No. of Eggs	Incubation
Turkey	12 to 15	26 to 30 days
Guinea	15 to 18	25 to 26 days
Pea Hen	10	28 to 30 days
Duck	9 to 12	25 to 32 days
Goose	15 to 18	27 to 33 days
Hen	12 to 15	19 to 24 days
Pigeon	2	16 to 20 days
Canaries	3 to 4	13 to 14 days

SETTING EGGS

Dates to be Born	Moon's Sign & Phase	Set Eggs
Jan 7, 1:23 pm- Jan 8, 10:31 am	Capricorn, 1st qtr.	Dec 17-18
Jan 10, 12:32 pm- Jan 12, 2:37 pm	Pisces, 1st qtr.	Dec 20-22
Jan 14, 5:37 pm- Jan 16, 9:58 pm	Taurus, 2nd qtr.	Dec 24-26
Jan 19, 3:58 am- Jan 21, 12:03 pm	Cancer, 2nd qtr.	Dec 29-31
Feb 6, 9:53 pm- Feb 8, 10:19 pm	Pisces, 1st qtr.	Jan 16-18
Feb 10, 11:46 pm- Feb 13, 3:23 am	Taurus, 1st/2nd qtrs.	Jan 20-23
Feb 15, 9:41 am- Feb 17, 6:34 pm	Cancer, 2nd qtr.	Jan 25-27
Mar 7, 12:20 pm- Mar 8, 8:37 am	Pisces, 1st qtr.	Feb 14-15
Mar 10, 8:26 am- Mar 12, 10:17 am	Taurus, 1st qtr.	Feb 17-19
Mar 14, 3:28 pm- Mar 17, 0:14 am	Cancer, 2nd qtr.	Feb 21-24

Mar 22, 0:25 am– Mar 22, 3:59 am	Libra, 2nd qtr.	Mar 1-1
Apr 6, 7:08 pm– Apr 8, 7:32 pm	Taurus, 1st qtr.	Mar 16-18
Apr 10, 10:59 pm– Apr 13, 6:32 am	Cancer, 1st/2nd qtrs.	Mar 20-23
Apr 18, 6:32 am– Apr 20, 7:14 pm	Libra, 2nd qtr.	Mar 28-30
Apr 20, 7:14 pm– Apr 20, 9:14 pm	Scorpio, 2nd qtr.	Mar 30-30
May 5, 5:47 am– May 6, 6:04 am	Taurus, 1st qtr.	Apr 14-15
May 8, 8:20 am– May 10, 2:24 pm	Cancer, 1st qtr.	Apr 17-19
May 15, 1:08 pm– May 18, 1:48 am	Libra, 2nd qtr.	Apr 24-27
May 18, 1:48 am– May 20, 12:17 pm	Scorpio, 2nd qtr.	Apr 27-29
Jun 4, 6:18 pm– Jun 6, 11:29 pm	Cancer, 1st qtr.	May 14-16
Jun 11, 8:32 pm– Jun 14, 9:12 am	Libra, 2nd qtr.	May 21-24
Jun 14, 9:12 am– Jun 16, 8:13 pm	Scorpio, 2nd qtr.	May 24-26
Jul 2, 11:00 pm– Jul 4, 8:38 am	Cancer, 1st qtr.	Jun 11-13
Jul 9, 4:31 am– Jul 11, 5:10 pm	Libra, 1st/2nd qtrs.	Jun 18-20
Jul 11, 5:10 pm– Jul 14, 4:32 am	Scorpio, 2nd qtr.	Jun 20-23
Jul 16, 1:02 pm– Jul 18, 11:42 am	Capricorn, 2nd qtr.	Jun 25-27
Aug 5, 12:29 pm– Aug 8, 1:06 am	Libra, 1st qtr.	Jul 15-18
Aug 8, 1:06 am– Aug 10, 1:03 pm	Scorpio, 1st/2nd qtrs.	Jul 18-20

Aug 12, 10:17 pm- Aug 15, 4:00 am	Capricorn, 2nd qtr.	Jul 22-25
Sep 1, 7:48 pm- Sep 4, 8:24 am	Libra, 1st qtr.	Aug 11-14
Sep 4, 8:24 am- Sep 6, 8:52 pm	Scorpio, 1st qtr.	Aug 14-16
Sep 9, 7:14 am- Sep 11, 2:03 pm	Capricorn, 2nd qtr.	Aug 19-21
Sep 13, 5:08 pm- Sep 15, 5:52 am	Pisces, 2nd qtr.	Aug 23-25
Sep 29, 3:48 pm- Oct 1, 2:54 pm	Libra, 1st qtr.	Sep 8-10
Oct 1, 2:54 pm- Oct 4, 3:30 am	Scorpio, 1st qtr.	Sep 10-13
Oct 6, 2:46 pm- Oct 8, 11:07 pm	Capricorn, 1st/2nd qtrs.	Sep 15-17
Oct 11, 3:38 am- Oct 13, 4:42 am	Pisces, 2nd qtr.	Sep 20-22
Oct 29, 9:28 am- Oct 31, 9:24 am	Scorpio, 1st qtr.	Oct 8-10
Nov 2, 8:47 pm- Nov 5, 6:10 am	Capricorn, 1st qtr.	Oct 12-15
Nov 7, 12:26 pm- Nov 9, 3:09 pm	Pisces, 2nd qtr.	Oct 17-19
Nov 11, 3:10 pm- Nov 12, 11:52 pm	Taurus, 2nd qtr.	Oct 21-22
Nov 30, 2:27 am- Dec 2, 11:43 am	Capricorn, 1st qtr.	Nov 9-11
Dec 4, 6:49 pm- Dec 6, 11:12 pm	Pisces, 1st/2nd qtrs.	Nov 13-15
Dec 9, 1:00 am- Dec 11, 1:16 am	Taurus, 2nd qtr.	Nov 18-20
Dec 27, 9:20 pm- Dec 29, 5:39 pm	Capricorn, 1st qtr.	Dec 6-8

Predetermining Sex
In Breeding Cows
by Louise Riotte

For the beef or dairy farmer, being able to predetermine sex can be of vital importance. Finding a way to suggest a solution to this problem has not been easy. In a very old *Moon Sign Book*, I found this method of predetermining sex in human children: "Count from the last day of menstruation to the day next beginning, and divide the interval between the two dates into halves. Pregnancy occurring in the first half produces females, but copulation should take place when the Moon is in a feminine sign (Taurus, Cancer, Virgo, Scorpio, Capricorn, and Pisces). Pregnancy occurring in the latter half, up to within three days of beginning of menstruation, produces males, but copulation should take place when the Moon is in a masculine sign (Aries, Gemini, Leo, Libra, Sagittarius, and Aquarius). From this three-day period, to the end of the first half of the next period, again produces females."

The cow is probably the nearest to the human mother in many ways, each taking approximately nine months to produce offspring, each producing usually only one, and each having the possibility of being bred at any time during the year. There are, of course, important differences but in a general way there is comparison.

Fertilization

This is the union of the male and female germ cells,

sperm and ovum. The sperm are deposited in the vagina at the time of service and from there ascend the female reproductive tract. Under favorable conditions, they meet the egg and one of them fertilizes it in the upper part of the oviduct near the ovary.

In cows, fertilization is an all or none phenomenon, since only one ovum is ordinarily involved. Thus the breeder's task is to synchronize ovulation and insemination so that large numbers of vigorous, fresh sperm will be present in the Fallopian tubes at the time of ovulation. This presents a big problem.

First, there is no exact way of predicting the length of heat at the time of ovulation (it has been determined that ovulation usually takes place toward the end of, or following, the heat period; however, it may happen during the heat period or as late as thirty-six hours after it). Second, as with all biological phenomena, there is often considerable individual variation. Third, the sperm cells of the bull remain viable only twenty-four to thirty hours in the reproductive tract of the female. Fourth, an unfertilized egg will not live more than approximately six hours. Fifth, it may require less than one minute for sperm cells to ascend the female reproductive tract of a cow.

From these proven facts it is easy to see that a series of delicate time relationships are involved and must be met, making it necessary for breeding to occur at just the right time. Therefore, for the maximum rate of conception, it is advisable that breeding be done during the latter part of the heat period; but, since the duration of heat in cattle is very short (seldom exceeding twenty hours), waiting too long may result in the cow's being out of heat when mating is attempted. Cows that are in heat in the morning should be bred during the afternoon of the same day, and those in heat in the afternoon should be bred late that evening or early the next morning.

As noted, the problem of breeding at the correct time is not an easy one to solve. In general, cattle that are bred when out on pasture or range are mated under environmental conditions approaching those of natural selection of mating time. Among such animals less breeding trouble is usually encountered than among beef or dairy animals that are kept in confined conditions and under forced production.

But, following the methods of predetermining sex in humans, it is suggested that for females copulation should take place when the Moon is in a feminine sign and for males, in a masculine sign. As for the phase of the Moon, there is an old saying among horse breeders, dating back to Colonial times, that may be of some help: "If you want horse colts, breed your mare before the Full of the Moon and when the Sign is below the heart."

Age of Puberty

Naturally the animal must be of the proper age to breed. Old-timers will know all this, but for those who do not, the normal age of puberty of cattle is eight to twelve months. It is to be understood, however, that the age of puberty varies in different breeds, smaller breeds attaining this earlier and the larger breeds being characterized by attaining maturity more slowly. Also, nutritional and environmental factors have an influence because puberty usually occurs when animals have reached about one-third of their adult size.

Heat Periods

The period of duration of heat—that is, the time during which the cow will take the bull—is very short, usually not over sixteen to twenty hours, although there may be a variation of six to thirty hours. Cows usually follow a definite pattern of estrus behavior—that is, they generally come in heat during the morning hours and go out of heat in the evening or early part of night, and then ovulate approximately fourteen hours after the end of heat.

Females of all species bred near the end of the heat period are much more likely to conceive than if bred at any other time. The heat period recurs approximately every twenty-one days, but may vary from nineteen to twenty-three days in certain individuals.

In most cases cows do not show signs of estrus until some six to eight weeks after parturition, or possibly even longer. Occasionally, an abnormal condition develops in cows that causes them to remain in heat constantly. Such animals are called nymphomaniacs.

Signs of Estrus

There is an old saying that indicates the signs of estrus: "The cow that stands is the cow in heat," and this is considered the best single indicator of the heat period. Also, cows in heat generally exhibit one or more of the following symptoms: rough hair on tailhead; soil marks on side when the ground is wet; nervousness; bawling; frequent urination; mucus on rump and tail; and a moist and swollen vulva. Dry cows and heifers usually show a noticeable swelling or enlargement of the udder during the heat period, but lactating cows are likely to have a sharp decrease in milk production. Also, it has been noted that a bloody discharge may be present for a day or two following the heat period.

Modern science, as in everything else, has now to some extent solved the problem of heat detection and there are several devices on the market. Properly used, these aids will improve heat detection but are by no means replacements for visual observation, nor will they solve all problems. Other factors that need attention are:

1. Proper nutrition. Cows must have adequate nutrition to cycle at a satisfactory rate for successful breeding. A cow in good health is more likely to follow a definite pattern.

2. Rest interval. This is of great importance, as cows must have calved at least sixty days prior to breeding for satisfactory performance. And a dairy cow especially should be as well and as carefully fed during a dry period as she is when lactating.

3. Appropriate facilities. They should be adequate for handling and breeding the cow herd. It's best to locate them where the cows tend to gather—generally the watering hole.

4. Personnel. Trained personnel are needed to do heat detection, gather the in-heat cows, and breed the herd.

Gestation Period

The average gestation period of cows is 283 days, or roughly about nine to nine and a half months. Though there may be considerable variation between individuals (the breed also influences the length of the gestation period), it is estimated that two-thirds of all cows will calve between 278 and 288 days after breeding.

Calving Season

There are many advantages to having calves spring-born. They are more likely to be larger and stronger—and the cows were bred during the most natural breeding season, when on pasture and gaining in flesh and most likely to conceive. The calves are old enough to use the cows' abundant milk supplies as they feed on lush spring pasture. Spring-born calves require litle or no supplemental feeding and make use of the maximum amount of pasture and roughage if marketed at weaning. Also, spring-born calves are ready for sale in the fall, usually when demand for feeder calves is greatest.

Dehorning and Castration

Cattle should be dehorned early in life, preferably before they are two months old, so as to minimize shock. Young calves are easier to handle, lose less blood, and suffer less setbacks. Select a date when the Moon is **not** in Aries, Taurus or Pisces, and is within one week before or after the New Moon.

For castration, select a date when the Moon is **not** in Scorpio, Virgo, Libra or Sagittarius, and is within one week before or after the New Moon.

Gardening In The South And West

by Louise Riotte

If you live in a climate with hot, dry summer weather, don't despair. You can beat it at its own game. Yes, you can—even if the Sun bakes your garden and the skies do not cooperate with rainfall, you can have a productive garden filled with flowers and vegetables. And I'm going to tell you how! Just follow these ten tips from Bedding Plants, Inc., an educational group that disseminates information on flower and vegetable gardening.

1. *Choose varieties that are heat and drought tolerant.* These would include zinnias, ornamental peppers, cosmos, vinca, portulaca, verbena, celosia, ageratum, cleome (spider flower), gazania, gerbera, and kochia (remember that flowers are planted in the sign of Libra); for the vegetable garden, try okra (Cancer, Scorpio, Pisces, Libra), lima beans (Cancer, Scorpio, Pisces, Libra, Taurus), amaranth (Cancer, Scorpio, Pisces, Libra), or other varieties developed for the Southern garden.

2. *Get a head start.* Buy bedding plants at the garden center or greenhouse and set them out as soon as possible when there is more soil moisture and cooler temperatures. Or, as an alternative, start your own plants indoors and have them ready at an opportune time. Grow cool-season vegetables, such as broccoli (1st quarter, Cancer, Scorpio, Pisces, Libra); kale (1st, Cancer, Scorpio, Pisces); cabbage (1st, Cancer, Scorpio, Pisces, Libra, Taurus); radishes (3rd, Libra, Taurus,

Pisces, Sagittarius, Capricorn); lettuce (1st, Cancer, Scorpio, Pisces, Libra, Taurus—late sowings); kohlrabi (1st, Cancer, Scorpio, Pisces, Libra); and cauliflower (1st, Cancer, Scorpio, Pisces, Libra), in late spring or fall, turning the summer garden over to heat lovers.

3. *Mulch.* Using mulch will help to conserve soil moisture, limit weed growth, and keep plant roots cooler. Use organic mulches like pine needles, bark, dried grass clippings (spread in thin layers, building up progressively so that they will not heat), straw, compost or leaf mold, or even a layer of black plastic if you have nothing else, covered with an ornamental topping.

4. *Prepare the soil well.* Dig deeply and work in plenty of organic matter such as sphagnum peat moss, compost or decayed manure (manure with straw in it is excellent). Not only does this help the soil to hold moisture, it also allows the plants to develop deeper, more drought tolerant roots.

5. *Water deeply.* This encourages deep roots. Water in the early morning to lower evaporation potential, about once a week if there is no rainfall, when the top one-half to one inch of soil is dry. To save time, effort, and precious water resources, consider using a soaker hose or drip irrigation system, which uses less water than a sprinkler—and there is also less evaporation. If it is extremely hot or windy, you may need to water more than once a week. Water in the signs of Cancer, Scorpio, Pisces, or Libra for the best results.

6. *Plant in raised beds.* You can plant more densely than you can if you use conventional rows. The plant foliage forms a canopy that shades the soil, keeping it moist and cool as well as reducing weed growth and the need for frequent irrigation. Raised beds also prevent the soil from becoming compacted and restricting root growth.

7. *Utilize windbreaks and shade.* This helps to reduce drying winds and loss of moisture from the ground and the plants' foliage. Open fences, trellises, and hedges slow down winds while still allowing for good air circulation.

8. *Harvest vegetables and fruits regularly and remove faded flowers.* This encourages continued growth and production. For keeping qualities, fruits and vegetables are best harvested in the 3rd and 4th quarters in the signs of Aries, Leo, Sagittarius, Gemini, and Aquarius. This applies particularly to root crops.

9. *Save water.* In case of drought, collect rainwater in barrels (better than tap water, which often contains chemicals), and save rinse water from clothes and dishes that has not been contaminated with bleach, high-phosphorus detergent or fabric softeners. Apply the water directly to the soil and check the pH annually to see if adjustments need to be made. And remember that water is more effectively used by the plants if given in a moist sign—Cancer, Scorpio, Pisces, or Libra. Plants absorb water better when they receive it in a watery sign.

10. *Avoid planting near large trees and shrubs.* Your flowers and vegetables will have to compete for much-needed moisture and nutrients if you put them near trees and shrubs. Speaking of nutrients, fertilize in proportion to the amount of water that the garden will receive, lowering fertilizer applications when water is scarce. Also, never apply fertilizer to dry ground. I prefer organic fertilizer, which is best given in the 3rd or 4th quarter in Cancer, Scorpio, or Pisces. For those who wish to use chemical fertilizer, use the 1st or 2nd quarter also in Cancer, Scorpio, or Pisces.

Cultivate when needed in the 4th quarter in the signs of Virgo, Leo, and Gemini, and start your compost heap in the 4th quarter under Cancer, Scorpio, or Pisces.

Even in a hot, dry climate nature is occasionally beneficent and you will find mushrooms. They are most apt to be plentiful at the time of the Full Moon. Just be sure you recognize the species you are picking.

Even during summers of adequate rainfall and normal temperatures, there are some hot and dry spots around the garden where plants will struggle. These include areas along pavement, at the edge of retaining walls, and on the south side of the house. Take extra care to treat plants in these areas with a little extra tender loving care. Whether from natural conditions or from location, plants stressed by heat or lack of moisture are more susceptible to pests and never grow, flower, or fruit to their full potential. By planning ahead, you can enjoy beautiful flowers and a bountiful harvest, no matter what the weather.

For a free tip sheet outlining plants for the hot and dry garden plus a suggested planting plan, send a self-addressed, stamped envelope to *Four Versatile Garden Environments*, Bedding Plants, Inc., 210 Cartwright Boulevard, Massapequa Park, NY 11762.

Designing the Sunny Garden

There's a place in the Sun . . . and it could be your garden. Those who garden in a somewhat milder climate may consider themselves lucky if they have a spot bathed in Sun all day, where a mind-boggling assortment of flowers could grow. If you are so gifted, plan your sunny garden in advance so that it is well designed, attractive and fun.

Think of color first. Do you want to create a soft, cool garden, or one that is a riot of color? If the cool garden is your choice (for a lovely spot for you to rest and think), stick with blues and violets with accents of white, silver, or grey. This can be done with lobelia, ageratum, blue and violet petunias, or cornflower, with accents from dusty miller or a number of white flowers. If, on the other hand, you want a bright, exciting garden, select red, orange or yellow tones. A yellow-gold-orange garden in a warm area can be created with a variety of marigolds. In cooler areas, the same effect can be achieved with calendula. Celosia (cockscomb) in a rainbow of bright colors brings such color to the garden that it is almost bizarre. And celosia now comes in an infinite variety of shapes and heights.

Perhaps you prefer tones of red, salmon, coral, or pink. If so, geraniums are one of the best choices. The hybrid (seed-grown) geraniums are more heat resistant and the better choice for massed beds over the cutting-grown types. And you can grow them yourself from seeds. If you use them in an area lighted at night, select a white or pastel shade so that they will be more visible. For red accents, salvia is another excellent choice. And the new varieties are very long blooming.

Consider your growing conditions. Is it sandy? Petunias in all colors do best in hot, dry, sandy locations. Something else for hot and dry? Zinnias will bring a rainbow of colors in a variety of flower shapes; plus they will not mildew as easily under these conditions. Is it cool and moist? Then select pansies, annual phlox, or snapdragons. Need red, white, and blue to celebrate the colors of the flag? You can do it with petunias, verbena, or geraniums and ageratum.

Before planting, put your plan on paper so that you can be sure it looks just right and so that you know how many plants to purchase. Soil should be prepared in advance by adding organic matter such as peat moss or compost and

fertilizer such as 5-10-5 (following label directions). When
you select your plants (the best way to an instant garden),
look for green, healthy, disease-free plants. Set into place as
soon as possible after frost damage has passed, watering
well after planting and through the summer as needed.
There is indeed a place in the Sun; let it be your flower garden, better and more attractive than ever before.

Designing for Shade

What could be more pleasant on a hot summer day than
relaxing in the cooling shade of an arbor or clump of trees
surrounded by colorful flowers? This enticing image is just
one of the reasons why more and more gardeners are finding shade gardens desirable.

Before selecting young plants to color your shade garden, take a moment to evaluate your growing conditions.
While a large group of annuals will grow in a partially
shaded area, only a few will tolerate a relatively heavy
shade.

The intensely colored, easy-to-grow impatiens is the
flower most chosen for the shade garden. Both the fibrous-
and tuberous-rooted begonias are also popular for shady
conditions. What the coleus lacks in flower appeal it more
than makes up for with its multicolored leaves in a variety of
shapes and textures.

Besides these three favorites, don't overlook some of
the other annuals that grow and flower in a partially shaded
garden. One of the best-known annual flowers for lightly
shaded gardens, especially in the spring and fall, is the perky
pansy. With just a few hours of Sun daily, the vibrant red,
blue, salmon, or white spikes of salvia will unfurl from late
spring until frost, as will the fuzzy clusters of ageratum, in
misty blue, white, or pink. These two annuals look especially
attractive together in flower beds. Putting together plants
that harmonize or contrast attractively with each other is
another form of companion planting (for more on this subject see *Roses Love Garlic*, published by Storey Communications). Massed beds are also very appealing when
filled with the multi-tones and wonderful scent of nicotiana,
the flowering tobacco.

A wonderful way to edge lightly shaded flower beds is
with sweet alyssum. The ground-hugging and fragrant plants

are covered with tiny white, lavender, or pink blossoms for months on end. Another good edging plant is lobelia. Where summers are hot, its blue or purple flowers will thrive only if shaded during midday. In shaded patio planters or hanging baskets, try browallia, which has cascading stems filled with starlike blossoms in blue or white; or fuchsia, which has hoop-skirt flowers in mixed colors.

An eye-catching choice for deeply shaded cool areas is mimulus, also called monkey flower. This increasingly popular bedding plant boasts two-inch-wide blooms that are flamboyantly patterned in shades of yellow and red. Equally attractive are foot-tall torenia, the wishbone flower, whose unusually shaped blooms are painted deep violet and yellow, and the deeply veined and unique salpiglossis.

Plants may have to compete with the roots of the trees under which they will be grown, and the soil may be very dry there also. For the greatest success, create high, more open shade by pruning away some of the trees' lower branches. If you have a choice in flower bed location, select a spot that receives morning Sun and afternoon shade. Where tree roots are a problem, seen especially under maple trees, you may want to consider slightly raised beds or gardening in flower pots plunged into the ground. When preparing the soil, add extra organic matter to overcome the dry soil problem by increasing water retention potential, and for best results, be sure the shade garden is in reach of the garden hose.

Designing the Cool Garden

Gardening shouldn't be thought of as a hot weather, summertime activity only. Increasing numbers of gardeners are discovering the possibilities and advantages of growing cool-season flowers and vegetables. There are literally dozens of these types of plants that can be set into the ground long before the last spring frost and again in mid to late summer for lengthening periods of color enjoyment and for early and late vegetable harvest. This is particularly of interest in the South and West, where a long growing season is possible. Even in Southern Oklahoma I have something growing in my garden for most of the 365 days in the year. Delicious Chinese cabbage and Brussels sprouts are possible in late fall. Jerusalem artichokes, left in the ground and mulched, may be dug most winters all winter long.

Butterhead lettuce grows well in the fall and sometimes all winter. Parsley will freeze and thaw out and be as good as ever. I have picked spinach after a light snow. Kale is another hardy vegetable that will stand a lot of cold.

Flowers and vegetables are divided into two groups. The hardy, cool-season plants can withstand light frosts in spring and fall and grow best where temperatures stay cool. The tender warm-season plants are killed by either spring or fall frosts and need warm summer temperatures to grow and flourish. With proper planning, your garden can utilize both types and give you the longest growing season possible.

Some of the cool-season flowers to consider include annual phlox, snapdragons, forget-me-nots, ornamental cabbage and kale, pansies, sweet alyssum, sweet peas, African daisies, baby-blue-eyes (beloved of cats), baby's breath, cornflower, salpiglossis, everlastings, poppies, larkspur, calendula, wallflowers, and monkey flowers. You can use these as spring or fall sources of color or as all-summer flowers where the climate is always cool, such as at high altitudes, in Northern areas, and along some seashores. Many of these plants suffer from summer heat unless protected by mulches and light shade. Fountains and pools also have a cooling effect.

The outstanding vegetables for cool-season growing, in addition to those previously mentioned, are many members of the *Brassica* family—cauliflower, kohlrabi, rutabaga, broccoli, mustard, cabbage, turnips, collards. Others that can be grown in the spring and fall gardens, as they are not harmed by frost, are carrots, beets, onions, radishes, chard, chicory, endive, leek, salsify, peas, and parsnips.

Planting the Poolside

Two requirements are necessary when choosing to landscape swimming pool areas. Never plant anything bristly, prickly, sharp, or thorny because such plants are likely to annoy or injure pool users. Your flowers and shrubs should also be as litter-free as possible—and what litter they do produce should be large enough to be removed by hand from the pool rather than passing into the pool's filter. Shrubs such as camellia, jade plant, Japanese fatsia, kupukatree, juniper, Japanese pittosporum, wheeler's dwarf, *Raphiolep-*

sis, African hemp, *Ternstroemia gymanthera*, and David viburnum are good. Trees such as *Cordyline, Cupaniopsis, Dracaena*, Abyssinian banana, *Ficus auriculata*, fiddle-leaf fig, Chinese parasol, *Montanoa arborescens*, banana, palm, *Schefflera*, tall firewheel, bird-of-paradise, and *Travesia* are suitable. If you want vines for screening, try Easter herald's trumpet, *Cissus, Fatshedera lizei, Solandra maxima*, and *Tetrastigma*. There is a wide variety of perennials to choose from—agapanthus, agave, soap aloe, shellflower, artichoke, parlor palm, canna, Kafir lily, elephant's ear, *Cyperus, Dianella tasmanica, Dietes*, gazania, *Hedychium, Hemerocallis*, torch lily, *Liriope*, philodendron (treelike types), *Phormium*, sedum, bird-of-paradise, succulents, yucca, and Mascarene grass.

Fire-Retardant Plants

For those who live in dry, hot areas, fire is an ever-present threat. While no plants will completely resist burning, there are some that will slow down a fire's progress. Remember that winds carry sparks from a fire and that even protective fire-retardant plantings can be breached.

Certain trees and shrubs are helpful. You might try planting the following types about your home: *Callistemon*, St. John's bread, California holly, *Myoporum*, rose bay (dwarf types), *Prunus lyonii*, buckthorn, smoke tree (evergreen kinds), rosemary, pepper tree, Brazilian pepper tree, and *Teucrium chamaedrys*. If perennials or vines are needed, plant *Achillea*, agave, aloe, *Artemisia* (low-growing varieties), *Atriplex* (some types), *Campsis, Convolvulus cneorium*, gazania, ice plants, *Limonium perezli*, portulaca, *Santolina vivens*, winter savory, *Senecio cineraria*, potato vine, and trunkless types of yucca.

Plants That Attract Bees

Keeping a few hives of bees is particularly profitable in warm climates. The bees will fertilize vegetables and fruit, give you honey for household use, and add interest to your days. Certain warm-climate flowers are particularly noted for drawing bees and will invariably attract them when in bloom. You may even find that you enjoy their humming on warm days as you lie in your hammock. However, if you wish to minimize their presence you would be wise to omit such flowers from your landscape. The following plants are their special favorites: trees such as acacia, avocado, citrus, *Crataegyus erubitirta japonica*, eucalyptus, honey locust, Brazilian pepper, *Sorbus aucuparia*, and *Tilia cordata;* and shrubs such as *Abelia*, acacia, *Artemisia, Buddleja, Callistemon citrinus*, heather, *Ceanothus*, Mexican orange, *Cotoneaster, Echium, Erica, Escallonia, Feijoa sellowiana*, California holly, privet, satinwood, firethorn, rosemary, *Syzgium, Teucrium chamaedrys*, and star jasmine. Perennials and vines you may use are dusty miller, *Eriogonum*, gladiolus, ice plants, *Lavandula augustifolia*, sweet alyssum, *Lonciera japonica halliana, Phyla nodiflora, Polygonum capitatum*, garden sage, winter savory, *Thymus*, and wisteria.

What Not to Plant

Sometimes it's just as important to avoid certain plants as it is to plant others for special purposes. In certain areas, air pollution adversely influences plants as well as humans. The effects will range from poor appearance to poor performance, or both. To the home gardener, damage to plants by polluted air is disconcerting, but the damage can be even more critical to commercial growers of vegetables and flowers.

At present the plants most tolerant of different types of air pollution are revealed by good to excellent performance in smoggy areas. In the absence of scientifically established resistance, this implied resistance is your best guide. Study the gardens around you when you plan your new planting, even along highways. Ask a knowledgeable neighbor or a reputable local nurseryman to suggest plants that perform well in the area. Plants propagated in polluted areas for the nursery trade are most likely to be among the resistant.

Here is a list of the plants—fruit, vegetable, and ornamental—that are no longer grown commercially in heavily air-polluted areas: almond, apple, apricot, avocado, bean, broccoli, cantaloupe, carrot, cherry, citrus, corn, cucumber, fig, grape, lettuce (head and romaine), nectarine, onion, parsley, peach, pepper, plum, prune, radish, spinach, tomato, maple, maidenhair fern, snapdragon, pot marigold, catalpa, chrysanthemum, *Coleus blumei*, cyclamen, carnation, sweet gum, stock, mulberry, orchid, petunia hybrids, mock orange, philodendron pine (many types), plane tree, sycamore, rhododendron (including azaleas), *Senecio cineraria*, violet, pansy, and zinnia.

Companion Planting

VEGETABLE	HELPER	HINDERED BY
Asparagus	tomatoes, parsley, basil	
Beans	carrots, cucumbers, cabbage, beets, corn	onions, glads
Bush Beans	cucumbers, cabbage strawberries	fennel, onions
Beets	onions, cabbage, lettuce	pale beans
Cabbage family	beets, potatoes, onions, celery,	strawberries, tomatoes
Carrots	peas, lettuce, chives, radishes, leeks, onions	dill
Celery	leeks, bush beans	
Chives		beans
Corn	potatoes, beans, peas melons, squash, pumpkins, cucumbers	
Cucumbers	beans, cabbage, radish, sunflowers, lettuce	potatoes, aromatic herbs
Eggplant	beans	
Lettuce	strawberries, carrots	
Melons	Morning Glories	
Onions, Leeks	beets, chamomile, carrots, lettuce	peas, beans
Garlic	summer savory	
Peas	radish, carrots, corn, cucumbers, beans, turnips	onions
Potatoes	beans, corn, peas, cabbage, marijuana, cucumbers	sunflowers
Radishes	peas, lettuce, nasturtium, cucumbers	hyssop
Spinach	strawberries	
Squash, Pumpkins	nasturtium, corn	potatoes
Tomatoes	asparagus, parsley, chives, onions, carrots marigold, nasturtium	dill, cabbage, fennel
Turnips	peas, beans	

HERB	COMPANIONS AND USES
Anise	Coriander
Basil	Tomatoes, dislikes rue, repels flies & mosq.
Borage	Tomatoes and squash

Buttercups	Clover hinders delphiniums, peonies, monkshood, columbines and others of this family
Chamomile	In small amounts it helps peppermint, wheat, onions, cabbage; destructive in large amounts. Makes spray for damping off.
Catnip	Repels flea beetle
Chervil	Radishes
Chives	Carrots. Spray against apple scab, powdery mildew.
Coriander	Hinders seed formation in fennel.
Cosmos	Repels corn earworm
Dill	Cabbage. Hinders carrots & tomatoes
Fennel	Disliked by all garden plants
Garlic	Aids vetch, roses, hinders peas and beans. Deters Japanese beetles. Spray against late blight on tomatoes and potatoes.
Gladiolus	Strongly inhibits peas and beans
Horseradish	Repels potato bugs
Horsetail	Makes fungicide spray
Hyssop	Attracts cabbage fly away from cabbages. Harmful to radishes.
Lovage	Improves hardiness and flavor of neighbors
Marigold	Pest repellent. Use against Mexican bean beetles, nematodes. Makes spray.
Marijuana	Beneficial as neighbor to most plants.
Mint	Repels ants, flea beetles, cabbage worm butterflies.
Morning Glories	Corn. Helps melon germination.
Nasturtium	Cabbage, cucumbers, squash, melons, radish. Deters aphids, squash, bugs, pumpkin beetles.
Nettles	Increases oil content in neighbors.
Parsley	Tomatoes, asparagus.
Purslane	Good ground cover.
Rosemary	Cabbage, beans, carrots. Repels cabbage moth, bean beetles, carrot flies.
Sage	Repels cabbage moth and carrot flies.
Summer savory	Deters bean beetles.
Sunflower	Hinders potatoes. Improves soil.
Tansy	Roses. Deters flying insects; Japanese beetles, striped cucumber beetles, ants, squash bugs.
Thyme	Repels cabbage worm.
Yarrow	Increases essential oils of neighbors.

Keeping The Harvest

by Louise Riotte

The freezer space is limited and you've used up all the canning jars—so what can you do now to preserve summer's bountiful harvest for winter meals? There are a lot of ways that predate either freezing or canning that you can use just as the old-timers did. They will work just as well now as they did in years gone by and help you to keep your foot out of the supermarket door. *Drying* is another method of preservation dating from the beginning of agriculture. It's an easy, practical and space-saving way to prepare and store food for winter use.

Air-Dry—Simple, Takes Little Equipment

This way is particularly good for beans and peas. Plan your strategy in advance when you garden in the spring by choosing the right types. You can let Horticultural, Navy, Pinto, Red Kidney, White Marrowfat, Soy and Mung Beans, as well as Alaska Peas, mature on the plants. Beans should be planted under the signs of Cancer, Scorpio, Pisces, Libra, and Taurus in the second quarter. Peas should be planted under Cancer, Scorpio, Pisces, and Libra, and also harvested in the second quarter. But both beans and peas should be harvested in the third or fourth quarter under the dry signs of Aries, Leo, Sagittarius, Gemini, and Aquarius, if possible. If wet weather threatens near the end of the growing season, pull up the vines with the pods attached and hang them in a warm, airy place. When the pods are completely dry, shell the seeds.

One of my friends once told me how her grandmother did this. "Many is the time I've gone with grandma to the corn fields," she said, "where row after row of cornfield beans intertwined with wild morning glories and wrapped themselves around and around each stalk of tall corn. (We have it from the Indians that wild morning glory is beneficial to corn—but you should remember that if it is allowed to go to seed it can become a great pest, coming up for years afterward).

"We would pick the full pods of beans in basket, bucket, or apron laps. They were picked over several times. When mature pods were turning from yellow to a dry brown these were spread to dry on paper, old cloth, or planks. Then they were poured into a burlap bag to be shelled. Sometimes grandma would say I could stamp on them with my feet, but most of the time she beat on them with a stick. This she called 'frailing.'

"When she thought most of the shells or hulls were broken up she would then dump the entire contents of the bag in her tub (a wooden barrel that had been sawed in half). Then the cleaning process started. At first the tub was shaken and bounced around to make the broken hulls and chaff come to the top. This was taken off, but there were those shiny beans in the bottom with lots of small broken bits of hulls still in them. We picked up the beans by the handful, blowing as we poured them from hand to hand. At last they were free of all the chaff and were put in a nice clean white bag with a few dried herbs to keep out the bugs."

Keeping out the bugs is still important and a few dried herbs still help but I would advise you also to heat your dry shell beans for about 30 minutes in a 140° to 150° oven to prevent insect infestation during storage. Let the seeds cool, then seal them in airtight containers.

You can also dry green snap beans. Remove the ends, strings, and any spots on the beans with a knife. Prepare a stout string with a big darning needle or use white crochet thread using a large-eye needle. Sometimes the beans were strung from one end, but the preferred way most often used was to run the string through the center of the beans. Hang string of beans on clothes line in full sun. Take inside at night. Usually they will dry in two or three days. Then slide dried beans from string onto cookie sheet and place in a previously warmed oven for five minutes. BE SURE oven is turned off. Store in glass jars.

To cook, take beans out, break up in small pieces and wash. Place in a large cooker and cover with water (fill cooker to top). Leave overnight. Pour water off next morning, then add fresh water. Bring to boil, lower heat, season to taste and cook slowly until tender.

Corn—Harvest ears of sweet corn and pop corn when the stalks, leaves, and husks are thoroughly dry. Hang the ears by the husks or spread out the ears in baskets in an airy place. Shell when the kernels will come off with a moderately aggressive twisting motion of both hands. Popcorn will usually shell off by rubbing two ears together. Store the kernels in sealed containers.

Here is another way the pioneer housewife used to dry corn. Cut sweet corn from the cob and spread in pans lined with absorbent paper. Cover pan with clean cloth and set in full sun. Stir often, take in at night. It will dry in two days. Pour corn into clean white cloth sack. Hang up for three days in warm place. Store in glass jars with tight lids. To serve, soak overnight in water. The corn will take up water best if soaked in one of the moist signs—Cancer, Scorpio or Pisces. Add one teaspoon salt and simmer one hour. Add butter or cream. One cup (dried) serves six.

Peanuts—Before frost in the fall, dig entire peanut plants (under a dry sign) with the peanuts attached to the roots. Hang the plants in a dry, airy place. Remove the pods when they are well-dried and roast at 350° for about 20 minutes. Store the peanuts in the pods in a cool, dry place, or shell them and keep in sealed containers. Peanut hay is relished by livestock or may be placed on the compost heap.

Hot Peppers—Pick hot peppers when they are mature and red. String them and hang them in a dry, warm, airy place or pull entire plants and hang them. Be careful not to get juice on your skin or in your eyes. Wearing gloves is a good idea for the juice can burn. Store completely dry peppers on their strings in a handy warm, airy place. Or seal them in small, airtight containers. A little hot pepper goes a long way. Years ago when I traveled extensively in Colorado and New Mexico, it was interesting to see great strings of large hot peppers strung up around the houses, on the porches, festooned from the rafters and even worked into designs, drying in the hot Southwestern sun.

Onions—Do not cut tops off. Tie **tightly** in large bundles. Hang up from rafters in garage where they will be out of the sun but where air can circulate around and cure them. Then, when you need an onion, all you will have to do is pick the size needed and pull it off. Onion separates easily from tops and others stay in place until needed.

Carrots, Parsnips and Salsify—Can be left in the row. Pull a ridge of dirt up and cover with dead grass. Place a marker at end of each digging.

Sweet Potatoes—Wrap each sound sweet potato in paper, place in a large box or barrel, and store in a room away from heat (garage or tool shed is ideal).

Vegetable Keg—Place a layer of straw in the bottom of a nail keg and then lay the keg on its side. Add another layer of straw, and fill about one-half full of white potatoes, layer of straw; then add a layer of carrots, more straw. Add a layer of beets, more straw, and fill remainder with head lettuce or your favorite vegetable *except any of the cabbage family*! Add straw around last item and on top of barrel after it's set upright. Set keg in deep trench and cover with dirt. When you take it into the kitchen, laundry or utility room, cover with a round plastic tablecloth and you will have a nice little stand for a flower pot. This one might be called the "Keg-of-the-month" plan, if you have enough to prepare several. This gives variety in each keg and saves opening and closing three or four large storage pits.

Here is another way to "put summer in a keg":

Apples and Pears—If you are not certain how to pick and store such fruits as apples and pears, here are a few pointers. Be sure to pick under one of the dry signs previously given. The more mature the fruit is, the less likely it will keep for a long period of time. Pick the fruit when it is slightly imma-ture. In my opinion, pears such as Kieffer are not good until they have ripened for a time in storage, when they will be mellow and sweet. The time honored test for determining *maturity* in an apple is to lift the fruit gently upward and see if it parts from the tree. But you must also be careful not to pick the fruit when it is too immature for it may shrivel or develop disorders and fail to ripen perfectly. Experience is the best teacher in deciding when to pick fruit.

Especially important is the care you take in actually picking fruit. Bruises, no matter how slight, will eventually cause decay after only a short time in storage. Grasp the fruit in the palm of your hand, not with the fingers, and be careful that fingernails do not puncture fruit skins. *Place* the fruit in the gathering receptacle; do not throw or drop fruit in receptacle. Look over fruit carefully from all sides, wrap only that which is most perfect in thin tissue paper. As you place fruit in keg or box, pack it with dried nettle hay. Fruit packed in nettle hay is hastened in its ripening. At the same time this weed deters fermentation, keeps fruit free from mold, and bestows upon it good keeping qualities.

Cabbage—To store cabbage for winter use, dig a trench about one foot wide and one foot deep. Line bottom and sides with dead grass, straw, or hay. Place cabbage heads in topside up. Cover with grass or straw, then pile the dirt back on top, building up a ridge. Cabbage will improve in flavor and texture until early spring.

How many today ever ate dried pumpkin butter? This was made from pumpkin with skins cut off, the pumpkin cut in round slices, and hung from a pole to dry, most times behind the old wood-burning kitchen range. The slices, when used, were cooked down low in the old-fashioned blackstrap molasses or maple syrup and offered as a dessert.

Here are some other uncommon ways of preserving foods: dried ripe tomatoes, cooked and dried like pumpkins, golden dried applies in the Sun and carefully preserved for winter pies. Mustard greens and turnip greens were preserved in a large earthen-ware crock. A layer of greens, a layer of salt, another layer of greens, another layer of salt, until the crock was full. It was then covered with water. A dinner plate or a piece of wood cut to size for this purpose was laid on top and weighted down with a clean stone. The crock was covered with a clean, heavy cloth and tied securely to keep out dust, dirt, and the hateful sour gnats.

Potatoes—Never dig potatoes for storage while the tops are green; they won't keep well. Best time to harvest late potatoes is several weeks after a killing frost (but never allow tubers to freeze in the ground). To determine best storage potatoes, rub skins. If a skin rubs off easily, that potato is still green and should be set aside for kitchen use. Choose a dry sign in the third or fourth quarter for digging.

The day you dig potatoes for storage should be above 45° and the soil should not be wet. Keep them protected from the sun and wind and handle carefully to avoid bruising. Brush off dirt. Place outside in the shade to dry off and set skins. Cure potatoes 10-14 days at 80-85° to decrease losses in storage. Place in a slatted crate or basket; store in a dark, humid place. Some people believe that a light sprinkling with lime will deter sprouting. Cover with bags or newspapers to keep out light. At about 50° potatoes will remain in good condition several months. For longer storage, hold at 50° for two weeks after digging, then store at 34-41° to prevent sprouting. If sprouting occurs in early spring, sprinkle lightly with table salt. Never store potatoes with apples.

Pumpkins—Slip a board underneath ripening pumpkins to keep them from turning white or rotting where they touch the ground. Once orange skin color darkens, the skin becomes tough and vines dry up, they're ready, but must be protected from hard frosts if left in the garden. Pumpkin leaves usually give ample protection during light frosts, but a couple of handfuls of straw are a good safeguard. When harvesting for storage, *cut* (don't pull) pumpkins from the vines and leave a 3-4 inch stem or they won't store well. Handle fruit very carefully to avoid bruises or scratches. Don't wash fruits before storing.

Squash (winter)—Pick only mature, ripe squash. Acorn squash should have a dark green color, be hard, and have an orange or yellow spot where it touches the ground. Butternut squash will have a hard skin and will be a buff or tan color when mature. Buttercup squash will have a very hard rind and be a dark green color with a few small yellow or orange striations in the "cap" when mature. Leave on vine until stem shrivels. Pick after vines have dried but before frosts. The skins should be hard enough to resist the pressure of your thumbnail. Leave about a 4 inch stem on each fruit (under no circumstances should the fruit be stored without a stem). It is well to place both squash and pumpkins on storage shelves in such manner that the fruits do not touch each other. Undamaged fruits will keep for months and perhaps even to spring.

Here are a few general hints to remember when harvesting crops for storage: Vegetables to be stored should be left in the ground as long as possible without danger of freezing.

Only sound, top-quality produce should be stored. Because of the fast spread of decay organisms, any injured vegetables should be set aside and used first. Handle crops reserved for storage carefully to avoid bruising or the slightest scratch or scrape. Squash and pumpkins, for example, should be handled "like eggs." Mature, hard-ripe vegetables store the longest. Green garden crops should not be stored. Right size and maturity for storage comes mostly from summer sowing. Large beets, carrots, etc., sown in the spring are too large and woody for top quality storage; these should be used in mid-summer for table use and canning.

Root Crops—Digging fork is best to avoid injury to roots. Always cut off tops of root crops—but not closer than ½ inch to crown—as soon as removed from soil. Considerable moisture is lost from roots through leaves if leaves are left on and this causes shriveling of the roots.

Vegetables for storage should not be washed. Use a soft brush to remove any soil. All should be stored with a dry surface (celery and similar crops should have moisture around the roots, *but the foliage must be dry to avoid rot*).

Shriveling in vegetables needing moist conditions (beets, carrots, parsnips) can be prevented by sprinkling walls and floors with water as needed during the winter. Pans of water also may be set out in storage area. Wooden apple boxes, if used indoors for storage, should be stacked with furring strips between units and the floor to permit full air circulation. Orange crates, mesh bags and discarded nylon hoses are excellent for onion storage. Fruits should never be stored with potatoes, turnips, or cabbage. Gases released from apples in respiration can sprout potatoes; cabbage and turnips transmit their odors to pears and apples.

Herbs—Again, be sure to harvest in a dry sign and cut your herbs on a bright day before they bloom. Lavender, Oregano, Sage, Sweet Basil, Sweet Marjoram, Summer Savory and Thyme all dry well. Tie in bunches, label and hang in a dry, airy, dustless place. When leaves are dry enough to crumble, strip leaves from the branches and place in dry jars with tight fitting lids. Cover and label jars. Watch for a few days and if any moisture appears on the glass, remove leaves and dry longer.

I dry my herbs in brown paper bags (not plastic). This keeps off dust, catches loose particles, and permits herbs to "breathe." Herbs which are grown for seed should be harvested just before the seed starts to drop—and in a dry sign. Gather the seed pods and spread on paper or cloth to dry. Thresh out the seed and remove all rubbish. Spread clean seeds in a thin layer to cure thoroughly. Store in glass jars with tight fitting lids. Anise, dill, and fennel are raised for seed.

If you wish to dig root crops for seed it should be done during the time of the Full Moon. They will keep longer and are drier. Never dig potatoes when the Moon is in a water sign or they will become soggy and sprout.

Great grandmother had no appliances for drying, but with care and patience she was able to achieve a good product by using the drying qualities of the Sun. The Sun is still available. Slices of tomatoes and various fruits, placed in single layers and covered with screening or cheesecloth, will still dry in time. But I see no reason why we should not avail ourselves of modern appliances, and many are gaining popularity to aid gardeners in drying foods. Some are heated with electricity to a low temperature that dries food quickly and evenly. Others are systems of trays that are placed in a warm oven. Microwaving is the newest way.

Many foods can be dried besides the familiar staples like grapes (raisins), plums (prunes), apricots, and sliced apples and bananas. These fruits and others including peaches and pears develop a concentrated, sugary sweetness which makes them delicious as healthy snacks and party foods. Dried fruits are also nice for dessert compotes and other cooked dishes in winter. Vegetables, too, retain much of their flavor in drying. When reconstituted by soaking in water, they are handy to fortify soups, stews and casseroles.

Beans, of course, are perfect candidates for drying—not just limas and soybeans, but also less familiar ones like horticultural beans, pinto beans and kidney beans, as well as chickpeas and blackeye, crowder or field peas. If you have so many green snap beans you can't keep up with them, let some pods mature on the vines, shell them and use them like other dried beans.

You'll be eating well come winter, and saving some money on food bills, if you preserve parts of your garden bonanza this summer and fall. All that extra bounty you put away will make tasty dishes that are lickin' good when the wind blows cold!

Growing Small Fruits
by Louise Riotte

I've often wondered why more people don't grow small fruits in their home gardens. They take little room and offer so many advantages, not the least of which is the pure pleasure of picking. Picking is, in itself, fun. You can pick one or two big red apples and enjoy eating them but it's lots more fun to pick several dozen strawberries or raspberries, choosing one each time that is just to your liking—ripe, juicy and unblemished. It's a form of outdoor recreation.

All of the major small fruits—strawberries, raspberries, blackberries, blueberries, currants, gooseberries, and grapes—may be grown successfully depending on where you live. There is also a new one called the Tayberry, and in the Southern states you may want to grow boysenberries, dewberries, dewblacks, and other variations. You may not be able to grow currants and gooseberries in certain states or certain sections as they are alternate host plants for blister rust, which is a serious disease of white pines. For this reason they are prohibited in areas where white pines are planted, such as federal, state, and county forests, parks, nurseries or other native or planted white pine areas. But if you are permitted to grow them, currants and gooseberries are a truly delightful addition to the home garden. Currants are under the rulership of Jupiter and gooseberries under Venus. Berries, in general, should be planted in the second quarter under Cancer, Scorpio or Pisces.

A well-planned garden will supply fresh fruit from early spring to the first killing frost in the fall. The fruits produced in the garden will be appreciated for their pleasing taste and for their dietary value as sources of vitamins, minerals and acids. Fruit of the best varieties harvested at peak quality from a home garden cannot be matched in the market, and surplus production can be canned, frozen, or preserved for use during the rest of the year. Just think how good those berry pies and cobblers will taste when the cold winds blow!

Aside from the benefits of superior quality, cultivating small fruits at home can provide much pleasure. Careful selection of early and late varieties of different kinds of small fruits will supply fresh fruit over the longest possible season. Success, of course, depends upon careful attention to cultural details.

First of all you should consider your own taste. Grow the kinds of fruit that your family likes. A few plants, well cared for, will produce more than a large, neglected planting. On the average you can expect to harvest sufficient fruit for one person from a combination of any two of the following: fifty strawberry plants, twelve blackberry, six boysenberry or four grape vines. To figure the number of plants needed for your family, select two kinds of fruit and multiply the number suggested by the number of persons in your family.

When To Plant

Fall planting in the Southern states is preferable for strawberries, grapes and one-year-old blackberry or dewberry plants. Tip-rooted plants such as black raspberries should be planted in the spring. In northerly areas any of the small fruits may be spring planted.

Soil Preparation

Prepare land to be set to small fruits in early fall. Plow it deep, turning under an application of barnyard manure if possible. Work the soil into a firm seedbed by disking and harrowing before planting. Cultivating is best done in the fourth quarter under Virgo, Leo or Gemini. This is the best time to kill weeds and destroy insect pests in the soil. You may also plow in Aries, Aquarius and Sagittarius. If your home garden is not large enough to include the fruit planting, enlarge it during the winter. And it is always advisable to protect small fruit plants with a good fence.

If well-rotted manure is available, apply 4 bushels per 100 square feet in the summer or fall before planting. Thoroughly work the manure into the soil. Compost, decomposed leaves, or lawn clippings may also be used. Weeds can be reduced by planting small fruits where row crops have been cultivated for one or two years. The cultivation and hoeing destroy many weeds and help provide good soil conditions by thoroughly mixing organic matter in the soil.

Planting Stock

Healthy, vigorous plants are essential to establish a successful small-fruit planting. It is generally wiser and cheaper, in the long run, to buy the best plants available. Reputable nurseries supply disease-free and true-to-name plants. Gift plants may or may not be healthy and disease-free. You should obtain catalogs from several nurseries. Place your order early to obtain the varieties you want; December or January is not too early to order plants for the following spring. The delivery date and method of shipment should be specified when placing the order.

One-year-old plants of medium to large size are generally best. The added cost of older or extra large plants is usually not justified, the exception being blueberry plants, which should be two years old.

Choosing Varieties

Varieties for home small-fruit plantings should be selected for high quality—either for eating fresh, preserving or freezing. Many varieties of high-quality small fruits are not suited to commercial production, so the only source of these quality fruits may be your own garden. Winter hardiness and resistance to diseases and viruses should be considered. Careful selection of early and late maturing varieties will provide a harvest of fresh fruit during a longer period. Read the descriptions given in the catalogs carefully. The use of several varieties of your favorite small fruit may also help to ensure a successful planting as one variety may perform highly satisfactorily in one location but not in another.

Care of Plants on Arrival

Most plants are dug by nurseries in late fall or early spring when they are dormant and then shipped from cold storage as orders are received. Such plants, when handled properly, are usually superior to freshly dug varieties.

Open the packages and examine the plants as soon as they arrive. Do not let the plants dry out. If the plants are dry when they arrive, soak the roots in water for one or two hours and plant immediately, if possible. If planting must be delayed more than one day, the plants may be placed in cold storage or "heeled-in."

For cold storage, moisten the roots if they are dry, but be careful not to overwet the plants or they may mold and rot. Plants in plastic bags may be kept satisfactorily for a week in your home refrigerator. Do not allow plants to freeze.

To "heel-in" plants, select a location that is well-drained, shaded and protected from the wind. Dig a trench deep enough to permit covering the roots and long enough to spread the plants side by side one layer deep. Water thoroughly and keep shaded until ready to plant. Do not leave plants heeled-in any longer than absolutely necessary.

Irrigation

Lack of rain while new plants are becoming established— during bloom and harvest and during late summer and fall when fruit buds are forming—can reduce the quantity and quality of fruit. Irrigate when the Moon is in a watery sign— Cancer, Scorpio, or Pisces. You may also use Libra. Most small fruits require at least one inch of water per week during the growing season for optimum growth. Irrigation to supplement rainfall is especially important for soils with a shallow hardpan, which restricts development of a deep root system.

If possible, locate the small-fruit garden where adequate water is available for irrigation. Sprinklers, porous soaking hoses, and perforated hoses are suitable for applying water. Irrigate to thoroughly wet the soil that is occupied by the roots. Shallow watering is of little value and may even be harmful.

Pruning Tools

Correct pruning and training are necessary for top production of brambles, blueberries, currants, gooseberries, and grapes. The tools needed are neither expensive nor complex. Hand shears are useful for cutting back small branches and lateral shoots, and for summer topping. The bramble hook is a specialized tool for removing entire canes of the brambles. Lopping or long-handled shears are needed for larger branches and canes that cannot be cut with the hand shears. A pruning saw may be needed for grapes.

Pruning tools in good cutting condition are necessary for good pruning. Tools should be cleaned after use and their cutting surfaces wiped with an oily cloth to retard rust. The cutting edges must be kept sharp so as to make smooth, rapid-healing cuts.

Pruning checks limb growth, prevents too much spreading of the branches and produces better fruit. Trim during the decrease of the Moon while it is in a fruitful sign. The third quarter and the sign of Scorpio are an ideal combination.

The Home Landscape

If space is at a premium you need not necessarily set aside land for growing small fruits. Individual or groups of small fruit plants can be included in the landscape to provide fresh fruit when space is not available for a defined garden. Strawberries, particularly ever-bearing varieties, can be useful for ground-cover plantings. Grape arbors or hedge plantings of erect blackberries, raspberries, or blueberries can be used effectively to partially screen or separate parts of the lawn or garden. Blueberries, especially, have attractive foliage coloring in the fall and therefore are useful as ornamental plants. A little imagination and careful planning can result in an eye-pleasing as well as appetizing planting.

In my book *The Complete Guide to Growing Berries and Grapes* details are given for making a "strawberry barrel." If it is placed so it can be turned to get Sun on all sides, you can get very good production from ever-bearers.

Strawberries

Strawberries are the most popular of the small fruits. They are the first fruit to ripen in the spring and are highly nutritious. A single portion of fresh strawberries supplies more than the minimum daily requirement of vitamin C. Satisfactory crops may usually be produced in the home garden with minimum care. Strawberries are under the rulership of Jupiter, Venus and Libra and should be planted in the third quarter in Cancer, Scorpio or Pisces.

Strawberries will grow satisfactorily in most garden soils but they require a relatively high level of soil fertility for optimum production. Fertilize with well-rotted manure or compost if possible but be careful, for too much will cause excessive vegetative growth, reducing yields, increasing losses from fruit and foliar diseases, and resulting in winter injury. Application of fertilizer during the spring of the fruiting year is not recommended.

Remove Blossoms

The flower stems should be removed from newly set plants during the first summer as soon as they appear. Allowing the fruit to develop during the first season will reduce the crop the next year. Flowers that develop after about July 1st on ever-bearing varieties should be left for a late summer or fall crop.

Weeds

Cultivation and hand-hoeing should begin soon after the plants are set. This will control weeds and help runners take root. Repeated cultivation every 10 to 14 days is most effective since weeds are easiest to kill when they are small. Cultivation should be shallow around the plants to prevent injury to the roots. Cultivate in the fourth quarter in Virgo, Leo or Gemini.

Mulching

Strawberries should be mulched to protect the plants during extremely cold winter weather and against damage from heaving during alternate freezing and thawing weather. Mulching also conserves soil moisture, keeps the berries clean, and provides better picking conditions. Use a loose organic material such as clean, seed-free wheat straw. As mentioned in my book on companion planting, *Carrots Love Tomatoes* (Storey Communications), pine needles alone or mixed with the wheat straw make an extra fine mulch, and it is said to give the berries a distinctive flavor more like the wild variety. Spruce needles may also be used as a mulch, and in some areas chopped alfalfa hay is very good, if available. A spruce hedge is also protective. Strawberries do well with such companions as bush beans, spinach and borage. Lettuce is good used as a border and pyrethrum (the "bug-killing daisy"), planted alongside, serves well as a pest preventative.

Brambles

Raspberries ripen shortly after strawberries and are a very popular fruit. Plantings that are well cared for may produce good crops for ten years or more. Red, black, purple, and yellow fruit types are available.

Because of virus diseases, black and purple raspberries should be planted about 600 feet from red varieties. Raspberries are ruled by Venus.

Blackberries

Blackberries, also ruled by Venus, are well suited to the home garden. Both erect and trailing types are available and each requires a different culture. The trailing varieties require support and are not very winter-hardy. Plant breeders are developing hardy thornless blackberry varieties which should increase interest in this luscious fruit. A blackberry cobbler is a never-to-be-forgotten taste thrill.

Blackberries are best planted in early spring, using the same care as for planting raspberries. Most erect blackberries can be grown without supports, spaced 4 to 5 feet apart in rows 8 to 10 feet apart. Set the plants at the same depth as they were planted in the nursery. Cut the tops back to 6 inches.

Most trailing varieties are best grown in Southern areas but may be grown farther north with special protection, such as covering lightly with soil or straw after they become dormant in the fall. When danger of severe cold weather is past in the spring, uncover the canes, do the dormant pruning, and tie the canes to a support.

Blueberries

Blueberries are delicious when eaten fresh, tasty in pies, and easily frozen. But they have very exacting soil and cultural requirements, requiring an acid soil relatively high in organic matter. A soil pH of 4.2 to 5.2 is best for optimum growth. The addition of soil-peat is helpful. If you are determined to grow blueberries, try providing the soil they like and grow them in 50-gallon drums with drainage holes cut in the bottom.

First, burn out any residue that might be injurious. Bury the drum in a sunny area and leave 1 to 2 inches of the rim above ground level. Fill the tub with an acid soil that is high in organic matter; make a mixture with acid peat moss if necessary. Set one blueberry plant in each tub.

Blueberries are shallow-rooted and grow best where the water table is 14 to 22 inches below the soil surface. Don't attempt to grow blueberries unless you can supply needed water when the rainfall is not adequate. In addition, the soil must freely drain as blueberry plants cannot tolerate standing water. The blueberry is ruled by Jupiter and Venus.

Currants and Gooseberries

These plants are very easy to grow and require much the same culture. Currants are ruled by Jupiter and gooseberries by Venus. As previously mentioned, they should not be grown where white pines are planted. They grow best in cool, moist and partially shaded locations. The north or east side of a building, fence, or arbor may best provide these conditions.

Plants can be set in either fall or spring. Spring planting must be done early, before buds begin growth. Vigorous, well-rooted, one-year-old plants are best. Prune off damaged roots and cut the top back to 10 inches. Set the plants with the lower branches a little below the soil to encourage a bush form to develop. Space the plants 4 to 6 feet apart in rows 6 to 8 feet apart.

Currants and gooseberries are heavy feeders but have rather shallow root systems. An annual application of barn manure is probably the best source of fertilizer. Strawy manure may be applied each fall (November or later) and maintained 4 to 6 inches deep to provide soil mulch. Sawdust, corncobs, straw, lawn clippings, or similar materials may also be used.

Grapes

Grapes are so beautiful and so tasty that they have always been a popular fruit for home gardens. Some grape varieties ripen from early August until mid-October, thereby providing a long season of fresh fruit. Grapes also offer a wide range of flavors, can be used for making juice, wine, and jelly, and the trellises and arbors on which they grow make attractive shaded areas which can be useful in landscape planning for screening undesirable areas.

Cultivation of grapes makes a whole chapter in itself, too lengthy to go into here. For detailed directions I suggest you obtain a copy of *Small Fruits for the Home Garden*, Circular 432, from the Department of Agriculture. Or, check with your library to see if it has a copy of my book *The Complete Guide to Growing Berries and Grapes* (Garden Way Publishing).

Grapes should be planted in early spring as soon as the soil can be prepared. Cut off long or broken roots so that they can be spread evenly in the planting hole. Set the plant slightly deeper than it grew in the nursery, arranging the roots so that they are not bunched together.

Grapes are ruled by Venus and the Sun—and it is interesting to know that grapes ripen because of the *Sun on their leaves*, rather than upon the grapes themselves, which are often hidden by the foliage.

As for grape varieties, the *Buffalo* has excellent dessert quality and this beautiful blue grape is also great for juice and jelly. The *Concord* is both hardy and reliable and there is now a *Concord seedless*, especially good for pies. The golden *Ontario* is vigorous and productive. The small pink *Delaware* is another grape with excellent dessert qualities. These are only suggestions and by no means exhaust the list. Look through several nursery catalogs and decide for yourself which varieties are best suited to your individual needs.

Other Berries

The *Tayberry* is a new fruit that was developed in Scotland. It is a hybrid cross between a blackberry and a raspberry. The berries, when ripe, are large and flavorful and are excellent for pies, jams or jellies. The fruits are about 50 percent larger than regular raspberries. And Tayberries do well in the Northern states.

Many nurseries now carry the Tayberry and if you live in Canada you can obtain it from McFayden Seed Co., Ltd.

The *Saskatoon* is a blueberry type, hardy in the far North. This upright shrub reaches 4 to 6 feet in height, producing a fluffy mass of showy, white flowers in early to mid-May, making it also desirable for landscaping. The berries are reddish-purple to nearly black. Though it looks like it, it is not a true blueberry. It is also known as the *shadblow* or *serviceberry*.

A wonderful new type of hardy raspberry, the *Bababerry* has been developed by Mrs. Gertrude Milliken, and they are presently being grown by the L. E. Cooke Wholesale Nursery.

The boysenberry, the dewberry and the loganberry are varieties popular and easily grown in the Southern states. They are good fresh, frozen or made into juice, wine, jellies and jams.

Elderberries are popular for homemade wine and the shrubs have white blossoms in June and loads of purple fruit in late summer. You must plant at least two for cross-pollination.

Berries, in general, are ruled by Jupiter and should be planted in the second quarter under the signs of Cancer, Scorpio or Pisces. Fertilizing is best done in the third or fourth quarter, also in Cancer, Scorpio or Pisces. Cultivate in the fourth quarter in Virgo, Leo, Gemini. To increase growth prune in Cancer, Scorpio or Pisces. Harvest for best keeping qualities in the third or fourth quarter in Aries, Leo, Sagittarius, Gemini, or Aquarius.

Berries are so delicious and versatile that they should be better known and more widely planted. You might even want to consider Uva Ursa, sometimes known as Upland cranberry or bearberry, whose leaves are medicinally useful in treating diabetes, Bright's disease, and all kidney disorders.

Many berries and their leaves have been used for centuries for medicinal purposes. In her book *Herbal Handbook for Farm and Stable*, Juliette de Bairacli writes concerning raspberry (*Rubus idaeus, Rosaceae*): "The plant is a very important one in medicine, mainly on account of its influence on the female organs of reproduction. The foliage of the raspberry shrub possesses a very active principle called *fragrine*, which exerts a powerful influence on the muscles of the pelvic girdle, especially when administered during parturition. The foliage is highly tonic and cleansing, improving the condition of the organism during pregnancy, ensuring speedy and strong expulsion of the foetus at birth. Raspberry herb becomes especially potent for female use when blended with feverfew plant. Use three parts of raspberry to one of feverfew when making tea."

The blackberry is useful for treating all gastric weaknesses, failing appetite, diarrhea, impoverished nerves and skin disorders, and externally for cure of all types of eczema. The Gypsies say that fresh-plucked leaves warmed over a fire will heal most diseased places. The white underside draws when applied to the skin; the green upperside soothes. The pulped leaves are applied to burns and foot blisters.

The black currant—sometimes called "Quinsey berry"—is useful in the treatment of all fevers, mouth and throat ailments, bladder ailments, dysentery, and pregnancy weaknesses. It is anti-abortive.

The red currant is similar in type and properties but is more laxative and more cooling than the black species. It does not possess the anti-abortive qualities of the black but is useful in treating blood disorders, constipation and jaundice. The dose is one cupful of berries twice daily.

Grapes are a good blood and body builder, the juice being easily assimilated and a source of quick energy. They are indicated in treating cases of anemia, cancer, tuberculosis, constipation, emaciation, low blood pressure, poor circulation, poor appetite, rheumatism, acidosis, jaundice, pimples and skin diseases, diarrhea, gallstones, liver disorders, gout, arthritis and nerve exhaustion. They contain vitamins B1, C and A. Fresh grape juice is truly a "nectar for the gods."

Cranberries may be crushed and made into a poultice in cases of erysipelas, carbuncles and boils.

Blueberries are a good blood purifier. Use them for anemia, constipation, poor complexion, dysentery, diarrhea, obesity and menstrual disorders.

Dewberries have medicinal value similar to blackberries.

Elderberries, long a source of medicinal wine, are also useful for bronchitis, sore throat, coughs, asthma, colds, catarrh and constipation. They also induce perspiration.

Gooseberries are useful for dyspepsia, constipation, sluggish liver, congested gall bladder, bad blood, poor complexion, obesity, arthritis and nephritis.

Huckleberries are indicated in cases of high blood pressure, obesity and diarrhea. Crushed berries make a good poultice for sores and wounds.

Strawberries are one of the best skin-cleansing foods known. If they cause one to break out with a rash, he should eat more of them than ever for they will give the skin a good cleansing and they are not likely to cause skin eruptions after the toxins have been driven from the skin. They contain vitamins C, B_2, A and B_1.

Strawberries have even found their way into "magic." In his book *Cunningham's Encyclopedia of Magical Herbs* (Llewellyn Publications), Scott Cunningham tells us: "Strawberries are served as a love food and the leaves are carried for luck. Pregnant women may wish to carry a small packet of strawberry leaves to ease their pregnancy pains." Uva Ursa, or bearberry, may be added to sachets to increase psychic powers. You may place blueberries beneath the doormat to keep undesirables from your property or entering your home. This protects from evil as well.

"Make blueberry pies or tarts and eat when under psychic attack; this gets the protection inside you and increases the herb's effectiveness.

"The elder was used in burial rites in ancient British long barrows. It is sacred to many Mother Goddess figures, due to its white flowers. Witches and spirits were thought to live within the elder; this was why it "bled" red sap when cut. Before felling an elder the following formula was recited:

> Lady Ellhorn, give me of thy wood,
> And I will give thee of mine,
> When I become a tree.

"This is recited kneeling before the tree, prior to making the first cut, and allows the spirit within the tree time to vacate."

Elder is very magical, warding off attackers of all kinds. Grown in the garden it protects the household and shields it from lightning. "To bless a person, place, or thing, scatter the leaves and berries of the elder to the four winds in the name of the person or object to be blessed."

Huckleberries placed and carried in sachets are luck-inducing. "To make all your dreams come true, burn the leaves in your bedroom directly before going to sleep.

"Pictures of grapes can be painted onto garden walls to ensure fertility, as was done in ancient Rome. Eating grapes or raisins increases fertility, as well as strengthens mental powers."

Whether you "believe" or not, *Cunningham's Encyclopedia of Magical Herbs* is a terrific book, the "magic" of its contents endlessly fascinating!

Grow some "small fruits" and have yourself a ball!

Miniature Veggies
By Moon Sign

by Louise Riotte

Is your yard small, or do you have just a small area in the sun for a vegetable garden? Or maybe you live in a penthouse and garden on a rooftop or in window boxes or pots on the patio. Or perhaps you live in a trailer-house and garden in hanging baskets.

If so, good news! Space-saving vegetables take little room and give big returns of tasty produce, and some of the leafy vegetables can even be grown in partial shade or filtered sunshine.

For several years now the trend has been toward more people living in cities and adjacent suburbs. Yards and space for gardens is getting smaller, yet almost everyone is a farmer at heart. So how can people reap big harvests from their mini-gardens? As with everything else worthwhile it usually takes a little planning. But even the planning can be fun.

"To meet this future need," says Ted Torrey, vegetable research manager for the W. Atlee Burpee Company, Burpee started a program to develop and introduce space-saving vegetables. And, under the direction of Glenn Goldsmith of Gilroy, California, who has developed many outstanding vegetable varieties, Park Seed Company is also offering a number of fascinating mini-vegetables which are also suitable for container growing.

TOMATOES (plant 2nd quarter under Cancer, Scorpio, Pisces), along with corn, are considered to be America's favorite vegetable. And you apartment dwellers can have fresh, bright-red, vine ripened tomatoes, too. *Pixie Hybrid Tomato*, introduced in 1971, is the answer. This tomato pioneered the way in Burpee's space-saving vegetables. It was an immediate success and continues to be very popular today. Pixie is so versatile anyone can grow and enjoy it.

Pixie tomatoes do not take much room. Space the plants one to one-and-a-half feet apart each way in your garden. Insert a short stake near each plant to give support as the fruit clusters develop. *Pixie* tomatoes are ping-pong ball size and ripen very early, in just 52 days from the time you set out transplants. You'll smack your lips at *Pixie's* "big tomato" flavor—and oh! how pretty they look in salads—long before large-fruited tomatoes are ready to pick. After *Pixie's* first crop is finished, water and fertilize the plants (preferably 3rd or 4th quarter and under Cancer, Scorpio or Pisces). They usually will flower again and produce more tomatoes.

If you have no space for gardening, *Pixie* is "at home" in containers—both outdoors on a sunny patio (or rooftop) or inside on sunny windowsills or under plant lights. Grow one plant in each pot at least 8 inches deep and across or several in a longer box. It's great fun to grow *Pixie* as a winter "houseplant" and to pick tomatoes out-of-season, fresh for salads.

New for 1982, *Basket King Hybrid Tomato* is both productive and decorative. This space-saver was developed especially for hanging baskets, window boxes and other containers. Numerous sturdy branches cascade over the sides of the container, bearing clusters of tasty, thin-skinned, red tomatoes about 1¾ inches across. Like *Pixie*, *Basket King* tomato also produces fast and supplies welcome fruit for early summer salads. A few containers of Basket King look pretty as a picture on your patio or terrace and are so handy for picking. A basket 8 or 9 inches across is sufficient for one *Basket King* tomato plant.

Tomato City Best VFN hybrid, a Park exclusive, is also a great container plant. This determinate or bush-type tomato bears an abundance of very tasty medium-sized red fruit. The plants have lush foliage, also very decorative, with self-supporting branches.

CUCUMBERS (1st quarter, Cancer, Scorpio, Pisces). Cucumbers fresh from your garden, chilled and sliced in salads or for the relish tray, are always a refreshing taste treat (and they are the dieter's "best friend"). Most varieties of cucumbers, however, have rampant vines that take up too much room to be practical in a small garden. You can solve the problem by growing bush-type cucumbers that save space.

Through cooperation with Dr. Henry Munger of Cornell University, Burpee introduced *Spacemaster* cucumber in 1978, and *Bush Champion* two years later. Both of these cucumbers skyrocketed to best sellers because they bear big crops of crisp slicers in minimal space. Plants grow well one foot apart in rows three feet apart. Even in a big garden bush cucumbers are neat and handy to grow. There's no tangle of vines to trip over as you tend the plants and pick the cucumbers.

Park Seed Company has introduced *Cucumber Bush Whopper* with really big cukes 6 to 8 inches long, on dwarf, mound shaped plants. The short vines have no runners at all. The cucumbers are thick and deliciously crisp. Bearing profusely in any climate this cucumber is ideal for container growing.

MELONS (2nd quarter, Cancer, Scorpio, Pisces). What could taste better on a hot summer day than a wedge of watermelon, picked ripe and sweet from your garden? No longer need you say, "I don't have room!" Burpee's *Sugar Bush* is popular with gardeners everywhere because you can grow it in just 6 square feet of garden space. Plant 4 to 6 seeds 2 to 3 inches apart in groups 3 feet apart each way. Later thin each group to 2 to 3 plants. Each *Sugar Bush* bears 2 to 4 oval "icebox"-type melons weighing 6 to 8 pounds each.

Park Seed Company's watermelon *Bushbaby* hybrid is another delight for the home gardener. The dwarf determinate plants produce generously round-oval 8-pound fruit of the highest table quality with light green striped skin and rich pink flesh. Plants are very prolific and ripen fruit in just 80 days.

SQUASH (2nd quarter, Cancer, Scorpio, Pisces, Libra). If you are wondering "why Libra?" it is because of the beautiful squash blossoms. And I would like to mention here that I have just started receiving calls from readers of my gardening column in *The Daily Ardmorite* (Ardmore, OK 73401) asking me why their squash, which is flowering abundantly, is not bearing. Squash plants bear both male and female blossoms (as do cucumbers), but the male blossoms come first and many drop off. Don't get upset. The female blossom will come along presently, the girls will marry the boys, and then set fruit. You can tell a lady squash blossom by the little "knob" which develops back of the blossom. This is a tiny squash fruit "in the making," so just be a little patient and you will have lots of squash babies.

Is butternut squash one of your favorites to bake, mash, or use in pies, puddings and cookies? Why not grow your own supply to have on hand this fall and winter? You can, even if your garden is small, but save a sunny space for it. Burpee's *Butterbush,* introduced in 1978, is the first bush-type butternut squash. It's ideal for small gardens because its compact plants take only one-quarter the space of the usual vining type.

Allow one or two plants every 3 feet in rows 3 feet apart. Each plant bears 4 or 5 butternut-shaped fruits that are just the right size to cut in half and bake for two servings. The deep reddish-orange flesh is extra delicious and attractive. I like to scoop out the seeds and fill the cavity with brown sugar, butter, and a sprinkling of cinnamon and ginger. Butterbush stores well and is a taste-tempter for winter meals.

Do you want a yellow summer squash? Try Park's *Creamy Hybrid.* This high performer produces squash in just 55 days on space-saving dwarf plants only 18 inches across. It is prolific over a long season and withstands extremes in temperature. This is a Park exclusive.

CARROTS (3rd quarter, Cancer, Scorpio, Pisces, Libra). *Baby-finger Nantes* will give you carrots in just 50 days. This brightly-colored, miniature selection was developed in Europe as a baby carrot for canning or pickling whole. Roots are very tender when young and must be harvested early.

At Stokes Seed Company you will also find *Baby Orange,* 53 days. *Baby Orange* is an improved selection of the popular French variety *Amstel.* Roots are bright orange and less fibrous foods. When processed for frozen than *Little Finger. Baby Orange* and *Amstel* are both selections from Amsterdam types.

SWEET POTATO (3rd quarter, Cancer, Scorpio, Taurus, Libra, Capricorn and Sagittarius). *Vardaman Sweet Potato* (Henry Field) will give you sweet potatoes in 110 days and has been especially developed for small gardens—and does not run. Highly productive, it yields a full crop of sweet potatoes with deep orange, tasty flesh. It is also very ornamental.

CANTALOUPE (1st or 2nd quarter, Cancer, Scorpio, Pisces, Libra). Henry Field's hybrid *Bush Star* cantaloupe can be grown in tubs on the patio. The vines grow just 3 feet long and it is ideal for containers or small gardens. Producing 2-pound melons, they mature in mid-season, and are fully netted with light sutures. The fruits are sweet, juicy and full of flavor and the firm flesh makes them ideal for melon balls.

STRAWBERRY (3rd quarter, Cancer, Scorpio, Pisces) If you are a strawberry lover you must have this one—*Bordurella Strawberry*. It is a prolific, bush-like everbearer and just great for a strawberry barrel, or may be planted in an herb jar. This strawberry comes to us from France, where it is very popular and bears loads of berries. The compact plants grow like bushes without long runners. (Henry Field).

LETTUCE (1st quarter, Cancer, Scorpio, Pisces, Libra, Taurus). Try *Tom Thumb*. This miniature butterhead is exceptionally crisp and sweet. The midget tennis-ball-size heads are served whole with dressing as individual salads at many famous hotels. *Tom Thumb* and many of the loose leaf lettuces such as *Green Ice, Red Sails, Black Seeded Simpson, Salad Bowl, Oakleaf* and *Slo-Bolt*, as well as green onions for the table, will tolerate partial shade or filtered sunlight.

Gurney's 1986 nursery and seed catalog has an interesting grouping under the heading "Adopt A Baby Vegetable." With this you will receive one packet of sixteen miniatures.

Herbs For Your Windowsill

There are lots of herbs suitable for windowsill gardening, some requiring sun and others that will grow reasonably well in shade. It is something good to know that pots of herbs and other plants on a windowsill gain sun benefit by adding a reflecting backing board covered with aluminum foil.

Basil is delicious with tomatoes, and will grow well in their shade, particularly if the tomatoes are trained to grow upward so they will not sprawl over it.

Bedstraw forms a dense ground cover and likes ample moisture.

Catnip is easy to germinate and its seed remains viable for 4 to 5 years. I love catnip in salads and it is very good with pork sausage.

Chervil prefers well-drained, fairly rich soil and shade or partial shade.

Mints come in a wide range of flavors. They will grow just about anywhere, sun or shade.

Sweet Woodruff, used mainly as a ground cover, grows a dense, 5-inch-tall mat, likes moisture and shade.

Both Parsley and Chives will grow well on windowsills but should have sun for at least part of the day.

Build A Garden You Can Reach

Since so many people, young as well as senior citizens, have back problems and find bending over painful, why not bring the gardens up to them? This can be accomplished in several ways: build boxes, preferably using redwood lumber, two feet wide by four feet long, setting them on sturdy 2-by-4 legs at the height most convenient for the individual to work. Vary the depths of the boxes according to what you will plant, making some eight inches deep and others twelve.

These raised beds have an added advantage. You can place them anywhere you want, out from the shade of your large trees, or your neighbors'. If at all possible, though, consider putting them near a southern house wall—the best location.

To produce well, of course, the boxes must be filled with good garden soil—a sandy loam into which plenty of organic matter (compost or well-decomposed manure) has been added. If you do not have access to such soil, try buying it from a florist or garden store. Or you might get someone to deliver a truckload of fairly good soil which you can gradually build up to a higher state of fertility for your concentrated gardening. Of course, a well-tended compost heap, supplemented with kitchen refuse will help here just as much as it does with other gardening methods.

One chore remains before putting soil in the boxes. Half-inch holes should be drilled in the bottoms for drainage and covered with copper screening. You can provide uniform and gentle watering by setting the hose nozzle deep in a tall glass jar buried in the soil, its top just level with the surface.

As water flows up and out of the jar in a gentle stream it will spread evenly throughout the bed. And don't let water go to waste when it begins to seep through the bottom of the boxes. Set a plant or two below to take up what soaks through.

This type of gardening has many advantages, not the least of which is being eye-to-eye with any insect pests which may decide to invade. Weeds are quickly spotted, too, and just as quickly pulled from the loose, friable soil. And no-stoop harvesting is a real joy!

Hang It All!

Especially where space is at a premium, don't overlook the possibilities of a hanging garden, both for decorative effect and edibility; combine tomatoes and cucumbers with trailing petunias or nasturtiums. Or take geraniums, for instance. Besides the common type, there are peppermint, lemon, nutmeg, ivy and oakleaf geraniums, as well as the rose geranium which has leaves useful for flavoring. Real strawberries, as well as the strawberry geranium, also may be good choices for hanging pots.

Take a walk through a mobile home park and you'll see hanging gardens everywhere—under awnings, on step railings and anywhere else that they conceivably fit. They give more foliage and blossom for the space than any other type of gardening.

Choose your containers with care. The best choices for warm or windy locations are wood. Plants in wood containers usually will need only about half the water as those grown other ways.

Containers should always be lined with sphagnum moss, then filled with soil. This spongy, water-retentive mixture keeps evaporation to a minimum. Even so, watering once a day may be necessary, and in very warm weather take your plants down once a week and soak them in a tub.

Container Grown Fruit Trees

Dwarf fruit trees lend themselves very well to growing in large containers. They will blossom and bear fruit splendidly if tended with care and they have the added advantage of being movable if you should decide to change locations. Boxes of redwood, cedar and other rot-resistant woods are best, but be sure that there are enough holes in the bottom for drainage. Consult the *Moon Sign Book* for best planting quarters and signs for a particular variety, just as you would for standard trees.

PERSONAL
HOROSCOPES

Your Ascendant is the following if your time of birth was:

If your Sun Sign is:	6 to 8 am	8 to 10 am	10 am to Noon	Noon to 2 pm	2 to 4 pm	4 to 6 pm
Aries	Taurus	Gemini	Cancer	Leo	Virgo	Libra
Taurus	Gemini	Cancer	Leo	Virgo	Libra	Scorpio
Gemini	Cancer	Leo	Virgo	Libra	Scorpio	Sagittarius
Cancer	Leo	Virgo	Libra	Scorpio	Sagittarius	Capricorn
Leo	Virgo	Libra	Scorpio	Sagittarius	Capricorn	Aquarius
Virgo	Libra	Scorpio	Sagittarius	Capricorn	Aquarius	Pisces
Libra	Scorpio	Sagittarius	Capricorn	Aquarius	Pisces	Aries
Scorpio	Sagittarius	Capricorn	Aquarius	Pisces	Aries	Taurus
Sagittarius	Capricorn	Aquarius	Pisces	Aries	Taurus	Gemini
Capricorn	Aquarius	Pisces	Aries	Taurus	Gemini	Cancer
Aquarius	Pisces	Aries	Taurus	Gemini	Cancer	Leo
Pisces	Aries	Taurus	Gemini	Cancer	Leo	Virgo

If your Sun Sign is:	6 to 8 pm	8 to 10 pm	10 pm to Midnight	Midnight to 2 am	2 to 4 am	4 to 6 am
Aries	Scorpio	Sagittarius	Capricorn	Aquarius	Pisces	Aries
Taurus	Sagittarius	Capricorn	Aquarius	Pisces	Aries	Taurus
Gemini	Capricorn	Aquarius	Pisces	Aries	Taurus	Gemini
Cancer	Aquarius	Pisces	Aries	Taurus	Gemini	Cancer
Leo	Pisces	Aries	Taurus	Gemini	Cancer	Leo
Virgo	Aries	Taurus	Gemini	Cancer	Leo	Virgo
Libra	Taurus	Gemini	Cancer	Leo	Virgo	Libra
Scorpio	Gemini	Cancer	Leo	Virgo	Libra	Scorpio
Sagittarius	Cancer	Leo	Virgo	Libra	Scorpio	Sagittarius
Capricorn	Leo	Virgo	Libra	Scorpio	Sagittarius	Capricorn
Aquarius	Virgo	Libra	Scorpio	Sagittarius	Capricorn	Aquarius
Pisces	Libra	Scorpio	Sagittarius	Capricorn	Aquarius	Pisces

1. Find your Sun Sign (left column);
2. Determine correct approximate time of birth column;
3. Line up your Sun Sign with birth time to find ascendant.

SOPHIA MASON

Sophia Mason is a professional astrologer with over 20 years of experience as a lecturer, counselor, author, and radio and television personality. Sophia is an Advanced Member of the American Federation of Astrologers, Inc. (AFA), the National Council for Geocosmic Research (NCGR), the Lake County Astrological Association (LCAA) and a professional member of Western States Astrology (WSA).

Sophia has an active astrological counseling practice in Parma, Ohio, and she teaches astrology four evenings a week through the continuing education department of Valley Forge High School. She is the founder and director of the Aquarian-Cancerian Tape Company, and is a staff astrologer for the "Live on Five" TV show. Sophia has also produced a "Progressed Report Writer" for Matrix Software and a synastry program for Hettigers Computer Software.

Sophia has authored more than seven books on astrology, including *Delineation of Progressions*, which has been hailed as one of the best books on the interpretation of progressions.

Sophia attended Western Reserve University, Cleveland Institute of Art, and Tri-C College for law enforcement. Her work with the local police department has won her several commendations for assistance in locating missing children.

ARIES
The Ram

March 21 to April 20

Quality: cardinal
Element: fire
Principle: active
Ruler: Mars
Gem: diamond
Lucky Day: Tuesday
Anatomy: head, face, brain
Key phrase: *I am*

Glyph: ram's horns
Natural sign of: first house
Opposite sign: Libra
Color: red
Lucky Numbers: 1 and 9
Flower: geranium

Key word: *activity*

Positive Characteristics:
pioneering
executive
competitive
impulsive
eager
courageous
independent
dynamic

Negative Characteristics:
domineering
quick-tempered
violent
intolerant
hasty
arrogant
brusque
lacks follow-through

ARIES

Aries is the most personal sign of the Zodiac. Your main concern is the immediate future and your own personal affairs. Your are the pioneers, forever seeking new and challenging avenues of expression and experiences. Fiercely independent, optimistic and aggressive, you must be a leader. Aries women often get along better with the opposite sex than their own. If she is wise, she will learn to control her bossy and competitive spirit when working with men, or in the handling of her love relationships. Patience is the one virtue that Aries must learn to develop at an early age.

In your youth, you ran before you learned to walk. This impatient attitude often resulted in an accident that would leave a scar, mole or mark on your head or face.

One can easily spot an Aries by their brisk manner and quick reaction to conditions that surround them at the moment. You are fearless individuals with the ability to make snap judgments. This highly qualifies you for any vocation requiring a decisive mentality. It is this one capacity that often draws you into such fields as nursing, medicine, police work, or an executive position. Some Aries have a combative quality that often results in the use of force rather than tact in the achievement of their aims. This gives others the impression that Aries are aggressive, arrogant and difficult to deal with. When, in reality, the Aries are so eager to get their ideas across that they lack tolerance with those that must ponder their decisions or course of action.

Never underestimate an Aries, for they are the most protective of all signs, especially with the underdog or those of whom they feel were unjustly treated. Loyalty, support and devotion are given freely to your immediate family members and to those you love dearly. You expect the same consideration in return. You are noted for your quick, hot temper which can diminish just as fast, and seldom do you ever hold a grudge. You will never intentionally hurt the feelings of another. You regret such action and you try to make amends as soon as possible. Never attempt to remind an Aries of past slights, for they regard the past as over and done with.

JANUARY

Enjoy the company of others on New Year's Day, but don't rely on promises made by one particular person or you'll be disappointed. The 2nd and 6th are excellent for clearing away old debris and paperwork and for developing new work methods to replace worn out procedures. The New Moon of the 7th in your 10th House of careers holds the promise of a long overdue salary increase or bonus. Others may receive a gift from a distance or a final resolving of a long standing lawsuit. If you have been desirous of furthering your education, look into the possibility of a company paid program or a scholarship. The main issue at this time is to avoid the impulse to hasten or push personal interests. Accept the fact that certain conditions require more time to develop in order for greater success. The afternoon hours of the 10th are ideal for seeking a promotion or a raise. Easy come, easy go may be the theme on the 12th, when unforeseen gains arrive in the morning only to leave in late afternoon due to your having to repair or replace an old appliance. The Full Moon of the 21st cautions against extravagant expenditures.

FEBRUARY

An unexpected invitation or gift may arrive on the 1st. Your ruling planet, Mars, is in your 2nd House and you may expect a past due refund around the 3rd or 4th. The New Moon of the 6th hints at unexpected financial drains through clubs, organized activities, children and friends. Caution is especially advised between the 11th and the 16th of the month. You are uncannily intuitive as a troubleshooter at work on the 7th and 8th. Social plans made on the 9th are apt to undergo an abrupt change on the 11th. A demanding or possessive relationship may start to lose its luster between the 15th and 19th. Someone new unexpectedly enters your life after the Lunar Eclipse of the 20th highlights the ruler of your 11th House. Professional individuals can look forward to a major advance in their careers during the months ahead. The 21st and 22nd offer challenging insights into a complex job situation. Keep a watchful eye on your financial budget and checking account during the last few days of the month because you might find errors.

MARCH

Whether at home or at work, the early morning hours of the 2nd and 3rd will produce surprising results in the solving or reorganizing of past issues. If someone owes you money, or if you have been seeking financial aid, the 4th may be the last time this year you will have the chance to push forth with positive results. The Solar Eclipse of the 7th in your 12th House may appear to hinder progress, but in reality it is preparing you for greater future rewards in exchange for past efforts and hard work. Other Arians are likely to obtain a long awaited financial gain through insurance, legal settlements, or other unforeseen benefits around the 8th or 9th. Watch for electrical or mechanical problems during morning hours of the 10th, but don't be too concerned— you may discover by late afternoon that the repair will be less costly than first anticipated. Mars joins Jupiter in your 3rd House on the 11th. A new vehicle may be in your future; don't be impatient to purchase. Give vans, station wagons, or small trucks first consideration. After the 22nd, you'll be glad you did, as another party offers excellent suggestions for utilizing a larger vehicle profitably.

APRIL

Don't be fooled on April Fool's Day. Prepare yourself for exciting and unexpected events involving communications, invitations, short trips, and even a possible gift on the 1st. The 3rd is not favored for pushing personal interests or pet projects; you will only be blocked at every angle. But it is an excellent day for researching material necessary for tomorrow's special events. The 4th is your day, so proceed full speed ahead in areas of romance, advertising, promotion, or the undertaking of new ventures. All is reinforced by the position of the New Moon in your 1st House on the 5th, introducing more than one avenue of personal interest that should keep you very busy in the weeks ahead. Romance, sports and creative interests are enhanced on the 15th. The latter part of the month, especially the 25th and 26th, favors refunds, dividends or gains through mutual resources as the Full Moon of the 20th highlights your 8th House of joint funds. Look for a financial roadblock to lift after the 28th, when more than one lucky offer comes your way.

MAY

You will have greater success and avoid possible conflicts on the 2nd if you handle pet projects yourself, and not involve disinterested family members. The 4th is favored for purchase of home appliances or remodeling of living quarters. The New Moon of the 5th sparks up the financial picture. Be sure you maintain enough in your checking account to cover forgotten insurance premiums or taxes that may be due this month. The 7th, 8th and 9th are emotionally depressing days when nothing seems to go right, but the evening hours of the 9th and 13th should bring you back into proper perspective. Someone extends an invitation to travel on the 16th, but you may have to refuse or place the offer on hold, due to family or personal responsibilities. You've had an intense desire to change your environment or vocation but have been held back by restrictive conditions. However, after the 20th, you will have the willpower to forge ahead along these lines. Have an alternative set of plans for the 21st, as changing conditions require re-routing several situations. Read between the lines around the 27th and be careful what you sign; much confusion and hidden elements prevail.

JUNE

The 1st of the month may find you reviewing your financial budget, updating and clearing away old, past due bills. The New Moon of the 3rd falls in your 3rd House. This is an excellent time for taking trips or planning your vacation. Consider the option of a variety of short excursions within driving range. If you have been feeling rather bored and restless lately, a new sport could do the trick—perhaps tennis, golfing or hiking. This is also a good time to contact or visit those living in distant cities. The 4th is a good day for a family outing as Venus highlights your 4th House. A luncheon with someone special on the 6th may pay off with valuable ideas. Last month's option for travel with someone crops up again on the 13th with more promising results. The Full Moon of the 19th may bring unexpected assistance from an old friend. Between the 26th to the 30th, the door to travel possibilities opens as personal and family problems are temporarily placed on the back burner.

JULY

The afternoon hours of the 1st can be busier than usual with many diversified duties and communications from those near and far. Short excursions or travel plans for Sunday the 2nd may have to be placed on hold due to other commitments. The New Moon of the 3rd is in your 4th House. You may expect a possible refund, due to overpayment of a utility bill or other property matters. Children or a romantic partner may attempt to borrow money or a possession on the 5th. An expansive, optimistic feeling prevails during early hours of the 6th, formulating several creative ideas. If you didn't yield to the demands of others yesterday, more pressure is likely to be exerted on you today, the 6th, and again on the 26th. Be aware that loaning money or your car to unreliable persons can prove costly or create animosity. Guard against hasty and unwise decisions on the 7th, and give serious consideration to even the minor details. The Full Moon of the 18th may find you concerned with the affairs or health of a close family member. The month ends with the promise of a lasting and stabilizing relationship that will soon enter your life.

AUGUST

Last month's close relationship continues to hold its special meaning and appeal on the 1st. The New Moon of the 1st falls in your 5th House of romance and children. If you have yielded under their pressures last month, you may suffer the consequence of a minor financial setback. New changing situations, developing after the 4th, may open the door to vocational opportunities that can be operated from the home base, or close to home. It appears to be an occupation you have never handled before—possibly through communications, computer, civil service, the police department, or security. The only drawback may be a requirement to work the evening shift or irregular hours. You should hear something positive by the 23rd; just don't permit another person to discourage or sway you from accepting this new position. Best not to reveal your intentions at this time, as another party may also be interested and work against you with deceptive tactics. The month ends with a promise of a new job and a responsible position that you have long desired.

SEPTEMBER

The Solar Eclipse of August 31st in your 6th House reinforces the indication of a new vocational change. A decision will be required concerning domestic affairs and job respon- sibilities, forcing you to come to terms on these two issues. Can you take time away from home to attend a training pro- gram if necessary? Or, handle other interference and demands that may curtail time spent with the family? The end results, however, promise long range security, monetary increase and better job benefits. There appears to be someone from your immediate environment who may try to place a few obstacles in your attempt to succeed with this job. Be aware of this tendency on the 3rd, 7th, 15th, 19th, 21st, and 24th. Afternoon hours on the 7th are excellent for seeking legal counsel, taking tests or enrolling in fall classes. Seek answers from within on the 14th, as your intuitive or psychic ability will be uncannily accurate. The Full Moon of the 15th in your 12th House may require you to "walk quietly, but carry a big stick," as the saying goes. Its opposition to Mars in your 6th House may create conflicting interests with those of a co-worker.

OCTOBER

You may be forced to clarify three important issues in your life at this time, concerning relationships, home and career as the former New Moon of September 29th creates a stress- ful atmosphere. Conflicts arise between the 1st and the 4th, offering a possible job change that could produce financial increase, yet on the other hand, undue restrictions that you feel are your responsibilities, which could curtail job accep- tance or proper handling of duties. Although you are totally confused, only you can make the right choice. Mercury retrogrades back into your 7th House and the sign of Libra on the 11th. Between the 12th to the 18th, it is best to be your own counsel, as the advice of others will not be con- ducive to your well being. An upsetting change of plans during early afternoon hours of the 22nd does a turnabout resulting in an entertaining and socially enjoyable experi- ence. Heated discussions on the 27th and 28th can lead to arguments unless you exercise extreme caution, tact, and diplomacy.

NOVEMBER

The month starts out on the 1st with the possibility of financial refunds or gains through forgotten or past incidents. An invitation is extended or a gift is sent from someone at a distance on the 2nd. Money looks good on the 3rd, so charge a few items if necessary to enhance the home decor. The afternoon and evening hours of the 5th can be especially enjoyable in the company of family and friends. Be cool and collected when someone tries to boss or dominate you after the 6th. This person could be of constructive assistance to you around the 7th or 8th. Overly aggressive or assertive actions during morning hours of the 10th will only hinder personal affairs, especially if it concerns a financial matter. Take family members into your confidence and try to reach a monetary compromise during the next two weeks, after the Full Moon of the 13th activates your 8th House of joint funds. Too many hidden elements prevail on the 14th, 15th and 16th, so don't attempt any important decisions. You are mentally and psychically astute on the 17th, 19th and 20th. Make major purchases or do your Christmas shopping on the 21st. The New Moon of the 28th highlights your 9th House of legal matters and travel.

DECEMBER

Apply for a raise in pay during afternoon hours of the 1st if you work; otherwise, it is an excellent time for collecting an old personal debt. Unexpected good news or communication from a distance is possible on the 4th. The super excellent ideas you had on the 5th may run into a few drawbacks on the 7th; give them another try on the 18th. The Full Moon of the 12th confronts you with two important decisions, involving home vs. career and travel vs. education. Travel or enhancing an educational skill may be your first choice on the 13th, but others may try to frustrate your attempts. Wait until after the New Moon of the 27th before you make a decision. Christmas Day may find you celebrating the holiday season away from home in the company of someone you really admire. The 30th draws the year to a close with the promise of possible marriage developing from this special holiday sojourn. For a more enjoyable time on New Year's Eve, select a few choice friends to help welcome in the New Year.

TAURUS
The Bull

April 20 to May 21

Quality: fixed
Element: earth
Principle: passive
Ruler: Venus
Gem: emerald
Lucky Day: Friday
Anatomy: throat, neck, vocal chords, thyroid, mouth, tonsils
Key phrase: *I have*

Glyph: bull's head and horns
Natural sign of: second house
Opposite sign: Scorpio
Color: blue
Lucky Numbers: 6 and 4
Flower: violet

Key word: *stability*

Positive Characteristics:
patient
conservative
domestic
sensual
thorough
dependable
practical
artistic
loyal

Negative Characteristics:
self-indulgent
stubborn
slow-moving
argumentative
short-tempered
possessive
greedy
materialistic

TAURUS

The main characteristic of the Taurus is their steadfast ability to stick with their objectives until they have reached their goal. You have the will power and the perseverance to plod along in spite of any obstacle. You understand the importance of methods, routine and details. You realize that you must first organize and assimilate the proper knowledge before you can lay a firm foundation in any enterprise.

Your ruling planet, Venus, causes you to put high value on peace and harmony. Seldom do you lose your temper or provoke an argument, but if pushed to the limits like the bull that governs your sign, you will explode and charge your opponent. You must have a harmonious atmosphere or you can become tense; any strife upsets you greatly and nerves can suffer badly. If you come across a person you don't like, or one that annoys you, you would just as soon avoid them.

Taurus has a strong love of beauty, luxury and personal comfort. You prefer to entertain at home where others can see and appreciate your beautiful surroundings. This Earthy sign loves to work in the garden, growing vegetables and lovely flowers to enhance the surroundings. You are very hospitable and have a knack for putting people at ease. Others trust your advice because of your high integrity and reliability. You give deep thought to matters and are never offhand or careless in reaching conclusions.

Although you are one of the most ruggedly healthy members of the Zodiac, you should seek a job in which you can move around a little, for too sedentary a job can make your system overly sluggish. When choosing a career, your priority is one that offers stability. You believe in putting in a full day's work.

Feeling and desire are one and the same. You want to belong to your romantic partner and own him or her in return. Exclusively. You can be terribly possessive and jealous. You have the power to soothe and can assure others that all is well. This quality is important in your love relationships, for it tends to relax them.

JANUARY

Distant relatives or in-laws may be a source of irritation or upset your sense of balance during afternoon hours of the 1st. Productivity increases during afternoon hours of the 2nd if you heed sound suggestions of others. A previous commitment for travel with your partner or associate is coming up for review, as the New Moon of the 7th highlights your 9th House. Pass up offerings you may encounter on the 10th as they could entail heavy restrictions. Discuss these outside issues with mate or partner on the 11th for better results. Don't be surprised if confusing elements between the 12th to the 14th put these plans temporarily on hold. Playing the waiting game after the 15th will prove financially beneficial in the long run. Something crops up on the 16th from the past with a golden opportunity for career advancement and monetary gains, with a good possibility of more than one source. Mars enters your 1st House on the 19th, increasing your energy span and in some cases a tendency toward impatience. Use caution with hasty actions on the 20th, 21st, and 25th, which could upset career goals. The 31st is your day for culminating latent opportunities to your best advantage.

FEBRUARY

Mercury has retrograded back into your 9th House, giving you ample time to reorganize, alter and make important changes in regard to future travel commitments. Contact influential people at a distance, who can be of constructive assistance in the way of possible career or monetary advancements on the 1st. If someone from the past owes you money, payment may arrive on the 3rd or 4th. The 7th and 8th are excellent days to work on a joint project that you have been thinking about for some time—one that could merit you long range financial returns. You're feeling ambitious on the 11th, and may want to get rid of useless articles no longer of value; just be sure that none are connected with business or organized activities. Watch finances between the 14th to the 19th to avoid possible embarrassment from bounced checks or past due bills. Depending upon your personal status, the Lunar Eclipse of the 20th can introduce a new exciting romance or the promise of a grandchild.

MARCH

Organized activities, friends, clubs and organizations, or a possible job in a distant city may be brought to your attention with favorable results on the 2nd and 3rd. The 4th is the last time that you can successfully finalize travel plans, as Jupiter will soon be entering your 2nd House of money. Any problems you encounter on the 6th, in regard to money that an organization or company owes you, should be resolved by the 11th. The Solar Eclipse of the 7th in your 11th House of aspirations holds the promise of money coming to you through a partner or mutual funds. Look for financial offerings to come through more than one source after the 11th—even funds that you may have forgotten about will surprise you. A letter or phone call on the 13th may leave you feeling very confused and mixed up. Contact an outside authoritative figure who can clarify this matter with ease. Before you sign any important papers or contracts between the 14th and 20th, make sure you understand the responsibilities involved. The Full Moon of the 22nd may introduce more than one job opportunity through the intervention of another individual. Look for positive results on the 22nd, 25th, 27th, or 29th.

APRIL

The new and totally unexpected events of the 1st may require a low key profile until after the Full Moon of the 20th. Be especially careful on the 2nd and 3rd not to make any careless disclosures of your pet projects that you may later regret. Although you may be mentally stimulated into action on the 4th, it is not advisable to speak openly about your recent private endeavors at this time. The afternoon hours of the 4th could bring several outlays of financial or material gain. You may find yourself expressing resentments against those in authority because nothing appears to be going in the right direction. The New Moon of the 5th in your 12th House continues to hinder or restrict personal interests. With cooperative efforts of family members on the 14th, it may be possible to wind up this private project. You will be faced with the difficult task of having to choose between several financial offerings on the 25th. Practical insights will aid in making the right choice.

MAY

The 1st of the month should bring a pleasant luncheon invitation or possible gift as a small token of appreciation from a friend. The 2nd bears conflicting situations; you are motivated by new concepts and ideas, but may have difficulty getting them off the ground floor when an emotional family crisis demands your personal attention. The energetic planet, Mars, has recently entered your 3rd House, motivating you into new realms of money making ideas on the 4th. The New Moon of the 5th highlights your 1st House. Past issues involving joint partnership funds come up for review. Try to avoid confrontations with family members and those you work with on the 7th, 8th, and 9th. Your ruling planet, Venus, enters your 2nd House of money on the 11th, joining Mercury and Jupiter therein. Expect several diversified sources to produce monetary gains and, at various times, produce a few setbacks. Partners or close associates offer excellent and sound ideas on the 19th, which may have to be revised on the 20th when the Full Moon of the 20th reaches your 7th House. Several lucrative offerings will have to be decided upon before this month is over.

JUNE

The focal point of the 1st is on you, with contacts from someone at a distance, or possibly an authoritative figure. This event will require coming to terms with your partner on an important decision. The New Moon of the 3rd suggests that the issues of the 1st are likely to involve news or travels to a distant place. Through some stroke of luck, it appears that your travel expenses may be covered by sources other than your own. The 4th is a beautiful Sunday, bringing you in touch with family members that arouse your tender emotions. Be careful on the 6th, as you hurry to keep a luncheon appointment, that you do not drive carelessly and create an accident. Children or a romantic partner can be a source of inspiration on the 10th. The Full Moon of the 19th in your 8th House reinforces monetary gains through distant matters. These funds appear to be connected with your company or an organization. Should someone confront you on the 26th with a mixed up situation, assure them that it will be resolved on the 30th.

JULY

The 1st is one of the best days for those who deal in sales or advertising. If you are not in this field of operation, you might consider a new investment program or joining a church credit union. The New Moon of the 3rd is in your 3rd House and throws a favorable light to your House of partners. A short trip is around the corner for the two of you and the best time to take the trip or to formulate these plans is on the 4th. Don't permit others to push you into doing something on the 9th, when your energy level is not up to par. If you have hidden an important document for safekeeping and can't locate it during morning hours of the 11th, you have a good chance of finding it during late evening hours. The Full Moon of the 18th in your 9th House may require some answers. Whether your travel demands are for vocational reasons or for visiting distant relatives, can you afford to go? Will it upset your emotional sense of security should expenditures get out of hand? Take a weekend pleasure trip on the 22nd and 23rd with someone whose company you enjoy. The practical side of your conservative nature is exceptionally strong on the 25th, as you question the feasibility of lending funds to a relative.

AUGUST

You may be feeling rather resourceful on the 1st, and may have the ability to take a useless or discarded item and transform it into something constructive. It is not going to be easy, but you may have to curb the spending habits of a family member or partner, either in business or marriage, as the New Moon of the 1st suggests they may be spending too lavishly on entertainment, children, romance, gambling, or investments. These issues are likely to turn up around the 4th. If you have been wanting to better organize your storage space, the 5th is a good day to shop for shelves, bookcases, or home/office furniture. Seek assistance from an authority figure between the 8th and 11th who can assist with the finer details of improving your investment program. The Lunar Eclipse of the 17th occurs in your 10th House. New, exciting and unexpected opportunities will advance career matters during the coming year. Do not become discouraged if success is slow at the beginning; all indications reveal a steady climb.

SEPTEMBER

The recent Solar Eclipse of August 31st highlighted your 5th House. All matters that have been pending for some time can be culminated to a fruitful conclusion. A romantic affair hampered by past responsibilities may soon result in marriage, a long desired grandchild may become a reality, or a creative enterprise finally achieves long overdue recognition. Whatever your interest may be, just rewards for past efforts through diligent handling of matters will be yours in the coming year. Pay close attention to details on the 1st, to avoid criticism through a co-worker. A tranquil weekend is not in the books for the 2nd and 3rd as others bombard you with their emotional problems. Mental confusion at work rears its head during morning hours of the 7th, but by late afternoon you'll have the matter untangled. Venus enters your 7th House on the 12th; a surprise invitation may be extended on the 13th from an old friend. Unforeseen opportunities may arrive in the mail on the 14th with a travel offer for you and a partner that is too good to refuse. The New Moon of the 30th in your 6th House of work may require the acceptance of additional responsibilities, just to maintain peace and harmony at work.

OCTOBER

Last month's New Moon in your 6th House of work continues to create upsetting conditions through co-workers on the 2nd, 4th, and 12th. The Full Moon of the 14th reinforces hidden matters prevailing at your place of employment. Keep a low profile and don't confide in others, even if you want to defend an injustice that has been operating against you, especially on the 17th, 18th, and 20th. Don't object to a change of plans on the 22nd that a family member or child wants to enforce; you will discover later that it was the best thing that could have happened. Nervous tension and excessive energy can create an explosive combination on the 27th and 28th. Lack of cooperative efforts on the part of others may give way to feelings of anger and resentment. Help is around the corner as the New Moon of the 29th activates your 7th House of partners and close relationships with offerings of constructive assistance in the resolving of an old problem. Don't hesitate to seek the counsel of an influential person.

NOVEMBER

The 1st of the month reflects the favorable conditions of the
October 29th New Moon. Seek the advice of a knowledgeable person and let them inaugurate the action. They
can help to bring about favorable changes in your profession through the offer of sound advice and assistance. The
2nd may bring contacts from someone at a distance who will
offer new insight in vocational matters. Review past efforts
between the 3rd and 5th and determine how you can advance
or improve future goals. The 7th and 8th are two of the best
days of the month. Nothing is impossible if you apply the
willpower and the stamina to tackle and finish a very difficult yet rewarding task. Whatever you are attempting, you
do not have to do it alone. You will discover that several
loyal and responsive friends and associates are eager and
ready to assist. A long cherished dream can become a reality
at this time. Perhaps a cruise or travel to faraway places or
obtaining a certificate in a specialized field. You may have to
contact someone on the 10th to correct some mixed up
paperwork. The Full Moon of the 13th is a good time to seek
those who can assist in helping you update your car, home,
life insurance or investment package. The New Moon of the
28th in your 8th House may produce financial gains through
joint resources.

DECEMBER

Your partner or close associate is likely to receive an insurance refund, a dividend check, or a bonus through the
government or their place of employment between the 1st
and 4th of the month. An invitation to future travels spurs an
interest on the 5th. This expense paid trip may be within
range of visiting a distant relative. The news you hear on the
13th may require an impromptu trip, in spite of heavy work
loads or present lack of immediate funds. If you have
domestic pets, converse with children on the 18th, who will
cooperate in caring for them, should you decide to travel.
For last minute Christmas shopping, the evening hours of
the 18th will be successful in finding practical gifts at terrific
bargain prices. A very special gift awaits you under the tree
on Christmas morning.

GEMINI
The Twins

May 21 to June 22

Quality: mutable
Element: air
Principle: active
Ruler: Mercury
Gem: agate
Lucky Day: Wednesday
Anatomy: lungs, collar-bone, hands, arms, shoulders, nervous system
Key phrase: *I think*

Glyph: Roman numeral 2
Natural sign of: third house
Opposite sign: Sagittarius
Color: silver
Lucky Numbers: 5 and 9
Flower: Lily of the Valley

Key word: *versatility*

Positive Characteristics:
  dual
  congenial
  curious
  adaptable
  expressive
  quick-witted
  literary
  dexterous

Negative Characteristics:
  changeable
  ungrateful
  scatterbrained
  restless
  scheming
  lacking in concentration
  lacking in follow-through

GEMINI

The Gemini nature is adaptable to almost any given situation. You possess both manual and mental dexterity, giving you the ability to handle a great variety of tasks, and very often simultaneously. Your nature is restless with a high degree of nervous energy and your attention span is quite short. You bore easily, must be constantly on the move, doing things and visiting friends. You have such an easy, flowing manner of talking that you are able to manipulate words to such a degree of persuasion that you often succeed in finding out valuable bits of information or secrets from others that would not have been revealed otherwise. Geminis are not what one would call deceptive, but rather, they are improvisers who either change or leave out pieces of information that best suit their purposes.

The Gemini dualistic nature makes it extremely difficult for others to understand them. At certain times you can be quite charming, gay, interesting and full of good humor. At other times, your attitude can be altogether different; extremely moody, irritable, full of sarcasm or cynicism, leaving others to wonder what they said or did to make you react that way. You have a marvelous way of bouncing back after a defeat. The present moment is most important and you give into it completely. You would make an excellent lecturer, teacher or salesman, for you enjoy a heated discussion. You love to explain and show others how to do things. You are very witty, fond of telling jokes and stories which are accompanied by illustrated gestures and mimicry.

Because of your natural talkative ability and quick wit, you are also well suited for such occupations as journalism, radio and television work, comedy acts, as well as writers of short stories, articles or plays. You need a job where there is complete freedom of movement and no dull routines, where each new day holds exciting challenges for you. A job that offers constant change, something that keeps you on the go and on your toes with flexible hours.

In partnerships and romance, you are selective and desire mental compatibility above all else.

JANUARY

The past few years have been very difficult trying to stabilize close relationships. All indications this year promise a favorable change in the domestic sphere and, for those who were divorced, new and lasting ties. A social affair on New Year's Day may prove disappointing when one particular person is unable to attend. Money someone owes you is repaid, or an increase in earnings appears likely around the 2nd. The New Moon of the 7th puts the spotlight on mutual funds. Concentrate during the weeks ahead on clearing personal debts and collecting money that others owe you—especially on the 10th, 14th, 15th, and 16th. An old relationship may try to make a re-entry into your life between the 12th and 14th; it would not be conducive to your well being to encourage it. Accept social invitations on the 16th; it may bring you in touch with prominent individuals who can be of valuable assistance in the near future. Mars joins Jupiter in your 12th House on the 19th. A partner or close associate will integrate a new idea into what has already been established. The Full Moon of the 21st in your 3rd House, however, suggests that you try and keep the expansive ideas of this person from getting out of hand and costing more than you intended.

FEBRUARY

Due to Mercury's retrograde motion, it will remain in your 8th House until the 15th, creating minor worries over past due payments or Christmas purchases. The 1st of the month may catch you off guard with one particular bill that you may have misplaced, lost, or forgotten to pay. Money matters ease up during afternoon hours of the 4th, when a stroke of luck produces an avenue of hidden gains. The New Moon of the 6th in your 9th House offers a brief respite from the winter blues through an unexpected invitation to travel. Be careful; it could strain the purse strings. You are highly inspired on the 7th and able to troubleshoot the most difficult problems at work. If you are self employed, the 7th can open new doors to business and financial advancements. The Lunar Eclipse of the 20th is likely to bring favorable changes in your immediate environment during the coming year. Some will gain an inheritance or a long awaited financial settlement. Others might make the final payment of a heavy mortgage.

MARCH

The 2nd and 3rd are favored for clearing up perplexing problems that have been troubling you for some time. The 4th is the last time you will have an opportunity to put the finishing touches on a private project. Travel interests that continue to involve financial burdens will ease up after the 10th. The Solar Eclipse of the 7th will produce many unforeseen changes in your career and public interests during the coming year. Be careful of those "who may try to ride on your coat tails," so to speak. The 10th is the last time that you will experience upsetting conditions involving financial commitments and close associations. Both Mars and Jupiter will enter your 1st House on the 11th. Be careful in your haste to tackle the many diversified interests, that you do not become careless in travel. You are feeling so energetic and expansive, now that all those hidden influences are behind you. More than one opportunity for entering into new enterprises will come your way—especially on the 17th, 22nd and 25th. The Full Moon of the 22nd in your 5th House may introduce a new romance that could result in a partnership, a new creative project, or a mutual cooperative enterprise involving a child.

APRIL

A spanking new offer comes from a distance or a friend that you cannot possibly resist on the 1st day of the month. It is not an April Fool's joke, so be sure to take full advantage of this new opportunity. You will have to exercise caution on the 3rd as one particularly new friend does not have your best interests at heart; an air of deception prevails with this relationship. The afternoon and evening hours of the 4th highlight social affairs, invitations, and the possible meeting of a new romance. The New Moon of the 5th in your 11th House will generate loads of activity during the weeks ahead involving clubs and organizations, new friends, and many, many social functions to attend. You are on a roll, so to speak, so enjoy what life has to offer at this time. The Full Moon of the 20th in your 6th House of work has all the earmarks of financial increase through hard work and past efforts. An unexpected financial matter may crop up again after the 28th. Resolve it with the aid of a legal advisor.

MAY

Job offers sound enticing on the 1st; clarify monetary issues before you take them too seriously. Mars' recent entry into your 2nd House of money could precipitate an unwise acceptance of this offer on the 2nd. There is no need to make impulsive decisions. The 2nd clearly indicates more than one opportunity, placing you in a position of being able to pick and choose. Several financial gains appear likely on the 4th. One comes through personal resources and the other through joint funds. With the New Moon of the 5th in your 12th House, it may be best to stick to regular routines for the next few weeks. Sounds boring, but it is necessary, now, to transform work related duties into more constructive outlets. Research ways to become more productive, materially as well as financially. Don't permit emotions to get in the way of logic between the 7th and 9th when confronted by errors in joint finances. You have the records to back you up. Disturbing family problems may create nervous stress and emotional upsets between the 13th and 20th. You will have to determine your priorities on the 21st as others attempt to pull you in too many diversified directions.

JUNE

The New Moon of the 3rd takes place in your 1st House. You are feeling optimistic and expansive and eager to begin new projects that may require some travel. Don't be too anxious to start, as your ruling planet, Mercury, is retrograding in your 12th House. Apparently there are a few issues behind the scenes that have to be ironed out. A dinner invitation on the 4th can result in a very emotionally rewarding experience. The 13th holds the promise of a new romance, but you may have difficulty yielding to their tender responses. Are you still suffering from the emotional scars of the past few years? The 14th and 15th can transform these emotional feelings and open the door to greater awareness and sensitivity. The Full Moon of the 19th takes place in your 7th House. If you are so inclined, marriage in the near future is a possibility. Those already married may consider extensive travel that they have never undertaken before. The 30th is a good day to garner these ideas for travel.

JULY

Communication from those near and far demands your personal attention during afternoon hours of the 1st. Sunday afternoon of the 2nd may be an ideal time to clear the deck of all these neglected correspondences; however, family interference may push them temporarily on the back burner. The New Moon of the 3rd is in your 2nd House of money. Financial or material gain is in the picture for the 3rd, 4th and 11th. A power struggle between you and a child on the 6th can result in a heated argument. Be careful; this could be a turning point in the parent/child relationship. The 9th is not favored for giving a baby or wedding shower or other social gathering. Even if you are invited to either event, in all likelihood it will be terribly boring. If you can take time off from work on the 12th, do so, and enjoy a pleasurable short trip in the company of someone you admire. If you have not yet taken your vacation, Saturday the 22nd is an excellent day for travel. A certain luxury item you have been wanting for some time may be available on the 25th at bargain prices. The greater protector, Jupiter, is entering your 2nd House of money and will assist in helping you pay for it. The 31st hints of a valued item with impeccable taste decorating the interior of your home.

AUGUST

The weather is perfect and your mind is on pleasurable pursuits rather than work related details. The New Moon of the 1st hints of errors in judgment at work due to lack of concentration. Someone may jolt you back into reality on the 4th when the serious error results in a financial loss. For others, it may be an upsetting car repair that may not be covered by the manufacturer's warranty. Caution your children to drive carefully; a minor accident on their part could increase your insurance premiums. If you are house hunting or just thinking of remodeling your present home, you'll have the energy on the 5th to tackle these projects. The Lunar Eclipse of the 17th highlights your 9th House. For those who lecture, teach or deal with electronics, radio and TV, this will be a banner year. For others, group travel tours, attending conventions, or the study of new subjects will be of prime interest in the months ahead.

SEPTEMBER

The recent Solar Eclipse of August 31st in your 4th House
will initiate new and favorable changes in personal and
domestic affairs. During the months ahead, you will close the
door on an old, stagnant condition, only to open another that
will lead you to new experiences and opportunities. Do not
look for immediate results, but rather, enduring ones that will
enhance future growth and expansion. This could be the real-
ization of a cherished dream that is soon to become a reality.
Children, your own or those of others, may be a source of
financial drain or create emotional stress on the 1st, 2nd, 7th
and 15th. Career and finances take a giant step forward on
the 14th, 18th, and 19th through several diversified interests.
Family matters require your personal attention in the resolving of a mini-crisis on the 21st. Romance and social affairs
take the spotlight on the 23rd and 24th. The New Moon of
the 29th, however, may require you to cut back on entertainments and pleasurable pursuits due to work responsibilities
and several heavy commitments. Gambling should also be
avoided, especially on the 30th.

OCTOBER

A difficult task that has to be completed during morning
hours of the 2nd is best handled personally. Make a special
note to comply accordingly during early evening hours when
others disappoint you through lack of cooperative efforts on
their part. Your ruling planet, Mercury, retrogrades back into
your 5th House of romance, children, and speculation. An old
financial or emotional problem in regard to these matters
will require your attention again on the 12th, 17th, 18th and
20th. You may have to contend with or yield to the wishes of
another individual when the Full Moon of the 14th takes place
in your 11th House. Try to seek a balance between children
or romance vs. friends and outdoor activities. The fall weather
is lovely in many parts of the country. A short excursion on
Sunday the 22nd, with someone whose company you enjoy,
can make you feel vibrant and alive. You may have to guard
your temper on the 27th and 28th; an emotional upheaval
involving a love relationship or a child can result in temporary separation. The New Moon of the 29th can increase
business acumen through use of new methods.

NOVEMBER

A special invitation, gift, or even an engagement, is probable during evening hours of the 2nd. There may be an increase in your payroll check of the 3rd, possibly due to overtime or a bonus. If self employed, concentrative efforts and hard work are paying off through expansion of business. Past errors at work involving shipments or services may have to be rectified on the 6th or 7th. You have excellent organizing ability, perseverance and willpower to handle the most difficult of tasks that may confront you on the 7th and 8th. Listen to your psychic or intuitive impressions on the 8th to assist in making the right moves for both business and financial advancements. Avoid the misguided advice of well meaning friends on the 10th. The Full Moon of the 13th falls in your 12th House. You may have to personally unravel confused issues involving incoming and outgoing financial expenditures. Embarrassing moments can occur between the 14th and 16th when a bounced check or past due bill is called to your attention. Your best day for clarifying this situation is on the 17th. Thanksgiving festivities can affect your health through intestinal upsets on the 26th and 27th if you are not careful.

DECEMBER

You are both admired and respected on the 1st by those in authority who recognize your capabilities, decisive action, and the concentrative manner in which you discharge your duties. The 4th brings exciting and surprising news and unlooked for opportunities from a distance. Someone from the past may call unexpectedly on the 10th—a magnetic person that hints of romantic appeal. The best day for Christmas shopping is on the 18th. Avoid the 20th and 21st; you may spend unwisely in your haste to finish your last minute gift shopping. The presence of a special someone from a distance adds a happy note during morning hours on Christmas Day. If you are single, the glitter of the holiday social gatherings between the 27th and 30th adds a glowing touch of romance as the two of you renew and rekindle an old love affair. Although your close friend or love relationship may have to return home on the 31st, there is the promise of future visits that makes the parting less painful.

CANCER
The Crab

June 22 to July 23

Quality: Cardinal
Element: water
Principle: passive
Ruler: Moon
Gem: pearl
Lucky Day: Monday
Anatomy: beast, stomach, upper lobes of liver
Key phrase: *I feel*

Glyph: crab's claws
Natural sign of: fourth house
Opposite sign: Capricorn
Color: white
Lucky Numbers: 3 and 7
Flower: larkspur

Key word: *devotion*

Positive Characteristics:
tenacious
intuitive
maternal
domestic
sensitive
retentive
sympathetic
emotional
traditional

Negative Characteristics:
brooding
touchy
negative
manipulative
too cautious
lazy
selfish
sorry for self

CANCER

Cancerians are often called the orphans of the Zodiac. Children born under the sign of Cancer do have the highest incident of being separated from one parent or of being brought up in a one parent home environment. In many cases where both parents exist, the Cancerian often experiences an invisible barrier between themselves and one of the parents. There is the inability to communicate with or to establish an emotional bond with this parent. As a result they feel love-starved and emotionally deprived and spend most of their life searching for the affection they think they missed.

Cancerians have a sympathetic and understanding regard of people. Being ruled by the Moon you are highly emotional and sensitive. Because you are also quiet and reserved, others may not realize how easily your feelings are hurt. Cancerians are idealistic about relationships, loyal to your friends. There is no limit to your generosity and helpfulness when you want to express your appreciation. You have sound intelligence and excellent memory recall of past events. However, you should curb the tendency to dwell on the past or self-indulgent reminiscing; rehashing old hurts and unintentional slights from others, and expanding them out of proportion.

Although you have good business sense, you do not have aggressive ambition and you do not care for hard work. You would prefer to inherit money or gain it through other sources so that you needn't be concerned with career efforts. And yet, many Cancerian women continue to marry men with limited incomes, requiring them to work after marriage out of fear of insecurity. Your financial needs are large; a home in which to establish your roots, comfortable furniture and a well stocked cupboard. Cancerians work well with the general public. This enables you to excel in fields such as restaurant work, catering, social work, public speaking and nursing.

Your emotions can be hazardous to your health. You turn to excessive food and drink to balm the hurt you feel inside. It is very easy to establish bad eating habits. Cancerians require a sensible diet and regular naps for they tend to tire easily.

JANUARY

Don't take it personally if someone at your social gathering on New Year's Day does not appear to be enjoying themselves. You can't mother everyone who has a depressing problem. A belated Christmas gift may arrive on the 2nd. The focal point for the next few weeks is on partnerships and close allies as the New Moon of the 7th falls in your 7th House. They may be harboring secret thoughts between the 11th and 15th, of relocation or changing jobs. Take an objective view at close relationships on the 15th and 16th. Decide for yourself if they have worn out their appeal; if so, take the necessary steps for positive changes. Something you discover on the 19th in regard to a close association might result in a rude awakening on the 20th. The Full Moon of the 21st in your 2nd House is liable to create disharmony among friends should you decide to lend them money or a personal possession. A close tie can be very charming in their appeal for funds on the 22nd. Best to refuse them than to lose them on the 23rd. An impromptu invitation may have to be refused due to a previous commitment that you feel is your duty to keep. The month ends on the 31st with an invitation from someone you have long admired and loved.

FEBRUARY

Mercury has been retrograding in your 7th House; minor worries and concerns in regard to partnerships continue until the 15th. Whomever you date or have a close contact with on the 4th is likely to be around for a long time. There appears to be an enduring and steadfast connotation to this relationship. The New Moon of the 6th highlights your 8th House of joint finances. If you have not heeded last month's advice against lending money or possessions to a friend, or anyone for that matter, then you are in for a jolt. Watch for problems along this nature on the 6th, 11th, 14th, 15th, 16th and 19th. The Lunar Eclipse of the 20th in your 3rd House places the spotlight on short travels and many diversified interests. There appears to be a new sideline that offers additional income through organized activities or associations. Partially paid travel expenses to attend conventions or those connected with groups of people will play a dominant role.

MARCH

Distant matters take precedence between the 2nd and 3rd of March. Contacts with friends or relatives residing in far-away places will wipe away the winter blahs. The 6th is the last time that friends or organizations will have an adverse effect upon joint finances, as Mars and Jupiter prepare to leave your 11th House. A chance to travel may indirectly come your way on the 7th, through the intervention of another individual. These offers of travel are reinforced with the presence of the Solar Eclipse of the 7th in your 9th House. It is apparent that you will not be traveling alone. You may hear from an old friend from a distant city on the 9th. Both Mars and Jupiter will enter your 12th House on the 11th. You can derive many varied benefits through your vocation if you are willing to handle work related duties that require working in solitude. The new job position will not be boring by any means, merely confining or isolating, so to speak. Personal contacts with important individuals on the 16th and 18th can enhance future aspirations. The Full Moon of the 22nd falls in your 4th House. Just when you're beginning to feel neglected, someone praises your efforts between the 22nd and 29th, concerning the way you have handled a difficult task.

APRIL

An exciting and unexpected offer may come your way on the 1st that could open the door to a new vocational interest or position. You may have to clear the ground, so to speak, of old, past conditions before you start preliminary, constructive action into this new field of endeavor. Jealousy rears its head between the 3rd and 5th, when someone at your place of employment resents your getting the new job offer. The 4th finds you handling loads of paperwork or writing job resumes. The New Moon of the 5th in your 10th House confirms the possibility of a positive job change or of vocational duties. It looks like it is in management, and the news may reach you on the 15th. The Full Moon of the 20th highlights your 5th House of romance and children. If single, you may meet a prominent, romantic individual on the 25th or 26th—if married, monetary gains through speculation and gambling, or one of your children announces an engagement.

MAY

A little surprise gift may come your way on the 1st or 2nd. Your job situation is going along well, except for one bossy individual whom you would love to tell off on the 2nd. With the New Moon of the 5th in your 11th House, a new friend will enter your life. This relationship has all the earmarks of a romantic connotation, but you will have to respect their need for personal independence and freedom to turn it into an enduring one. These compromises will be required of you between the 7th and 9th. Wherever you go or whatever you do during afternoon hours of the 13th, take time to double-check the information or instructions. Errors, misunderstandings and misinterpretations are par for the course. The evening hours, however, are fine for dating or social engagements. The Full Moon of the 20th finds you in a rather peculiar dilemma; you are torn between a new romance and yet somewhat tied to an old one. Take time out on the 21st to visit several individuals who are confined in the hospital for minor ailments. Your mail brings a surprise windfall or other financial gains on the 25th or 26th. The month closes on the 30th with a sigh of relief as Mars gets ready to leave your 1st House.

JUNE

It may sound boring, but the New Moon of the 3rd may keep you working behind the scenes with lots of paperwork to contend with. Friends will continue to be a source of concern or irritation until after the 10th. With Venus's entry into your 1st House on Sunday the 4th, make it a special day for a family gathering and plan a picnic or an outing. You've got loads of energy on the 6th; use it to catch up on neglected repair work around the home or apartment. Then, go out for dinner with a friend in the evening. If you haven't taken your vacation yet, give it serious consideration after the Full Moon of the 19th, at which time you will be feeling rather restless and itching for a change of pace. If you have been unhappy about conditions at work, it may be time to take a firm stand on the 26th and seek a raise in salary. If you apply logic rather than resort to emotions on the 30th and illustrate in a positive sense why you are entitled to an increase, you have greater chance for success.

JULY

The 1st and 2nd are excellent days for tackling neglected correspondences and visiting those that are confined. The New Moon of the 3rd falls in your 1st House. Take advantage of all opportunities that could produce extra cash through gambling or speculative offers. These financial gains are favored on the 4th and 11th. Avoid gambling or extravagant tendencies on the 5th, 6th and 9th. Nervous tension and emotional anxieties prevail between the 7th and 10th when others interfere with personal plans or block your attempts for progress. Be like the Moon and show others only what you want them to see, and on the 11th, you will have the willpower to accomplish what you first set out to do. Someone surprises you with a very special gift on the 12th. For the singles, it could well be an engagement ring. The spotlight is on your 7th House of partnerships as the Full Moon of the 18th falls therein. Someone gives you an ultimatum, perhaps concerning relocation. A decision on your part may be required by the 25th.

AUGUST

The 1st of the month begins with good news or a long awaited article from afar. The New Moon of the 1st is in your 2nd House of money. It is ill-advisable to make major purchases during the next 4 weeks or lend money to children or romantic partners. Note especially the early evening hours of the 1st and the afternoon hours of the 4th. You should be feeling a major change in the air, as Jupiter enters the sign of Cancer and your 1st House. No longer will you have to work behind the scenes in an isolated atmosphere. You will be in a very expansive mood with the foreknowledge that the future holds brighter opportunities. Because you are feeling so terrific, you may overdo the food intake. Weight gain is one of the major sore spots of this placement. Consider a short trip on Saturday the 5th to expand your knowledge by attending lectures or seminars. The company of another person will make a short excursion more enjoyable. News that you've been wanting to hear for some time arrives on the 9th. You'll be making major changes with joint financial issues with the Lunar Eclipse of the 17th in your 8th House.

SEPTEMBER

The recent Solar Eclipse of August 31st throws a favorable light on your 3rd House. There are tremendous opportunities in the months ahead for possible relocation, or a job offer in a different area or county. This offer may bring you closer to the home of a romantic partner or child. A family member, however, may not be very happy to hear this news and may show their displeasure around the 1st or 2nd. You may receive an unexpected refund check in the mail on the 12th, only to have part of it go out for another expenditure. Look for a surprise gift or unexpected invitation on the 13th. If a lie detector test is required before you can get that new job, you'll pass with flying colors on the 14th. The Full Moon of the 15th in your 9th House requires adjustments and decisions in regard to new working conditions and travel. An enduring romance is in the air on the 18th. Others should accept social invitations that could lead to a new association of prominence and future assistance. Romance is being steadily nurtured on the 19th, 20th and 23rd. Additional data need revising as Mercury retrogrades back into your 3rd House on the 26th.

OCTOBER

The previous New Moon of September 29th brings family matters into the spotlight. You may have to contend with family interference between the 1st and 4th, concerning your personal affairs. Mercury re-enters your 4th House on the 12th and already you are under stress trying to balance the scale between family or home conditions and close associations. You'll have to take a firm stand on these issues after the Full Moon of the 14th takes place in your 10th House. You need to get away for a short respite between the 17th and 22nd to a little hideaway place with someone special to retain your sense of balance and relax your nervous system. You'll later emerge with a different perspective in the handling of those stressful outside conditions. Control your temper on the 27th and 28th; you won't want to say something you will later regret. If you are single, the New Moon of the 29th will endow you with the willpower to do what you feel is best as far as romantic interests are concerned. Those in business can form a profitable partnership at this time.

NOVEMBER

The 1st of the month favors all matters to do with children, investments, partnerships and financial dealings for long-term gains. Accept a social invitation for the evening of the 2nd; you'll have a marvelous time. You will be able to communicate your innermost thoughts to those you love on the 3rd and 5th. And much to your surprise, the spoken word may not be necessary, as messages transcend between the two of you through mental telepathy. If you have been spending too much on children, romance or entertainment, you'll have to pay the piper on the 6th or 7th. Take advantage of every opportunity that may come your way on the 8th. It may involve travel, romance, children, grandchildren, attending seminars or promotion of a creative project. Personal interests will have to be set aside on the 16th as you yield to the wishes of others for the sake of peace and harmony. The 17th, however, is your day to escape from it all and do what you wish. Love relationships continue to thrive on the 19th, 20th, 21st and 26th.

DECEMBER

For those so inclined, a romantic affair is developing into a lasting relationship. Others may receive a thoughtful gift from a close associate. Decision making is combined with clear logic on the 4th, and thus you are able to handle complex work problems with ease. You are faced with several troublesome decisions with the Full Moon highlighting your 12th House. One may contain a job change, which may not be to your best interest. It may require your return to an old position which you disliked. The 13th is not favored for reaching any decision as you may be emotionally off balance in your judgment. Put it off until the 18th, at which time you will be more discriminative and conscientious in thought. The evening hours of the 18th are also excellent for winding up your last minute Christmas shopping. Unique, enjoyable and interesting experiences await you on Christmas morning. The New Moon of the 27th takes place in your 7th House of partnerships. You are undecided on the 29th, whether or not you should go on that short trip with a close associate. The gentle persuasion of a magnetic person sways your thinking and you are off to experience a new adventure on the 30th.

LEO
The Lion

July 23 to August 23

Quality: fixed
Element: fire
Principle: active
Ruler: Sun
Gem: ruby
Lucky Day: Sunday
Anatomy: heart, sides, upper back
Key phrase: *I will*

Glyph: lion's tail
Natural sign of: fifth house
Opposite sign: Aquarius
Color: gold
Lucky Numbers: 8 and 9
Flower: marigold

Key word: *magnetism*

Positive Characteristics:
dramatic
idealistic
proud
ambitious
creative
dignified
romantic
generous
self-assured
optimistic

Negative Characteristics:
vain
status conscious
childish
overbearing
fears ridicule
cruel
boastful
pretentious
autocratic

LEO

You have complete faith and trust in humanity. This can prove to be a handicap, when one becomes blinded to the faults of others. You are a loyal and generous friend who will help another in genuine need without being asked. You have a great deal of pride and tend to keep your private life to yourself. You permit no one to pry into your personal affairs. In general, you radiate an air of friendliness and charm in a very dignified manner. You will not tolerate dishonesty.

Your father may have played a strong role in your character development during your early years. The type of relationship between the father and child can be detected in the Leo personality. The secure Leo does not lack in self confidence, indicating there was good rapport between the two of them. Should the Leo be a loud boaster and require constant attention, he or she may have been neglected by their father or there has been a severe lack of communication between the two of them. The person who marries the latter type of Leo will have to provide a great deal of encouragement and flattery to rebuild their spouse's deflated ego and esteem.

Leos love to command, protect and lavish favors. Your main goal in life is to hold a position of authority. You should have no trouble gaining prestige and advancements through your career, for you are a highly responsible person and a perfectionist. If you cannot find a job where others can recognize your worth, then you would be wise in starting a business of your own.

Basically, your health is sound, for you have excellent recuperative powers. It is stress that can take its toll on your blood pressure or your heart. You should also be careful to lift heavy objects with your knees bent rather than use your back muscles. Slipped disks are another problem that often plague the Leo sign.

You are an idealist when it comes to romance. You learn rather early in life that love is not all wine and roses. You want so much to attract the perfect mate that you can overlook one who could have been a real gem. You have to have pride in your lover, but no matter how it turns out, you will always remain loyal.

JANUARY

New Year's Day is a time for celebration—don't permit the misbehavior of a relative to spoil your afternoon. A heavy workload or added responsibilities are indicated by the presence of the New Moon of the 7th in your 6th House. This may restrict you from taking time off from work for the travel plans you've had in mind. On the other hand, you appear relieved, as though you secretly preferred to spend the time with neglected home repairs. You proceed to tackle these repairs between the 10th and 12th. Your partner or close tie may be terribly disappointed and decide to take the trip alone the weekend of the 13th. Keeping your nose to the grindstone, so to speak, is likely to pay off during the week of the 16th, when good news reaches you about a future salary increase or bonus. The Full Moon of the 21st is taking its toll on your personal relationships as it falls in your 1st House. If you want to improve rapport with partnerships, you will have to seek a compromise by reducing the time you spend at work. Try to take a few days off and reconsider that previous planned trip between the 29th and 31st.

FEBRUARY

Revising, changing, or correcting work-related data will undergo consideration as Mercury retrogrades back into your 6th House of work. The tedious paperwork should ease up after the 16th. Someone offers an interesting invitation on the 1st to attend or participate at a sporting event. You will have to take time out for a serious discussion with your marriage or business partner as the New Moon of the 6th indicates there may be over-extending expenditures. If you want to maintain your good credit rating, you will have to keep a watchful eye on these trends between the 11th and 19th. Your willingness to work overtime and even on Saturdays has not gone unnoticed. A figure of authority has been secretly observing your ability to handle complex and responsible duties. Monetary or career advancements and a possible management position appear to be right around the corner. This is reinforced by the placement of the Lunar Eclipse of the 20th in your 2nd House of money. You will appreciate the challenging and interesting aspects of this new job offer between the 21st and 22nd.

MARCH

Intuition plays an important role in troubleshooting a difficult problem on the 2nd and 3rd at your place of employment. The early morning hours of the 4th are favored for the completion of a long-standing project. The 6th and 10th will be the last time you will have to contend with the mental aggravation of having to work with uncooperative individuals. These conditions will soon be changing for the better. New acquaintances enter the picture after the 11th. One will play a competitive role in a sporting game that requires manual dexterity, such as golf, racketball, volleyball, or tennis. If you filed your income tax early, you may receive a tax refund or other mutual benefits on the 11th. If weather permits, join your new pal in a friendly yet challenging sport during the Sunday morning hours of the 12th. If you can get Friday the 17th off from work, a short trip with a friend for a special sporting event could prove interesting. Both the 22nd and the 25th indicate the possibility of winning an award for your participation in a sporting event.

APRIL

Spring is in the air and finds you and your mate or partner taking or planning a trip on the 1st. If you take this trip, then be sure to allow sufficient time for your return home Sunday the 2nd because of time lost on detours or mechanical breakdown. Otherwise, you may not make it home in time for work on Monday the 3rd. For those who are free to travel or are on vacation time, the 4th and 5th continue to hold your interest in distant places. Keep your phone line open on Saturday the 15th for contacts from influential people who can help advance future interests. The Full Moon of the 20th falls in your 4th House. The 25th and 26th are the best days to seek a compromise between home, career, and partnerships. Apparently you have reached an impasse with your mate or partner concerning these issues, as more stress is indicated on the 28th. The ideal solution is to take a short trip together Friday evening the 28th. Enjoy a nice dinner Saturday the 29th, and in a sensitive manner, try to understand the needs of your partner. Discontinue these discussions on the 30th because too much talk leads to confusion.

MAY

Inviting an influential person to lunch between the 1st and 4th can add a few "brownie points" to possible future advancements. With the New Moon of the 5th in your 10th House, this is certainly the best time of the year to work toward career goals. Accept all invitations to attend social affairs connected with work. Especially on the 11th and 16th, you are likely to meet a prominent person who can be of tremendous help in promoting your personal interests. The Full Moon of the 20th continues to place the spotlight on home matters vs. job responsibilities. This time, however, you are determined to seek a workable solution that includes future travel plans to visit relatives of your mate. A decision regarding a child, yours or another's, has to be reached on the 21st. The 25th and 26th are your most enjoyable days of the month. You are highly active with group-related activities, friends, social parties, or educational seminars and lectures. The 30th is the last time you will be experiencing a mini-emotional crisis in connection with distant relatives and travel.

JUNE

If you have not yet taken your vacation, the New Moon of the 3rd in your 11th House, conjoined with Jupiter therein, may indicate a good time to embark on one. It may offer you respite from Mercury's retrograde motion in your 10th House of careers. You will be able to get away from minor irritations at work and the critical, faultfinding tendencies of others. The 4th is excellent for staying at home and puttering around the yard in quiet solitude. Do not listen to the advice of well-meaning co-workers on the 12th—there are too many inconsistencies that will only confuse matters at work. Tomorrow is a far better day for balanced judgment and logical application in the making of decisions. The planet Mars enters your 1st House on the 16th, enhancing possibilities of travel, new enterprises, and lucky speculations. This is further emphasized with the Full Moon of the 19th in your 5th House of pleasures, romance, and gambling. The 26th is not favored for risky ventures as the emotions are likely to rule over logic. The 30th is your best day for gambling if you are interested in the races or other sporting events.

JULY

On both days of the weekend of the 1st, get together with close friends for a friendly game of golf, tennis, or other outdoor sport. If you have a step-child, plan a special outing that will help to establish better rapport and bridge the communication gap. The New Moon of the 3rd in your 12th House should provide the willpower and incentive to modernize or revamp your present home or apartment. This month is also favored for the purchase, sale, or rental of property. In any case, be sure the ground rules are understood and that proper security papers are drawn. You are likely to experience greater emotional intensity and contentment on this 4th of July than on any you have ever celebrated in the past. There is a deep sense of inner security in the knowledge that you are loved and are happily surrounded by those you love. The Full Moon of the 18th is in your 6th House of work. Unforeseen circumstances stemming from the past may require correction of misleading or deleted printed material that may be connected with your job. The weather is perfect on the 29th, so contact a friend and participate in an outdoor sport.

AUGUST

The New Moon of the 1st in your 1st House may spark up a power struggle between you and a child, family member, or romantic partner, and this struggle may explode on the 4th. If you are considering a change in vocation, the 5th is your best day for writing business letters and mailing out your resume. A new channel may be opening the door to an unusual occupation, one that you have not undertaken before. Do not become discouraged by apparent delays. The news you've been wanting to hear can arrive on the 8th, 9th, or 15th. The Lunar Eclipse of the 17th places the spotlight on partnerships, as it falls in your 7th House. Patience and understanding will be required on your part as the element of the unexpected throws a monkey wrench in the daily routine. Your partner or mate may be upset over news from a distance concerning members of his/her family between the 19th and 27th. If a friend or a sibling tries to borrow money from you on the 23rd or 24th, chances are you may not get it back. The 30th bears good news concerning health improvements in your mate or partner's family.

SEPTEMBER

The previous Solar Eclipse of August 31st in your 2nd House of money reinforces last month's promise of financial and career advancements, especially those involving a unique occupation or technical know-how. The 1st to the 3rd still find your mate or partner fretting over distant relatives, although the 5th and 7th appear to indicate that his/her fears and concerns over distant relatives may not be as serious as he/she anticipated. The Full Moon of the 15th seems to indicate that minor surgery for this family member may be necessary. By the 24th there is the possibility of travel to visit those confined in a hospital. You are going along with the idea of taking this trip because you want to ease the feelings of anxiety your partner is undergoing. If you don't leave on the 24th, in all likelihood you will leave on Friday the 29th, when the New Moon highlights your 3rd House of travels.

OCTOBER

Between the 1st and the 4th, distant relatives still play havoc with daily routines and continue to upset your partner's nervous system. Just when matters get back to normal, your partner receives more disturbing news on the 12th. The Full Moon of the 14th takes place in your 9th House of travels and opposes Mars in your 3rd. If you don't agree to visit your partner's family, a serious confrontation is likely. A solution is found between the 17th and the 20th. Don't buck any change of plans on the 22nd that may be contrary to what you wanted to do. Go with the flow, and you will later discover it was the best thing that happened. You may not be hot on letter writing, but answers to several correspondences received on the 27th and 28th will require an immediate response. The New Moon of the 29th in your 4th House brings routine matters and stability back into your everyday affairs and in regard to matters of distant relatives. The future looks brighter in the weeks ahead, endowing you with optimism, energy, and willpower that you have not felt in ages. It is an active period for painting, fixing, or renovating property. Luck is with you if you are thinking of selling or buying a home. Those with rental property will be surprised to find very considerate tenants.

NOVEMBER

There appears to be an opportunity on the 1st that is likely to bring an unusual job offering that may be operated from the home base. A discussion with your partner or close ally on the 2nd will reveal his/her eagerness to participate in this new venture. The benevolent planet Jupiter has been transiting your 12th House for some time in the sign of Cancer. This indicates that a lucrative idea may be beneficially operated from the home, but to succeed, it must be kept hidden until it is ready to be presented before the public. The 3rd through the 5th indicate that loads of paperwork are necessary to get the pet project off the ground. You and your partner must exercise caution on the 6th to avoid confiding in a friend who may want to get in on the bandwagon, so to speak. Whatever you have going for you at this time, whether it deals with selling property or operating a business from the home, the 7th, 8th, and 12th are your best days to forge ahead with confidence and the knowledge that you will succeed. Don't sign legal documents or make important decisions on the 10th. The balance of the month will be extremely busy—you will be making changes and adapting to new situations.

DECEMBER

The previous New Moon of November 28th highlights your 5th House of romance, children, and creative projects. Seek a legal advisor if you are buying or selling a home, or operating a small business from the home. The 1st of the month finds you working very hard on something you have been wanting to achieve for some time. Listen to your partner and legal advisor on the 4th, they have good advice to offer. You may taste the fruits of your past labors through financial gains on the 5th. The Full Moon of the 12th calls for a compromise. Perhaps you should consider revising a pet project for greater productivity. Past concentration pays off handsomely on the 18th. An enjoyable Christmas Day is spent with relatives of your mate or romantic partner in a distant city. If you are heading for home after the holidays, the weather conditions in many parts of the country will be unbearable on the 29th. Your best bet is to get an early start the morning of the 30th.

VIRGO
The Virgin

August 23 to September 23

Quality: mutable
Element: earth
Principle: passive
Ruler: Mercury
Gem: sapphire
Lucky Day: Wednesday
Anatomy: intestines, liver, pancreas, gall bladder, upper bowel
Key phrase: *I analyze*

Glyph: Greek for 'virgin'
Natural sign of: sixth house
Opposite sign: Pisces
Color: gray
Lucky Numbers: 3 and 5
Flower: pansy

Key word: *practicality*

Positive Characteristics:
industrious
studious
scientific
methodical
discriminating
exacting
clean
humane
seeks perfection

Negative Characteristics:
critical
petty
melancholy
self-centered
picky
pedantic
skeptical
sloppy

VIRGO

Virgos have a fine sense of discrimination with a keen eye for details. You have a deep interest in culture, perfection, thorough logic and education. Some Virgos can become too critical and fault-finding, too rational and too involved with education. You have to analyze everything and often worry too much. In your need to think things over before you act, you sometimes take too long and lose good opportunities. You can handle tasks that others consider monotonous, for you have the ability to stay with complex problems until they are completed. Your high sense of responsibility causes you to dedicate yourself to the job. You are a top-notch organizer and work best when left alone. You prefer methodical routine. You become easily upset when someone goes through your desk or file cabinets. A confused or chaotic atmosphere while you are trying to concentrate can make you highly nervous.

Virgos often have a working mother, either in an office or holding an executive position. This tends to make them critical of their husbands, who may not earn as much. This type of mother resents having to stay home and take care of the children. The Virgo mother will constantly stress the need for education, knowing full well it lays the foundation for the earning capacity. Virgos are hard workers and often overwork. This is especially true of the male Virgo who has developed a determination to be better than his father.

As a rule, Virgos are sharp dressers, impeccably neat and tidy. They almost always look at least ten years younger than they really are. Love is serious to you; it is nothing you take for granted. Virgos do have relationship problems, in that they are too selective. No one appears to be perfect enough for them. They have to work at developing sound relationships and many do not marry until after they have passed the age of 25.

You generally take good care of your health, having regular check-ups. You make a medical appointment at the first sign of a problem. In diet, you can be a health-food fad-dist. Fresh air and exercise are needed and you should set aside some leisure time, just for yourself.

JANUARY

If you haven't heard from your child or a romantic partner on New Year's Day, don't despair. They'll probably call or visit during the afternoon hours of the 2nd. The New Moon of the 7th is in your 5th House of children, romance, and speculation. The single Virgo may hear from an old lover on the 10th or 11th. Virgo parents can expect communication from a child that lives in a distant city. This period is not favored for gambling or investments. If you have more than one child, the second oldest may be a source of concern on the 12th. This child appears to be undergoing financial or career restrictions at this time and will require your patience and understanding. What's the good news on the 15th or 16th? Are you going to be a grandparent? Or, is there a chance for an unusual training program you have long desired? Or, are you going on a trip with your romantic partner? The answers to these questions depend upon your status. Secret transactions with someone at a distance are not favored between the 21st and the 23rd, as the Full Moon falls in your 12th House. All's well that ends well, as the 31st brings good news from a distant city—a child appears to be financially secured with a good job.

FEBRUARY

Mercury's retrograde motion in your 5th House may have you fretting and worrying more than usual over affairs of children. The single Virgo may experience a very disappointing time in the area of romance. Evaluate future prospects on the 4th, and if necessary, apply for a special financial grant or assistance to undertake a specialized study course. The single Virgo should accept invitations to attend social functions that could lead to the meeting of a prominent or influential person. This relationship may be slow in developing, but has all the earmarks of endurance. The New Moon of the 6th in your 6th House of work may introduce new equipment or technology. The requirement necessary to prepare for this new vocational technology may interfere with the studies you were planning to pursue. The Lunar Eclipse of the 20th places the spotlight on you, as it falls in your 1st House. You can expect extraordinary and pleasant surprises affecting your personal affairs during the months ahead.

MARCH

News of an engagement, wedding, or birth is likely to reach you between the 2nd and 4th. The 4th through the 6th may be your last chance to consider the option of taking a specialized study course. While it is true that demands at work may make this study course too difficult to fit into your work schedule, the Solar Eclipse of the 7th can help you through the assistance of an advisor or counselor. Listen to what that person has to offer between the 8th and 9th. It is time to slam the door on feelings of inadequacy on the 10th. Mars and Jupiter will soon be entering your 10th House. A new career interest lies before you, requiring personal initiative to learn new techniques. Your future and career outlook appear promising during the months ahead. You can look forward to a pleasant social gathering on the evening of the 16th. You may feel overwhelmed with studies or paperwork on the 19th and 20th. Seek assistance from others who are eager to help you on the 22nd, 25th, and 29th.

APRIL

It may be a weekend seminar that is tied in some way with your job, or you may have to work on Saturday the 1st. Whatever the situation may be, don't pass up the offer. You will be given an opportunity to garner unusual information or knowledge that will benefit future career advancements. Money you lend anyone on the 2nd or 3rd will not be returned. Think twice if you are asked to co-sign for a loan—matters are not as they appear on the surface. With the New Moon of the 5th in your 8th House of joint finances, there is the possibility you will impulsively go against your better judgment. Secret financial transactions appear likely on the 15th. From all indications, it looks like someone at a distance or a child will be in need of monetary assistance. If you are married and haven't told your mate, he/she will get wind of it on the 19th. The Full Moon of the 20th in your 3rd House throws a favorable light on your children's or romantic partner's financial picture. Past concerns about these areas will ease after the 25th and 26th. Your ruling planet, Mercury, enters your 10th House, increasing the amount of paperwork and studies you may have to deal with in the next few weeks.

MAY

Your marriage partner or close ally may receive an invitation, a gift, or hear good news on the 1st. The extra work demanded of you lately should be good for a salary increase. Why not give it a try between the 2nd and 4th? The New Moon of the 5th in your 9th House will activate contacts with those living in distant cities. An emotional crisis will develop between the 7th and 9th that will place you in a compromising position. You may have to sacrifice a personal interest and yield to the wishes of another. You can get a lot of work done on the 11th if others stop interrupting your train of thought. Matters concerning money or possessions take precedence on the 16th, and controversial issues develop in connection with children and their spouses or romantic partners. The Full Moon of the 20th is in your 3rd House. It may be time to change or update your car, life, or home insurance policies. Keep the communication lines open on Sunday the 21st—someone wants to discuss a matter of importance with you. The 30th is the last time you are likely to undergo a disturbing emotional crisis.

JUNE

The New Moon of the 3rd places the spotlight on your 10th House of careers. It is in close conjunction with the beneficial planet Jupiter. You should, in the weeks ahead, take advantage of all opportunities that are likely to enhance career advancements. This New Moon may also increase travel possibilities or opportunities to attend lectures involved with your vocation. The best days for pushing career interests are the 8th, 9th, and 13th. The 10th is your day and is favorable for pet projects, shopping, and catching up on correspondence. There is a good chance of a monetary refund or an insurance settlement on the 15th. The Full Moon of the 19th falls in your 4th House. If you haven't taken your vacation yet, this may be a good time to visit family members in distant cities. You can make your marriage partner happy on the 24th with offers to visit his/her family, or inviting them to stay at your home. Listen closely for a possible secret that is sure to reveal itself between the 26th and 30th. This exciting news is centered around the affairs concerning a child or a romantic partner.

JULY

The 1st and 2nd are apt to be extremely busy days, with diversified tasks dealing with phone calls, correspondence, and several short trips. Some individuals may have to contact siblings and discuss certain matters relating to the affairs of a parent. On the 3rd and 4th, a parent may require your assistance to straighten out matters of insurance, taxes, and other joint financial issues. The New Moon of the 3rd may prove rather depressing when an old past secret is revealed in connection with affairs of a child or romantic partner. This information may temporarily upset you emotionally or psychologically on the 5th and 9th. You regain your sense of balance, however, between the 10th and 12th when the hidden matters concerning these issues are clarified. The Full Moon of the 18th in your 5th House indicates that a thorough discussion may be necessary to clear the air of past misunderstandings and old issues with family members and close ties. The 23rd to the 25th are your best days for confrontations, as you are more likely to exercise caution in speech and care in your judgmental attitude. You will be able to present yourself in your best light.

AUGUST

The month begins with Venus in your 1st House. You are feeling exceptionally cheerful on the 1st and everything appears to be going well. The New Moon of the 1st in your 12th House may indicate unforeseen problems with joint finances or insurance, which can manifest either on the 1st or 4th. Exercise caution when driving; a young person who does not have insurance may damage your car, or your child drives the car and your insurance premiums are increased as a result. Mars and Mercury have entered your 1st House recently. A new and influential person may come into your life on the 5th and introduce a whole new concept that you have not considered before. Your marriage partner or other close tie is likely to rebel against this new undertaking. But you have a willful determination between the 8th and 15th to continue with this new pet project. The Lunar Eclipse of the 17th fortifies the entry of a new vocational interest as it occurs in your 6th House. A cutback in funds while learning this new trade may be the only drawback.

SEPTEMBER

The previous Solar Eclipse of August 31st places the spotlight on personal interests as it falls in your 1st House. In the months ahead, you will be drawn toward a new vocational interest, to something that you have long desired. It is difficult to specify the category, as much depends upon environmental background. It is apparent that some Virgos may enter the medical field. Others may go into spiritual or mental healing. Working with land, real estate, insurance, or mortgages is indicated for some Virgos. Whatever the job may entail, it is certain that you will venture into this new program with an assurance and self-confidence you never felt before. In any case, either someone attempts to discourage you, or financial gains will be very slow in the beginning. If you are in earnest, pursue the possibility of job changes on the 2nd, 5th, and 13th. The Full Moon of the 15th is in your 7th House. Someone will come to your assistance, either financially or through moral support, between the 14th and the 20th. You will be faced with many decisions on the 21st, but hold off on them until the 24th, at which time your intuitive ability will guide you in the right direction.

OCTOBER

You may have to provide financial assistance for a child or romantic partner between the 1st and 4th. Your ruling planet, Mercury, retrogrades back into your 2nd House of money. News that will place additional burdens on personal finances may reach you on the 12th. The Full Moon of the 14th falls in your 8th House of mutual funds. Between the 17th and 20th, you will have to draw the line on continual financial assistance to a family member. Don't try to handle this monetary crisis alone. Discuss this matter on the 27th and 28th with your partner or close ally, who can help you balance the situation. The New Moon of the 29th highlights your 3rd House of mental aspirations. It is time to take stock of yourself and determine what YOU want to accomplish. Luck, combined with determination, will be with you every step of the way. From this New Moon you have the assurance that no matter how difficult the learning process may be, you will overcome all obstacles and succeed. During the next few weeks, fate will open a new door for you and, at the same time, close an old door.

NOVEMBER

On the 1st, contact a figure of authority who can assist you with complex paperwork. Luck is with you on the 2nd in the area of finances. The 3rd is a busy day for writing letters, phone calls, and possible short trips for clarification of monetary assistance through your place of employment, perhaps to undertake a study course. If recent attempts have not been successful, then continue to write additional letters on the 5th as new sources will soon be opening up to you. Stressful conditions crop up at work on the 6th and it may be a good idea to shelve study interests for the day. The 7th and 8th produce surprising results as others get on your bandwagon and offer their assistance. The afternoon of the 8th finds you pursuing an objective with an intensity you have never felt before. Control impulsive tendencies on the 10th, or your actions may agitate others. The Full Moon of the 13th falls in your 9th House of travel and higher education. Being in close opposition to your ruling planet, Mercury, you are faced with a decision. Should you invest time and money on a new study course? You are filled with doubt and apprehension on the 23rd. But something happens between the 26th and 30th that enables you to reach a decision.

DECEMBER

A past-due refund check is likely to come through on the 1st. An interesting and unexpected change in circumstances may occur at work on the 4th. Previous misunderstandings through partnerships can be cleared up on the 5th. The Full Moon of the 12th will place you in the precarious position of having to make several important decisions. A compromise will have to be reached between career interests and family responsibilities. Rely on your sound, intuitive and practical senses to aid in the resolving of these issues on the 18th. The morning hours of the 20th are excellent for last-minute shoppers. Be sure to include in-laws or distant relatives in your Christmas celebration on the 25th, plus a new friend that you may have met at work. The New Moon of the 27th in your 5th House bears good news from distant places. The 28th and 29th should bring you in contact with friends that you have not heard from in a long time. Accept an invitation from a friend or co-worker for a festive night out on Saturday the 30th.

LIBRA
The Scales

September 23 to October 23

Quality: cardinal
Element: air
Principle: active
Ruler: Venus
Gem: opal
Lucky Day: Friday
Anatomy: kidneys, lower back, adrenal glands, appendix
Key phrase: *I balance*

Glyph: the scales
Natural sign of: seventh house
Opposite sign: Aries
Color: blue
Lucky Numbers: 6 and 9
Flower: rose

Key word: *harmony*

Positive Characteristics:
cooperative
persuasive
companionable
refined
judicial
artistic
diplomatic
sociable
suave

Negative Characteristics:
fickle
apathetic
loves intrigue
peace at any price
pouting
indecisive
easily deterred

LIBRA

With Libras, it is sometimes yes, sometimes no, but most often it is a definite maybe. Does this sound as though Libras are indecisive? Not necessarily, it is just a matter of making the right decision. You try so hard to see both sides of an issue, to reach a fair and just conclusion. Libras are great at solving other people's problems, becoming diplomats, judges, counselors, attorneys or arbitrators between labor and management. But on the personal level, they seldom learn how to solve their own problems. The reason for this is that spending so much time being a peacemaker for others necessitates their concealing even from themselves, the fact that they have emotional needs, become angry and frustrated. Should you allow these emotions to surface, your social image would be impaired.

Libras are attracted to beautiful things and like to fill their environment with it. Those that don't enter politics, become interior decorators, artists, designers, hair dressers or salespeople of cosmetics and jewelry. Libras are intelligent, tactful and diplomatic. You have the ability to take ideas or material developed by others and determine the best way to present it to the public in the most acceptable form. Your manner is pleasant and poised. Creativity is important to your career for you loathe ordinary work and routine dismays you. Seek to climb to successful heights so that you may be free of monotony. Work in an area where you will no doubt need to give yourself a push. You enjoy laboring with people and anything connected with justice or public welfare.

Your social life is quite important to you. You can be the most attractive person at any social event, for you know how to wear clothes and your speech is charming. Libras are people oriented and need to have them around. You can't say no to anyone or anything. Your one main psychological fear, is going through life alone.

For your health's sake, you should live in a harmonious atmosphere. Disruptive home conditions can make you ill and throw you off balance. Water is an important necessity in keeping your kidneys flushed.

JANUARY

An unpleasant incident from the past is likely to be a source of irritation during the afternoon hours of the 1st. A gift on the 2nd, possibly from a co-worker or close friend, may have to be kept on the quiet side. The New Moon of the 7th falls in your 4th House. Family responsibilities have been weighing rather heavily on your shoulders lately. You may want to go on a short trip with a friend on the 11th or 12th, just to get away for a while. But your marriage or business partner may be opposed to the idea. In the face of a possible argument, you are still interested in your friend's invitation and are likely to accept on the 14th or 15th. You are feeling rather repressed at the moment. But an unexpected phone call during the evening hours is apt to lift your spirits. You may be due for a rude awakening, as the Full Moon of the 21st occurs in your 11th House, and you discover the unreliability of a friend. Be aware of this trend on the 22nd, 23rd, 25th, and 26th. But all is forgiven when a social invitation is extended on the 31st.

FEBRUARY

Mercury retrogrades back into your 4th House and you are again faced with some minor problems concerning a family member. Perhaps it is a child that needs your logical advice in connection with school or other personal matters. Take time out for a serious conversation with this person on the 1st and help him/her seek a workable solution. Consult with your partner or an advisor on the 4th and discuss a possible loan if the child is being faced with a monetary crisis. The New Moon of the 6th falls in your 5th House of children and romance. The family member may be overly independent and rebel against your offer of financial aid. Best to turn the entire matter over to your partner or a counselor who will broach the subject from a different angle on the 7th or 8th. The Lunar Eclipse of the 20th in your 12th House comes up with an unexpected and surprising solution to the long-standing family problem. There is the promise of a job offer, through a figure of authority or a government official, for this child or romantic person, possibly on the 21st, 22nd, 25th, or 26th. The starting salary may be a disappointment.

MARCH

You are enjoying the present atmosphere at your place of employment, which is rather congenial as co-workers and those in authority collaborate in cooperative efforts on the 2nd and 3rd. The 4th and 5th are excellent days for furniture shopping or searching for other decorative items to enhance the home decor. The 6th should be the last time that you are likely to experience difficulty through children (or romance) and their financial affairs. The Solar Eclipse in your 6th House of work should produce favorable results in regard to a wage increase and improvements in your health insurance coverage. This is always a good time to get a thorough physical and change your dietary food habits if you have gained a sufficient amount lately, paying attention to fruits and vegetables, and fiber. If you have not yet received that long overdue pay raise, the 8th and 9th are good days to try for it. Jupiter enters your 9th House on the 11th, and your mate or partner may feel an urgency to visit several members of his/her family, both near and far. One trip may be undertaken shortly after the Full Moon of the 22nd and quite possibly before the 29th.

APRIL

Surprise your mate or loved one on April Fool's Day and invite him/her out to a nice dinner. The 3rd finds your partner concerned about the welfare of a distant relative. Both of you may have to make a decision on the 4th concerning a short trip in the near future. This is emphasized with the New Moon of the 5th in your 7th House of relationships. In all likelihood you and your mate or close ally will be taking a short excursion, quite possibly on Saturday the 15th. This person that you and your partner are thinking of visiting may be confined in a hospital, but do not worry as there does not appear to be any real cause for concern. The Full Moon of the 20th highlights your 2nd House of money. You may receive a bank statement or bill calling an error to your attention on the 25th or 26th. Much to your surprise, the error is in your favor benefitting you. Mars enters your 10th House of careers on the 28th. Your actions and ambitions will be governed by instinct during the weeks ahead.

MAY

You might be permitted to take slightly damaged or otherwise unsaleable merchandise home from work on the 1st. With the New Moon of the 5th in your 8th House, you may have to consider spending some time and money on home improvements or repairs. Sunday the 7th doesn't appear very tranquil—animosity is running rampant among family members. Family tension continues to weigh heavily on the 8th and 9th. If you are not careful, you can be drawn into this sticky domestic situation on the 16th. There is a good chance on Saturday the 20th, the day of the Full Moon, to smooth over family squabbles. Be flexible on Sunday the 21st when expected plans are altered and lead to different directions. The unexpected good news of the 25th or 26th should uplift your spirits after the past few depressing days you've experienced. Don't overreact on the 27th or 28th—the news you hear has all the earmarks of being a mix-up. The household atmosphere will become less tense and more relaxed after the 30th.

JUNE

The New Moon of the 3rd enters your 9th House of travels and joins Jupiter therein. Vacation plans and distant family visits make for a pleasurable month ahead. It is not too early to think about the fall college quarter and the study courses you may want to take. If your company is planning a summer festivity or picnic on Sunday the 4th, be sure to include the entire family as the day promises to be an enjoyable one. You can lock horns with management during the morning hours of the 9th, and it may be best to keep your opinions to yourself. You won't be able to please anyone during the evening hours of the 12th, so don't even try. Good luck comes your way through several resources on the 13th, so be alert to all opportunities and take advantage of them. If you work the evening shift, there is a good chance of bringing home something special on the 14th or 15th. The Full Moon of the 19th highlights your 3rd House of short travels. Consider an afternoon outing with a youngster or a special friend. Let your partner handle any emotional flare-ups that may occur on the 26th, which may involve a child. Your partner has the finesse and the know-how to handle the problem effectively.

JULY

It is unlikely that you will be spending the 4th of July in your own surroundings. All the activity connected with the holiday weekend of the 1st appears to be in the company of distant relatives. You'll be catching up on a lot of family news on Sunday the 2nd. The New Moon of the 3rd may provide you with one of the most emotionally rewarding times you have ever spent with your family. Go along with any change of plans that relatives are likely to make on the 4th of July because the end result will be memorable. A daughter- or son-in-law or a step-child may be a source of financial drain on the 5th, 6th, or 9th. It may be time for a family discussion concerning this matter on the 10th or 11th. The Full Moon of the 18th brings an old family problem into view as it highlights your 4th House. For the sake of peace and harmony, it may be best to keep your opinions to yourself at least until the 22nd, at which time you can broach the matter objectively. Jupiter enters your 10th House of careers on the 30th. Be alert for new opportunities for financial and employment advancements.

AUGUST

You are very compassionate on the 1st and would make a good mediator for past family grievances. The New Moon of the 1st is placed in an uncomfortable position. As a result, a power struggle may exist between you and a daughter- or son-in-law or a step-child, and is likely to explode on the 4th. Don't worry if you hear news on the 5th of a relative being hospitalized. There is a strong shield of protection surrounding that person. Your intuitive ability is also uncanny at this time, so you should research new avenues for mental improvement and a possible new business opportunity. You can gain at this time through secretive sources or a private project. Take time to investigate these matters on the 8th, 9th, 12th, 13th, and 15th. The Lunar Eclipse of the 17th falls in your 5th House of creativity. An unusual hobby that can be operated from the home could produce financial gain. Seek the advice of an authoritative figure on the 14th. Family problems may temporarily throw you off balance mentally on the 27th. A few more details are required on the 30th before you can get your private project moving.

SEPTEMBER

The recent Solar Eclipse of August 31st in your 12th House places the spotlight on pet projects. There appears to be something you have had in the back of your mind that you have been wanting to perhaps incorporate into a business. It may be a discovery that you uncovered at your place of employment, a new service or commodity that could be very productive financially. Should you go ahead with this private venture, don't expect dramatic monetary advancements. But most certainly there will be long-range benefits and security as the end results. You are likely to experience difficulty convincing others of the feasibility of your idea on the 1st and 2nd. Without any fanfare, contact a knowledgeable person on the 5th and get that person's constructive views. The Full Moon of the 15th is in your 6th House of work and the sign of Pisces. Mercury, ruler of your 12th House of secrets, is retrograding in your 1st House. Someone is not "gung ho" on the idea and may require convincing. Do some additional research on your secret project and maybe redo or reconsider some of the previous plans. It is a shame, but someone may throw a monkey wrench into your personal project and try to discourage you from venturing further as the New Moon of the 29th falls in your 1st House.

OCTOBER

With the previous New Moon of the 29th in your 1st House, it may be a good idea to get a physical checkup. There is the possibility of an old health problem flaring up again in the next few weeks. Limit your salt intake and drink lots of water to balance your system, keep the kidneys flushed, and prevent any possibility of an infection. Don't do anything strenuous that could result in an injury to the muscles of the lower back. Also, keep a weather eye on past conditions concerning varicose veins. Dates to watch for possible health upsets are between the 1st and 4th. The Full Moon of the 14th emphasizes 7th House matters. Be your own counsel during the next two weeks as others are apt to disapprove or disagree with your ideas or actions, especially between the 17th and 20th. The 22nd is a perfect day for an outing. To avoid any cause for regret later, investigate thoroughly all alternatives before you reach any hasty agreements on the 27th or 28th.

NOVEMBER

The recent New Moon of October 29th took place in your 2nd House of money. Do you need extra funds to meet household expenses or to fulfill family responsibilities? This month is favored for gain through joint monetary resources. It may be a forgotten insurance refund, a dividend check, an inheritance or a long-overdue salary increase. If you are employed, the 1st is a good time to apply for a raise. A possible financial gain is likely on the 2nd through your partner. The 3rd appears to favor a payment from an insurance company or the settlement of a small legal matter. The 8th indicates a beneficial change in working conditions or a possible advancement in which you may be placed in control of a situation, machinery, or individuals. The Full Moon of the 13th in your 8th House of joint finances calls for an assessment of mutual funds. Evaluate your budget and see where you can add to, or open, a new savings account. Your emotions are apt to carry you away between the 14th and 16th when news reaches you of an ill family member who either resides at a distance or is an in-law. The 26th and the 27th are likely to see the end of an old condition, forcing new beginnings.

DECEMBER

The previous New Moon of November 28th highlighted your 3rd House of communications. With the Christmas season just around the corner, it may be a good idea to correspond with relatives in distant places and discuss getting together for the holidays. Your marriage or business partner may be awarded an insurance settlement or other financial returns through mutual resources on the 1st. Sunday the 10th can be one of those depressing days when you decide to balance your checkbook and find an upsetting discrepancy. Everything is still up in the air as far as visiting relatives at Christmas time because the Full Moon is in a changeable sign and in your 9th House of travels. Christmas may find you staying close to home and spending the day with close friends and with relatives of your mate. The New Moon of the 27th takes place in your 4th House. You appear rather depressed, perhaps your having to return to work on the 28th was disappointing as you were looking forward to a long holiday vacation. The extra money, however, will be handy.

SCORPIO
The Scorpion

October 23 to November 23

Quality: fixed
Element: water
Principle: passive
Ruler: Pluto
Gem: topaz
Lucky Day: Tuesday
Anatomy: the genitals, bladder, rectum, reproductive organs
Key phrase: *I desire*

Glyph: scorpion's tail
Natural sign of: eighth house
Opposite sign: Taurus
Color: burgundy
Lucky Numbers: 2 and 4
Flower: chrysanthemum

Key word: *intensity*

Positive Characteristics:
motivated
penetrating
executive
resourceful
determined
scientific
probing
passionate
aware

Negative Characteristics:
vengeful
temperamental
secretive
overbearing
violent
sarcastic
suspicious
jealous

SCORPIO

You are a very emotional, intense and sensitive individual. No one can fathom the depths of your magnetic forces, which can be personally constructive or highly destructive. You have a way of ferreting out information from others without disclosing any of your own. You are a very secretive person. You love to observe others and you go about your affairs in a quiet manner. You give your complete trust and loyalty to others and demand the same intensity in return. If your trust has been betrayed, you will seek to get even no matter how long it takes. You have the patience to wait for this opportune time. Scorpios on the higher plane are more likely to say, "God will take care of them for me".

Your mind is very active and loves to engage in complex games such as difficult jig-saw puzzles or cross-word puzzles. You want to be the master of your own fate. You resent outside interference that may upset your power of self-control. Power is what you would like to have over others or over any situation at hand. You have strong likes and dislikes, often at first sight. Some Scorpios like to work alone and hidden from the outside world, while others can climb to fame rather easily. Don't hide your talents, soar to the heights, for you have so much to contribute. You are a leader, not a follower. Just make sure your leadership is not manipulative.

Scorpios are supposed to be the sex symbol of the Zodiac, especially the male Scorpios. Actually, the average Scorpio is not really all that interested in sex. It may be true that they discovered sex rather early in life, earlier than the other Zodiac signs. Sex for the Scorpio is used more as a means of seeking the affection that was absent when he or she was a child. You have to learn to give affection in order to get it.

Scorpios have a phenomenal memory and are terrific researchers. You are excellent as detectives or undercover agents. Psychic healing, the occult, or the medical profession are other fields open to Scorpios. However, you'll find the average Scorpio in banking, insurance or as an attorney. Your reproductive organs and elimination systems are your chief areas for health concerns.

JANUARY

You are in the mood to spend New Year's Day in quiet solitude, but others seem determined to impose upon your privacy. Although you may have to return to work on the 2nd, you don't seem to mind. In fact, your art of visualization finds you planning your day's work so well that all tasks are completed before you leave. The New Moon of the 7th is in your 3rd House. You are very well organized and working on future projects that promise larger monetary returns. Romance beckons on the 10th and 11th, with an unexpected phone call from someone out of your past. An aggressive newcomer appears determined to upset your methodical work methods through the introduction of something totally new and different between the 12th and the 14th. What starts out to be a beautiful, romantic morning on Sunday the 15th may end in a squabble due to differences of opinion later in the day. You can get a great deal of work done during daytime hours on the 16th by the cooperative efforts of others. Later in the evening accept that unexpected invitation to help ease nervous tension. You are likely to lock horns with someone at work on the 21st and 23rd through stubborn adherence to ideas.

FEBRUARY

As Mercury continues to retrograde in your 3rd House, you may have to redo, change, or alter previous job commitments. Exchange of ideas and views with others on the 1st might help you to arrive at a workable solution for an old problem. If you hesitate and exercise care in what you say during the evening hours of the 3rd, you will be able to smooth ruffled feathers that resulted earlier through a disagreement. The New Moon of the 6th falls in your 4th House. You may be caught off guard by an unexpected bill created by someone staying at your home. Sound ideas on the 3rd can lead to future marketable projects. Whoever is sharing your home or apartment at this time seems to be creating a great deal of emotional stress and tension. You will have to exercise patience with that person on the 15th, 16th, and 19th. The Lunar Eclipse of the 20th falls in your 11th House. New friends will enter your life in the months ahead. One friendship will develop into a romantic relationship and generate a transforming effect upon your personal life.

MARCH

No matter what type of work you do for a living, your inner senses will be in tune with the finer intricacies of the task at hand on the 2nd. Whatever work-related problems have beset you in the past can be resolved at this time. Your ability to combine the art of creativity and practicality on the 3rd is both remarkable and productive. The 6th is the last time that you will undergo a serious confrontation with a household member. The Solar Eclipse of the 7th highlights your 5th House of romance, children, and hobbies. A new romance should have entered the single Scorpio's life recently. They may have to think seriously of eliminating their present household guest on the 10th. Romance goes into full steam on the 11th. All other Scorpios will be faced with the reality that a new phase is before them, but in the process, they will have to let go of something or of someone. You can effectively deal with that at a distance on the 16th. Business and finances take an upward trend on the 17th. The Full Moon of the 22nd in your 12th House hints of romantic involvement with someone you may have met through contacts at work. It is difficult to say why, at this time, the relationship must be kept behind the scenes.

APRIL

There is a great deal of activity surrounding the home front on the 1st. Apparently, you are making some positive changes in the right direction. Don't work to the point of exhaustion during early evening hours, and don't place too much reliance upon promises of others later in the evening. The indications for mental confusion, delays in communications or a mix-up, and disappointments through others continue on the 2nd and 3rd. The New Moon of the 5th in your 6th House of work will activate both creative and mental application along new lines of endeavor. Several new diversified interests are favored with the promise of financial increase. The Full Moon of the 20th falls in your 1st House. There are exceptional and dramatic changes in store for you during the next two weeks. You will either go on a short trip on the 25th or 26th with someone special, hear good news that will alter personal affairs, or make an important change in your residence. Distant matters are activated on the 30th.

MAY

There is the possibility of receiving a luncheon invitation or a gift on the 1st day of the month. Haste makes waste, so if you must deal with published material or important papers connected with your job on the 2nd, don't try to rush it through. Errors are possible, so put that task off for another day or have someone double-check your material. The afternoon hours of the 4th may bring pleasant communications or news from a distance. The New Moon of the 5th places the spotlight on other people as it takes place in your 7th House. A long-lasting and satisfying relationship may emerge during the month ahead for the single Scorpios. Others are likely to have a busy round of social functions, weddings, or parties to attend. Your mental and physical senses will be tirelessly active on the 20th, which should enable you to reach a decision that you have been pondering for some time. The 25th and 26th are excellent days for contacting individuals concerned with finances and payroll. Marriage may be in store during this time for the single Scorpio who has recently met someone of wealth and influence.

JUNE

The New Moon of the 3rd conjoins the beneficial planet Jupiter in your 8th House of mutual funds. Money should be coming in through several sources during the weeks ahead. If you are due for a salary increase, apply for it on the 8th or 9th. The 13th indicates profits through a creative project. Even a forgotten refund is likely to come your way. The 4th will remain in your memory for a long time as you receive a phone call or a visit from someone special. This might be a good time to take or plan your vacation. Don't involve others with your pet projects on the 12th—they are apt to hinder progress because of their confusion. Whether married or single, your emotional responses are in high gear during the late evening hours of the 14th. You are still on a high excitable plane on the 15th. Perhaps you can take the day off from work and go on a short, pleasurable outing to relieve your inner tensions. The Full Moon of the 19th indicates that several financial dealings are likely or in the offing. The news will be very unexpected, stemming from a past issue and involving printed material.

JULY

The 1st and the 2nd of the month find you quite busy working on financial statements, signing contracts, or writing letters to distant places connected with mutual funds or royalty benefits. The month ahead should be extremely beneficial for you personally as the New Moon of the 3rd in your 9th House throws a favorable light on your ruling planet, Pluto, in your 1st House. Push this sideline that you have been working on, whether it is teaching, publishing, or lecturing. The 4th is a good time to formulate these long-range plans for the future. Contact an authoritative figure who can beneficially promote your intellectual interests. Be ready to travel if necessary. A personal career goal or pet project may have to be temporarily set aside on the 5th, 6th, and 9th, due to other commitments. The Full Moon of the 18th falls in your 3rd House. Be sure to double-check paperwork or published material for possible deletion of an important item. You may have to contact a publisher or someone at a distance and have the printed matter corrected. Someone comes to your rescue between the 25th and 31st, and a cherished dream may become a reality.

AUGUST

Your intuitive and creative abilities are at their highest peak during the morning hours of the 1st. You may even be surprised at the practical ideas that are likely to emerge from within. The New Moon also takes place on the 1st in your 10th House of careers. It may be wise at this time to keep your pet projects or creative hobbies to yourself, especially on the 4th, when the management where you work may want to incorporate them into its business. Whatever the project may be, once you give control of it to others, your earnings from it will not be as great. Jupiter has recently entered your 9th House and will instill an interest in travel and publications. Listen to a friend between the 5th and 15th, who will have your best interest at heart. That friend's shrewd sense and practical approach will guide you in the right direction concerning published material, legal matters, and travel. The Lunar Eclipse of the 17th indicates an abrupt change is likely at your place of residence in the months ahead. Moving or relocation is a good possibility.

SEPTEMBER

The previous Solar Eclipse of August 31st falls in your 11th House of hopes and wishes. There is something you have begun in the past that will transpire during the months ahead. It appears to be related to publications, travel, furthering your education, or the settlement of a lawsuit. The patience and perseverance you have applied to this matter will not have been in vain. There is the promise of personal financial gain as a result of your laborious efforts. Sign nothing and make no important decisions between the 1st and 3rd because there is a strong element of misrepresentation or misunderstanding that could impair your good judgment. Seek the counsel of a trusted friend on the 5th, who may guide you in the right direction. Venus's recent entry into your 1st House will activate social affairs, especially on the 13th, 18th, 19th, and 20th. The Full Moon of the 15th in your 5th House is likely to bring hidden elements out in the open. There is a chance that you may break away from someone, possibly a friend, due to fraudulent tactics on that person's part.

OCTOBER

If you have been too trusting in the past or have not protected yourself with proper legal documents, you may be hit rather hard through the unforeseen actions of another individual. The previous New Moon of September 29th was not well situated in your 12th House of secrets. The 30th of last month and the 1st through the 4th of this month will be very trying times. Betrayal, deception, or fraudulent action by someone you trusted is in evidence at this time. One can only speculate about the hidden elements involved. It appears that publications, creative projects, romance, children, or legal actions may be the source for concern. Mercury retrogrades back into your 12th House on the 11th, and more hidden paperwork or upsetting documents come out into the open on the 12th, 13th, 18th, and 20th. A compromise may be reached on the 27th or 28th. The New Moon of the 29th will eliminate past problems as it occurs in your 1st House, fortified by excellent planetary configurations. You will succeed in overcoming the previous injustice recently experienced because you now have the willpower to overcome all odds.

NOVEMBER

The 1st of the month finds you successfully clearing away
the remains of a confused or mixed-up situation involving
an important document or published material. Legal counsel
or advisors will operate in your behalf on the 2nd or 3rd, and
those efforts will result in a financial settlement, but not
without some compromise on your part. Your mental outlook
is much better on the 5th, due to the clarification of an old,
confused issue. The 7th and 8th find you eager and ready to
embark on new projects and enterprises. The Full Moon of
the 13th places emphasis on partnerships for the next few
weeks. Partners may attempt to have you alter or change
some of your preconceived ideas between the 14th and
16th. You will have the finesse and the right amount of tact
to present your own position in no uncertain terms between
the 17th and 21st. If you are prone to bladder infections or
problems with other areas of elimination, be on the alert for
possible health hazards on the 26th and 27th. Because the
New Moon of the 28th is in your 2nd House of money, it may
be a good time to work on your Christmas shopping list.

DECEMBER

You are very well organized on Friday the 1st, so whatever
task you have on hand that must meet a deadline will be
completed on time. Money will come your way after the 5th,
through distant matters or a legal settlement. Venus enters
your 4th House on the 10th, indicating a good time to think
about decorating your home base for the Christmas holidays.
The Full Moon in your 8th House may be good for winding up
Christmas shopping, just don't be surprised if you purchase
doubles of identical items. Indecision about which relative
to spend the coming holiday with may beset you on the 13th.
Your choice may be a friend who extends a warm invitation
on the 18th. It's a delightful Christmas Day, full of enthusiasm,
joy, and hope for brighter days ahead. The 27th appears to
be an extended holiday vacation for many, as you travel
about in the pleasant company of a warm companion. The
New Moon of the 28th in your 3rd House is likely to bring a
check in the mail or a bonus from your place of employment. Wrap up belated correspondence on the 29th and take
care of bills and charges made over the holidays.

SAGITTARIUS
The Archer

November 23 to December 22

Quality: mutable
Element: fire
Principle: active
Ruler: Jupiter
Gem: turquoise
Lucky Day: Thursday
Anatomy: hips, thighs, upper leg
Key phrase: *I understand*

Glyph: archer's arrow
Natural sign of: ninth house
Opposite sign: Gemini
Color: blue
Lucky Numbers: 5 and 7
Flower: narcissus

Key word: *visualization*

Positive Characteristics:
straightforward
philosophical
freedom-loving
broadminded
athletic
generous
optimistic
scholarly
enthusiastic

Negative Characteristics:
argumentative
exaggerative
talkative
procrastinating
self-indulgent
blunt
impatient
a gambler
pushy

SAGITTARIUS

You are a generous, independent, free-spirited individual. You love freedom of movement in your job and daily activities. You cannot stand being confined in a small area or with a boring, routine type of work. You love variety and anything that has a hint of challenge to it. You believe in justice and fair play. You will not tolerate underhanded tactics. Your cards are always on the table and others know exactly where they stand with you. You have a light and breezy nature, sparked by pure intelligence. You enjoy festivities and being among crowds of people. You open your arms to everyone, from all walks of life, backgrounds, race and religion. You can become quite indignant about such things as bigotry. Travel and adventure lure you, and you hope that each day will bring new and exciting experiences. You are an optimist. Your one main fault is the tendency to get involved with too many activities and projects. You often make plans or promises that are difficult to fit into your already busy schedule. Consequently, this causes you to miss an important appointment or break some of your promises. Procrastination is another bad trait. You always think you have more time than you actually have. Invaribly, you are late and will probably be late for your own funeral.

Although you have many on your list of friends, you tire of them easily once they cease to stimulate and hold your interest. You have a marvelous sense of humor, especially about sex. Many are drawn to your genial nature and smiling face. They often come to you for help in solving problems, and you give them impartial advice. You want to make a lasting impression on people. But, more than anything, you want to be a complete person. You should not work alone. You are happiest when using your education, experience and wisdom to make things better and easier for others. You are the perpetual teacher always ready and eager to instruct someone in any field of endeavor.

You are born with reasonably good health, but you take on too much, often to the point of exhaustion. Outdoor activities and a daily exercise program is what you need.

JANUARY

You've been rather busy these past few weeks because Venus is transiting your 1st House. It was an exciting time for social affairs and visits with family and friends. The 2nd through the 6th may bring a refund check, a gift from a parent, or a bonus from your employer. The New Moon in your 2nd House of money reinforces the possibility of financial gain through past resources. Keep your ears open between the 10th and 12th because secret negotiations may be underway that may result in back pay, a bonus or a salary increase. Watch your driving on the 21st, since you won't relish a traffic ticket. Distressful news concerning the ill health of an aunt, uncle, or a distant relative may reach you on the 22nd or 23rd. If you feel that you are not adequately compensated for the amount of work you do, the 24th and 25th are the best days to present your case for a wage increase. You are under a lucky trend on the 31st. Either a new job, a promotion or a large pay increase is heading your way.

FEBRUARY

Mercury has been retrograding in your 2nd House of money. This is a good time to take care of past-due bills and work on a budget to increase future savings. Don't attempt to purchase anything new until after the 6th. You're on a roll as far as your energy level is concerned, and you can accomplish a great deal of work on the 3rd. Since your intuitive ability is astute during the afternoon hours of the 3rd, try for the lottery if you have one in your state. Lucky, lucky you. Terrific bargains at tremendous savings and the opportunity to purchase a van or truck come your way on the 4th. The male Sagittarian has been wanting one for some time, one that he can incorporate into a sideline business. The New Moon of the 6th falls in your 3rd House of transportation and communication. There is the possibility you may have to forego the idea due to lack of adequate funds. Perhaps a figure of authority or a parent can be of financial assistance on the 7th or 8th. The prospects are looking better for a new car or larger vehicle between the 9th and 11th. The Lunar Eclipse of the 20th throws a beneficial light on your 2nd House of money. A company boss or parent might come through with a loan. You should hear the good news by the 25th.

MARCH

Since you may want to make a few dramatic changes in your home surroundings, secretly mull these arrangements in your mind on the 2nd and 3rd. On the 4th don't ponder too long on that large purchase you want to make; the opportunity for a good bargain could pass you by. The Solar Eclipse of the 7th in your 4th House confirms the previous secret desire for changes. There is a strong desire to have a place of your own, and in some cases, for personal privacy so to speak. This is nothing new, for it has been in the back of your mind for some time. In all probability, if you live with your parents or a parent-in-law, you are likely to find a place of your own. Other Sagittarians sharing their homes with friends may look forward to their friends' moving out. The main problem appears to be restriction of privacy and of personal activity. You are likely to take action along these lines before the 11th. With Jupiter and Mars simultaneously entering your 7th House on the 11th, it is apparent that the change of residence may also involve another individual. All apprehension leaves you as the Full Moon of the 22nd shines a favorable light on your 7th House of partnerships. You will realize in the weeks ahead that you and that special someone have made the right decision to obtain a place of your own.

APRIL

Saturday the 1st is likely to be the busiest day of the month. There is much driving about, and changes and excitement are in the air. If you are moving or altering some aspect of your home, by all means don't overdo it, and try to stop before 6:00 p.m. EDT. There is a chance of an accident or a muscle strain through carelessness or exhaustion. Be careful on Sunday the 2nd so that you do not, in haste, break something old and of traditional value. The New Moon of the 5th finds you and a partner involved in several creative projects. The Full Moon of the 20th in your 12th House may bring an unexpected financial gain, which should come through by the 25th or 26th. If you have been experiencing financial difficulties, they should ease after the 28th. A loan or other financial assistance that you've been seeking for home repairs or remodeling should be available on the 30th.

MAY

Someone offers you good advice around noon on the 2nd. If you don't heed that advice, you will suffer the consequences through a financial setback that may occur during the late afternoon hours. You have the ability on the 4th to see a difficult task through to completion, which does not go unnoticed by those in authority. The New Moon of the 5th may catch you off guard when a past-due bill comes due again, which you misplaced or forgot to pay. You should get wind of this monetary incident between the 6th and 9th. Some of you may have to work on Saturday the 13th, which may be good for extra funds but creates a problem if it interferes with a previously planned affair. Something is in the air on the 16th; an announcement of a pending engagement or marriage of a brother or sister may come your way. Don't be surprised if you hear that two family members may be getting married within a short time of each other. Don't make personal plans for Sunday the 21st; they will be subjected to change due to interference by relatives. You are likely to be drawn into the exciting events surrounding the affairs of siblings or close relatives on the 23rd, 25th, and 26th.

JUNE

The New Moon of the 3rd highlights your 7th House of social affairs, and places additional emphasis on last month's indications of pending marriages within the family circle. Sunday the 4th is an excellent day for family members to get together for a baby or wedding shower. If you have not yet embarked on your vacation, Friday the 9th is favored for travel or for planning future trips. A confused matter involving personal funds appears out of nowhere between the 12th and the 14th. Through the assistance of another person, you should be able to untangle the financial situation on the 15th. The Full Moon of the 19th places the spotlight on you as it occurs in your 1st House. You don't have to travel to faraway places for an enjoyable vacation. If you cannot afford an extensive trip at this time, a nearby resort can be just as exciting. You and your partner should go out on Saturday the 24th and search for a wooded area that offers camping, fishing, and boating. An emotional upheaval on the 26th is resolved on the 30th.

JULY

A busy time is scheduled for the 1st and 2nd of the month.
There appears to be a great deal of running about, short
trips, phone calls, and other activity involving partnerships
and close family members. The New Moon of the 3rd is in
your 8th House. This is a propitious time to clear the deck of
past financial difficulties. Out of the blue, something is likely
to appear that may enable you to finalize old debts or mortgage payments on the 4th. If a relative should enter the hospital on the 5th or 6th for chest or back pains, it does not
appear to have serious repercussions. Although additional
concern may be aroused on the 9th, the good news you hear
on the 10th and 11th should erase these fears. The Full
Moon of the 18th falls in your 2nd House of personal funds.
You may get a little depressed when you discover that you
have less money in your checking account than you first
anticipated, due to a past error in calculation. The 22nd
and 23rd are super nice days for planning a family outing.
You'll find a solution to previous money problems after
the 25th.

AUGUST

You are unusually lucky during the morning hours of the
1st. If your coworkers engage in a check pool, you should
give it a try since you may have the winning numbers. The
New Moon of the 1st takes place during the late afternoon,
in your 9th House. You may, around the 4th, hear news of a
health problem involving a distant relative or an in-law. Oh,
how you hate to work on Saturdays during the summer
months! The 5th may be one of those days that you should
not refuse. There is an indication that conscientious efforts
and a willingness to work overtime can help you get a pay
raise in the near future. This may disrupt a previously
planned social outing and upset a family member or partner,
but more money could be a big help now. The Lunar Eclipse
of the 17th highlights your 3rd House. A new position may
be opening at your place of employment. Learning new
techniques and skills may be part of your "on-the-job" training program during the months ahead. When complex work
problems arise on the 24th, do not turn to a newcomer, for
that person's advice may be misleading. Seek, instead, the
assistance of an authoritative figure.

SEPTEMBER

The previous Solar Eclipse of August 31st places the spotlight on your 10th House of careers. Once you have completed the necessary learning process to develop the new techniques and skills necessary for your new position, the indications are highly favorable that the end results will markedly improve your finances. For many Sagittarians, this may open the door to complete independence. If you are living with your parents or with a parent-in-law, you may soon be able to afford a place of your own. On the 1st, be careful that emotions do not get in the way of logic and cause you to make errors at work. The 5th is your chance to show those in authority that you have the capacity to work alone and without supervision, for it is apparent that a boss may be quietly observing your work methods. The Full Moon of the 15th falls in your 4th House. Previous monetary situations have been improving at a steady rate, and you may be secretly thinking of making changes connected with your home base. You are likely to experience friction with a parent, parent-in-law, or boss between the 15th and 24th. This is further emphasized by the New Moon of the 29th. If you lose control of your temper on the 30th, you may create an irreparable rift.

OCTOBER

It appears that you are still trying to promote peace and harmony among family members between the 1st and 4th. Since Mercury retrogrades back into your 11th House, you will have to weigh your words to avoid creating further animosity, especially on the 12th. The Full Moon of the 14th seems to indicate most of the problem stems from relatives through marriage or business relationships. Emotional upsets continue to create disharmony within the family circle between the 17th and 20th. Sunday afternoon on the 22nd may be your best time to approach close kin and seek a balance in mutual understanding. The New Moon of the 29th in your 12th House will provide the insight and intuitive ability that will psychologically enable you to smooth over past slights and hurts. Other Sagittarians are likely to gain financially, through working overtime in a rather isolated condition or maybe switching temporarily to the second shift.

NOVEMBER

The afternoon and evening hours of the 1st indicate great rapport with bosses, parents, and authority figures. Past misunderstandings appear to be resolved now. Venus is in your 1st House. If you extend a dinner invitation on the 2nd, it will help to smooth any remaining ruffled feathers. It looks like you have forgotten to save money for house or auto insurance premiums, so you may be short when the reminder arrives after the 6th. Don't worry; a parent or other authority figure rescues you between the 7th and 10th. You have creative and yet practical ideas on the 12th for decorating your home in the traditional holiday fashion. The 14th through the 16th is not favored for entering into controversial issues with close family members. If some minor irritation has been bothering you, discuss it during the evening hours of the 17th, when you have more emotional control. Expect to make adjustments or a change of plan on Saturday the 18th, due to possible upheavals through the affairs of children or close ties. One of the parties may feel that the other is being too possessive or domineering and may try to sever the bonds. Because the New Moon of the 28th is in your 1st House, it may be time to consider important personal changes, such as looking into new and different ways to increase personal funds.

DECEMBER

You have excellent concentrative powers on the 1st, coupled with the necessary perseverance and discipline to complete the most difficult of tasks, whether at work or at home. Any unexpected change of plan that may occur on the 4th is apt to work in your behalf. You can expect previous problems involving living arrangements or in-laws to be favorably resolved after the 5th. The Full Moon of the 12th is centered around partnerships and close kin. There are some emotionally charged changes you have been wanting to make that will be met with strong opposition on the 13th. Christmas Day may catch you off guard, when you rediscover the bonds of affection that tie the family members together. The New Moon of the 27th takes place in your 2nd House. The New Year is about to begin and you feel it is time for major changes that are long overdue.

CAPRICORN
The Sea Goat

December 22 to January 21

Quality: cardinal
Element: earth
Principle: passive
Ruler: Saturn
Gem: garnet
Lucky Day: Saturday
Anatomy: knees and lower leg
Key phrase: *I use*

Glyph: seagoat's horn
Natural sign of: tenth house
Opposite sign: Cancer
Color: brown
Lucky Numbers: 2 and 8
Flower: carnation

Key word: *ambition*

Positive Characteristics:
cautious
responsible
scrupulous
conventional
perfectionist
practical
hardworking
economical
serious

Negative Characteristics:
egotistic
domineering
unforgiving
fatalistic
stubborn
brooding
inhibited
status-seeking

CAPRICORN

You take life rather seriously and are a firm upholder of tradition and authority. Because you are so dependable, others tend to rely on you for help and your practical advice. It takes a while for you to warm up to people. This gives others the impression that you are cold and detached. This is far from the truth, as you are extremely sensitive and affectionate once they get beyond that barrier. This austere nature has been ingrained into your personality from early childhood. Your parents were hard working and conservative people who may have lacked the ability to convey love and affection. Thus, you have very limited experience with affection. Capricorns seem to be born already "grown-up" because of their remarkable mental maturity. You learn early in life how to manage people, by observing the way your mother handled your father, who may have been repected in his community, yet could not run his own household. The average Capricorn, in their early years, did not relate well with those of their own age. You preferred the company of older individuals or those who were very young in age, enabling you to act the role of parent toward them. However, as you advance in age, this trend reverses itself. You become more attractive in your features, appearance and style of dress which inclines toward youthfulness. You begin to attract, and even prefer, companions who are of the same age or younger than yourself.

You are extremely loyal and dedicated to your mate and expect the same in return. When you are betrayed by your loved one, you are devastated. Should you develop an inferiority complex as a result of this experience you may build an invisible protective wall around you. No one will ever penetrate it again. No one will ever get a chance to hurt you again, because they will have to work long and hard to prove their love and devotion for you.

Capricorns are conscientious in fulfilling their obligations and not afraid of hard work. At sometime in their life, they will be required to work the night shift. Their main concern is brittle bones and arthritis with advancing years.

JANUARY

Don't permit the minor irritations of others to spoil the afternoon hours of New Year's Day. For those who don't have to return to work on the 2nd, it is an interesting day for doing something different that you have not tackled before, perhaps ice fishing or skiing. With the New Moon of the 7th occurring in your 1st House, it may be time to review past conditions—perhaps an old appliance in the home that needs to be repaired or replaced. Others are likely to receive money that is owed them through a bonus, overtime pay, or an insurance dividend. Someone may introduce an unusual creative item that you will be able to incorporate into a money-making hobby between the 10th and 12th. Mars enters your 5th House of children and creative projects on the 19th. A child may be a source of financial drain on the 20th, or you may be spending more than you should on a pet hobby. The Full Moon of the 21st continues to stress a financial crisis involving the affairs of a child, gambling, or an investment. These conditions are likely to prevail on the 22nd, 23rd, and 25th. Mercury retrogrades back into your 1st House on the 29th. An important document or news you've been waiting for may take longer to reach you. Through a stroke of luck on the 31st, money comes your way.

FEBRUARY

An invitation to attend a family celebration may arrive on the 1st. You would like to go full steam ahead on a pet project during the morning hours of the 3rd, but other commitments may temporarily hinder progress. A lack of adequate funds may place another block in the path of your aspirations during the evening hours of the 3rd, but if you persevere and proceed slowly, there is no reason why you should not eventually succeed. Rid yourself of pessimism on the 4th and study the practicality of that new venture; it could produce long-range benefits. Since you've always had to work hard for your earnings, the New Moon of the 6th in your 2nd House of money may psychologically deter you from attempting what you fear may be an expensive project. The Lunar Eclipse of the 20th can provide an opportunity in the near future that will enable you to get your inventive project off the ground, through the assistance of an outsider.

MARCH

The 2nd is an ideal day for dispatching your backlog of correspondence. Be alert for interesting news and secrets that could come out at this time. The 4th may be your last chance for an opportunity to promote your personal projects. The Solar Eclipse of the 7th is in your 3rd House. Past creative ideas may have an opportunity to present themselves again, through the intervention and assistance of others. An organized system and well-laid plans are your best defense against those who may not be in agreement with you, especially on the 8th, 9th, or 10th. Mars and Jupiter enter your 6th House of work on the 11th. Luck is in your corner if you are in the market for new employment. There is the possibility that your new position may require on-the-job training, for it appears to be something you have never handled before. Scan the employment section of your Sunday newspaper on the 12th before noon, otherwise you are likely to be deterred and miss a marvelous job opportunity. If you are mailing resumes on the 13th, take the time to double-check them. Make sure the address or other pertinent information is correct. The Full Moon of the 22nd in your 10th House of careers throws a favorable light on your 6th House of employment. You may have to choose between several job offers before the month closes.

APRIL

Saturday the 1st may be one of your busiest days of the month. There appear to be loads of activities, including shopping and buying items to enhance home decor. Just be sure to call it quits before 5:00 p.m. EST, or you may go over board with credit charges. Don't jump to conclusions on the 2nd; your first impression could be wrong. The new week begins on the 3rd and already you feel that those in authority are making unnecessary demands of you. Your irritability might carry over into the evening hours, so be careful anger doesn't interfere with your driving. Better yet, let someone else do the driving for you. If you have been bored with past routine jobs or duties, the New Moon of the 5th may introduce something new, interesting, and diversified. On the 26th, news may reach you of a pending birth or wedding. Your partner may be the bearer of good news on the 30th.

MAY

On the 1st, your art of visualization runs along practical lines, endowing you with the ability to troubleshoot any complex problem that may arise at work or at home. Be patient with partners or close ties on the 2nd; they are in an emotionally upsetting mood, and may flare up at the least provocation. The New Moon of the 5th falls in your 5th House. A strong difference of opinion concerning a past financial situation involving children, romance, or hobbies could lead to a serious confrontation if you do not exercise control. Your partner or close ally may try to draw you into an argument in connection with these matters between the 7th and 9th. You get a brief reprieve on the 13th, only to undergo another crisis on the 16th and 18th. You will have the emotional stability and the willpower to bring these upsetting past conditions under control on the 19th and 20th. A compromise may be necessary if your partner does not yield; it may be in your best interests if you do so. The 23rd through the 25th may introduce an interesting innovative change of duties at your place of employment. At first you may be apprehensive about your ability to handle the job, but on the 30th someone will be willing to instruct and assist you.

JUNE

Saturday the 3rd would be a good day for starting your vacation as the New Moon offers a brief respite from your everyday work routine. Your mate or other close ties are feeling rather festive and may plan a picnic or outing for the 4th. They may also exercise a difference in opinions or views on the 5th; a good time can be had by all if you are willing to compromise. The center of attention is still on partnerships, and on the 6th and 7th your partner may want to go somewhere that offers a variety of activities, such as a fair or an amusement park. Be careful that you don't overspend on entertainment on the 9th. It appears that you are having a marvelous time on Saturday the 10th. Something happens on Monday the 12th that may require your return to the work-a-day world. The Full Moon of the 19th may bring to light a hidden matter concerning a past financial issue. Don't interfere with your partner's small crisis of the 26th; your partner will resolve it him- or herself by the 30th.

JULY

The 1st and 2nd may mark the beginning of an extended weekend for many Capricorns. These two days are favored for escaping from the humdrum activities of daily life; you embark on an enjoyable short excursion. The New Moon of the 3rd highlights activities surrounding partnerships. Partners have excellent ideas, which feature an interesting change of pace, for celebrating the 4th of July. You should take the initiative on Friday the 7th when making plans for the evening's recreation, even if your partner has other ideas. A little tact and diplomacy can go a long way on the 10th if the working Capricorn wants to seek a raise in pay. The Full Moon of the 18th falls in your 1st House. Self-centered interests may have to be temporarily set aside as you concentrate on family matters connected with your partner or close ties. Through your overspending on entertainment or while on vacation, unexpected bills may arrive around the 25th, but apparently your budget has enough set aside to offset your concern.

AUGUST

Listen to your intuition during morning hours of the 1st; it can help you to solve matters confronting you. The New Moon of the 1st occurs later in the day and affects your 8th House of mutual funds. You may receive a notice on the 4th that you forgot to pay, or overlooked, an insurance premium or credit charge. Your mate or partner hears good news on the 5th, which in some way will have a positive bearing on your personal life. Important news that you've been wanting to hear for some time is likely to reach you on the 9th or 11th. A new job position may be available after the 15th. This is further indicated by the presence of the Lunar Eclipse in your 2nd House of money; this Eclipse means that an apparent change affecting one's earning capacity is likely to occur during the months ahead. Monetary issues and health benefits are highly favored if you are going for a job interview on the 24th. Be careful with your speech, however; it is better to say less at this time than to say too much and jeopardize your position. The month closes on the 30th with the promise of a new job offer for a position that may require additional responsibilites, but it will be financially compensated.

SEPTEMBER

The previous Solar Eclipse of August 31st highlights your 9th House and throws a beneficial spotlight onto your 1st House of personal affairs. Depending upon each person's environmental condition, some Capricorns will travel, return to college, or favorably resolve an old legal matter. Others are likely to gain financially through marriage or business partnerships. In all probability, you should be able to fulfill your fondest dream during the months ahead. Between the 1st and 3rd, caution your partner or close ties to not sign important papers at this time. Someone does not have their personal interest at heart. You may be under the illusion that all is well during the morning hours of the 12th, only to be thrown a right wringer during the afternoon hours. Don't reach any hasty decisions on the 15th until you have taken additional facts into consideration. Matters are not as they appear on the surface. Your sense of logic will be more astute between the 18th and the 20th. Be careful, because tempers flare up easily on the 21st. The New Moon of the 29th is in your 10th House. There appears to be some resentment through those in authority, and it may be brought to your attention on the 30th.

OCTOBER

Sunday the 1st is not the best day for dealing with in-laws or distant relatives; there is much animosity in the air. You are on a roll during the morning hours of the 2nd, and have the ability to complete even the most difficult of tasks at work or at home. Isolate yourself during the evening hours if you can; others in your midst are out to create upsetting conditions in your life. Mercury retrogrades back into your 10th House of careers on the 11th. An annoying or faultfinding individual at work is likely to irritate you on the 12th, 17th, 18th, and 20th. Don't permit a lack of funds to force you into staying home on Sunday the 22nd; a drive through autumn's colorful countryside can be both relaxing and inexpensive. On the 27th and 28th, you are likely to take a decisive stand on an important issue that involves a family member. The New Moon of the 29th is in your 11th House. News will reach you shortly, concerning a beneficial financial gain through conditions surrounding your partner.

NOVEMBER

Many of the hopes and wishes formulated at last month's New Moon have a good chance of becoming a reality on the 1st, 3rd, or 5th of this month. Social activities are on the agenda for the 7th, as several invitations are likely to come your way. A new friend offers sound advice that you should listen to on the 7th and 8th. The 12th and 13th are excellent days for planning your Thanksgiving festivities. Don't be too disappointed if you are notified on the 14th and 15th that several family members will be unable to attend. Because extravagant tendencies prevail on the 18th and 19th, postpone holiday shopping until a later date. You can find terrific bargains if you shop during the morning hours of the 21st, or have someone do it for you if you must work during those hours. A power struggle appears to be a problem among family members on the 26th and 27th. The New Moon of the 28th falls in your 12th House. You would like nothing better than to be left alone to renew your spiritual resources and inner strength. Unexpected incidents on the 30th, however, impose on your desired peace and tranquility.

DECEMBER

The 1st opens up the possibility of making new friends, perhaps at your place of employment. The 5th is not too soon to take care of your Christmas mailing and shopping. The Full Moon of the 12th falls in your 6th House. Double-check paperwork, shipments, and work-related data to avoid confrontations with bosses over possible errors. Call or write distant relatives on the 18th to clarify holiday plans and activities. You'll find that even your best-laid plans tend to go out the window through mixups on the 20th and 21st. There will be a special gift under your Christmas tree this year, one that you have always hoped for. If you have to return to work after a holiday vacation, you may find it difficult to get into the swing of things on the 27th. The position of the New Moon in your 1st House does little to lift your spirits; you are depressed by the dull, lifeless atmosphere. The very idea of work seems to weigh you down on the 28th and 29th. You are both mentally and physically low in spirit. Thank goodness for Saturday the 30th, when you can look forward to another long holiday weekend.

AQUARIUS
The Water-Bearer

January 21 to February 20

Quality: fixed
Element: air
Principle: active
Ruler: Uranus
Gem: amethyst
Lucky Day: Wednesday
Anatomy: the ankles
Key phrase: *I know*

Glyph: waves of water
Natural sign of: eleventh house
Opposite sign: Leo
Color: blue
Lucky Numbers: 1 and 7
Flower: orchid
Key word: *imagination*

Positive Characteristics:
 independent
 inventive
 tolerant
 individualistic
 progressive
 artistic
 scientific
 humane
 intellectual

Negative Characteristics:
 unpredictable
 temperamental
 bored by detail
 opinionated
 shy
 eccentric
 radical
 impersonal
 rebellious

AQUARIUS

Aquarians are independent people and revolutionaries in the real sense of the word, because they stand out as being square pegs in round holes. By the time everyone finds out how much fun this can be, the Aquarian is off on another idea. Many Aquarians are concerned with making life easier for their fellow man. You thoroughly research a theory with much probing and investigation. If you should discover a new or better method of doing something, you immediately pass it along as quickly as possible. You are one of the finest types of researcher or scientist, for you will introduce this new discovery even if you must abandon some of your former views and theories. At an early age you may have felt different or set-apart from others, as though there were something wrong with you. This was due primarily to your sense of humor and approach to life, which was more advanced than those of your own age level. As you matured, you wanted to belong somewhere, so you began joining or starting clubs and groups. Aquarians do not live a normal routine, kind of existence. Even their early childhood was marked with a different home environment. Many unexpected events and abrupt changes were par for the course. You were often faced with a good deal of hostility because you wouldn't follow conventional lines of thought and action. You go your own way, often defying public opinion. You do not judge others and feel they should not sit in judgment of you.

The well balanced and self-developed Aquarian who has learned to control his or her peculiar behavior or concepts can rise to great heights in any specialized field. Whatever your chosen career, you were often referred to as a "border-line genius". In similar fashion with Thomas Edison, you too have an inventive mind, the capacity to come up with unique ideas on the spur of the moment. You are a people watcher. You love to observe their actions and note their style of dress and who they are with. You offer a willing hand to all your friends, but you bow down to no one's command.

Health problems stem from poor circulation resulting in cold feet and hands.

JANUARY

Don't neglect your in-laws or distant relatives on New Year's Day; take the time to wish them the best during the year ahead. Those of you who may have to return to work on the 2nd may not mind. You seem to relish the opportunity to get away from the turmoil of family holiday gatherings. The New Moon of the 7th falls in your 12th House. There is an old project that you have been working on rather steadily, and you would just love to wrap it up, but an aggressive individual persists in making inroads on your valuable time. Perhaps a family member can succeed in diverting this person in a different direction temporarily. Working in a self-imposed, isolated condition to complete a job should pay off financially between the 10th and 12th. Whether you are in the employ of others or in business for yourself, don't attempt any work on Saturday the 14th. Your state of mind is not conducive to laborious efforts, and errors can result. Shopping at the mall with friends or family may hold more interest. On Sunday the 15th, you were looking forward to a lovely day of isolation and serenity. Unfortunately an unexpected visitor disrupts your desire for a quiet afternoon. The Full Moon of the 21st falls in your 7th House. You may have to put a curb on your partner's spending habits, especially on the 22nd, 23rd, and 25th.

FEBRUARY

Mercury's recent retrograde motion in your 12th House indicates that you have not met the deadline of a particular project or that you may require additional data to see it through to completion. Keep your nose to the grindstone on the 1st even if you are bored and desirous of something new and different. Monetary rewards for past laborious efforts should come forth by the 3rd or 4th. The New Moon of the 6th falls in your 1st House. There appears to be conflicting interests between you and a family member that need to be resolved. Be alert on the 7th and 8th; you may be able to save the company a great deal of money by detecting an error that would have been costly. The Lunar Eclipse of the 20th highlights your 8th House of mutual funds. Financial gain through the intervention of another person and the involvement of a private project is possible in the months ahead.

MARCH

On the 2nd or 3rd, there is the possibility of unforeseen financial gain stemming from the past. Perhaps a retroactive pay raise, a medical refund, or other joint monetary gains. If, on Sunday the 5th, you decide to balance your checkbook during the morning and find a discrepancy, the chances are that the tables will be turned in your behalf. The Solar Eclipse places the spotlight on personal finances for the months ahead. A private project you have been working on in the past should be given the "go ahead" signal. You can reduce the monetary risk by starting on a small scale. Luck is with you for financial protection on the 8th and 9th. Something in your immediate surroundings will be altered after the 10th, and this change will ease any friction that may have resulted between you and a family member. Mars and Jupiter enter your 5th House on the 11th. The single Aquarian may have to choose between several romantic partners. The married Aquarian may expand the family through a possible birth during the year ahead. The older Aquarian may hear surprising news of an expected grandchild. In some cases, twins are a good possibility.

APRIL

It's no April Fool's joke; the entire day's events on the 1st will focus on personal affairs. Several challenging opportunities you have never encountered before will be presented. Engulf yourself with these new ventures and ideas, jotting notes of importance, then set it all aside after 6:00 p.m. EST to avoid overestimation of the project. Leave the new enterprise alone the 2nd and 3rd; too much discussion will only confuse the issue and expand it out of proportion. The New Moon of the 5th falls in your 3rd House. Additional insight about a new pet project is likely to hold your interest. Social invitations will be on the agenda for others; look for a special one to arrive on the 15th. You have excellent concentrative ability during the morning hours of the 18th. Put it to good use on tasks requiring deep mental application. The Full Moon of the 20th is in your 10th House. You will have the willpower to make the necessary changes in a positive sense in regard to personal, vocational, and home interests. You can successfully pursue these matters on the 25th and 26th.

MAY

Have extra cash on hand if you go out for lunch or shop on the 1st; a very lovely and unusual item is sure to catch your eye. It may be difficult to concentrate at work on the 2nd, after family members have discarded their personal problems on your shoulders. The month of May is a good time to think about sprucing up the home or apartment as the New Moon of the 5th highlights your 4th House. Try to complete the painting or remodeling of your property before the 11th, at which time Venus enters your 5th House and activates the social aspect of your life. Accepting too many invitations after the 13th can deplete your financial resources and may put a big dent in your savings account. On the 19th a new job offer or change of position may place you in control of employees or of a department. The Full Moon of the 20th emphasizes this opportunity as it falls in your 10th House of careers. You may be confronted, however, with a major decision that is likely to affect family members. The new position appears to have some restrictions that may take you away from the home for long periods, perhaps due to lengthy hours or travel time. You should be able to reach a decision by the 30th.

JUNE

The New Moon of the 3rd falls in your 5th House. A busy, busy month lies ahead in connection with parties, weddings, baby showers, theater productions, and several dinner invitations—all of which are just some of the possibilities. Mark your calendar for these special days to watch: the 8th, 9th, and 13th. The 5th and 6th are emotionally charged days, and it won't take much to get you to lash out against those you must work with every day. Cooperative efforts will be lacking on the 12th, so make up your mind to handle job-related duties by yourself. There is an indication on the 15th that you may soon change your line of work. The Full Moon of the 19th brings into play your 11th House. Joining a health spa for health and exercise is a possibility. Others are likely to hear from old friends who live in distant cities. On the 24th, the financial picture looks pretty good except for one bill (perhaps it is your phone bill) that should be double-checked due to a possible error. Interesting mail arrives on the 30th.

JULY

Saturday the 1st is another one of those busy days. You're either playing golf, driving your children about, shopping with friends, or leaving for a weekend trip with someone. Be flexible on Sunday the 2nd, as everyone comes up with different ideas for the afternoon's entertainment. Last month's hint of a possible job change appears eminent as the New Moon of the 3rd highlights your 6th House of work. Not necessarily a change of company as much as one of department, which should be evident on the 4th. Be sure to discuss the important details of a wage increase and health benefits on the 7th. Contact in-laws or distant relatives on the 9th and 10th, as they may be experiencing a health problem. The Full Moon of the 18th falls in your 12th House of hidden influences. You may have to call someone's attention to a document that does not contain important information; perhaps it was your name that you felt should have appeared. Or, you are not given credit for a job well done. Go on an outing on the 22nd and 23rd, participate in sports, and deal with young people. Avoid older individuals or those with a negative attitude who might put a damper on a festive weekend.

AUGUST

The spotlight is on marriage or business partnerships as the New Moon of the 1st takes place in your 7th House. There appears to be a power struggle between you and another individual. Unless one of you yields to the other, a serious confrontation could result on the 4th. The 8th and 9th are your best days for conscientious efforts in the handling of a difficult task that you have set aside in the past, due to the amount of work involved. The Lunar Eclipse of the 17th falls in your 1st House. You have been rather restless lately. There is a strong desire for personal change in new directions. You want to break away from stagnant conditions and enter into something new and different that you have not experienced before. Events of the 23rd may give you the incentive and the willpower to branch out into challenging and untried territory. The month closes on the 30th with the possibility of an unexpected job opportunity or an additional sideline—one that offers you the freedom and control you desire.

SEPTEMBER

The previous Solar Eclipse of August 31st beneficially enhances your 8th House of mutual funds. This month, as well as those in the future, should produce financial gains through a private project that you have been working on for some time. There is the promise of long-range gains and in some cases the possibility of prolonged receiving of royalty checks as a result of a personal enterprise in collaboration with another person. The 5th is your best day to get a project off the ground floor, especially if you require financial assistance. For those who are not professionally oriented, a health, insurance, or accident settlement may soon come to a fruitful conclusion. This may be a propitious time for senior Aquarians to consider retirement. Those at a distance may contact you on the 7th or 12th for possible travel in the near future. Money comes your way through more than one source on the 13th and 14th. The Full Moon of the 15th reinforces the possibility of increase through personal funds, especially on the 18th, 19th, 20th, and 23rd. On the 24th your partner hears good news that opens the door for additional travel opportunities. Since Mercury retrogrades back into your 8th House on the 26th, it may be a good idea to review your budget and bring charge payments up to date.

OCTOBER

Sunday the 1st may be a good day to visit in-laws or distant relatives whose health has not been up to par. Catch up on neglected job duties and bring them up to date on the 2nd, just in case you have to take time off from work to visit an older family member who may be hospitalized. Mercury re-enters your 9th House on the 11th, bringing unexpected news of a confined person. The Full Moon of the 14th falls in your 3rd House of communications. The next few weeks may be quite busy with short trips and frequent phone calls, especially on the 17th, 18th, 20th, and 27th. The New Moon of the 29th in your 10th House of careers may instill the necessary willpower to enforce the beneficial job changes that have been so frequent in your life. Those who are not employed may gain through governmental affairs. Disability, social security, and an increase in your monthly retirement are all possible in the weeks ahead.

NOVEMBER

Don't hesitate to seek the assistance of a government official or an authority figure on the 1st, should you run into a complex problem. A friend who is at a distance is likely to contact you on the 2nd. Financial or career advancements are possible through a stroke of luck on the 3rd. The 5th is a good time to write, call, or visit relatives near and far. You have the "Midas Touch" on the 7th and 8th, as money comes in through past efforts, a lucky streak, and through more than one source. The Full Moon of the 13th falls in your 4th House. Family plans for the upcoming Thanksgiving holiday may require a few revisions. There appears to be much opposition between the 14th and 16th as to where the dinner should be held. Whatever decision you reach on the 17th will be altered on the 18th or 19th. You may be in a resentful mood, being placed in a position of dominance by others. This explosive situation is likely to break loose on the 26th or 27th through a heated argument. The New Moon of the 28th in your 11th House can clear the air with the philosophy that the holiday season is a time to forgive and forget past grievances.

DECEMBER

The 1st is excellent for the employed Aquarian who needs to organize and at the same time eliminate a lot of debris at work. The unemployed Aquarian won't find a better time to clean out the attic or basement and rid him- or herself of useless items. Good news awaits you during the morning hours of the 4th. The evening of the 5th is favored for early Christmas shoppers seeking exquisite items at bargain prices. The Full Moon of the 12th falls in your 5th House. A round of entertainment and parties will keep you busier than usual this holiday season. Pre-Christmas sales should help you wind up last-minute gift purchases during the evening hours of the 18th. You may have to forego social invitations on the 20th and 21st in lieu of family or job responsibilities. It looks like a friend from a distant city may be spending Christmas with you. The New Moon of the 27th may find you in a rather restrictive situation. It appears you've gotten behind in your work—you may have to isolate yourself to meet a belated deadline. Watch for an interesting event to occur on the 30th.

PISCES
The Fish

February 20 to March 21

Quality: mutable
Element: water
Principle: passive
Ruler: Neptune
Gem: aquamarine
Lucky Day: Friday
Anatomy: the feet
Key phrase: *I believe*

Glyph: two fish tied together
Natural sign of: twelfth house
Opposite sign: Virgo
Color: blue-green
Lucky Numbers: 2 and 6
Flower: water lily
Key word: *understanding*

Positive Characteristics:
compassionate
charitable
sympathetic
emotional
sacrificing
intuitive
introspective
musical
artistic

Negative Characteristics:
procrastinating
over-talkative
melancholy
pessimistic
emotionally inhibited
timid
impractical
indolent
often feels misunderstood

PISCES

You are born into this world with terrific psychic and intuitive ability. Your creative Piscean imagination provides us with the largest proportion of the worlds' greatest artists, actors, writers and musicians. You are gullible to a degree, but only because you want so much to believe in people. Friends, and those in your immediate environment, have the wrong impression of you. They think you are an easy mark. What they do not realize, is that they have only one chance with you. When someone betrays your confidence or deceives you, there is no direct confrontation. Instead you quietly, but firmly, dismiss them from your life. You will make it a point to be busy every time this person calls to invite you out. After awhile, they get the hint that you no longer want their friendship.

Pisceans are emotionally sensitive and caring people. You willingly give of your time and energy to friends and those you love. But, you need to feel that your efforts are appreciated. Just a short thank-you note, a phone call or an inexpensive gift would make you feel that someone noticed and cared.

Pisceans cannot tolerate the harshness and reality of life. When it becomes too unbearable, you often retreat into a world of your own. Perhaps a stroll in the woods to listen to the birds or watch the squirrels might be just the tranquilizer to soothe your nerves. Others love to listen to good music, paint or go fishing.

Piscean mothers, under stress, may jump back into bed after the children have left for school. They pull the covers over their heads and retreat into a world of dreams of what they thought marriage should be. There is nothing wrong with these methods of temporary escapism. It is the Piscean that begins to rely on addictive drugs or alcohol that should seek outside help.

In health, the Piscean is often sensitive to certain medication. Be sure to check with your doctor about possible side-effects before taking medication. The feet are the most delicate area, therefore you should purchase good quality shoes to avoid corns, bunions and other painful foot problems.

JANUARY

It's difficult to spend a quiet New Year's Day by yourself when others want to include you in their festivities. You'll have plenty of time for solitude after the 2nd, as Mercury enters your 12th House. There appears to be loads of paperwork, research, or correspondence that will tie up much of your free time. Try to wrap up as much as you can because the New Moon of the 7th will activate social affairs and contacts with friends. Invitations are likely through an old friend on the 10th. Fortunate trends prevail during the morning hours of the 12th, placing you in the right place at the right time. Your mind is quick and alert on the 13th; you can catch up on a lot of paperwork as long as you don't permit friends to interrupt your train of thought. The 14th and 15th are not conducive for mental application. Take the weekend off and enjoy a few social gatherings with close friends. A large sum of money or an expensive gift may arrive through an old friend or through a political figure on the 16th. The Full Moon of the 21st falls in your 6th House of work. If you have been socializing too much and neglecting your job, repercussions will crop up on the 23rd and 25th. Mercury retrogrades on the 24th in your 12th House, indicating that private projects require additional attention and possible revision.

FEBRUARY

You may have to temporarily tear yourself away from private mental projects due to Mercury's retrograde motion into your 11th House of friends. Communications with political parties, old friends, organizations, and prominent individuals will have to be handled at this time. You will have until the 15th to wrap up these important issues. Don't impulsively latch onto a business offer that may be presented on the 1st. Between the 3rd and 5th you may discover the offer requires more money than you care to invest. The New Moon of the 6th falls in your 12th House, rudely indicating a deadline is near for the paperwork you should have concentrated on. The Lunar Eclipse of the 20th is in your 7th House. A profitable venture involving a friend, travel, published material, or other creative projects will dominate your time and energy during the months ahead.

MARCH

The first ten days of the month will be centered around your personal interests and affairs. Through the assistance of a helpmate on the 2nd, you can succeed in the completion of a long-standing project. An invitation or a gift may come your way on the 3rd. You have the capacity on the 5th to take hold of an upsetting situation and make it work to your advantage. The 6th and 10th are the last times you will experience the underhanded tactics of so-called friends operating behind your back. The Solar Eclipse of the 7th places the spotlight on you, indicating that changes are certain to occur during the months ahead. Push ahead on the private project you have been working on for some time, especially during the morning of the 8th and the afternoon of the 9th. Mars and Jupiter enter your 4th House on the 11th, and it is apparent that some of the altering conditions are apt to affect your home base. A different arrangement in the rooms of your home or office may be necessary to accommodate the new equipment you will be adding. The Full Moon of the 22nd in your 8th House is likely to indicate the start of one of the many new devices you will soon be purchasing. Be sure to shop during the morning hours of the 25th if you are seeking something both useful as well as attractive.

APRIL

There are many hidden elements that are working in your behalf on the 1st, but they may not reveal themselves until a later time. If you loan money to someone on the 2nd or 3rd, accept the fact that your chances of getting paid back are slim. The 4th is excellent for purchasing equipment, bookcases, or file cabinets for the home or office. The New Moon of the 16th highlights your 2nd House of personal earnings. There appears to be more than one avenue of financial gain through several new enterprises. You should concentrate on organizing your budget and bookkeeping system on the 4th, because you'll have the mental capacity for this type of detailed work. The Full Moon of the 20th falls in your 9th House. A royalty check, refund, or insurance dividend is likely to furnish you with unexpected funds, which are necessary to finish an old project. An invitation to a family gathering may arrive on the 29th.

MAY

You are the focus of attention on the 1st, being the recipient of interesting mail or news. An emotional trauma may explode on the 2nd through romance or children who may be a source of financial drain. The New Moon of the 5th in your 3rd House should bring old matters to a head in connection with contracts or important documents. You will discover on the 11th that matters relating to your immediate environment are more productive than those located in distant cities. Mercury and Venus are conjoined in your 4th House on the 16th. In the home there are many diversified interests that you are eager to embark upon. They may, however, have to be set aside temporarily, due to outside interference. The Full Moon of the 20th is in your 9th House. Travel and faraway places can be productive of financial gains if you can come to terms with opposite parties. On the 21st you will have to choose between many offers for travel ventures involving trips both near and far. Caution on your part is indicated on the 27th and 28th if you are requested to sign important papers or agreements. Make sure you fully comprehend your end of the bargain.

JUNE

The New Moon of the 3rd is sure to produce an abundance in connection with your home or office. More than one opportunity exists for expansion that will enable you to purchase new furnishings or office equipment. If you have been thinking about a tax shelter, a duplex or an apartment building may be a wise investment at this time. Sunday the 4th is a lovely day for a family gathering or for a wedding or baby shower. The 9th and 13th are your most opportune days for expansion, either in business or real estate. Listen to the valuable advice of a partner on the 10th, whose views are both constructive and practical. The 12th and 14th may find you unaware of a financial crisis connected with affairs of children or your romantic partner. The Full Moon of the 19th highlights your 10th House of careers. You may stumble upon an old solution to a perplexing problem connected with your job. Money will be flowing in a bit easier through several resources after the 26th. Be sure to take advantage of the many offers that will come your way on the 30th.

JULY

Saturday the 1st is one of those days in which you can garner an abundance of material that will advance both real estate and professional interests. The New Moon of the 3rd is in your 5th House. This is a good month for those inclined to gamble. Give due consideration to creative hobbies that you can turn into a profitable future enterprise. A child may be awarded a scholarship. Others will look forward to future travel and vacation trips. For those who must ship merchandise out of the state, use extra care to avoid costly errors on the 5th, 6th and 9th. If you ordered something for your home from a distant city, it may arrive on the 11th. The Full Moon of the 18th falls in your 11th House of organizations. What you want to do may be hampered by what is expected of you, especially on the 20th. Past errors in shipments of merchandise can be corrected with little effort on the 25th and 29th. Accept social invitations extended on the 31st; in all probability, you may meet a prominent person who can be of valuable assistance in the near future.

AUGUST

The New Moon of the 1st falls in your 6th House. You have been working very hard lately and are under a great deal of pressure through demands of others. It is imperative that your health be given first consideration. Should you experience chest pains, it does not necessarily indicate a heart condition, but it is a warning signal that you are overdoing something. While it is true that no one can do the job as well as you, delegating it to others will ease a lot of tension and stress. Be particularly watchful of your health during the afternoon hours of the 4th. You won't have to seek outside help on the 5th if you approach family members in the right way. Whether it be family, friends, or a partner, they will be of enormous assistance to you on the 8th, 9th, 12th, and 13th. You have the stamina to wind up a long-standing complex problem on the 15th. The Lunar Eclipse of the 17th highlights your 12th House. Success in the months ahead will be promoted by the correct handling of a private project. Important contacts reach you on the 23rd through those at a distance. The 30th indicates the possibility of professional success through past organized activities.

SEPTEMBER

The previous Solar Eclipse of August 31st places the spotlight on partnerships as it falls in your 7th House. Past cooperative efforts on the part of others could produce a turning point in your life through an unexpected set of circumstances. This once-in-a-lifetime opportunity could bring you into the limelight or before the public at large. Give your partner or close ally full rein on the 5th as his/her ideas are invaluable. You are likely to receive a gift or invitation on the 13th from someone at a distance. You have a golden opportunity on the 14th to partake in an unusual arrangement that could merit material or financial gain. This is fully emphasized by the presence of the Full Moon of the 15th in your 1st House. Money appears to be rolling in from a distance between the 18th and 20th, as a stroke of luck combined with intuitive insight produces advantageous results. Mercury retrogrades back into your 7th House on the 26th; you have a few more details to work out before signing important contracts. The New Moon of the 29th falls in your 8th House of mutual funds. Be careful on the 30th because friends with little capital will attempt to ride on your bandwagon.

OCTOBER

The morning hours of the 2nd are best for handling group-related projects. Do, however, avoid financial commitments after 4:00 p.m. EST because an air of monetary deception prevails. Continue to be on guard where mutual funds are concerned on the 4th and 12th. The Full Moon of the 14th falls in your 2nd House of personal finances. This is not the time to get involved with cooperative enterprises if money is an issue. Friends and organized activities can be a source of financial drain or deception on the 17th, 18th, and 20th. Be assertive on the 27th and 28th, and demand to see papers or purchase agreements that are in discrepancy with your findings. The New Moon of the 29th falls in your 9th House. If you must, seek legal action to clarify past monetary problems. Others may decide to take a group tour or a cruise for the first time. The following month is also favored for visiting children or loved ones residing in a distant city. For those interested in gambling or football pools, the next four weeks can be very lucky.

NOVEMBER

The evening hours of the 1st and 2nd should keep you rather busy running to meetings and visiting friends. This is a good time to ask favors of those holding influential positions. You have boundless energy on the 2nd, which should give you the upper hand over your competitors. Attend social functions on the 3rd, since a lucky chance meeting could bring you in touch with prominent individuals. Sunday the 5th is an excellent day to contact those at a distance and plan for Thanksgiving visits. On the 7th and 8th you may be asked to volunteer your time for a worthy cause or organization. The Full Moon of the 13th falls in your 3rd House of communications. You may have to contact someone at a great distance to correct a financial matter. You'll have greater success, however, if you wait until the 17th or 21st. The New Moon of the 28th falls in your 10th House of careers. An old problem dealing with matters at a distance may crop up unexpectedly on the 30th.

DECEMBER

You may have the opportunity on the 1st to meet and make new and powerful friends by attending social or political functions. Be alert for chances to befriend influential people who can help you realize some of your major aims and goals in life. Use your excellent intuitive powers on the 4th and 5th to resolve past issues connected with your job, finances, and distant matters. A surprise phone call from an old friend or someone from the past is likely to catch you off guard on the 10th. The Full Moon of the 12th highlights your 4th House. It is difficult to get family members to agree on anything on the 13th; they all seem at odds with one another. Someone who can play the role of mediator on the 18th can help reconcile the family differences. Some dissension still prevails on the 20th and 21st, but all is forgotten and forgiven come Christmas morning. The New Moon of the 27th falls in your 11th House of friends. You may hear of an old friend being hospitalized due to the return of a problem. On the 29th, reach out and touch someone that you have not seen in a long time. The 30th can be a fun-filled, festive day. Invite close associates to share it. Celebrate New Year's Eve in the quiet atmosphere of your home with a few choice friends.

WORLD
EVENTS

Weather Predictions
Earthquake Predictions
Stock Market Forecast
Political Forecast

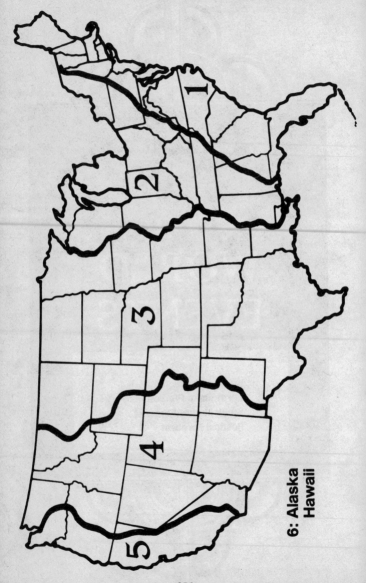

6: Alaska
Hawaii

356

Weather Predictions
by Nancy Soller

While the Saturn/Uranus conjunction brought drought to many parts of the country in 1988, the Saturn/Neptune conjunction in 1989 will bring excess moisture. The year will be marked by low barometers, abnormally damp weather, flooding in low-lying areas, fog, mist, haze and at times temperatures well below normal.

The year will begin with a **winter** marked by a loose conjunction of Uranus, Saturn, Neptune and Mercury all in Capricorn. Saturn and Uranus will be three degrees apart, influencing the weather to be cold and dry. Neptune and Mercury will be in conjunction with each other and with them bringing fog, haze and stagnant air to many parts of the country. Since the portents of this planetary configuration are mixed, the weather will often seem to be erratic. In certain times and certain places excess moisture will predominate bringing cloudiness and snows. In other times and places dryness and extreme cold will predominate under bright skies. The full effect of the Saturn/Neptune conjunction won't be felt until spring when Saturn overtakes Neptune.

The month of *January* should be interesting for weather watchers. Three times during the month Venus and Neptune form hard aspects to each other promising three days of extremely heavy snowfall over many parts of the country. January 1 is the first date, so the year should begin with a big snowstorm. Other dates to watch are January 19 and January 27. Besides the Venus/Neptune aspects, Venus will aspect Saturn three times promising more heavy precipitation. Dates to watch in connection with this are January 4, January 16 and January 24. On January 12, Venus and Uranus are conjunct and a nation-wide sharp drop in temperature can be expected.

February does not have as many aspects promising heavy precipitation, but Venus, which brings precipitation, will still be active. On February 4 and February 10, Venus aspects Mercury bringing wind and snow to many parts of the country.

It won't be until the end of the month of *March* when the effects of the Saturn/Neptune conjunction will take full effect. March will have several strong snow dates before then, including March 2 when Saturn and Neptune aspect the Sun. Other dates to watch for precipitation are March 3, 9, 11, 14, 18 and almost the whole week following March 20. Since Mars and Jupiter are in conjunction on the March 20 ingress chart, thunderstorms will characterize the last week of the month and continue in record number throughout the spring. *Tornado dates* this month include March 10, 18, 24, 25, 28 and 30.

The **spring** of 1989 is the first season to find Saturn and Neptune in close conjunction. Uranus continues to conjunct both of them, but is a little farther away. This season should see much of the East Coast innundated, and also much of coastal British Columbia and the Alaskan Panhandle. Precipitation all over the country, however, should be in excess of normal.

A busy day weatherwise in *April* should be April 10 when seven different weather changing planetary aspects are in effect. These aspects are associated with both wind and precipitation, and tornados are a great possibility that day. Rain will be generous throughout the month in many parts of the country. *In addition to April 10, April 3 and 19 are dates suspect for tornados.*

May will be a month marked by generous amounts of precipitation throughout the country. Rains and winds that may spawn tornado activity will occur May 16 and 17. *A tornado watch will also be in effect on May 7, 20, 21, 23 and May 27.*

June will continue to find heavy precipitation throughout the country. After June 21, the forecast for extremely heavy precipitation shifts to the entire country east of the Mississippi River and that forecast will be in effect all summer. The Alaskan Panhandle will see heavy precipitation also. *Tornado activity in June will be most likely on June 6, 7 and June 26.*

The **summer** ingress charts show Saturn and Neptune exactly conjunct forecasting one of the *wettest* summers in memory. In the lower forty-eight states the heaviest amounts of precipitation will fall east of the Mississippi River, and the driest parts of the country will be the Eastern and Central Rockies. Coastal British Columbia and the Alaskan Panhandle will get the greatest amount of precipitation in North America during this season.

July will be noted for excessive precipitation and also winds. Wind-driven rain may cause damage to crops. *July 7* is a day for especially destructive winds.

August will continue to see excessive rainfall over most of the country, especially east of the Mississippi and on the Alaskan Panhandle. An unseasonably sharp drop in temperature will occur nationwide on August 19. Winds will continue to be associated with rain, especially *the last two weeks* of the month.

September continues the same weather pattern of excessive precipitation east of the Mississippi and on the Alaskan Panhandle until the last two weeks of the month when the excessive precipitation will center over the Eastern Rockies. Two dates this month are associated with destructive winds: *September 24 and September 27.*

Fall will continue to see excessive rainfall in our country, but this time it will center over most of the continental divide. Saturn and Neptune are on the Midheaven of ingress charts set for the fall season for locations in this area. Streams that drain the divide will be swollen, and flooding may be expected downstream to both the east and west. The prediction for excess moisture will extend from the Rockies to the West Coast. In addition, lower than normal temperatures will center over Salt Lake City and points directly north and south. Jupiter is on the Nadir of the fall ingress charts set for the Eastern Rockies and will contribute to many pretty days between rains. Central Alaska will also see some excess moisture.

October will continue to be a month of precipitation, especially in the Rockies, to the west and in Central Alaska. Winds will be prominent on October 12, 17, 27 and on October 29. A nationwide sharp drop in temperature will occur October 13.

Heavy precipitation should continue throughout the month of *November*. Dates associated with heavy precipitation are November 7, 13, 15, 16 and 21. A sharp drop in temperature should occur nationwide November 8.

December will see plenty of snow over most of the nation. Heavy snows are predicted for December 3, 4, 6, 8, 10, 13, 15, 17, 18, 19, 26 and December 27. The snow coming December 4 will be accompanied by strong winds and a sharp drop in temperature. Winds will cause drifting on December 10, 15, 17, 18 and December 27. Winds will cause drifting in snow areas on December 28.

The year 1989 will be one of excess moisture. Even desert areas in the Southwest will see precipitation. Areas under the Saturn/Neptune conjunction influence will be drenched throughout the year, and areas to the east of these areas will see excess moisture also.

NOVEMBER 1988 WEATHER

ZONE 1: Wet weather is predicted for New England during the month of November. Temperatures there should be normal. Much of the Middle Atlantic States area will be dry and warmer than is usual. The southern part of this zone will be warmer than is usual, and precipitation will fluctuate from wet to very dry. Precipitation, when it comes, will be heavier the first week of the month.

ZONE 2: Temperatures in most of this zone will be warmer than usual except in the states bordering the Mississippi where it will be colder than usual. Precipitation will be heaviest in the eastern portion of this zone, and erratic in states bordering the river. Winds will be severe along the Mississippi and the heaviest precipitation of the month will come during the first week.

ZONE 3: Weather may best be described as erratic in this zone during the month of November. The drying effect of the Saturn/Uranus conjunction in a prominent spot on ingress charts wars with the wet influence of Neptune also prominent on ingress charts. Near the Mississippi, temperatures should be colder than is usual and strong winds will be frequent. The southern part of this zone may be warmer than is usual.

ZONE 4: The Rockies west of Cheyenne and east of Salt Lake City will be warmer than usual during the month of November. Fog will be prominent there throughout the month. East of this area it will be drier than is usual and without fog. Temperatures in other parts of this zone will range from very cold to warmer than usual. Winds will be strong in the eastern portion of this zone.

ZONE 5: Dry weather is forecast for this zone during the month of November. Winds will be strong in all portions of this zone throughout the month. Temperatures will fluctuate from cooler than usual to warmer than usual. Precipitation may be sparse, but a dumping of precipitation is likely when any occurs. Winds will be prominent along the coast driving rain when it comes.

ZONE 6: Alaska should have a warmer and drier November than is usual. Throughout the state skies should be unusually blue for this time of year. Wet is the forecast for most of Hawaii for the month of November. Temperatures should be normal, but even desert areas should get wet. The island of Hawaii itself, however, may be relatively dry. Precipitation should center on Oahu and islands to the west.

Dates to Watch:
Watch for rain on the 1st, 2nd, 3rd, 5th, 6th and 11th.
Watch for snow on the 16th, 23rd, 24th and 30th.
Watch for winds on the 3rd, 5th, 10th, 14th, 25th and 30th.

DECEMBER 1988 WEATHER

ZONE 1: New England will have little precipitation the first part of the month of December, and abnormally warm temperatures at the end of the month. The Middle Atlantic States will have an unusually warm and dry December. To the south the weather will also be warm and dry, especially in Georgia and Florida. The end of the month will see some extremely wet weather in Florida.

ZONE 2: Unusually warm weather is forecast for much of this zone during the month of December. Cold and windy weather, however, is forecast for those states in this zone that border the Mississippi River. After the twenty-first, temperatures in the western part of this zone should rise, but a dumping of precipitation is predicted for Ohio, Eastern Kentucky and Eastern Tennessee.

ZONE 3: The very eastern part of this zone will have unusually cold temperatures the first part of this month. To the west, the weather will be cold and dry. Westerly winds will prevail in much of this zone during the month. The last week precipitation along the Mississippi River may be generous, and beautiful skies and warmer-than-usual temperatures will be found to the west.

ZONE 4: Cold and dry is the forecast for the eastern portion of this zone during the month of December. Between Cheyenne and Salt Lake City temperatures will be higher than usual. The last week of the month should find warmer temperatures in the eastern portions of this zone and erratic weather to the west with some wide fluctuations in temperature and precipitation.

ZONE 5: Weather in this zone during the month of December will be erratic with wide fluctuations in temperature. Precipitation during the month will be abnormally low except for the last week of the month when a dumping of precipitation is likely to occur in much of this zone. The year is likely to end with a heavy storm in this zone, but drifting is unlikely.

ZONE 6: Unusually high temperatures and less than normal amounts of precipitation are likely to prevail in Alaska throughout most of this month. After the twenty-first the weather will become erratic in the panhandle with dumpings of precipitation and wide fluctuations in temperature. The rest of the state will remain warmer than usual. Wet is the word to describe Hawaiian weather throughout most of the month.

Dates to Watch:
Watch for snow on the 1st, 3rd, 4th, 7th, 16th, 20th, 24th, 26th and 31st.
Watch for winds on the 1st, 4th, 7th, 14th, 16th, 20th, 22nd, 25th, 28th, 30th and 31st.

JANUARY 1989 WEATHER

ZONE 1: The forecast for New England is for relatively dry, warm weather during the month of January. To the south there will be excessive precipitation in Western New York State, Western Pennsylvania, Washington, D.C., Maryland, Central Virginia and the coast of North Carolina. Even heavier precipitation is slated for Georgia and Florida. Except for New England, temperatures will be well below normal throughout this zone.

ZONE 2: Excessive snowfall is forecast for the northern portion of this zone during the month of January. To the south rainfall will be generous. Temperatures throughout this zone will be lower than normal, but in areas bordering the Mississippi River temperatures will be more seasonable. Also, along the river, skies will not be as overcast as in the rest of this zone. Watch for many heavy storms throughout the month.

ZONE 3: Precipitation will be generous and temperatures will be lower than usual throughout the month of January in this zone. However, along the 100th meridian a break in the low temperatures should occur along with a break in the incessant precipitation. The Saturn/Neptune conjunction, in effect throughout 1989, portends overcast skies for most of the country this month, but this zone should see some blue skies.

ZONE 4: Low temperatures and generous precipitation will characterize most of the country in January, but the eastern portion of this zone will have slightly warmer temperatures and less snowfall. Occasional heavy snows are forecast, however. In the western portion of this zone cold temperatures and excessive snowfall will prevail. Strong winds are also forecast for the western portion of this zone.

ZONE 5: Excessively low temperatures and heavy snowfall are predicted for this zone during the month of January. Winds will be strong. In the south, heavy rain will substitute for snow, and the warming and drying effect of an angular Pluto will help alleviate the effects of an angular Neptune/Mercury conjunction. In the north heavy snows are forecast for the entire month of January.

ZONE 6: Very cold weather and heavy precipitation are predicted for the Alaskan panhandle during the month of January. The rest of the state will be cold with generous amounts of snow, but the warming influence of an angular Mars may be felt here from time to time. Since Hawaiian ingress charts show a prominent Uranus and Saturn, Hawaii should be cooler than usual during the month.

Dates to Watch:
Watch for snow on the 1st, 2nd, 4th, 5th, 8th, 12th, 14th, 16th, 19th, 22nd, 24th, 27th, 30th and 31st.
Watch for winds on the 1st, 2nd, 12th, 25th, 26th and 31st.
Watch for a nation-wide sharp drop in temperature on the 12th.

FEBRUARY 1989 WEATHER

ZONE 1: February will be cold with generous amounts of precipitation in most of this zone. Temperatures slightly higher than usual may occur some days in New England, but excessive amounts of precipitation are predicted for parts of New York, Pennsylvania, Maryland, Virginia, North Carolina and especially Georgia and Florida. Snowfall will be heavy in the northern portions of this area, and rainfall generous in the south.

ZONE 2: Very cold temperatures and generous amounts of precipitation are predicted for this zone during the month of February. Snowfall will be very heavy near the Great Lakes and snow will fall as far south as Mississippi and Alabama. Near the Mississippi River, temperatures will be more seasonable and the sky will not be as overcast as other parts of this zone.

ZONE 3: The forecast for February for this zone calls for low temperatures and generous amounts of precipitation to the east and slightly higher temperatures in much of the Dakotas, Nebraska and Kansas. Drier weather is also forecast for the western portion of this zone. The eastern portion of this zone will have blue skies when snowfall ceases and some relatively warm days in this area.

ZONE 4: Cold and snow are forecast for most of this zone during the month of February. To the east temperatures may be a little warmer and skies bluer, but from Salt Lake City westward the sky should be overcast and temperatures very low. Snowfall will also be generous in the western portions of this zone, more so near the Cascades and the Sierra Nevadas.

ZONE 5: Very cold temperatures and very generous amounts of precipitation are forecast for this zone during the month of February. Snowfall should be extremely heavy in the north, and flooding is possible when snowfall melts during the warm spells. Skies should be overcast frequently in much of this zone throughout the month and warmer days should see much fog. Desert areas in the south will be cold.

ZONE 6: Low temperatures and much precipitation are forecast for Alaska for this month. The Panhandle will have some extremely cold weather with very generous snowfall. Winds in this area will be strong. However, in the central part of the state some days will be warmer than usual. Hawaii will have slightly lower temperatures than usual and generous amounts of rainfall. Breezes during this month will be pleasant.

Dates to Watch:
Watch for snow on the 1st, 5th, 8th, 10th, 12th, 15th, 16th, 21st, 26th and 28th.
Watch for winds on the 1st, 4th, 10th, 14th, 15th, 16th, 23rd and 28th.

MARCH 1989 WEATHER

ZONE 1: The forecast for the first three weeks of March is for slightly higher temperatures than usual for New England. To the south temperatures should be normal, but precipitation will be very generous. The last week of the month a dumping of precipitation should occur in New England and it should be chilly. Generous precipitation should occur to the south all month.

ZONE 2: Generous amounts of snow and rain are forecast for this zone during the month of March. In the western portion of this zone temperatures will be seasonable until the last week of the month when it should turn chilly. The eastern part of this zone will also be cold toward the end of the month. Winds at this time will be very high.

ZONE 3: Precipitation should be generous over most of this zone during the month of March. Temperatures should be seasonable. Along the 100th meridian and to the west temperatures should be slightly higher and it should be drier. It should be chilly along the Mississippi River at the end of the month. Winds will be strong there also. The last week in the west will be warm.

ZONE 4: The eastern portion of this zone will get smaller amounts of precipitation during the month of March than most of the rest of the country. Temperatures in the eastern portion of this zone should be normal for the month. In the very western portions of this zone precipitation will be generous and temperatures will be lower than normal. Strong winds are forecast for the western portion of this zone.

ZONE 5: Extremely wet weather and normal temperatures are forecast for most of the month in this zone. Smog should be frequent and haze will be a problem in wide-spread areas in portions of this zone. The last week of the month additional precipitation will fall and flooding may be a problem in some areas. Desert areas to the south will not be exempt from precipitation.

ZONE 6: The Alaskan Panhandle will be chillier than usual during the month of March and precipitation will be generous. The rest of the state will have normal temperatures and plenty of snow and rainfall during the month. Temperatures in Hawaii should be slightly lower than normal for most of the month. Rainfall there will be especially generous the last week of the month.

Dates to Watch:
Watch for snow on the 2nd, 3rd, 9th, 11th and 14th.
Watch for rain on the 18th, 23rd, 24th, 25th, 28th and 30th.
Watch for winds on the 10th, 11th, 18th, 24th, 25th, 28th, 29th and 30th.
Tornado watch in effect on the 10th, 29th and 30th.

MAY 1989 WEATHER

ZONE 1: Very generous amounts of precipitation are forecast for most of this zone during the month of May. New England will have the greatest amounts of precipitation, but heavy rainfall is predicted all along the coast. Temperatures should be a little cooler than normal and winds should be brisk. Watch for a generous amount of rainfall around the middle of the month and also toward the end of the month.

ZONE 2: Rainfall should be generous here, but not as heavy as in Zone One. Temperatures should be a little cooler than normal, and brisk winds should whip through this zone. Toward the west temperatures should be a little warmer and winds not as strong. Watch for heavy rainfall in the middle of the month and again at the end. Temperatures in Wisconsin may be a little warmer than other states in the northern portions of this zone.

ZONE 3: Zone Three should be the driest part of the country in May. Although most of the country will experience heavy rainfall this month, much of Zone Three will be warm and dry. Rain, when it comes, will be in the form of thunderstorms, especially in the western portions of this zone. The closer the location is to the Rockies, the wetter it will be.

ZONE 4: This zone will have generous amounts of precipitation during the month of May, especially in the form of thunderstorms. Temperatures should be seasonable. Watch for strong winds over much of this zone throughout the month. Watch for heavy thunderstorms throughout the month, and especially around the middle of the month. Rain, without wind, should fall on the 12th and again on the 28th.

ZONE 5: Precipitation will be generous in this zone during the month of May. Temperatures will be chilly, but breezes gentle. To the north, in British Columbia, along the coast some extremely heavy rainfall is due. Mudslides, flooding and other complications will be coming from the extreme dampness. Watch for some extremely heavy rainfall toward the end of the month. Prepare for flooding after this.

ZONE 6: Generous amounts of rainfall should come to the state of Alaska during the month of May. The Alaskan panhandle should receive some extremely heavy precipitation; also temperatures should be chillier than usual and winds very strong. Winds in the rest of this state should be normal. Hawaii will also receive generous amounts of precipitation, and temperatures will be a little cooler than usual and breezes gentle.

Dates to Watch:
Watch for rain on the 2nd, 4th, 12th, 16th, 17th, 18th, 20th, 21st, 23rd, 27th and 28th.
Watch for winds on the 4th, 7th, 16th, 17th, 18th, 20th, 21st, 23rd and 27th.
Tornado watch is in effect on the 7th.

APRIL 1989 WEATHER

ZONE 1: New England will have some extremely damp weather during the month of April. The forecast for generous precipitation extends south along the coast. As far south as Florida, precipitation will be heavier than usual. Watch for many foggy days and temperatures ranging from normal to cool in this zone. Winds should be strong throughout the area.

ZONE 2: Generous amounts of precipitation are forecast for this zone during the month of April, although rainfall will not be as heavy as in zone one. Temperatures should range from normal to cool and fog will be noticed often. Winds throughout this zone should be strong during the month. Areas near the Mississippi River should be a little warmer than the rest of this zone.

ZONE 3: Generous amounts of rainfall are predicted for those portions of this zone which border directly on the Mississippi River, but to the west, about the 95th meridian, the month should be very dry. Temperatures here should be warmer than usual also. The rest of this zone should be relatively dry and temperatures should be warmer than the norm. Wind is predicted for this zone during the month.

ZONE 4: Precipitation in this zone during the month of April should be heavier than on the plains, but less extensive than in the east. Temperatures should be seasonable. Haze and fog will occur at some locations, but there will be many days of pleasant temperatures with clear blue skies. Winds will be strong on occasion and thunderstorms will be frequent. Flash floods are a possibility in this zone this month.

ZONE 5: Pleasant weather is forecast for this zone during the month of April, although precipitation should be generous. Temperatures will be seasonable. Watch for haze and fog in many areas throughout the month, watch for frequent thunderstorms and watch for flash floods after heavy precipitation. North of the border in British Columbia record-breaking precipitation should occur.

ZONE 6: Alaska south of Juneau should have extremely heavy precipitation. Temperatures should be chilly also. The central part of this state should also have generous amounts of precipitation. Temperatures here will not be unseasonably cold, but slightly cooler than is usual. Generous amounts of precipitation, slightly cooler than usual temperatures and stiff breezes are forecast for Hawaii. Winds will be prominent in Hawaii.

Dates to Watch:
Watch for rain on the 2nd, 3rd, 4th, 12th, 15th, 18th, 21st, 22nd, 26th and 28th.
Watch for winds on the 3rd, 4th, 14th, 19th, 25th and 28th.
Tornado watch in effect on the 14th and 19th.

JUNE 1989 WEATHER

ZONE 1: Very generous amounts of precipitation are forecast for New England and the northern portions of this zone. In the southern parts of this zone there will be less precipitation the first three weeks of the month, but temperatures will be a little lower than normal. The last week of the month there will be very heavy rainfall throughout the entire zone. Winds should be strong this month.

ZONE 2: Rainfall should be generous throughout this zone during the month of June. Temperatures should be a little cooler than usual. Winds will be strong throughout the month, and when combined with heavy rain will make this month memorable. The last week of the month should see some especially chilly weather in the western portions of this zone. At this time even heavier rainfall will mark the east.

ZONE 3: The eastern portion of this zone will see some heavy rainfall throughout the month of June, but a little to the west it will be drier and also warmer. However, thunderstorms are predicted for the very westernmost portions of this zone, and the last week of the month rainfall will be generous everywhere except the foothills of the Rockies. There it will be dry.

ZONE 4: Thunderstorms are forecast for zone 4 during most of the month of June. However, the last week of the month will begin a trend toward dryness which will continue through the summer. This is especially true of the Eastern Rockies. Temperatures will be seasonable throughout the month, but the last week of the month will see above average temperatures in the eastern portion of this zone.

ZONE 5: Rainfall in this zone will be very heavy throughout most of the month. Desert areas of this zone should not be exempt. The last week of the month, however, should be drier. Temperatures should be seasonable throughout the month, and winds normal. To the north of this zone, in coastal British Columbia, record-breaking rainfall should occur. Watch for flooding, mudslides and other complications of excessive moisture.

ZONE 6: Heavy rainfall is predicted for most of Alaska during the month of June. This is especially true of the panhandle. Throughout most of the month, temperatures will be low in the panhandle too. In the central part of this state temperatures will be lower the last week of the month. Rainfall will be generous in the state of Hawaii during the month. Temperatures should be seasonable.

Dates to Watch:
Watch for rain on the 8th, 11th, 14th, 15th, 20th, 23rd, 24th, 26th and 29th.
Watch for winds on the 6th, 7th, 8th, 24th, 25th and 29th.
Watch for an unseasonable sharp drop in temperature on the 8th.

JULY 1989 WEATHER

ZONE 1: Extremely heavy rainfall is predicted for this zone during the month of July. Fog and haze will be common in low-lying areas and flooding is probable also. The prediction for heavy rainfall covers all areas along the eastern seaboard, but the northern portions of this zone will feel the dampness the most. Temperatures will range from seasonable to a little cooler than normal.

ZONE 2: Generous amounts of precipitation are predicted for this zone during the month of July. This is especially true for Ohio, Michigan, Indiana, Central Kentucky and Central Tennessee. Along the Mississippi River it will be a little drier, but rainfall should be above normal here too. Temperatures throughout this zone during this month should range from normal to cooler than usual. Winds will be strong also.

ZONE 3: Generous amounts of precipitation are predicted for this zone during the month of July, but this rainfall will be slightly less than that falling east of the Mississippi. In the very westernmost portions of this zone it will be relatively dry. Temperatures throughout this zone during the month of July will range from normal to slightly below normal. Winds will be strong in the eastern portion of this zone.

ZONE 4: The Eastern Rockies will be dry during the month of July with hotter than usual temperatures. The prediction for heat and dryness extends as far west as Salt Lake City and a little beyond. In the westernmost portion of this zone precipitation will be more normal, and temperatures should fluctuate from the very high to very cool. Winds will be featured throughout this zone during the month of July.

ZONE 5: The weather in Zone Five should be pleasant during the month of July. Precipitation should be normal and temperatures seasonable. North of this zone, in British Columbia, extremely heavy rainfall should occur. Haze, fog, flooding and other complications of excessive moisture are predicted. Temperatures here will vary from normal to cool. Winds will drive much of the precipitation. Record-breaking rainfall is predicted.

ZONE 6: Rainfall will be generous in Alaska during the month of July and extremely heavy rainfall is predicted for the Panhandle. Here record-breaking rainfall is predicted. Temperatures in Alaska will range from normal to cool in the Panhandle to cooler than usual in the rest of the state. Precipitation will be generous in Hawaii, and temperatures here may be slightly below normal. Gentle breezes are predicted for Hawaii during this month.

Dates to Watch:
Watch for rain on the 2nd, 9th, 10th, 11th, 12th, 15th, 19th, 22nd, 25th and 31st.
Watch for winds on the 2nd, 4th, 5th, 6th, 7th, 9th, 10th, 11th, 12th, 15th, 16th, 18th, 24th and 26th.
Tornado watch is in effect on the 6th, 7th and 26th.

AUGUST 1989 WEATHER

ZONE 1: Generous amounts of precipitation are predicted for this zone during the month of August. Rainfall will be heavy all along the coastal states, but Georgia and Florida will have a little less than the rest of this zone. Temperatures will be a little lower than normal and winds will help to drive the rain. The farther south a location is within this zone, the more seasonable the temperatures.

ZONE 2: Rainfall will be heavy in this zone during the month of August. This is especially true of the eastern portions of this zone. Areas bordering the Mississippi River will be drier. Temperatures in this zone will be a little lower than the norm. Winds will be strong and skies blue when rain is not falling. In the western portions of this zone temperatures will be a little higher.

ZONE 3: Precipitation will be plentiful in this zone during the month of August, but it will not be as heavy as precipitation east of the Mississippi. In the very westernmost portions of this zone it will be dry. Temperatures will be a little lower than usual in the eastern portions of this zone and range from normal to above normal near the Rockies. Winds will be strong in the west.

ZONE 4: While most of the country sees heavy precipitation during the month of August, most of the Rockies will be extremely dry. Heat will be associated with the dryness. The driest part of this zone will encompass most of the continental divide. Areas in the westernmost portions of this zone will have a little more normal precipitation and a little more normal temperatures. Winds will be strong in the eastern portion of this zone.

ZONE 5: Rainfall will be generous in this zone during the month of August. Temperatures will fluctuate from above normal to a little below normal. Winds will be strong. North of this zone, on the Canadian coast, extremely heavy rainfall is due. Records for precipitation should be broken, and haze, fog and flooding are predicted. Temperatures here will be a little cooler than the norm.

ZONE 6: Rainfall should be generous during of August in Alaska; especially in the panhandle where rainfall records will be set. Temperatures will fluctuate from a little below normal to higher than usual, except in the central part of Alaska where temperatures will be lower than normal. Winds should be strong. Hawaii will see plenty of rain and temperatures a little below the norm.

Dates to Watch:
Watch for rain on the 1st, 3rd, 9th, 11th, 15th, 18th, 19th, 20th, 21st, 23rd, 26th, 27th and 30th.
Watch for winds on the 4th, 5th, 8th, 19th, 20th, 24th and 27th.
Hurricane watch in effect following the 13th of the month.

SEPTEMBER 1989 WEATHER

ZONE 1: The forecast is for heavy precipitation in this zone during the month of September. The northern portion of this zone will have the heaviest rainfall. Temperatures will be below normal throughout this zone and especially in the south. The last week of the month will be relatively dry in both the northern and southern sections of this zone. Temperatures will be higher then also.

ZONE 2: The entire eastern portion of zone 2 will have heavy precipitation during September. Heavy rainfall is forecast for much of northern zone 2 also. Temperatures should be below normal, and winds will be strong. The last week of the month precipitation may abate somewhat in the south, and temperatures will be normal for this time of year. Humidity should be high then.

ZONE 3: Generous amounts of rainfall are predicted for this zone during the month of September. Temperatures will be a little cooler than is usual and winds will drive much of the rain. When rainfall is absent, however, skies should be blue. In the very westernmost reaches of this zone it will be dry. High humidity will characterize the last week of the month.

ZONE 4: While most of the country is deluged with rainfall this month, this zone will be very dry. The forecast for dry weather extends from Cheyenne in the east to past Salt Lake City in the west. However, the last week of the month will see a deluge in the easternmost portions of this zone and chilly weather in the central sections. The southern part of this zone will see higher temperatures.

ZONE 5: Heavy rainfall is forecast for this zone during the month of September. Temperatures will be a little lower than usual and winds will be strong. The last week of the month will continue to see the heavy precipitation. Temperatures then will be very low. Extremely heavy rainfall is forecast for much of British Columbia north of the border during the first three weeks of the month.

ZONE 6: A deluge of precipitation is forecast for the Alaskan panhandle during most of the month of September. Generous amounts of rainfall are forecast for the rest of the state, and temperatures in the central portion of the state will be chilly. Hawaii will see generous amounts of precipitation and pleasant breezes. Temperatures may be a little below normal the first three weeks of the month.

Dates to Watch:
Watch for rain on the 2nd, 3rd, 7th, 8th, 10th, 13th, 16th, 19th, 20th and 30th.
Watch for winds on the 1st, 3rd, 7th, 16th, 18th, 19th, 21st, *24th*, 25th, 26th, *27th* and 29th.
Hurricane watch in effect following the 15th and 24th.

OCTOBER 1989 WEATHER

ZONE 1: Precipitation will be plentiful in this zone during the month of October, especially in New England. Temperatures will be seasonable throughout this zone, but a little higher than normal in the south. Winds should be brisk most of the time and humidity should be high throughout the month, especially in the north. Rainfall should be generous the first two weeks of the month.

ZONE 2: Rainfall should be generous in this zone during the month of October. Temperatures should be seasonable. Humidity will be high and winds should be brisk. The driest weather in this zone during the month will come in the eastern portion of this zone. The wettest weather will be found along the Mississippi River. The first three weeks of the month will be the wettest.

ZONE 3: Rain should be plentiful in zone 3 during October, and especially generous in the western portion. Heavy storms to the west should cause streams and rivers to rise and flooding could occur in low-lying areas. Temperatures will be normal and winds should be brisk. Montana should feel the brunt of the excess precipitation, and the Missouri River may flood.

ZONE 4: The eastern portion of the Rockies is due for some extremely heavy precipitation during this month. Flooding is likely to occur in low-lying areas and rivers on both sides of the continental divide should be swollen. To the west of the continental divide, excess moisture is forecast also. This prediction includes all areas east of the coast. A chill is forecast for Salt Lake City.

ZONE 5: Heavy precipitation is forecast for this zone during the month of October. The heavy precipitation should cause flooding in low-lying areas in the north and even reach desert areas in the south. Temperatures will fluctuate between normal to chill. Winds will be brisk. The heaviest amounts of precipitation will come the first three weeks of the month. The last week should be dry.

ZONE 6: Heavy precipitation is predicted for central Alaska. The Alaskan panhandle will see less precipitation than it did in the summer. Temperatures will be relatively warm in the central portion of the state and normal elsewhere. Winds should be brisk. Moisture in excess of the usual is also predicted for Hawaii. Temperatures here should be normal and breezes gentle.

Dates to Watch:
Watch for rain on the 1st, 2nd, 4th, 7th, 8th, 9th, 13th, 15th, 17th, 18th, 20th and 21st.
Watch for winds on the 1st, 4th, 12th, 17th, 27th and 29th.
Watch for a nationwide sharp drop in temperature on the 13th.
Hurricane watch is in effect after the 8th, 10th and 12th.

NOVEMBER 1989 WEATHER

ZONE 1: The forecast is for generous amounts of precipitation in this zone during the month of November. Temperatures throughout this zone should be a little higher than normal. The air should hold much moisture when it isn't raining. This will be especially true in New England and also in Georgia and Florida. Winds should be brisk throughout this zone. Watch for record-breaking lows around the 8th.

ZONE 2: Precipitation should be generous throughout this zone during the month of November. Temperatures will be erratic, sometimes higher and sometimes lower than usual. Snow should come early to the northern portions of this zone and the south should experience some wet, sloppy weather. Temperatures may be a little higher than usual near the Mississippi River. Winds should be brisk in this zone.

ZONE 3: Precipitation will be generous in this zone during the month of November. This will be true in the westernmost portions of this zone, especially in Montana and Wyoming just east of the Rockies. Temperatures will range from higher than usual to very low. Skies will be blue when it isn't raining or snowing. Wind activity should be brisk throughout the month.

ZONE 4: Extremely heavy precipitation is forecast for the Eastern Rockies during the month of November. This part of the country should have the heaviest amount of precipitation this month. To the west, snow will continue to be generous, and extremely low temperatures will center on Salt Lake City and points directly north and south. Temperatures in other parts of this zone will also be chilly. Winds will be brisk.

ZONE 5: Snowfall will be very heavy in the northern portions of this zone, and rainfall will be generous in the south. Even desert areas in the southern portion of this zone should see moisture. Temperatures in this zone will be erratic; higher than usual at some times and chillier than normal at others. Wind activity will range from gentle to extremely brisk. Watch for a sudden, sharp drop in temperature around the 8th.

ZONE 6: The central part of Alaska will have some very heavy amounts of snow during the month of November. The panhandle will see less precipitation than other parts of the state. Between snows and rains the weather should be pleasant, although it should be chilly much of the time. Precipitation should be normal in Hawaii and temperatures there may be a little higher than the norm.

Dates to Watch:
Watch for rain on the 1st, 2nd, 5th, 6th, 10th, 14th and 15th.
Watch for snow on the 8th, 16th, 19th, 20th, 21st, 22nd and 29th.
Watch for winds on the 7th, 8th, 10th, 21st, 22nd, 25th, 27th and 29th.
Watch for a nationwide sharp drop in temperature on the 8th.

DECEMBER 1989 WEATHER

ZONE 1: Generous amounts of snowfall are predicted for the northern parts of this zone during the month of December. Generous amounts of rainfall are predicted for the south. Temperatures will fluctuate throughout this zone, sometimes higher and sometimes lower than normal. Heavy precipitation is forecast for all the month, but especially for the first three weeks of the month. Winds will be brisk throughout the month.

ZONE 2: Precipitation will be heavy throughout the month in most of this zone. Look for heavy snowfall in the north, and heavy rainfall near the Gulf of Mexico. The first three weeks of the month will see the heaviest precipitation. Temperatures will be erratic, sometimes higher and sometimes lower than normal. Winds will be brisk throughout this zone during the entire month. Watch for a sharp drop in temperature around the 4th of the month.

ZONE 3: Generous amounts of snowfall are forecast for this zone during the month of December. This will be especially true in the western portions of this zone just east of the Rockies. Look for heavy snowfall the first three weeks of the month in most parts of this zone. Watch for temperatures fluctuating from higher than usual to lower than usual. Brisk winds are also forecast.

ZONE 4: Extremely heavy snowfall is forecast for the eastern portions of the Rockies. This snowfall may well break existing records. The forecast for heavy snowfall extends to the western portions of the zone also. Very cold temperatures are forecast for Salt Lake City and parts directly north and south. Temperatures in other parts may fluctuate from the very cold to higher than normal. Winds will be strong. Watch for a sharp drop in temperature around the 4th of the month.

ZONE 5: Very heavy precipitation is forecast for this zone during the month of December. Snowfall will be very heavy in the north, and rainfall may even wet desert areas in the south. Temperatures will be erratic; sometimes higher than usual and sometimes lower than the norm. Winds will be strong. The greatest amount of precipitation will come the first three weeks of the month.

ZONE 6: The central part of the state of Alaska will see much snowfall throughout the month. This forecast extends to the western portion of the state, but not to the panhandle where precipitation will not be much higher than normal. Temperatures will be low, and winds brisk throughout the state. Hawaii will have generous amounts of precipitation, normal temperatures and pleasant breezes.

Dates to Watch:
Watch for snow on the 3rd, 4th, 6th, 8th, 9th, 10th, 13th, 15th, 17th, 18th, 19th, 26th and 27th.
Watch for winds on the 4th, 10th, 15th, 17th, 18th, 22nd, 26th and 28th.
Watch for a nationwide drop in temperature on the 4th.

Earthquake Predictions
by Nancy Soller

Most large earthquakes are eclipse-related. A Solar Eclipse occurs. Planets begin to form hard angles to the eclipse point as they travel through the sky. Finally a planet forms an angle to the eclipse point when another condition of heavenly stress is in effect and an earthquake occurs.

What is a hard angle? It can be either geocentric (involving the planet, the Earth and the eclipse point) or it can be heliocentric (involving the planet, the Sun and the eclipse point). The hard angles include the conjunction (zero degrees), the square (90 degrees), and the opposition (180 degrees).

What conditions of heavenly stress allow a planet to trigger an earthquake? Information is still being gathered on this, but here are some of the stresses which contribute to quakes:

1. *The Moon conjunct or squaring its Nodes.* In this case the Moon is either conjunct the equator or at a high point or low point in relation to it.
2. *A second planet aspects an eclipse point along with the first.*
3. *Mars and Neptune form a geocentric hard angle to each other.*
4. *Multiple planets form hard angles to multiple eclipse points at the same time.*
5. *A heavy outer planet aspects the eclipse point while the Moon forms a hard angle to a cluster of planets.*

6. *A planet is conjunct the Sun at the time of the eclipse.* In this case the earthquake closely follows the eclipse.

Geocentric eclipse-related earthquakes generally precede heliocentric eclipse-related earthquakes. Typically a heliocentric eclipse-related earthquake follows a geocentric eclipse-related earthquake, involves the same eclipse-point and is triggered by the same planet that triggered the original quake. It appears as though a given eclipse-point may be involved with a number of earthquakes; sometimes all associated with the same planet and sometimes associated with different planets.

Making the job of earthquake watching difficult is the fact that many large quakes go unreported in the news media. If an earthquake occurs in an unpopulated area and does little damage it may not make the news.

High Risk Dates for Earthquakes

One recent eclipse point bears special watching during the year of 1989. This is the *October 3, 1986 eclipse-point at ten degrees of Libra. During the year, Mars, Jupiter, Saturn and Neptune all aspect this eclipse-point under conditions that suggest a quake.*

On May 16 Mars will aspect the eclipse-point while Mars and Neptune form hard aspects to each other. A quake is possible. On *October 6* Mars and Jupiter will together form hard angles to the eclipse-point. Again, a quake is possible.

A quake may occur *between November 10 and November 20* when Jupiter, Saturn and Neptune all aspect the eclipse point at the same time, or a quake may occur when these planets aspect the eclipse point separately.

Since Saturn and Neptune will both be retrograde at ten degrees of Capricorn part of the time during the year, each will have *three* periods of time when they aspect the eclipse point. Jupiter will aspect it once. Since these planets move relatively slowly, there will be *large periods of time* when there will be danger of quakes.

Neptune will form hard angles to the eclipse point between *January 4 and January 31*, between *July 5 and August 13* and between *October 29 and December 3*.

Saturn will form hard angles to the eclipse point between *February 10 and February 20*, between *June 28 and July*

11 and between *November 10 and November 20.*

Jupiter will form hard angles to the eclipse point between *October 6 and November 21.*

All of the above dates are suspect for earthquakes. When a quake occurs, it will probably be discovered that the Moon was forming a conjunction, a square or an opposition to a cluster of planets fine-timing the quake. Other suspect dates are listed below:

Dates associated with the May 30, 1985 eclipse at twenty-eight degrees of Taurus: February 28, March 9, **July 3 and 4** and December 16.

Dates associated with the November 11, 1985 eclipse at twenty degrees of Scorpio: February 20.

Dates associated with the April 9, 1986 eclipse at nineteen degrees of Aries: November 26.

Dates associated with the March 29, 1987 eclipse at eight degrees of Aries: May 13, September 19, October 2 and **October 3 to 5**.

Dates associated with the September 9, 1987 eclipse at zero degrees of Libra: January 11, April 30, August 3, **September 15-17, September 21-31** and November 6.

Dates associated with the March 18, 1988 eclipse at twenty-eight degrees of Pisces: August 17.

Dates associated with the September 11, 1988 eclipse at nineteen degrees of Virgo: Probably none this year.

Dates associated with the March 7, 1989 eclipse at seventeen degrees of Pisces: An earthquake is likely to coincide with this eclipse because Mercury will be forming a wide conjunction with the Sun at the time of the eclipse.

Dates associated with the August 31, 1989 eclipse at eight degrees of Virgo: Probably none this year.

Bold type indicates a heliocentric quake is possible.

Postmortem on Some 1987 Earthquakes

March 5 and 6, 1987; Ecuador: There were several forms of heavenly stress in effect when this earthquake occurred.

1. Mars was square the point of the July 31, 1981 eclipse at eight degrees of Leo.
2. Jupiter was square the point of the June 2, 1982 eclipse at zero degrees of Cancer.
3. Saturn was opposing the point of the June 11, 1983 eclipse at twenty degrees of Gemini.

As all three planets formed hard angles to recent eclipse points the stress helped to set off the quake. Mars, the fastest moving of the three, probably acted as the trigger.

June 10, 1987; Midwest: Venus was conjunct the May 19, 1985 eclipse point at 28 degrees of Taurus. A wide Mars square Neptune provided the additional stress needed to trigger the earthquake.

October 1, 1987; Los Angeles: This quake occurred when the earth formed a heliocentric conjunction with the March 29, 1987 eclipse point at eight degrees of Aries.

The *November 16, 1987 earthquake in Alaska* occurred when Saturn was opposing the June 11, 1983 eclipse point at twenty degrees of Gemini and the Moon was conjunct its north node. In addition, Mars was forming a heliocentric opposition to the March 29, 1987 eclipse point of eight degrees of Aries.

Economic And Stock Market Forecast For 1989

by Pat Esclavon-Hardy

We have a new President and since this writing occurred in the latter part of 1987, I cannot confirm whether we are in a Democratic or Republican Administration. I can only speculate by saying the economy does not seem to approve of the newly elected! My thoughts are that it is not the President who helped the bull market of 1982-1987, but the Federal Reserve Chairman, Mr. Paul Volker! Since his retirement in August 1987, the economy has lacked direction and is confused. October 19, 1987, was an immediate reaction of the confusion that snowballed!

The year 1989 will commence a new Saturn/Neptune cycle of 35.87 years. This particular cycle comes on the heels of last year's significant Saturn/Uranus 45.363 year cycle. For these two cycles, which usually occur ten years apart, to manifest in this time window only one year from one another announces significant changes associated with these three planets of Saturn, Uranus and Neptune! In the following pages we hope to shed some light on what those changes may involve.

There have been only two other times in this century that this Saturn/Neptune conjunction occurred: 1953 and 1917! You may want to research these years and establish your own conclusions. One of the common denominators, which is particularly associated with Neptune, is a weakness in mass constitution, i.e., in 1917, the typhus epidemic sweeps

Europe and kills 3 million people in the next 4 years. In 1953, the Japanese deal with mercury poisoning in their waters; many die eating fish and shellfish the following several years. Another common denominator of this conjunction is that many companies and corporations find financiers to begin their dream, and other companies merge to keep their dream intact! The economy enters a recessionary period and the stock market declines, confirming a true bear market in both years! Saturn/Neptune seems to coincide with a contraction in the economy (deflationary) and is recession-oriented.

The Saturn/Neptune conjunction will occur three times this year—the first time on March 3, then as these planets appear in retrograde motion on June 24th, and finally in direct motion on November 14th. Another interesting factor is that these planets will travel in their orbits together within one degree of one another from February 21st, before the conjunction, to March 21st (Spring Equinox), after the first conjunction. Again June 5th, before the second conjunction, to July 4th. And finally November 5th, before the final conjunction, to November 27th. The conjunction finale will occur on November 14th! I would tend to think that the economy could accelerate recessionary attitudes during these above time windows. Yes, we are in a primary bear market! October 19, 1987, was the first clue!

The years 1988-89 will truly be years of economic transition, not only from a Presidential election year ('88) and new Administration ('89), but cyclically, we are dealing with a new attitude—a new attitude toward the way we acquire and use our resources. The country's budget deficit for example—we can no longer mortgage our future, and that doesn't mean ten to twenty years from now—it means near term . . . tomorrow, next week and next month! If we do not deal with this now, we could be in a major depression with other parts of the world looking at us as if we don't have it together any more. What's so sad is that it is true! We have become a nation in major debt without enough revenues (income) to pay for it. Are we any better than Mexico? Brazil? Or other debtor nations?

We are beginning to stop and take a long hard look at the reality we have created, and it isn't very pleasant. The positive thing about this is that we are AWARE and taking

ACTION. Hence, a transition in our economy. Realize that it took over 50 years to create this debt; it isn't going to go away slowly. The 1980's are known as "the transition years" and they are coming to a close, which means the transition process has been taking place, and recently it has been accelerated. These are crucial years, and as this fine tuning process takes place, we somehow must keep the attitudes of the people optimistic (maybe a little Neptune idealism) and healthy so that we can continue to generate an economic healing process (Saturn conjunct Neptune)!

Let's take a closer look at what this all means. The stock market is explained to you in the pages ahead. But what about the mass psychology? The stock market is known as the barometer of mass psychology. How does it affect you and me, together and separately? Basically, since this is a 35.87 year cycle, this cycle occurs in the sign of Capricorn, while the 1953 cycle occurred in Libra and 1917 in Leo. Saturn rules Capricorn, so its energy can be expressed freely. Neptune is in its fall under the sign of Capricorn. While Saturn in Capricorn is big business, politics, everything that is materialism and worldly, Neptune deals with the intangible realms and the next dimension. The Neptune factor dissolves the materialism of Saturn. Neptune is the higher octave of Venus (resource, values, love). Neptune tries to achieve final attainment, usually by intangible means.

Psychologically there is a positive variation and a negative one. Negatively, there appear to be pockets of mood variations that can be rather strange or negative-pessimistic, resulting in confusion, self-doubt, uncertainty and a general tendency to look at life from the worst possible point of view. There is a sense of uncertainty about what is real in a person's life, sometimes resulting in a sense of fear or free-floating anxiety. This is because Neptune is the unreal and Saturn is the real. When the two categories of reality blend, they become difficult to separate. A negative-minded person unfortunately would attract the more difficult variation!

The positive, constructive side of this aspect can be one of ability to make extraordinary self-sacrifices or sacrifices that could be common sense actions that each of us must do for the betterment of all, a more balanced, conservative approach in our daily lives to help the economy get back on its feet for all of us. The emphasis is that we must all participate in the betterment of our material universe! There is a higher purpose we must keep in mind to do the things necessary to better our lives and keep them spiritually and economically healthy in the future! The common denominator is that perceptions of reality at this time are quite different from times in the past, and we should take this into consideration when making any plans for the future. We are embarking on a new 35.87 year cycle taking us into the year of 2024!

It is a time to update your metaphysics, your spiritual beliefs, and bring them into reality—not just preach them on the Sabbath, but incorporate them in our lives and live them DAILY. If each one of us gets in touch with the intuitive awareness within each of us, this blends into the mass psychology and sparks an attitude of wholeness for the economic structures Saturn has presented to us. This creates beliefs and inspirations, and bridges the gap to our future reality. This could help the transition years of the 1980's reach a finale as we leave the doors open to the 1990's!

Here are some ideas that would fall along the lines of this Saturn/Neptune energy that may incorporate into our economy: prescription drugs by mail-order; pay TV for newly released movies; religion vs. politics as a major issue; secrets, covert activities, and missing people being exposed. Our drinking water NEEDS to be PROTECTED from chemical waste. Our drinking water is being polluted more and more each day, and this awareness needs to happen very QUICKLY! Our forests, too, are at stake with the chemical pollution, and acid rain de-mineralizing the trees and soil; a major erosion issue could be at hand. Possible bridge or construction decay; refurbishing programs may be needed since most bridges and buildings are now over 80 years old! The liquor and tobacco industries could be near their peak as these personal "vices" may be on the decline. Places of confinement, penitentiaries, could undergo renovation and re-evaluation of processes. Hospitals creating new divisions for specialized illnesses or even preventive medicine. Hospitals and penitentiaries may become privately owned with investors along with those that are state and federally owned. New Age beliefs that could be used in corporate seminars, medicine, politics, athletics, motivation lectures, etc. In other words, putting some structure to the New Age ideas, and formulating them into everyday life and REALITY—the

New Reality!

The primary focus of 1989 is the Saturn/Neptune conjunction. Much like 1988, there was major focus on the Saturn/Uranus conjunction which produced activity around the time when the Moon triggered the conjunction. Pay attention to the Moon cycle this year. The Moon acts like a timer to something (Saturn/Neptune) already set to go, and when the Moon is in one of these signs, which lasts approximately 2.5 days each, it should trigger (much like a gun) things into (e)motion. The Cardinal signs of Aries, Cancer, Libra, and Capricorn will activate this planetary conjunction.

For those of you who would like to research how this timing affects you, personally, look these Moon dates up monthly and jot them down in your personal calendar, and then make notes of the outcome as you go through the year. Pay attention to the news at that time also, as it may benefit you in your career or financial plans and goals. You will start to become more aware of lunar timing and its interaction with man and the cosmos.

Moon

PLANET	HOUSE(S) RULED	CORRESPONDENCES
Sun	5th	Money, investments, gold, government, brokers, stock exchanges.
Moon	4th	The public, mass psychology, silver, aluminum, soybeans, fluctuations, homes and property.
Mercury	3rd & 6th	Business in general, contracts and agreements, communication, travel, wheat and oats.
Venus	2nd & 7th	Partnerships, investments and valuable possessions, copper, national treasures, securities, accumulation, wheat.
Mars	1st & 8th	Activity and energy (used wisely or unwisely), national defense, steel and metals in general, manufacturing.
Jupiter	9th & 12th	Optimism, over-spending, national budget, international relations, judicial system, stocks, tin, financial gain.
Saturn	10th & 11th	Conservatism, agriculture, cattle, barley, rye, grains in general, lead, financial losses or limitations, recession.
Uranus	11th	Inventions, technology, sudden change, uranium, earthquakes, civic and humanitarian organizations, public media (radio, TV, broadcasters & reporters).
Neptune	12th	Inflation, chemicals and pharmaceuticals, medicine, oil industry, unseen influences, idealism.
Pluto	8th	Underground resources, institutions, transformations, rebuilding, space exploration & oceanographic research, insurance, plutonium, atomic energy.

General Trends for 1989

One of the most noticeable factors for minor trend changes in the markets for the next 90 days will be the position of the Moon in the Cardinal signs of Aries, Cancer, Libra and Capricorn. Consult the pages of this book to find the dates of the Moon in these signs!

JANUARY: Happy New Year—As we ring in 1989, this is the month to inaugurate our new President. The markets in general appear to be somewhat depressed. Since we are truly in a bear market and recessionary aspects are upon us, this President will have to pull some rabbits out of the hat to ward off the prey of a failing economy. Unemployment may be picking up again, and this time with the higher-end white collar executive. The fat is truly being trimmed in the higher echelons of corporations. Mercury goes retrograde on the 16th and lasts through February 5th. Caution in signing contracts or other documents. Fix those mechanicals and cars before this time frame as it could cost you more now! The Dow Jones should be mixed to down this month and possibly starting the year with falling prices with a mid-month rally for the inauguration. Gold and other metals should be falling also. Soybeans may still be enjoying the latter part of its bull market, but coming to a close by spring. If you followed the previous Moon Sign Books, my advice was to be out of the market August 1987! Small percentage in stocks in 1988 and out of the market 1989! Unless you are a strong speculator and know the ropes in options and futures, your money should be in safety now. Money should have already been placed in liquid instruments such as money market, CD's, and government secured bonds. Not a time for speculation with investments as it could get hairy this year. End of January and first week in February you may want to be selective with certain stocks that are going to pay any sort of dividends. There seems to be speculation in dividend paying stocks for these few days. This is a real short term play for speculators!

FEBRUARY: Aerospace may be highlighted this month as purse strings could be pulled even tighter than last year due to all the problems NASA has had after the Challenger incident and the past 18 months. The space program must be kept alive as this is where our technology is important for other economic and medical applications. Possibly private enterprise may come into the picture more for commercial uses. Airline deregulation could create more airfare wars and cheaper traveling rates may be seen—could have started last month, too. Early part of February may be more optimistic, but by mid-month a significant sell-off in the stock and most commodity markets. Bond market may take a hit here too. Full Moon Eclipse this month right on the ascendent of the New York Stock Exchange Chart! Emotional period on Wall Street! Changes in the market policies are occurring independent of the FED or SEC. New rules and regulations may try to be enforced.

MARCH: The Saturn/Neptune conjunction occurs on the 3rd in between two eclipses! This accentuates recessionary issues, and negative news may be a bit overwhelming at times. I think the media may be overdoing it a bit with the economic news, and most of it must be clarified and many questions asked. Saturn/Neptune issues, as mentioned in the previous pages, may be highlighted now. Solar Eclipse on the 7th keeps the markets in a turmoil. Volatility across the boards. Stock market may be looking better after Jupiter enters Gemini around the 12th! Mars and Jupiter conjunct, and this usually indicates a minor bottom and the start of a rally. Still a little cautious on the 14th, as this sets off an eclipse point which could drop the market for the day considerably. Then off to complete the rally. Portfolio adjustments taking place due to the end of the first quarter.

APRIL: Buckle your seat belts for the first week in April as the 3rd through 5th are some of the MOST ASPECTED days of the year. Significant cycles at play here and the markets can be most volatile and even going in both directions within the day. Real whipsaw days! Appears mostly negative aspects for the stock market. Possible selling off in the markets to raise cash for tax purposes or just a specific message being sent to the FED/SEC/President about some important issue within the economy. Stock market seems to rebound later in the month. Sugar, lumber and soybeans may be in focus this month.

MAY: This month appears to be "resting" or moving sideways a bit after the last few months of re-adjusting. Stock market could move sideways this month, not giving any real clear cut signals as to what it will do. The economy is sluggish and not much is moving it. The manufacturing and export business may be looking brighter. Mercury turns retrograde on the 12th signaling a good bit of confusion from many different directions. Whether this is a problem or an opportunity is up to you. Pay attention to details, as they could trip you up. Clarify communications which could lead to misunderstandings. Caution in paperwork, mails, communications and travel as there may be delays or unexpected changes in plans. Try to remain flexible and give yourself a little more time in between scheduling appointments. This lasts through June 5th. This time frame could allow you to get caught up on office work that has lain around for some time. Use this time to get organized with work up to present. Avoid initiating new projects after the 5th, as they may have a tendency to be more hassle than expected. Could be a slight market rally after mid-month. Soybeans in the spotlight; may be peaking out.

JUNE: Mixed to up for the stock market the first two weeks in June, but as we approach the Saturn/Neptune conjunction on the 24th, bearishness creeps back in. As we end the second quarter and first half of the year there appears to be a sell-off in stocks. Influences most of the month and into July activate this Saturn/Neptune volatility in the market place. Remember to watch for the Moon in Cardinal signs this month to activate these influences. Unions in the news and strikes, or at least labor disputes. Watch the drug, chemical, pharmaceutical, liquor and oil industries for changes and possible hassles. Oil spills, chemical pollution, waste problems may be in the news.

JULY: Happy Birthday, America. Choppy to up action creating some minor volatility through the 18th. Full Moon on the 18th could provide some minor relief, although it could just move the market sideways and become overly boring to try to speculate in options or futures. Time will erode price sometimes faster than price movements in a wrong trend. Pluto goes direct and Mars sets off an eclipse point of August

17th on the 24th of July. Watch those bonds. Gold and metals could rally in here.

AUGUST: Uranus trines a Solar Eclipse point. Something I usually don't use much is the trine aspect, but I think it important for the market this time. Could produce an unexpected rally, short term, but at least helpful to the deteriorated market place. Full Moon Eclipse at Perigee (closest to the earth) on the 17th may bring the market back down, but expect the unexpected as this eclipse is in Aquarius, and since Uranus (ruler of Aquarius) trines the eclipse, this could prove to be better than we think! Another Solar Eclipse on the 31st in Virgo could keep the market in an unexpected up trend. There are still many changes trying to take place with the new structure of the stock market and the exchanges between New York and Chicago.

SEPTEMBER: There could be a rally lurking in here. Positive aspects are beginning the month as September may be re-aligning itself for portfolio adjustments. We are ending the third quarter. Saturn turns stationary direct on the 11th which was in a harmonious aspect with the recent Solar Eclipse on the 31st. This could help bring more optimism or at least some stability in the market place. Mercury turns stationary retrograde on the 11th also; you can make your outcome with this energy a problem or opportunity and remember the choice is yours. Be aware!

OCTOBER: Mercury turns direct on the 3rd, and the stock market in general appears to be mildly negative with some choppiness. A T-Cross sets up on the 4th to really ignite the market, and hopefully it will push prices higher. Emphasis on import/export issues. The latter part of the month remains a bit quiet. Jupiter turns retrograde and will remain there through February 1990. The stock market usually trends downward after the first 6 weeks of Jupiter under retrograde. New Moon at Apogee in Scorpio on the 29th (weekend) could help eliminate some of the downside pressures seen in the stock market lately.

NOVEMBER: The final Saturn/Neptune conjunction will take place on the 14th, although the 7th through 23rd put it in tight orb to activate its energies and influences. Mars sets off an eclipse point of upcoming Solar Eclipse on January 26, 1990. This could be an interesting month, and the stock market may again decline. Review stock market charts technically on the past two Saturn/Neptune occurrences to see what the results have been. Then you will be able to tell what this time window could produce. Soybeans may be on their lows, which may have started in October. Metals could be looking a bit better. Careful around the 27th.

DECEMBER: Another month where portfolio adjustments will take place. Coming down to the final quarter of the year and also the end of the year. I'm sure investors are asking, "What have my profits been this year?" Since the bear market in stocks has been evident, they would have to look to their "wise choice" of being in liquid positions and the safe areas of their money. Venus turns retrograde on the 29th and Mercury turns retrograde on the 30th, indicating a sell-off in the market place to end the year. Currencies may trend lower also. Bonds may show some signs of strength as there may be nowhere else to place money other than longer term instruments. The close of a decade and a Happy New Year!

JANUARY
MARKET FORECAST

Jan 1-8: Happy New Year! The stock market this week should open with volatility, but once again money needs to be placed. If one MUST be in the market, the specific stocks that are chosen will need to hold up under recessionary times, i.e., AT&T, food retailers, drug companies, chemical companies, pollution control and soft drink companies. Saturn conjuncts the midpoint of Uranus/Neptune, bringing in some negative selling in the market on the 4th. New Moon on the 7th may help to keep prices from falling. May take a little more time to ignite market activity as planetary patterns indicate frustrated decisions, hence more traders/investors on the sidelines waiting for the "right" moment!

Jan 9-15: Most of the week will be choppy except for Friday the 13th; the Moon will be 90 degrees (square) Uranus/Venus/Saturn/Neptune all within trading hours. Look for a dramatic sell-off in the markets. There could be some trouble for beans, hogs, and currencies. This is usually a tough week in bear markets; confirmation may come that this market isn't holding together as well as anticipated. Mercury turns retrograde on the 16th, adding to the confusion.

Jan 16-22: Venus conjuncts Saturn on the 16th, which could continue selling pressures from last Friday. This could continue through the morning of the 20th. The 19th shows a significant down and possible bottom the morning of the 20th, when Jupiter turns direct, adding a bit of optimism. Full Moon on the 21st. This is inauguration week and the markets will be nervous to all sorts of news. But hopefully a general optimistic market for a new administration?!

Jan 23-31: Mars is 120 degrees (trine) to Uranus on the 24th; this could produce a rally, especially in technology stocks—maybe a few computer stocks, too. IBM should hold its weight here. 25th and 26th have strong aspects to the Mercury retrograde, which usually produces large volume and doesn't do much for the markets except frustrate those who day-trade or play options or futures. Venus trine Jupiter can give the markets a little relief. Good for soybeans, bonds, pork bellies and sugar.

FEBRUARY
MARKET FORECAST

Feb 1-5: We could have a rally during the first two weeks in February. Mercury at station trines Jupiter and will last through the 10th—an unusual influence, since Mercury moves so fast. Mercury goes stationary direct on the 5th, but stays in harmonious aspect to Jupiter to bring some good news—hopefully economic news! Gold and metals could decline. Foreign affairs and currencies should be favorable. The dollar should be stronger. This planetary pattern favors all forms of business and commercial activity, and the making of long-range plans and goals. Excellent for signing contracts or concluding a deal.

Feb 6-12: A little caution on the 8th with the Mars/Neptune/Saturn aspect. Look back to the technical charts on January 18th and they may give you a clue as to the extent of the downside activity we could be facing in the indexes and DJIA. This is a good week to position for buying gold puts if you are so inclined to play options. Gold is having a hard time keeping bullish in any respect.

Feb 13-19: WOW! What a week—Mars is 180 degrees from Pluto, which is stationary and ready to turn retrograde within two days (16th), also being squared by Venus (the money, resource planet). Seems to be "trouble in black rock." Definitely a DOWN week for metals as well as the stock market in general. You may want to short the indexes and definitely the metals. There may be some sort of negotiation or power struggle with prominent person. Emphasis on the security sectors. Monetary policies in transition could be a major focus. Business and personal relationships being tested. Reevaluation of business productivity in focus.

Feb 20-28: Topping this off is the Lunar Eclipse on the 20th during trading hours; more downside pressure to an already gloomy market! Emotional activity as this eclipse conjuncts the Ascendant of the New York Stock Exchange chart! But be careful, as there may be a whipsaw in action here since this eclipse trines Uranus; expect the unexpected here! New challenges in trading. 22nd and 23rd look to be positive. Mixed to sideways for the remainder of the week. Grain markets also due to correct at the eclipse. Careful on the metals as they could do a turnaround. Try to keep your focus on the important issues and let the minor stuff ride.

MARCH
MARKET FORECAST

Mar 1-5: March 3rd is a day that could prove to be one of the most interesting of the year. Moon conjuncts the Saturn/Neptune conjunction, putting more emotional emphasis on this day. Could be one of fear or panic from a public standpoint, i.e., like October 19, 1987. There are also two midpoints being activated—Saturn/Uranus and Uranus/Neptune, and all this happens between two eclipses. Solar Eclipse occurs the 7th. This is the first conjunction of Saturn/Neptune out of three this year.

Mar 6-12: Solar Eclipse on the 7th may bring a bottom to this accelerated down pressure from last week. Grains could see some downside acceleration. Jupiter and Mars both enter Gemini on the 11th and this can be a very positive bolt of energy needed to grab the stock market by the bootstraps and get it going again! So there may be a significant low as buying opportunities in stocks may look attractive, especially since we are closing the first quarter in two weeks! Portfolio adjustments taking place.

Mar 13-19: Stocks may be slow in taking off from here, as it still has the 15th-17th to work through some sluggishness. Mixed prices keep stocks from going very far, but at least the drop has stopped! Gemini-type stocks should fare well during bad market weather; communication stocks, Federal Express, trucking, shipping (for exports), and automobile industry could have some interesting news this week. Options expirations emphasized a little more as we end the first quarter. Import/export activity in the news. Possible new regulations on this industry, as we try to target the trade deficit.

Mar 20-31: Spring Equinox occurs on the 20th and this usually signals a trend change. The remainder of the month could be better. Full Moon on the 22nd may produce the start of a sell-off as we merge into the holidays. Careful on the 28th and 30th if playing options or futures, as there may be a few setbacks. Financials, currencies, and beans may see some volatility. There seems to be news in the air, but the translation is mixed, and it's difficult to initiate a trend for the markets. Jupiter squares a Lunar Eclipse point from 2/20, adding some support and optimism. Portfolio adjustments for the end of the first quarter should be active now.

APRIL
MARKET FORECAST

Apr 1-9: This week contains one of the most aspected days of the year! April 3rd and 4th have it coming from everywhere. Some of the positives are Sun/Venus/Mercury sextiles (60 degrees); Mars/Jupiter, which shows some opportunities in optimistic stock prices, and then there are the negative aspects, which signal dropping stock prices! Sun/Venus/Mercury square Saturn/Neptune, and Sun/Venus/Mercury/Mars inconjuncts Pluto/Saturn/Neptune (heavy-duty planetary aspects). New Moon on the 6th sets it all off again. This one has too much to tell, but the feeling I get is heavy change and uncertainty, which may turn out for the benefit of all in the long run, but for now is a bit awesome! Soybeans, grains and pork bellies look positive and may provide an excellent buying opportunity to hold for the next several weeks.

Apr 10-16: Tax season is upon us and the new tax laws this year really take hold more strongly than the past few years, when they were just creeping in. We are having to take a hard look at the results of the tax cuts now, and they seem pretty ominous. Still a lot of planetary activity with the Moon triggering some of last week's energies into play. Neptune turns stationary retrograde and a possible rally could be seen into next week. (Neptune turns stationary retrograde on the 13th.) You may find that you are not as aware or on your toes as usual—a touch of spring fever or just spacey, trying to get used to the time-change schedule.

Apr 17-23: Mercury trines Saturn/Neptune and Uranus/Venus—definitely some unexpected news to brighten the week. Saturn turns stationary retrograde on the 22nd and may produce some downside prices. Drugs, pharmaceuticals and oil stocks in the news. Full Moon on the 21st! Moon sets off the Saturn/Neptune on the 19th—mergers, especially in drugs, pharmaceuticals, cosmetics and medical areas that concern the skin. Sensitivity to environmental influences.

Apr 24-30: Stock market appears to be optimistic this week with all the Venus and Mercury trines; subtle planetary energies, but effective. Beans, bonds, stocks, and the dollar look positive. A little washout could develop on Friday, so if you are an options or futures player, you may want to keep this in mind.

MAY
MARKET FORECAST

May 1-7: Saturn sextiles Pluto on the 2nd, and this could be positive if the technicals are poised to show this to be the case. It could be quite a mixed bag otherwise. Metals, bonds, grains, hogs, currencies and stocks all seem to be affected here. New Moon near Perigee on the 5th opposes Pluto; keeps the governmental strings tied to the markets, and controls may give mixed market weather. Keep an eye on the oil producers for some changes in policy. Products from the earth are in focus more this week—gemstones may show an increase in value. Jewelry appraisals may show you have a better investment portfolio than you thought. Employers may be taking a look at their work forces to check the productivity. A good time to ask for a raise if you know you have truly produced. A good time for personal achievements if you focus on your goal.

May 8-14: Moon opposes Uranus on the 8th, giving us a whipsaw day and possible news to where the markets may steer us. Mixed energies the rest of the week, but Jupiter semi-sextiles Neptune on the 12th along with Mercury turning retrograde. Some idealism is thrown in here to possibly give the markets a boost out of the doldrums. Carefully check your contracts or important papers to be signed as overlooked details could trip you up.

May 15-21: Happy Birthday New York Stock Exchange on the 17th! Positive market weather through the 18th, and a possibility of some downside activity in stock prices under Mars opposition to Neptune. Usually a bubble burst in some prices; check the technicals and if there are any stocks, indexes, or commodities that are looking pretty toppy, this aspect may reverse it. Full Moon on the 19th at 29 Virgo, which set last year's markets in a tailspin and also the eclipse point associated with October 19, 1987! I think the effects may be somewhat diminished by now, but proceed cautiously during this time frame.

May 22-31: Very few aspects this week to really pull from and they indicated mixed market prices. Good time to take that Memorial Day mini-vacation and stand aside from any market activity except for very long-term holdings if you already own them. A truly stand-aside week! Enjoy the warm weather.

JUNE
MARKET FORECAST

Jun 1-11: Mercury at stationary direct on the 5th, as the pace of business in general picks up. New Moon near Perigee on the 2nd closes to a conjunction with Jupiter. This may add some optimism through the 9th for market timers. Careful on the 5th as Mercury turns retrograde and the Moon sets off the upcoming Saturn/Neptune conjunction (second time, but now in retrograde motion). News of a more sobering nature may be in the winds. More limits, controls and governmental bureaucracy in the works. Where is Paul Volker when we really need him?

Jun 12-18: The Moon in Cardinal signs this month will help tune into the energies taking place with the Saturn/Neptune conjunction approaching. Choppy to up markets until the 14th, when Venus opposes the upcoming S/N conjunction. A little positive for the stock market may come into play the next day for a possible rebound, but only mildly. Emphasis on the soybeans, currencies and copper; may not effect other metals. Options expire this week (a short month) and portfolio adjustments are taking place as we close the second quarter.

Jun 19-25: Full Moon on the 19th sets up a wide conjunction with Saturn/Neptune. This should initiate some drama on the market front. Drugs, oil, gasoline, chemicals, and entertainment industries should be in the news. This aspect can work both positively and negatively for these industries, but definitely DOWN for the markets! We may be looking at a few weeks' downside trend in here from the Full Moon. Only breather rallies may be considered (if any)!

Jun 26-30: Moon squares the Saturn/Neptune conjunction on the 26th—more downside pressure. Portfolio adjustments and nonperforming stocks are being weeded out, and they are really weeding them out this week! The general performance of the economy and markets is not very positive, to say the least. Playing the market to the downside with put options or shorting futures may give you some ways of capitalizing on this whole weak market. Check with your broker to see how you can do this and be sure to pick one that has been doing it regularly, not just occasionally! End of the second quarter and first half of the year.

JULY
MARKET FORECAST

Jul 3-9: Happy Birthday, America! Moon in Cardinal signs also this month will accentuate the Saturn/Neptune energies on the markets. Emphasis on the 3rd and 5th Moon aspects for weaker stock prices. Venus/Mars square Pluto on the 6th usually provides a washout on the market. Looks like we are in for some selling pressures this week. May just be a good time to be on vacation, unless selling short is your bag! Resources in general are put to the test. It's not just making money anymore, but how you can preserve the capital you have and keep it from eroding. Emphasis is put on the creative investment that helps to preserve capital.

Jul 10-16: Starting the week off with Moon in the apex of the T-square with Mercury on one end and Saturn/Neptune on the other. A lot of pessimistic energy; news in general may be the culprit as it sometimes gets overdramatized. I'm sure statistics from the first half of the year may be hitting the streets. A pause that could refresh on the 12-13th. Avoid those utility and transportation stocks.

Jul 17-23: Moon again starts the week conjunct Saturn/Neptune. The signature of previous Moon aspects to this conjunction will enact again today the 17th. Close to the Full Moon on the 18th, too. Sun conjunct Mercury on the 18th may help provide some strong volume, and the markets could find support levels in here—moving sideways type of day. The rest of the week is just lackluster also, with nowhere to go. Could get boring to frustrated. Pluto turns stationary direct and Mars opposes the 8/17 eclipse point on the 23rd (weekend) to finish a major down trend within the next week. Metals could be down on the 23rd. Option traders may want to short it for a day trade. Keep an eye on the oil stocks and oil futures as they may take a dive also.

Jul 24-31: Some small signs of a rally could be lurking here, seen around the 25th, but there could be a setback for a few more days until the 31st. Gold and oil stocks, or just the metals themselves, may deteriorate in price this week through early August, as the stock market may be looking up soon.

AUGUST
MARKET FORECAST

Aug 1-6: New Moon on the 1st along with Uranus trine the February eclipse point may just be what the market needs to turn it around with more optimistic energy. After all, we've rallied in August the last six years, and even started a bull market once! So as soon as we clear out the 4th it should be more optimistic and a rally could be upon us. Movie industry and entertainment, drugs, liquor and pharmaceuticals could be part of the movers. Very short term though. Better to play the indexes or a specific commodity unless you want to pick up some bargains after all the previous downside just to tuck away in your LONG, long-term portfolio.

Aug 7-13: Markets are still looking up. Jupiter opposes Uranus on the 8th; could be positive for the market, especially technology stocks. Mercury trine Saturn/Neptune. More news, but hopefully with a bit more optimism. Media in general may get some slack, possibly from some controversial reporting. There seems to be a kind of "lucky" energy we are able to tap from. Maybe a trend develops that can be readily seen and you make money on it. A nice break from the market doldrums.

Aug 14-20: We start to come into the eclipse period once again. A Full Moon Eclipse on the 17th could bring the market down. The eclipse energies get triggered into action just a little sooner than anticipated by Mars conjunct the eclipse point on the 15th with a trine to Saturn/Neptune. There could be some constructive efforts by the government to improve the economy as things may have gotten somewhat out of hand with all the regulations and controls. Anyway, there seems to be a stabilizing effect (I hope) as this is such a weird combination of energies to be all in tight pattern so close to the eclipse point. BE CAUTIOUS. Expect the unexpected!

Aug 21-31: Most of the regular aspects are positive for the market this week except the 24th, when Venus squares Saturn. I'm just hoping last week's eclipse energies don't heavily override during this week. Since we are in between two eclipses this week, the markets could be very volatile! Be cautious! Solar Eclipse trine Saturn/Neptune on the 31st. These energies could be dramatic and run prices both ways. A truly confusing energy pattern.

SEPTEMBER
MARKET FORECAST

Sep 1-10: Labor Day weekend may be a bit more pleasant than we would have anticipated a few weeks ago. Just be sure to recheck plans and details of traveling as we are so near an eclipse. A lot of unexpected details could trip you up and cause delays or rescheduling. Try to remain flexible in travel plans and allow a little more time between appointments. Publishing, the media and bonds should be in the limelight now. What are those interest rates doing? Adding to more deflation down the road? Mercury turns stationary retrograde on the 9th. Check those mechanicals too, as anything that has needed repairs lately may demand it this week. Metals may open with a rally after Labor Day.

Sep 11-17: Full Moon on the 15th could bring some delays in communications such as driving, telephone, mechanical machines, wire transfers, and other data. Mercury just turning retrograde for these three weeks can give you an opportunity to catch up on that work you've been putting off. Time to clean out those closets, or clear up paperwork that has been shuffled under the desk mat for later. Later has arrived. Rally possible on the markets this week.

Sep 18-24: Portfolio adjustments are taking place as we close down the third quarter. Nonperforming stocks are weeded out. Downside pressures influence the fair market weather we may have been enjoying. The 19th could deteriorate with news and then action. Edit what you read, as rumors rather than fact could be the target of an important issue publicized. Neptune turns stationary direct; may also add to the sell-off and confusion or misunderstandings.

Sep 25-30: Mercury squares Uranus on the 25th and this could give a whipsaw-type day. Careful trading in here, as it could get pretty volatile. Technology, publishing and media/communication stocks could be the focus of the markets this week. If any of these are merger material—it may just be a rumor or a flash-in-the-pan attempt. Good bit of action last of the month, as the market could get very intense. New Moon conjunct Mars square Saturn/Neptune on the 29th and this should prove to be very explosive to the downside. Truly deflationary and much confusion as to the direction of the economy in general. Too much information to sort out and none of it may be very clear or defined right now.

OCTOBER
MARKET FORECAST

Oct 1-8: More of the New Moon energy being stimulated as Sun, Moon and Mars are at the apex of the T-cross with a square to Jupiter opposing Neptune/Saturn between the 1st-3rd. Mercury turns stationary direct on the 3rd. A lot of energy in here that could make the markets volatile in both directions. Or, if the markets are nervous enough, they just might cancel each other out and move sideways, giving a stagnant, frustrating market this month! The primary trend is still bearish. The pace of mental activity is accelerating and we may not be on top of things as readily as needed. Pay attention to details and remain cautious in driving or any hurried activities. Numbers in particular may be the culprits that cause problems or delays.

Oct 9-15: Still not much to work with from all the month's energy. Sideways to down this week, especially down around the 11th-12th. There are a good bit of Mercury aspects at the end of this week and beginning of next, which could bring some news that would give us a minor rally. It appears as if something has gone into motion for a change. IBM may be looking better the end of the week. Full Moon on the 14th. Negotiations and mergers in the news and a good bit of publicity may cause dramatic moves in the stock. Good time to study a particular subject or project, also increase your skills.

Oct 16-22: Finishing out those Mercury aspects by the 18th. There should be some kind of news event that helps the market. Bonds could have a minor trend change in here and possibly a rally. May need to take time out to just sit and think—reevaluate what is going on in your life and what changes you may want to make in regard to your investment strategies. Reflecting is important now after all these Mercury aspects to stimulate the mind in many directions. Make use of this mental stimulation to set goals or redefine them.

Oct 23-31: Sun sextile Uranus on the 25th, giving us an opportunity for a minor rally in stocks. New Moon on the 29th (with Moon at Apogee on the 28th) supports the possible rally to sideways move in stocks, but picking up momentum as November rolls around. Jupiter turns stationary retrograde on the 29th. Monday (30th) should be an up day after all the weekend planetary activity.

NOVEMBER
MARKET FORECAST

Nov 1-5: This week seems pretty positive as Sun/Mercury trine Jupiter at station and sextile Uranus, Saturn, Neptune! Your mind is eager for new experiences—try out new activities, experiences or approaches to your work; let it be a day when you make your job enjoyable; set your goals to do so and attract it! Technology stocks may be looking better this week too. More news surfaces that may cut into this rally. By the end of the week a little deterioration may creep in, so be careful. Airlines may be running special saver fares for the holidays—check to be sure you're getting the best price as there may be a lot of alternatives in attaining your destination.

Nov 6-12: Sun/Mercury conjunct Pluto, which usually produces a good down day on the Dow Jones. Keep an eye on bonds, pork bellies, soybeans and cyclical commodities, as the trends are changing. Transiting Moon in Cardinal signs should be watched this month as we are closing in on the major conjunction. A possible slight rally at the end of the week; it all depends on how the market interprets the news. Intensity in the air. Metals markets could have a trend change on the 7-8th.

Nov 13-19: Full Moon at Perigee on the 13th sets market timing up for the next day's (14th) Saturn/Neptune conjunction along with Mars squaring the 1/90 Solar Eclipse point. Jupiter opposes this Saturn/Neptune conjunction and this could make a difference with the market. It may not deteriorate as quickly and it may move more sideways. The big yawn, as these planetary energies struggle with each other to determine the trend. A good stand-aside market if this is the case! If there is any volatility, it could come in spurts—off and on this week as if the markets are deciding what position to take so close to the holiday season.

Nov 20-30: The Thanksgiving holidays and the start of this week could have some mild upside potential, but may deteriorate as we close the week and month. Downside is emphasized on the 23rd and especially the 27th, when Mars conjuncts Pluto (a two-year cycle). This could set the trend for the beginning of December, which is bearish. New Moon on the 28th. Good time to stand aside and get a head start on your Thanksgiving holiday.

DECEMBER
MARKET FORECAST

Dec 1-10: More bearishness as we come into the beginning of the month. So naturally there are no stocks to recommend. Bond markets, metals could be active now. If you are attuned to shorting the markets this may be a good time to play that side of it. Jupiter opposes the Saturn/Neptune/Moon conjunction on the 1st. Not signalling much optimism for higher stock prices. Sun/Saturn/Neptune aspects from the 4th-6th add to the bearishness. Gold could be in a rally phase as we come into the close of this year's gold cycle.

Dec 11-17: Full Moon on the 12th may help the market weather, but slacks off around the 15th with Mercury conjunct Neptune. Careful in making travel plans at the last minute. Check those details and remain flexible in your travel appointments. We are starting to see the Saturn/Neptune conjunction separate. Its effects have been sobering for this year, to say the least. There may have been a lot of frustrating moments, but the true lesson was tenacity and renewal of your faith. Breaking away from old habit patterns may have been forced on you and your perception of reality may have gone through many phases. You should be getting a better perspective on the conservatism needed to preserve your investments.

Dec 18-25: MERRY CHRISTMAS! Winter Solstice on the 21st is usually associated with trend changes on the market. Definitely a stand-aside market as we close down the year. Could be a bit boring in here just before the Christmas holidays, but the final week of the year has some potential.

Dec 26-31: The day after Christmas could catch many traders off guard as it tries to rally into the end of the year. This is the week most people take their holiday vacations and those left behind are going to gamble with the market; and its going to be the upside they're betting on. Volume may be low and the end of the day may only produce a few points. Venus turns stationary retrograde on the 29th, and with Mercury on the 30th. These energies may help you see patterns in your perception and experience. Traditionally favorable for financial and business dealings. Reflection on the turn of the decade is present for many and I wish you all a very happy and prosperous New Year.

Astrology, Politics And America

by Stan Barker

Can the future of America be forecast astrologically? Can the movement of the planets through the Zodiac predict what challenges lie ahead for our nation? If you believe the answer is yes, you are, of course, in powerful company. As the entire world found out in 1988, President Ronald Reagan thinks so, too.

The media had a field day last spring when former White House Chief of Staff Don Regan blew the whistle on First Lady Nancy Reagan's use of astrology to determine the President's schedule. As reporters developed the story, it was learned that the Reagans—Ronald as well as Nancy—had been consulting astrologers for nearly forty years . . . that much of Ronald Reagan's political career, from his successful first run for governor of the state of California to such Presidential decisions as the bombing of Libya, had been astrologically timed.

While scientists wailed and fundamentalists gnashed their teeth, those self-appointed "voices of reason," the political commentators, smirked and snickered. But they were so busy chuckling that they missed a crucial point.

For almost eight years, these very same astute political pundits had been trumpeting Ronald Reagan's amazing savvy—the quality that made him one of the most popular Presidents in our history, a leader with a Teflon coating who could seemingly do no wrong. Not a fumbler like Jimmy

Carter or Gerald Ford, not someone whom problems stuck
to like Richard Nixon or Lyndon Johnson . . . Ronald Reagan,
the pundits told us, was the most effective President we'd
had in years.

Well, he was also the first President in years to use
astrology . . . no wonder he'd led such a charmed electoral
life! If the commentators who'd spent so much time lauding
Reagan's political wisdom now wanted to laugh at his political "foolishness," the joke was really on them. Could any
one of them deny that the Reagans had gotten much better
advice from their astrologers than from such "rational"
advisers as Ollie North, Ed Meese, Bud McFarlane, *et al*?

An objective person would conclude that there just
might be something to astrology, if Reagan had obviously
done so well by its guidance. In the stories that followed Don
Regan's revelation, the press admitted that Reagan was not
the first President to seek answers in the Zodiac. Thomas
Jefferson, maintained a large astrological library at Mon-
ticello. Theodore Roosevelt was said to keep his birth chart
on hand for ready reference. During the critical illness that
incapacitated Woodrow Wilson, First Lady Edith Wilson
consulted an astrologer to determine her husband's schedule
of appointments . . . just like Nancy Reagan.

As it says in the astrological book of the Bible, Ecclesiastes,
"There is nothing new under the sun." Astrology's beginnings were as a means to guide kings and emperors in the
ruling of their nations. Astrology in the White House was
merely a modern setting for an age-old practice.

But wait—if Ronald Reagan had made so many good
moves with the help of astrology, why, by 1988, was his
second term losing its luster? Shouldn't astrology have predicted the troubles that followed his re-election . . . the Iran-
Contra scandal, the doomed campaign to seat Robert Bork
Supreme Court, the "sleaze factor" settling on Attorney General Meese's wheelings and dealings, the tiff between Donald
Regan and the First Lady that led to the flap over Oval Office
astrology—and the other "kiss and tell" revelations from
Larry Speakes, Michael Deaver and the rest which, all totaled,
were casting Ronald Reagan's place in American history in a
much less flattering light?

Certainly, astrology should have predicted trouble in the
President's second term . . . and certainly, astrology *did just*

that. I don't know what Nancy Reagan's astrologer was telling her, but I have been on record since before Ronald Reagan's 1984 re-election as predicting second-term problems.

In my book, *The Signs of the Times* (Llewellyn Publications, 1984), I documented the single most reliable method of forecasting America's future—the cycle of the planet Neptune through the twelve signs of the Zodiac, which has accurately predicted the events of American history since the time of Columbus' voyage. I explained that with Neptune entering the sign of Capricorn in January, 1984, and staying in this sign until 1998, this fourteen year period would echo the events of American history the last time Neptune was in Capricorn, from 1820-1834.

I described a parallel between Ronald Reagan and the last American President to run for re-election in the first year of a Capricorn "wave," James Monroe . . . among the similarities, the Monroe Doctrine, making the U.S. the "policeman" of Latin America, and Ronald Reagan's aggressive posture toward Grenada and Nicaragua. Written and published before the 1984 elections, *The Signs of the Times* contains the following prediction:

" . . . Ronald Reagan fits Capricorn better than any of the Democrats running, and thus has the best chance of being elected in November 1984. However, the Sign of the Times (Capricorn) indicates it will not be a happy second term for him.

"Remember the last President elected to a first term at the end of (Neptune in) Sagittarius and re-elected at the start of Capricorn. James Monroe's first four years were called the 'Era of Good Feelings'; he could do no wrong. Similarly, Reagan's first term has been called 'the Teflon Presidency'; despite various scandals, nothing has stuck to him. According to the polls, Reagan follows Monroe's pattern of being extremely popular in his first four years.

"But Monroe's second term quickly turned into the 'Era of Bad Feelings', and his only major success during it was the Doctrine. Why? He got caught in the change of waves.

"The same thing looms ahead for Ronald Reagan."

That was on page 284 of *The Signs of the Times*. Later, on page 286, I reiterated:

"POLITICS: If the Democrats do not run their 1984 campaign on Capricornian themes, then a second term for

Ronald Reagan, during which there will be economic slow-down or recession, U.S. interventionism in Latin America, and the President's popularity will fade."

Of course, all of that came true: the re-election, the worst crash in the stock market since 1929 followed by a slowdown in the economy, the sending of U.S. troops to El Salvador as well as the Iran-Contra affair and our entanglement with Panama's General Noriega, and the inevitable diminishing of Reagan's popularity.

Maybe I should have sent the First Lady a copy of *The Signs of the Times*. Or a videotape of my appearance on the PBS television series *Tony Brown's Journal*, taped on September 14, 1986, when I predicted that problems would begin to stick to the President as his "teflon" stripped away in the second term (two months before the Iran-Contra scandal broke), that the booming economy would experience big down turns (one year before the stock market crash of 1987), and that the heyday of the television evangelists was over, their influence having already peaked (again, nearly two years before the Jim and Tammy Bakker and Jimmy Swaggart scandals and the laughable performance of Pat Robertson in the 1988 primaries).

Obviously, the Reagans were right in believing that astrology can accurately predict what will happen in America's future . . . their mistake was in not using the Neptune Factor I used in *The Signs of the Times*. Each time Neptune enters a sign, history repeats itself around the same themes that were found the last time Neptune was in that sign. Also, events echo those that happened the last time Neptune was in the related sign—for example, Neptune is now in Capricorn, and Capricorn's related sign is Cancer. The last time Neptune was in Cancer was from 1901 to 1916. Teddy Roosevelt was President in that period, and like Ronald Reagan, was shaking a big stick at Latin America (especially Nicaragua and Panama), was characterized as a cowboy, and, as we've been recently told, used astrology in the White House.

Here's an example of how President Reagan could have used the Neptune Factor for the betterment of all Americans. Noting that previous Capricorn/Cancer periods have been times of transportation disasters, I warned in *The Signs of the Times* that we were in danger of seeing this awful history repeated. Specific mention was made, on page 273,

of airplane crashes and space shuttle malfunctions. If he had
heeded this warning when it was issued in 1984, Ronald
Reagan might have been able to prevent the tragedies that
followed—1985, the worst year for air crashes ever; 1986, the
terrible explosion of the space shuttle *Challenger*. Obviously,
Capricorn was the wrong period to approach by firing air
traffic controllers and trying to accelerate the shuttle program.
The problem of packed skies and overburdened planes (a
result of airline deregulation) is still with us, and NASA's
attempts to get the shuttle back on line have failed to date.

But one cannot undo the past. At least Ronald Reagan is
ending his administration in tune with *The Signs of the Times*,
thawing relations with the Soviet Union and achieving the first
treaty to eliminate a entire class of nuclear weapons, making
the prediction on page 294 of my book come true: "The arms
race will slow." Beyond this final achievement, the challenges
of Neptune in Capricorn will face a new administration.

What those challenges are can be determined by using
the Neptune Factor. Already the 1988 primaries are an
example of history repeating itself according to the Sign of
the Times. The last time Neptune was in Capricorn, in the
parallel election of 1824, when James Monroe stepped down
after his second term, the field was crowded with candidates. It narrowed to three, and interestingly enough, one
of these was a Southerner named Jackson... who was
defeated by a candidate from Massachusetts, who then
became President... John Quincy Adams.

Does this bode well for Massachusetts' current favorite
son, Governor Michael Dukakis? Maybe, but then again,
maybe not. A few years before Adams' election, a new state
was carved out of Massachusetts... the state of Maine, whose
present favorite son is, of course, George Bush. Then, too,
Adams, like Bush, was a member of the outgoing administration. So it seems that the Sign of the Times is presenting us
with a toss-up as to who the next President will be... but it is
definitely showing hisory repeating itself with the Massachusetts candidate (Andrew or Jesse), both times around.

What is more important is that, regardless of whether it
is Michael Dukakis or George Bush who is inaugurated in
January of 1989, the new President will have to deal with the
influence of Neptune in Capricorn on America's destiny
during his term of office. What lies ahead for the next

administration? Here's what the Sign of the Times indicates:

More Trouble in Latin America:

Because Capricorn is the sign of the Zodiac associated with Fathers, the United States during Capricorn periods tends to play the role of "Big Dad" toward our neighboring nations to the south. The same thing happens when Neptune is in the related sign, Cancer, associated with Mothers— then, the U.S. plays "Big Mom." This parental attitude of "Father (Mother) knows best" has resulted in American intervention in Latin American affairs in every Capricorn/ Cancer period in our history.

Thus, in the Cancer wave 1737-1752, colonial American troops, under British command, fought in Columbia, Panama, the then-Spanish possession of Florida, and planned to invade Cuba. In the Capricorn wave 1820-1834, James Monroe issued his Doctrine warning Old World nations to drop their plans to invade Latin America, which was then a hotbed of colonial revolutions and wars of national liberation. Spanish Florida, having been seized by General Andrew Jackson a few years before, became a U.S. possession at the beginning of the wave. In the Cancer wave 1901-1916, U.S. intervention in Latin America was consistent. We engineered the revolt of Panama from Colombia in order to build the Panama Canal (Teddy Roosevelt boasted, "I took the Canal Zone and let Congress debate"), and U.S. forces were sent for various reasons to Santo Domingo, Cuba, Honduras, Nicaragua and Mexico.

So it comes as no surprise that in Reagan's administration, Grenada, Nicaragua, Honduras, El Salvador, and Panama have been hot spots. . . with Capricorn once again the Sign of the Times, there is every indication that Latin American problems will plague the new administration as well. The growing awareness of the drug problem in the U.S., with its ties to such Latin American governments as Panama's Noriega regime, only adds fuel to the flames. Given this climate, circumstances may well force the new administration to follow the standard Capricorn/Cancer pattern of U.S. intervention south of the border.

Economic Unsteadiness:

Capricorn is an Earth sign, and like all Earth signs is

associated with business, labor, and the economy. As I pointed out in *The Signs of the Times*, this doesn't necessarily mean these are good periods for the economy, merely times when economic matters are up front in the public consciousness. For example, the Earth sign wave of Taurus, from 1874 to 1888, saw the rise of American Industrial capitalism in the "Gilded Age" of Rockefeller, Carnegie, and Morgan; the Earth sign wave of Virgo, from 1928 to 1943, almost extinguished American capitalism with the stock market crash of 1929 and the Great Depression of the 1930's.

Capricorn's historic record is one of big ups and downs in the economy. It is a time of technological revolution sparked by entrepreneurs; the High Tech revolution of the current time echoes the Industrial Revolution of the last Capricorn wave, 1820-1834. Both times around, the making of money is offset by a shift in the basis of commerce—in the earlier period, from agriculture to industry, in this period from blue collar to white.

So we may expect both bull and bear markets as speculators bring boom and bust, labor dissatisfaction as old jobs are lost, and another Capricorn constant: protectionism. In the last Capricorn wave, America's new Industrial Revolution was threatened by unfair competition from more established British industries; this time around, our High Tech businesses face the same danger from another overseas competitor, Japan. Since the solution in the earlier Capricorn wave was the passage of protectionist legislation, I predicted this happening again when *The Signs of the Times* was published in 1984. Since then, Congressional agitation for such trade measures has grown, along with proposed restrictions on American companies' ability to close plants— since Capricorn represents the principle of restriction and limitation, this, too, fits the Sign of these Times. The new administration will undoubtedly be wrangling with the pros and cons of these measures over the next four years, in addition to wrestling with a fluctuating economy.

Transportation Disasters:

As mentioned earlier, Capricorn/Cancer periods historically see these. . . it's only natural with Neptune moving into these "stay-at-home" signs from highly mobile signs like Sagittarius and Gemini. The basis for the current problem is that Capricorn's emphasis on restriction/limitation, caution, and responsibility is not being heeded.

If the new administration is to solve this crisis, new regulations will be needed to ensure better maintenance and safety standards for commercial transportation, cutting back the number of flights arriving and departing from overtaxed airports like Los Angeles', and rehiring experienced air traffic controllers to alleviate the problems of stress and burn-out. Stricter Capricornian control will have to be exercised over train and bus transportation, drunk drivers of automobiles, and, the space shuttle program, if NASA is to avoid another tragedy like *Challenger*. If such steps are not taken, travel will continue to be perilous in this period.

The Problem of AIDS:

Neptune in Scorpio (1955-1970) brought us *Playboy*, porno films, the Pill, and the Sexual Revolution. In "no commitment" Sagittarius (1970-1984), it resulted in singles bars and one-night stands. Cautious, restrictive Capricorn has put a halt to all of this with the sexually transmitted disease, AIDS.

Again, the Capricornian keywords here are *caution* and *limitation*, with such AIDS-preventatives as use of condoms, limitation of the number of sexual partners, and total abstention or celibacy. However, the historical record suggests that a cure can be found: in the last Capricorn wave, the fatal epidemic of cholera was blamed on those on the fringes of society—wastrels, prostitutes, etc. A cure was found, and cholera is rarely heard of today. Capricorn's resourcefulness can be brought to bear on the fatal disease, AIDS, as well.

More concern with America's Social Welfare:

Capricorn symbolizes the Teacher; education is a Capricornian priority. The new administration will be challenged to improve our nation's schools, a challenge that was recognized but not met by the outgoing Reagan administration.

Capricorn as Father, along with Cancer as Mother, puts a high relief on the social welfare of all Americans. Children, of course, are a special concern, which is why we've heard so much in recent years about missing and abused children. Home and family are also highlighted in these periods, and challenges are mounting. One is the need to strengthen family units, especially among black Americans. Another is the need to strengthen the concept of America as a family, to find Capricorn/Cancer homes for the millions of homeless in our cities, to provide sanctuary for Latin Americans who flee to our land from atrocities in their own countries.

Capricorn is a tricky time, when the emphasis on making money can send a nation onto the wrong track. It happened to England in the last Capricorn wave, and the novels of Charles Dickens still tell us of the poor houses, orphans in street gangs, and Scrooge-like businessmen evading social responsibility that were the result.

"Mankind was my business," Jacob Marley wails; like a warning from the Ghost of Capricorn Past, his words must be heeded in this present time. The new administration will face this challenge in its term, for 1991 is the midpoint of the current Capricorn wave. The challenges will peak around this time, and how the new administration responds may determine its fate, as surely as Scrooge determined his.

History records that the last time around, the administration of John Quincy Adams was tried and found wanting, lasting only one term. It was ousted by the farmers, workers, and the politically disenfranchised, who rallied around a candidate Adams had defeated four years earlier, in the parallel election to 1988's.

That candidate was Andrew Jackson, who founded the Democratic party to embrace all the little people crying for change. His triumph, called "the revolt of the common man," occurred at a similar Capricorn midpoint as that coming in 1991... when the first influences of the following Neptune in Aquarius period are beginning to be felt.

Aquarius is the sign of social change, the sign of brotherhood for all. If we do not live up to the Capricorn wave's demand that we be *responsible*, Aquarius ushers in sweeping changes to correct what we've let go wrong.

Will the new administration meet Capricorn's challenge... or will it, like Adams', be only a one-term stopgap? Will the Neptune Factor bring a new Andrew Jackson to the fore?

Will history repeat itself, as it has been doing for the past five years? We will have to wait and see.

RESOURCE
GUIDE

PROFESSIONAL CHART READINGS FROM LLEWELLYN

What is astrology and what can it do for you? The dictionary defines astrology as "the study that assumes and professes to interpret the influence of the heavenly bodies on human affairs." The forces behind the accuracy of the astrological interpretation have not yet been discovered. Therefore many astrologers consider it an art—a counselling tool. Astrology is not meant to be a fortunetelling device. It cannot answer specific questions, such as "will this person marry me?" or "will I get this particular job?" It can tell you of the influence and potentials, but you have free choice, as do the other people involved.

Astrology can help you to better understand yourself and your place in the world. It can help guide you through rough times and can help you to see the light at the end of the tunnel. It can help you ride out the cycles that are natural to everyone. It can point out areas where you may have to work harder than other people and areas that will come easy to you. Mostly, astrology gives you the keys to discovery.

There are many types of charts and ways to use astrological information. Llewellyn offers a wide variety of services which can help you with specific needs. Read through the descriptions that follow to help you choose the right service for you. All of our services are done by professional astrologers from around the country. The charts are set up by computer (the Matrix program) and the readings are tailored to your needs. The astrologer will try to answer your questions, but please don't ask him/her to answer questions that have no answers. Remember, astrology only points out possibilities; it will not be able to tell you that something will definitely happen. These astrologers are counselors and will try to help you with your problems. However, they cannot give you the magic solution to everything. Only you can decide what is right for you.

If you have never had a chart reading done before, we suggest that you order the Detailed Natal or the Complete Natal service. Please give us as much detail as possible about the areas that you want the astrologer to address. All information is held strictly confidential. Be sure to give accurate and full birth data: time, date, year, place, county, country. Check your birth certificate. We will not be responsible for mistakes made by you.

We require that all orders be in writing to avoid mistakes in gathering the exact birth data. You will receive some materials that will help you understand your chart with your order. Please allow 3–6 weeks for delivery. If you have any questions or problems with your order, please contact us in writing, or call (612) 291-1970.

You may charge your order ($15.00 minimum) on your Visa, MasterCard, American Express, or Diner's Club by giving us the account number, expiration date, your signature and your day phone number. Be sure that you have accurate birth data included for all people involved, that you have sent full payment, and that you have included a descriptive letter concerning your situation.

For those of you who are curious about astrology but don't want to spend the money for a full reading, check out the computerized *Personality Profile* offered below. We have several computerized services that will fit anyone's budget and that will give you plenty of good insights into yourself as well.

Please use the order form provided, send for our catalog with a full list of services offered, or just send in your order giving us all of the necessary data. Send to: **Llewellyn Publications, P.O. Box 64383-404, St. Paul, MN 55164-0383.**

COMPUTER SERVICES FROM LLEWELLYN

Llewellyn offers computerized readings for those of you who are interested in particular aspects of astrology, but don't want to spend the money for the more personal readings. We offer a variety and will be offering more in the future. Be sure to order our catalog to keep updated on new services.

APSO3-503-PERSONALITY-PROFILE HOROSCOPE: A complete character analysis and very thorough description of your talents, mental abilities, luck factors and more. Find out all about yourself at this low price...............................$10

APSO3-504 COMPATIBILITY PROFILE: Tells about you and one other person (can be lover, boss, friend, child, parent, etc.). Tells about how you approach relationships, how the other person approaches relationships and how the two of you relate $20

TRANSIT REPORT: Gives a day by day look at what's in store because of the planetary transits compared to your natal chart. Tells you what you might be able to accomplish on that particular day. Comes in three formats: 3 months, 6 months, and 1 year.

    APSO3-500: 3 Month Transit Report........................$12.00
    APSO3-501: 6 Month Transit Report.......................$20.00
    APSO3-502: 1 Year Transit Report $35.00

APSO3-510-ALPHA-NUMEROLOGY REPORT: This is the best numerology report on the market. It is based on your full name (be sure to give middle name) *and* your natal chart for double accuracy. Full instructions and a very thorough reading with lucky numbers are given..........................$19.95

APSO3-511-LUCKY LOTTERY REPORT: This is the *best* readout for you gamblers. It gives you sets of three numbers and lucky dates for the period of time specified. It is based on your full name (incl. middle name) *and* your birth chart for double accuracy..per month $10.00

PERSONALIZED ASTROLOGY READINGS

These chart readings are done by professional astrologers and will focus on your particular concerns. Please include descriptive letter.

APSO3-110-SIMPLE NATAL: Your natal chart done in whatever house system stated. With aspects and midpoints, Trop./Placid. unless stated. Computer chart print-out....$5.00

APSO1-101-COMPLETE NATAL: Natal chart, interpretation and forecast for the coming year. Describe interest areas $125.00

APSO3-102-DETAILED NATAL: Natal chart plus interpretation with focus on one area of your life as specified by you $65.00

APSO3-105-PROGRESSED CHART: Progressed chart with forecast for coming year. Include descriptive letter and interests..$75.00

APSO3-114-COMPATIBILITY CHART: This chart is based on the birth data of the two people involved. Give details. Indicates positive and negative characteristics of relationship $75.00

APSO3-116-COMPOSITE CHART: This chart is a combination of the natal charts of two people. Give location of relationship as well as birth data. More accurate than above for existing relationship..$75.00

APSO3-117-FERTILITY/FAMILY PLANNING: Use for birth control, sex determination, fertile dates, one year $25.00

HOW TO ORDER

Be sure to give all birth data (date, year, time and place) plus your full name for these reports. Order our FREE catalog for more services to be added this year! See the order form on the last page or the order form for the Personal Services on the next page.

PERSONAL SERVICES ORDER FORM

Service Name and Number _____

Birth Data:

Name _____

Time _____ □ am □ pm

Date_____ Year_____

Birthplace: City, State, County, Country _____

_____

Lat. and Long. if foreign country _____

Birth Data (2nd person):

Name _____

Time _____ □ am □ pm

Date _____ Year _____

Birthplace: City, State, County, Country _____

_____

Astrological Knowledge:
□ Novice □ Student □ Advanced.
Please include letter describing questions on separate sheet of paper.

Name _____

Address _____

City, State,Zip _____

Please make check or Money Order payable to Llewellyn Publications.
Send to:
LLEWELLYN'S PERSONAL SERVICES
P.O. Box 64383-404RC
St. Paul, MN 55164-0383
Allow 4–6 weeks delivery.

SPECIAL DISCOUNTS
ON LLEWELLYN ANNUALS

There are several money-saving ways of ordering Llewellyn's Annuals for next year. You can order a *four-year subscription* which entitles you to receive your books or calendars upon publication for the next four years at a fixed price, regardless of price increases. You also save money in the deal. You can also order *special combination packages* of just the books you want, at a discount. Or, you can order in *quantities of a dozen* (to sell or give as gifts) each of the Annuals for a big savings. And to top it off, we pay postage on all of these offers if sent in the USA!

FOUR YEAR SUBSCRIPTIONS: 1990—1993

Sub 1 Moon Sign Book (MSB)	$15.00
Sub 2 MSB and Astrological Calendar (AC)	$42.00
Sub 3 Sun Sign Book (SSB)	$15.00
Sub 4 MSB and SSB	$30.00
Sub 5 Daily Planetary Guide (DPG)	$28.00
Sub 6 Astrological Calendar	$28.00
Sub 7 All Four Annuals	$84.00
Sub 8 MSB and DPG	$43.00
Sub 9 MSB, AC, DPG	$69.00

SPECIAL COMBINATION PACKAGES
State 1989 or 1990
Combo

1	MSB and AC	$11.00
2	MSB and DPG	$11.00
3	MSB, DPG and AC	$17.00
4	AC and DPG	$14.00
5	MSB and SSB	$ 8.00
6	SSB and AC	$11.00
7	SSB and DPG	$11.00
8	SSB, AC and DPG	$17.00
9	SSB, MSB and DPG	$15.00
10	All Four Annuals	$21.00

QUANTITY ORDERS
Price per dozen—state 1989 or 1990

Moon Sign Book	$28.44
Sun Sign Book	$28.44
Astrological Calendar	$50.04
Daily Planetary Guide	$50.04

Remember, we pay postage on all of these orders.
Use order form on last page.

LLEWELLYN ORDER FORM
LLEWELLYN PUBLICATIONS
P.O. Box 64383-404, St. Paul, MN 55164-0383

You may use this form to order any of the Llewellyn books or services listed in this publication.

Give Title, Author, Order Number and Price.

_____

_____

_____

_____

_____

_____

_____

Be sure to include 50 cents per item and $1.00 for handling. Minnesota residents add 6% sales tax. Outside USA add $1.00 per item postage. You may charge on your ☐ Visa, ☐ MasterCard, ☐ American Express or ☐ Diner's Club.

Account No. _____

Exp. Date _____Phone_____

Signature_____

Name _____

Address _____

City, State, Zip _____

CHARGE CARD ORDERS (minimum $15.00) may call 1-800-THE-MOON (in Canada, 1-800-FOR-SELF) during regular business hours, Monday–Friday, 8:00 am-9:00 pm, CST. Other questions please call 612-291-1970.

☐ **Please send me your FREE CATALOG!**